Proclaiming the Gospel, Engaging the World

Proclaiming the Gospel, Engaging the World

Celebrating One Hundred Years
of Melbourne School of Theology

MICHAEL BRÄUTIGAM
PETER G. RIDDELL
JUSTIN T. T. TAN
EDITORS

Forewords by
Rosemary Wong and Tim Meyers

WIPF & STOCK · Eugene, Oregon

PROCLAIMING THE GOSPEL, ENGAGING THE WORLD
Celebrating One Hundred Years of Melbourne School of Theology

Copyright © 2021 Wipf and Stock Publishers. All rights reserved. Except for brief quotations in critical publications or reviews, no part of this book may be reproduced in any manner without prior written permission from the publisher. Write: Permissions, Wipf and Stock Publishers, 199 W. 8th Ave., Suite 3, Eugene, OR 97401.

Scripture quotations marked NRSV are from the New Revised Standard Version Bible. Copyright © 1989 National Council of the Churches of Christ in the United States of America. Used by permission. All rights reserved worldwide.

Scripture quotations marked ESV are from The Holy Bible, English Standard Version® (ESV®). Copyright © 2001 by Crossway, a publishing ministry of Good News Publishers. All rights reserved.

Scripture quotations marked NIV are from The Holy Bible, New International Version® NIV®. Copyright © 1973, 1978, 1984, 2011 by Biblica, Inc.™ Used by permission. All rights reserved worldwide.

Colin Kruse's contribution in this volume was originally published as a chapter in *Paul as Pastor*, edited by Brian S. Rosner, Andrew S. Malone, and Trevor J. Burke (London: T. & T. Clark, an imprint of Bloomsbury Publishing, 2019). Used by permission of Bloomsbury Publishing.

Steve Walton's chapter was originally published in the *Journal of the Evangelical Theological Society* 55 (2012) 537–56. It is reproduced here by kind permission of the editor of *JETS*.

Wipf & Stock
An Imprint of Wipf and Stock Publishers
199 W. 8th Ave., Suite 3
Eugene, OR 97401

www.wipfandstock.com

PAPERBACK ISBN: 978-1-7252-8678-8
HARDCOVER ISBN: 978-1-7252-8677-1
EBOOK ISBN: 978-1-7252-8679-5

01/20/21

Contents

Contributors   vii
Foreword by Rosemary Wong   xiii
Foreword by Tim Meyers   xv
Acknowledgments   xix
Abbreviations   xxi
Introduction   xxiii

CELEBRATING OUR HISTORY

1. "The China Connection": Influence of the China Inland Mission in the Founding of Melbourne Bible Institute   3
   RUTH REDPATH

2. The First Three Principals 1920–1970   19
   ROWLAND S. WARD

THEOLOGICAL AND SPIRITUAL APPROACHES

3. The COVID-19 Pandemic: The Global Mental Health Crisis and a Reflection on the Human Condition   45
   MICHAEL T. H. WONG

4. "The Wound of Love" and the Pursuit of Holiness: Frances Young's Spirituality in a Broken World   55
   JUSTIN T. T. TAN

5	Transformation through Contemplation: Reflective Liturgies that Transform Us THOMAS KIMBER	73
6	Challenge, Critique, and Celebration: The Role of Humor in Proclaiming the Gospel and Engaging the World BRIAN EDGAR	84
7	Sanctified Reason: Exploring the Why of a Christian Liberal Arts Education CHRISTOPHER GREEN	98
8	We Have to Change: New Strategies for Theology in Australia MICHAEL BRÄUTIGAM	111
9	To What Extent Does Theological College Contribute to a Deepened Sense of Spirituality? DELLE MATTHEWS	131
10	Between Two Worlds: The Gospel and the ANZAC Myth MICHAEL RAITER	144

BIBLICAL PERSPECTIVES

11	What Does "Mission" in Acts Mean in Relation to the "Powers that Be"? STEVE WALTON	163
12	Paul as Pastor in Romans: Theological Foundations COLIN KRUSE	190
13	Reflecting on a Wreck: The Book of Genesis and the Marginalization of Christianity in the West ANDREW BROWN	204

CULTURAL INSIGHTS

14	Making Christ Offensive Again: A Kierkegaardian Polemic against Soft-Pedal Evangelicalism ERNIE LASKARIS	231
15	Jesus and Modernity: Why the Twenty-First Century is the Most Christian Ever RIKK WATTS	255

16 Mindsets and Muslims   268
    RICHARD SHUMACK AND PETER RIDDELL

17 From Receiving to Sending: Healthy Principles to Mobilize the Church
    for CrossCultural Service—Insights from Ukrainian Evangelicalism 279
    ERIC OLDENBURG

18 Why Does Theology Still Matter for Chinese Christianity?
    A Theological Reflection on Contemporary Christian Mission
    in China   298
    JASON LAM

Contributors

Michael Bräutigam studied psychology in Germany (University of Trier) and theology in Scotland (University of Edinburgh). He teaches in both disciplines at Melbourne School of Theology. His doctoral dissertation focuses on the Christology of Swiss theologian Adolf Schlatter (1852–1938), published as *Union with Christ: Adolf Schlatter's Relational Christology* (Pickwick, 2015; in German with TVZ, 2017). Michael is an ordained minister with the Free Church of Scotland and he serves as the director of the Centre for Theology and Psychology at Melbourne School of Theology.

Andrew Brown grew up on the east coast of Australia before completing undergraduate degree studies in New York State and Tennessee. After theological studies back in Australia, he joined a pastoral team at a Baptist church in Brisbane. A six-year country pastorate followed. In 2011 Andrew took the position of Old Testament lecturer at Melbourne School of Theology. His PhD (University of Queensland) is a history of Christian interpretation of the creation week in Genesis 1:1—2:3. Andrew is married to Naomi and they have three children, Gilchrist, Timothy, and Kyria. They live in Montrose in Melbourne's outer east and enjoy bushwalking and music.

Brian Edgar is professor of theological studies at Asbury Theological Seminary (US) while still residing in Melbourne. He is married to Barbara and both were students at MBI and then BCV (1976–1978). They lived on campus again (1986–2003) when Brian taught theology and was academic dean. Brian is the author of numerous articles and *The Message of the Trinity* (IVP, 2004), *God is Friendship* (Seedbed, 2011), *Laughter and the Grace of*

God (Cascade, 2019) and winner of a Christianity Today Book of the Year section award for *The God Who Plays* (Cascade, 2017).

Christopher Green is senior lecturer and director of online learning at Melbourne School of Theology and Eastern College Australia. His doctoral work has been republished as *Doxological Theology: Karl Barth on Divine Providence, Evil and the Angels*, and with David Starling has edited the proceedings of the 2016 Theology Connect conference, *Revelation and Reason in Christian Theology* (2018). Christopher is originally from Bakersfield, California, and he enjoys running, films with theological themes, and conversations with friends about cultural differences.

Thomas Kimber is dean of faculty, senior lecturer in missional and pastoral theology, and coordinator of the doctor of ministry at Melbourne School of Theology. He has ministered for more than thirty years through teaching, preaching, writing, and mentoring. He and his wife, Sue, served as missionaries in Asia for nine years before returning to the United States, where Tom taught at Biola University. He holds both MDiv and PhD degrees from Talbot School of Theology. His area of research interest includes the integration of spiritual formation and spirituality in mission and pastoral theology.

Colin Kruse is an emeritus scholar of the Melbourne School of Theology. Following ordination into the Anglican ministry, he gained practical experience in parishes in Australia and the US. He worked as a missionary lecturer at a Christian university in Indonesia for five years before undergoing further studies in the US. He taught at Ridley College for sixteen years, then moved to Melbourne School of Theology in 1995. Colin is the author of *New Testament Foundations for Ministry* (MMS, 1983), *Paul, the Law and Justification* (IVP, 1996), the Pillar commentaries on *The Letters of John* (Eerdmans, 2020) and *Paul's Letter to the Romans* (Eerdmans, 2012), the Tyndale commentaries on the *Gospel of John* (IVP, 2015) and *2 Corinthians* (IVP, 2015), and the *Exegetical Guide to the Greek New Testament on 2 Corinthians* (B&H Academic, 2020). His chapter has appeared earlier in *Paul as Pastor*, edited by Brian S. Rosner, Andrew S. Malone, and Trevor J. Burke (London: Bloomsbury T. & T. Clark, 2018). It is reprinted here with kind permission from T. & T. Clark.

Jason Lam is originally from Hong Kong, joining MST in 2019. He is now senior lecturer in Christian thoughts, senior research fellow of the Australian College of Theology, and holds a professorship and a fellowship from different higher institutions in Hong Kong and PRC. He obtained his doctorate from the University of Cambridge in the field of hermeneutics and modern theology and endeavors to bring the Scriptures, philosophy, and contextual issues together for theological reflection. His recent books include *Sino-Christian Theology: A Theological qua Cultural Movement in Contemporary China* (ed.) and *Theology after Heidegger* (in Chinese).

Ernie Laskaris grew up in rural Australia, moving to Melbourne in his early teens. After being an atheist for the majority of his life, he was converted in 2015 and immediately began his theological studies. He graduated from Melbourne School of Theology with a bachelor of theology (honors) and he is now a PhD candidate at the University of Queensland, continuing his research on the religious and philosophical thought of Søren Kierkegaard. Ernie currently works as a regular preacher at Wattle Park Chapel, functioning as a pastor for the young members of the congregation, and he has also pastored a local house church for the last four years. Alongside his ministry, Ernie works as an academic research and teaching assistant for various lecturers at Melbourne School of Theology.

Delle Matthews was a member of Wycliffe Bible Translators and SIL International for twenty-two years as literacy coordinator for SIL Indonesia, serving in West Papua and teaching at SIL, Kangaroo Ground. She began working in educational administration while there and completed a masters in educational administration. In 2004 she took up the position of dean of studies at Melbourne School of Theology (formerly BCV) and completed her Doctor of Ministry researching the retention of theological students and how matters of faith impact students' decisions.

Eric Oldenburg is the academic coordinator of doctoral programs, extensions, and certificates at Talbot School of Theology, Biola University. He is also adjunct professor of biblical and theological studies at Talbot. From 2004 to 2016, Eric served as a missionary theological educator in Ukraine. In 2011 to 2014, as the area director of SEND International's Ukraine field, Eric worked with cross-culturally-minded leaders, encouraging Ukrainians to pray for and serve unreached people groups both inside and outside the country. He is currently a PhD student at Melbourne School of Theology. He lives in Whittier, California, with his energetic wife, Josie, and three rambunctious sons, Dietrich, Lev, and Max.

Mike Raiter is the director of the Centre for Biblical Preaching, which trains people in expository preaching. He taught in theological colleges in Pakistan. From 1997 to 2005 Mike was head of the Department of Mission at Moore College. He then served as principal of BCV/MST from 2006 to 2011. He is the author of over forty books and articles, including the 2004 Australian Christian Book of the Year, *Stirrings of the Soul*, and, more recently, *The Songs of the Saints* (with Rob Smith), *Shadows of the Cross*, and *Meet Jesus*. He is married to Sarah and they have four adult children.

Ruth Redpath graduated in medicine in 1964 and practiced as a radiation oncologist and palliative care physician in UK and Australia. In 1996, she became a carer for her husband and elderly parents, during which time she discerned God's call to ordained ministry. She then enjoyed eleven years in pastoral ministry until her recent retirement. Her interest in MBI's history springs from family involvement from its earliest years and an upbringing surrounded by friends whose pan-evangelicalism was so much part of its ethos. In her teenage years she devoured many China Inland Mission publications from the early twentieth century found on the family bookshelves.

Peter Riddell is a senior research fellow of the Australian College of Theology at MST and professorial research associate in history at SOAS University of London. He took his PhD in Islamic studies at the Australian National University and has previously taught at the ANU, the Institut Pertanian Bogor (Indonesia), SOAS, and the London School of Theology. He has published widely on Southeast Asia, Islam, and Christian-Muslim relations. His books include *Transferring a Tradition* (Berkeley, 1990), *Islam and the Malay-Indonesian World* (London, 2001), *Islam in Context* (with Peter Cotterell, Grand Rapids, 2003), *Christians and Muslims* (Leicester, 2004), and *Malay Court Religion, Culture and Language: Interpreting the Qur'an in 17th Century Aceh* (Leiden, 2017).

Richard Shumack is the director of the Arthur Jeffery Centre for Islamic Studies at Melbourne School of Theology. He is a research fellow at the Centre for Public Christianity and the academic director of the Ravi Zacharias International Ministries' Understanding and Answering Islam project. His publications include a training book, *Witnessing to Western Muslims*, a philosophical apologetic entitled *The Wisdom of Islam and the Foolishness of Christianity*, and the recent *Jesus through Muslim Eyes*.

Justin T. T. Tan graduated from King's College, University of London, researching on patristic spirituality, particularly Gregory of Nyssa and the Desert Fathers. He was awarded a PhD in 1995. He was vice-principal (academic) of MST until he stepped down to concentrate on research. He is currently senior lecturer and director of the Centre for the Study of Chinese Christianity and is a senior research fellow of the Australian College of Theology. Justin has been published widely on patristic studies and the Old Testament. His research interests include a structural analysis of biblical literature, Old Testament theology of suffering, the practice of spiritual theology in the Chinese church and the spiritual tradition of the early church fathers.

Steve Walton is professor of New Testament at Trinity College, Bristol, UK. He has taught at St. Mary's University, Twickenham, London School of Theology, and St. John's College, Nottingham. His present major writing project is the Word Biblical Commentary on Acts.

Rowland Ward is Melbourne born and has been a minister of the Presbyterian Church of Eastern Australia since 1976. He holds BA and Hons BTh degrees from the University of South Africa, a diploma from the Free Church of Scotland, Edinburgh and a doctorate from the Australian College of Theology, Sydney. He was founding pastor of Knox Presbyterian Church, Wantirna from 1987 to 2012 and is the author of numerous books on church history, theology, and worship. He has lectured in Australia and overseas and is currently research lecturer at the Presbyterian Theological College in Melbourne. He is married to Anna and they have five children.

Rikk Watts, a former lecturer at BCV, is a research professor of NT at Regent College, Vancouver. Initially trained in aeronautical and systems engineering (IBM), he undertook studies in art history, philosophy, and sociology, helped found *On Being* magazine, and worked with Truth and Liberation Concern. He has two masters degrees from Gordon-Conwell (OT/NT), and a Cambridge PhD. His primary interests are Scripture, the history of ideas, and marketplace design and innovation. A highly regarded biblical scholar, he has published several books and numerous articles, and speaks widely in Australia and internationally. Rikk and Katie have two adult children. They enjoy sailing, canoeing, Scandi Noir, good food, music, reading, and long walks.

Michael T. H. Wong is clinical professor of psychiatry at LKS Faculty of Medicine, The University of Hong Kong. He is Chair, Section of Philosophy and Humanities in Psychiatry, World Psychiatric Association and immediate past chair, Section of History Philosophy and Ethics, Royal Australian and New Zealand College of Psychiatrists. Professor Wong is also trained in theology and philosophy, holding a MDiv from the Bible College of Victoria and a PhD from Monash University on how hermeneutics integrates philosophy, neuroscience, psychiatry, and theology. He was formerly a member of the board of Melbourne School of Theology and Eastern College.

Foreword

Rosemary Wong, Chair, Melbourne School of Theology

THE COVID-19 PANDEMIC HAS thrown our world into the grip of convulsive changes such as many have not seen in their lifetimes. Melbourne has entered its second lockdown within a matter of a few months. Our ever-changing circumstances bring fresh understanding of the assurance of the One who is "the same, yesterday and today and forever," our Lord Jesus Christ (Heb 13:8).

Paradosis is a Greek word that means "tradition." It is a word that can cut in two opposing ways, bad and good. Jesus repeatedly rebuked the Pharisees and scribes for breaking God's commandments and imposing man-made rules, while Paul referred to the empty way of life handed down to the Jews from their forefathers (1 Pet 1:18). In contrast, and with resolute urgency, Paul reiterated the gospel tradition that he passed on, and that we at Melbourne School of Theology (MST) have endeavored by God's grace to pass on likewise: "For what I received I passed on to you as of first importance, that Christ died for our sins according to the Scriptures, that he was buried, that he was raised on the third day according to the Scriptures, and that he appeared to Cephas, and then to the Twelve" (1 Cor 15:3–5).

As we commemorate our centenary year, we give thanks to God for the founding principal of Melbourne Bible Institute (MBI, renamed Bible College of Victoria, and now Melbourne School of Theology), the Rev. C. H. Nash, its governing council and countless faithful supporters. MBI began not merely to train men and women for missionary work but as a response to a critical situation—that of a perceived drifting from traditional Protestant orthodoxy amidst a society that seemed no longer to acknowledge its Christian roots. Darrell Paproth wrote that MBI stood for interdenominational Evangelicalism in Melbourne (indeed, in Australia). According to David Bebbington, the four characteristics typical of Evangelicalism are an emphasis on the need for individual conversion to Christ, activism demonstrated in evangelism and missions, the divine inspiration and authority of the Bible, and the centrality of the cross to Christian life and thought.

Thus, it is apt that our centenary's *Paradosis* theme is "Proclaiming the Gospel and Engaging the World." Christian theology must serve pastoral ministry, evangelism, cross-cultural mission, interfaith dialogue, and indeed every sphere of human learning, endeavor and life. Theologian Karl Barth famously quipped that Christians should "take your Bible and take your newspaper and read both. But interpret newspapers from your Bible." Indeed, ". . . in Him, all things hold together" (Col 1:17). This volume of *Paradosis* does justice to our motto "Bible and Mission": with our anchor firmly rooted in Jesus Christ and his authoritative word, we can with God's help engage the world in all her vicissitudes. *To God be the glory!*

Foreword

Tim Meyers, Executive Principal, Melbourne School of Theology and Eastern College Australia

It is surely a great irony that in this, the one hundredth year of the Melbourne School of Theology (known initially of course as the Melbourne Bible Institute, and then the Bible College of Victoria), the entire world has become dramatically reacquainted with what one writer describes as "perhaps the oldest traveling companion of human history: existential fear."[1]

So it is that, rather than being free to gather publicly, as we had planned, to reflect, to worship, to reminisce, and to celebrate with thanksgiving the remarkable history of this school, our entire community—staff, students, faculty, supporters, partners in church and mission, and graduates—will likely end up spending much of this centenary year in relative social isolation, save perhaps for the now ubiquitous new world of virtual relationships and digital communication.

Nonetheless, as followers of Christ, and as a school, we are called to live above anxiety and fear, drawing upon the unlimited resources and riches that are ours in the great promises of God in Christ, sufficient to provide everything we need for "life and godliness" (2 Pet 1:3).

As a school, we remain commissioned and set apart to "equip men and women with transformational theology, biblical depth and a missional heart." So it is, then, that we must remain both confident and, indeed,

---

1. Lyman Stone, "Christianity Has Been Handling Epidemics for 2000 Years," in *Foreign Policy*, March 13, 2020, https://foreignpolicy.com/2020/03/13/christianity-epidemics-2000-years-should-i-still-go-to-church-coronavirus/.

profoundly hopeful, that in the midst of such global upheaval, as the writer to Lamentations stated nearly twenty-five centuries ago, "The steadfast love of the Lord never ceases; his mercies never come to an end; they are new every morning; great is your faithfulness" (Lam 3:22–23, ESV).

The Rev. C. H. Nash knew well the buffeting of adversity; personally, and throughout his remarkable life and ministry. Not surprisingly, the school he founded, now the Melbourne School of Theology, similarly has survived many seasons of turbulence: economic depression, global conflict, personal, theological and financial crises, and spiritual opposition. Yet Nash's legacy remains; rather than falling victim to fear, we are called to teach, and to proclaim with even more passion and vigor, the gospel of Christ.

Perhaps it is fitting, then, in this centenary volume of essays, to reflect on the words of a simple poem, penned by C. H. Nash, which speak of the source of his vision and the basis for his confidence.

THOU ART THE ROCK[2]

C. H. Nash

Thy changeless Word; firm, unshaken,
In unabated strength,
Has met the shocks of storm and flood,
Through two millenniums length.

Thou art our Shepherd, great and good,
Leading in pastures green;
Thy fickle followers seeking food,
And rest by streams serene.

Thou art the vine, the pulsing flow,
From root and strenuous bough,
To every branch gives power to grow,
And fruit, we know not how.

Thou art the bread of life, in ways
Beyond our power to think;
Through all our lean and hungry days,
Thou art our meat and drink.

Thou art the way, the truth, the life,
The way to heaven's goals;
The truth through errors' blinding strife,
The life within the soul.

---

2. Darrell N. Paproth, *Failure Is Not Final: A Life of C. H. Nash* (Sydney: Centre for the Study of Australian Christianity, 1997), 201.

Acknowledgments

This volume has been put together in challenging times. This year, 2020, was supposed to be a time of celebration for Melbourne School of Theology (MST) as the college commemorates its hundredth anniversary. A conference was originally scheduled to take place in July this year to showcase the rich history of what began as the Melbourne Bible Institute (MBI), later renamed the Bible College of Victoria (BCV), and the Melbourne School of Theology—three names but a single proud tradition of serving Christ.

The onset of the COVID-19 pandemic, of course, thwarted our plans, and we were forced to cancel the conference. We were reminded of our human inadequacies and our fallenness as we learnt afresh to rely on God's grace on a daily basis. The fact that we still exist and still equip people for the service in the kingdom of God is a witness to God's consistent faithfulness and grace throughout the past hundred years. We are immensely grateful to our speakers who still managed to contribute essay versions of their planned paper presentations for this volume. This has not always been a straightforward endeavor, since, for instance, many libraries were closed and therefore resources were not always as easily accessible as in pre-pandemic times. The underlying stress of working under several lockdowns in Victoria during the compilation of this volume is not to be underestimated and we give thanks to God who sustained our contributors in these challenging times.

Not all is lost, then! We are thrilled that with this special volume MST's birthday is still being celebrated in a worthy form. This volume contains eighteen essays by present and past members of the MBI/BCV/MST family and its friends. This volume contributes toward remembering the past while also looking forward to the future, acquiring a clearer sense of how we participate in God's mission in Australia and the world in post-pandemic times.

We would like to convey a particular word of praise to our editorial assistant, Diana Summers, who has not only proofread every essay with a careful eye for detail but has also assisted us greatly with several organizational tasks that accompany the responsibility of preparing a volume such as this. One could not ask for a more dedicated and talented assistant, and we express our deep gratitude to Diana.

We are also very grateful to our editor, Greta Morris, for her expertise and efficiency which allowed for a swift turnaround of this project. We would also like to express our thanks to Matthew Wimer and the team at Wipf & Stock for their encouragement and support.

May the content of this volume be a source of inspiration and encouragement for our brothers and sisters in Christ as they continue to proclaim the gospel and engage the world, to the glory of God.

Michael Bräutigam, Peter Riddell, and Justin Tan
Melbourne, November 2020

Abbreviations

AB	Anchor Bible
ABD	*Anchor Bible Dictionary*. Edited by David Noel Freedman. 6 vols. New York: Doubleday, 1992.
ANRW	*Aufstieg und Niedergang der römischen Welt: Geschichte und Kultur Roms im Spiegel der neueren Forschung*. Part 2, *Principat*. Edited by Hildegard Temporini and Wolfgang Haase. Berlin: de Gruyter, 1972–
ANTC	Abingdon New Testament Commentaries
BAFCS	The Book of Acts in Its First Century Setting
BDAG	Danker, Frederick W., Walter Bauer, William F. Arndt, and F. Wilbur Gingrich. *Greek-English Lexicon of he New Testament and Other Early Christian Literature*. 3rd ed. Chicago: University of Chicago Press, 2000 (Danker-Bauer-Arndt-Gingrich)
BDF	Blass, Friedrich, Albert Debrunner, and Robert W. Funk. *A Greek Grammaar of the New Testament and Other Early Christian Literature*. Chicago: University of Chicago Press, 1961
BETL	Bibliotheca Ephemeridum Theologicarum Lovaniensium
BSL	Biblical Studies Library
CIJ	*Corpus Inscriptionum Judaicarum*. Edited by Jean-Baptiste Frey. 2 vols. Rome: Pontifical Biblical Institute, 1936–1952
HThKNT	Herders Theologischer Kommenar zum Neuen Testament
ICC	International Critical Commentary

IGR	*Inscriptiones Graecae ad Res Romanas Pertinentes.* 3 vols. Edited by R. Cagnat et al. Paris, 1906–1927
IVPNTC	IVP New Testament Commentary
JETS	*Journal of the Evangelical Theological Society*
JPTSup	*Journal of Pentecostal Theology Supplement Series*
JSJSup	*Journal for the Study of Judaism in the Persian, Hellenistic, and Roman Periods Supplement Series*
JSNTSup	*Journal for the Study of the New Testament Supplement Series*
JSOTSup	*Journal for the Study of the Old Testament Supplement Series*
LCL	Loeb Classical Library
LNTS	The Library of New Testament Studies
MHT	Moulton, James H., Wilbert F. Howard, and Nigel Turner. *A Grammar of New Testament Greek.* 4 vols. Edinburgh: T. & T. Clark, 1906–1976
NAC	New American Commentary
NICNT	New International Commentary on the New Testament
PNTC	Pillar New Testament Commentaries
RGRW	Religions in the Graeco-Roman World
SBLDS	Society of Biblical Literature Dissertation Series
SNTSMS	Society for New Testament Studies Monograph Series
WBC	Word Biblical Commentary
WUNT	Wissenschaftliche Untersuchungen zum Neuen Testament

Introduction

"This is the end of the world."

So Europeans said and believed in 1348, when the bubonic plague ravaged the continent. Its terrors drove priests to abandon their parishes and parents their children while unharvested crops drooped in the fields, the air reeked with foul odors, and death knells tolled until nobody survived to pull the bell ropes. Bad theology exacerbated the damage. If the plague was not God's punishment for some unidentified mortal sin, it was the work of the devil or the stars or climate change or witchcraft or the Jews. Froissart's famous guess that a third of the population died was not based on any death-poll census but on his reading of Revelation 9:18, which predicted the death of a third of humanity from plagues—and surely those apocalyptic predictions were coming true in his own age.[3]

Five minutes of contemplating 1348 place 2020 firmly in perspective. Nobody believes that the COVID-19 pandemic will end the world. Nevertheless, 2020 is the year when everyone's plans have been disrupted. Most of us have been forced into unnatural social isolation, a healthy workforce has been forbidden to go out to work, and the economy is unpredictable but certain to suffer. At Melbourne School of Theology, we expected to celebrate our centenary with communal thanksgivings and a review of our history. We were to commemorate one hundred years of training God's people for overseas mission and domestic ministry and commit ourselves to whatever he required of us for the next century. Instead, we have been called to focus on the present. The pressing question is no longer, "What has happened at college?" but "How does God want us to serve him under such altered circumstances?"

---

3. Barbara Tuchman, *A Distant Mirror: The Calamitous Fourteenth Century* (New York: Alfred A. Knopf, 1978), 92–125.

Paradosis 2020 is not as we planned it; but nor has the world ended. Our need to understand God's actions and to stir one another up to love and good works is an invariable of the human condition. Therefore the need to share good theology is a constant, and this compilation includes articles on general truths as well as those specific to the present time.

The first section celebrates our college's history. Ruth Redpath (*The China Connection*) traces the cultural and spiritual forces that inspired Australian Christians to take the gospel to China. Melbourne Bible Institute was founded to train these missionaries, and although it came to provide a biblical grounding for many other kinds of ministry, it has supplied missionaries to China ever since. Rowland Ward (*The First Three Principals*) provides vivid pen portraits of the three men who were the college's principals over its first half-century.

Next we turn to theological and spiritual approaches. Michael Wong (*The COVID-19 Pandemic*) directly addresses the COVID crisis, its impact on mental health worldwide and some implications for discipleship. Justin Tan (*The Wound of Love*) confronts the problem of suffering in general by focusing on disability, reminding us that every person is flawed, that we should expect suffering to be normal in a fallen world, and that struggling through human frailty and misfortune is the usual pathway to holiness. Thomas Kimber (*Transformation through Contemplation*) writes of the human necessity to contemplate God's love, which secures our identity and dwelling place and transforms us into his image. He highlights the importance of community to experience that love and of liturgy to reinforce order and identity. Brian Edgar (*Challenge, Critique and Celebration*) presents the central place of humor in both the gospel and discipleship. Humor may serve a serious purpose—to challenge people to repent or to critique human folly—but, above all, "joy is the serious business of Heaven."[4] Christopher Green (*Sanctified Reason*) explores the sanctification of reason. Every academic discipline is sanctified when it recognizes the fallenness of every human endeavor yet extols the Father and conforms to the Son in the power of the Holy Spirit; and a Christian community is the right context to reorient our powers of reasoning. Michael Bräutigam (*We Have to Change*) reminds us of the sobering decline of theological education throughout the Western world but offers some hope for the future. Our civilization's lack of direction and meaning has become so desperate that theologians now have an opportunity—if only they know how to make use of it. Delle Matthews (*A Deepened Sense of Spirituality*) provides direct evidence that most students feel theological college helps to deepen their spirituality. However, most of

---

4. C. S. Lewis, *Letters to Malcolm: Chiefly on Prayer* (San Diego: Harvest, 1964), 93.

them mean "a better understanding of God" rather than a lived experience of faith, and it is not yet known why some students benefit more than others. Michael Raiter (*Between Two Worlds*) strikes an iconoclastic note in suggesting that Australia, having rejected Christianity, has created a substitute religion in sacralizing its Anzac heroes. Though its mythology bears little resemblance to the historical facts, this new religion meets humanity's unchanging search for ethics, identity, and a higher purpose.

The third section concerns biblical perspectives. Steve Walton (*"Mission" in Relation to the "Powers that Be"*) celebrates the willingness of the earliest Christian missionaries to challenge the Roman Empire with unpalatable truths, not only in declaring the gospel but in directly confronting the rulers' morality. Colin Kruse (*Paul as Pastor in Romans*) focuses on sanctification. He presents Paul's pastoral ministry to the Romans not primarily as "telling people what to do" but as "reminding people what God has done for them," with a right understanding of God's words as the basis for a healthy praxis. Andrew Brown's overview of the history of theories of the earth (*Reflecting on a Wreck*) reveals a reciprocal theme: the misunderstanding of God's words as an incitement to synthesize empirical science with Bible stories, to the detriment of both.

The final section offers some cultural assessments. Ernie Laskaris (*Making Christ Offensive Again*) probes how Western Evangelicals have self-imposed an agenda of never offending anyone; but by removing the offence of the gospel, they have removed the heart of the gospel itself. Only by being willing to embrace the scandal of offence can we present the gospel to the world truthfully. Rikk Watts (*Jesus and Modernity*) shows how Christian assumptions have become the basic assumptions of the modern West. Therefore, the civilization that declares itself hostile to the gospel is in fact by its own existence a testimony to the gospel's victory. Richard Shumack and Peter Riddell (*Mindsets and Muslims*) pay respect to the popular Muslim assumption that Islam is a rational and righteous religion before questioning whether it satisfies biblical standards of rationality or righteousness. They conclude that "the best response to Muslim religious zeal is Christian zeal." Eric Oldenburg (*From Receiving to Sending*) documents some recent trends in Ukraine, which was recently perceived as a mission field but whose churches are now sending missionaries to unreached people groups, and he challenges nations with longer-established churches to learn from the Ukrainian experience. Finally, Jason Lam brings our thoughts back to China as he reflects on its contemporary relationship between church and state (*Why Does Theology Still Matter for Chinese Christianity?*). He points to the necessity of developing a theology that is both possible and responsible for a persecuted church, a theology that must nevertheless become a voice in the public arena.

We thank all of our contributors for the grace and diligence with which they accepted the invitation to write for *Paradosis 2020*. Several of them were writing under the extraordinary pressure of living in interesting times. This centenary anthology is the result of their collaboration. While nothing else is what we expected, God's goodness has not changed.

Soli Deo Gloria.

Diana Summers

Celebrating Our History

1

"The China Connection"

Influence of the China Inland Mission in the Founding of Melbourne Bible Institute

Ruth Redpath

THE FIRST PRINCIPAL OF Melbourne Bible Institute—Rev. C. H. Nash—had joined the Australasian China Inland Mission (CIM) Council in 1916 at a time when the vision to provide theologically conservative, biblical instruction for people of all levels of educational attainment called to full-time service was being conceived. Existing theological colleges, in addition to their educational prerequisites for applicants, were increasingly influenced by the so-called "higher criticism" of the Scriptures. Hudson Taylor's initiative in the founding of the CIM in England in the mid-nineteenth century occurred in the context of the "holiness movement" and the flourishing revivalist preaching in the 1870s and 1880s, especially that of D. L. Moody. It so happened that Nash had been training for the Anglican ministry in Cambridge at the time of the Moody evangelistic campaigns and the sending to China of "The Cambridge Seven" by the CIM. The consequent dramatic increase in volunteers for overseas missionary service there and in North America was followed, not long after, by a similar surge in Australasia. In the establishment of MBI, Melbourne paralleled what had already happened a few years earlier in North America. Recruitment of many CIM personnel there had played a significant role in the founding of Bible Institutes in Toronto, Los Angeles, and other centers. Many of the early alumni of MBI left for China, and this continued. In present times, the circle is completed with the continuation of the Chinese Department at MST, having been established twenty-five years ago at the then named Bible College of Victoria.

There was nothing grand about the opening exercises of the Melbourne Bible Institute (MBI) on Monday morning, September 13, 1920. Two men faced one another across a desk in a schoolroom at the rear of the Prahran Congregational Church in inner suburban Melbourne, each with a Bible open in front of him. The younger of the two, the pupil, was Theo Lowther, who had, until 1919, been in military service and who now believed himself called to missionary service in China. The teacher, aged fifty-four, was the Rev. C. H. Nash, a commanding figure of solid build and graying hair in a double-breasted suit and clerical collar. He had been appointed as the first principal of MBI.

The public announcement of MBI's commencement had occurred just three weeks previously and, with this modest beginning, few if any would have expected the rate at which growth occurred, nor that it would later celebrate a centenary. Certainly, no one could have predicted that in 2020 MBI, now the Melbourne School of Theology (MST), would also be celebrating the quarter-century of its formal involvement with the training of Chinese-speaking Christians in Melbourne. Classes in the Chinese Department of what was then the Bible College of Victoria (BCV) commenced in 1995, but at a separate site, to meet the need of trained pastors for the increasing number of Chinese congregations in Australia. With the relocation of MST to Wantirna in 2011, colocation of the Chinese Department was enabled, and a flourishing and fruitful partnership has continued.

This recent turn of events gives added cause for thanksgiving, especially as the evangelization of China provided strong motivation for MBI's original opening. In its foundation in 1920, MBI was part of a pattern of global developments occurring among Evangelicals over the preceding three or four decades. Particular to it, perhaps, was that the appointment of C. H. Nash as principal was minuted by an already-constituted body—the Australasian Council of the China Inland Mission (CIM). Concurrently, a new, independent MBI council was being formed, and, not surprisingly, several of its members were also on the CIM council.

Though drawn from churches of several Christian denominations, members of these councils already knew each other well through Evangelical networks and through the socalled "holiness movement," whose influence and continued ministry had converged in the first Upwey Convention (now Belgrave Heights) held two years previously, in 1918, under the banner "All One in Christ Jesus."[1]

To understand the confluence of the various elements of Evangelicalism as then expressed in the CIM and MBI in a country that had only recently emerged from its colonial model of government, we need to return to events in Great Britain (the "mother country") in the latter half of the previous century and to meet members of the network of Evangelical leaders at that time.

MOODY AND THE NINETEENTH-CENTURY BRITISH REVIVAL MOVEMENT

The years from 1865 to 1890 provide a context for the later course of events in Melbourne. During these years, widespread spiritual revival was experienced. In 1858 to 1859, there were times of revival in Wales and other areas, and their effects had continued, albeit somewhat localized.[2]

The appeal of General Booth and the Salvation Army was reaching to the very poor. Much more far-reaching in both its immediate and its long-term gospel influence was the response to the American preacher, Dwight L. Moody, in the seventies and eighties.[3] Of minimal education, Moody's first job had been as a traveling salesman. Energetic and entrepreneurial, he abandoned ambitious plans to become a wealthy Chicago businessman, concentrating instead on the spiritual and material needs of that burgeoning city. This new focus resulted in the building of an independent church with a multifaceted ministry, and later, in 1890, the founding of Moody Bible Institute.

In 1867, just thirty years old, he visited London to learn from other Evangelicals engaged in similar city ministries. He was especially impressed by the Mildmay Centre established in 1864 by Rev. William Pennefather at St Jude's Church of England, Mildmay Park, in London's East End. As well as many activities to help the underprivileged, a Deaconess Training Institute was preparing hundreds of women for local community and missionary

---

1. Terms such as "holiness movement" and "higher life movement" described the networks, formal and informal, of Evangelical Christians who desired to have a deeper experience of the Holy Spirit in their lives. The Keswick Convention movement in England exemplified this, teaching the possibility of personal Holy Spirit renewal to give assurance of cleansing, victory over sin, and power for service. Others described a desire to walk with God all day long, with self displaced and Christ enthroned. Tan, *Planting an Indigenous Church*.

2. Bebbington, *Evangelicalism*, 116–17.

3. Pollock, *Moody*, 131; Bebbington, *Evangelicalism*, 162.

service. An annual Mildmay Conference had been commenced for "the enrichment of spiritual life" in a hall built to accommodate the thousands who attended.[4] Moody made a strong impression on his hosts.

Invitations to return to Britain for evangelistic missions followed. His first visit lasted two years, from mid-1873 to mid-1875, when missions were conducted in many centers, each often lasting several weeks. A profound impact was made, especially in Edinburgh and other Scottish cities. Moody returned for several months between 1881 and 1882 and then again in 1883 to 1884, this time mostly in London and its environs. The whole country was impacted by the simplicity of his message. His own assessment was that the church in Britain had been "dying in its own respectability." He "pierced the screen of [Victorian] hypocrisy."[5] The essence of his message was the need for individuals to respond to the love of God in Jesus Christ. "Him," he would say. "Not a dogma, not a creed, not a myth, but a Person."[6]

In November 1882, Moody conducted an eight-day mission at Cambridge University, having been invited by a group of students. The student body at Cambridge represented the younger generation of the aristocratic class, and the mission led to the conversion of many. It also kindled the zeal of students who were already Christians for evangelistic ministry.

BRITISH FOREIGN MISSIONARY ENDEAVORS

The eighteenth-century Evangelical revival in England and Wales had spawned missionary initiatives, and these continued into the next century, in an era of expanding British colonization and trade.

Interest in missionary service in India was associated with the pioneering work of William Carey and those who joined him, though their activities were severely limited by the power of the East India Company. When Britain took responsibility for the government of India in the midcentury, a new freedom was given to the many recruits eager to serve there.[7]

From the mid-nineteenth century, Africa's colonies also captured the imagination of British Christians as they learned of the opening up of the country by traders and by individuals like David Livingstone, who combined devoted missionary service with adventurous exploration.[8]

---

4. Bebbington, *Evangelicalism*, 159.
5. Pollock, *Moody*, 162, 163.
6. Pollock, *Moody*, 123.
7. Neill, *Christian Missions*, 223, 301.
8. Neill, *Christian Missions*, 266.

Interest in China had developed more slowly, with encounters driven by the commercial and political activities of the East India Company and by the trade in opium with China. The first Protestant missionary was Robert Morrison, who went to Canton in 1807. Because of his speedy acquisition of the language, the East India Company engaged him as a translator even as he worked on the translation of the whole Bible, and he enjoyed their protection. Otherwise, until the end of the First Opium War between Britain and China (1839–1842), Protestant missionaries did not reach mainland China. However, with the signing of the Nanking Treaty in 1842, missionaries recruited by CMS and other denominational groups were able to work in the five treaty ports, though not inland.[9]

THE FOUNDATION OF THE CHINA INLAND MISSION

Hudson Taylor, a Yorkshireman, had gone to China in 1856 at the age of twenty-one, earnest in his desire to bring the millions of that country to know Christ. His first four years there were a disappointment for many reasons, in part because it seemed to him that the small number of missionaries already there, who were confined to the treaty ports and settled in relative comfort, were lacking in passion for evangelism in unreached areas.[10]

Returning to England in 1860 for health reasons, he could not forget the almost four hundred million unevangelized people in China's inland provinces, and he addressed many meetings to arouse the concern of British Christians. In 1865 he committed, under God, to return to China with a band of twenty-four men and women, two for the evangelization of each of the untouched inland provinces, and he and his wife accompanied these first members to China the following year. Thus, the China Inland Mission (CIM) was born.[11]

Soon after taking this momentous decision, with a new clarity of vision directing his energies, he attended the Perth Conference for "the fostering of spiritual life." He asked for an opportunity to speak of his vision to the assembled company. The reply he received from the organizers was abrupt. "My dear sir, surely you mistake the character of the conference. These meetings are for spiritual edification." Undaunted, he persuaded them to allow him to speak. The effect was immediate in its supportive response and the offer of more opportunities to present his vision.[12]

9. Neill, *Christian Missions*, 238–40.
10. Pollock, *Hudson Taylor*, 33.
11. Taylor and Taylor, *Growth*, 31–33.
12. Taylor and Taylor, *Growth*, 9. "Hudson Taylor had a magnetic appeal to the

Convinced that men and women of little educational attainment could still be effective evangelists, the background of that first CIM party was humble. They had no professional experience, and little, if any, missionary training except what they received from Taylor himself on the long sea voyage, during which time they also began language lessons. On reaching China, they experienced the benefits of the new treaties made at the end of the Second Opium War (1856–1858), when more treaty ports had been created and the inland areas had been made more accessible.

Hudson Taylor returned to England in 1870, directing his team from afar, and deliberately made his recruitment base in East London near his friends at the Mildmay Centre.

At this time, there was no college for missionary training for the continuous stream of volunteers for service in China whose educational and social background did not meet the requirements of established theological colleges. Hudson Taylor recognized this gap. So when the older and experienced evangelist, Henry Grattan Guinness, applied in 1872 to serve in China, Taylor diverted him to the task of establishing "The East London Institute for Home and Foreign Missions" at Harley House. By 1900, one thousand students had been trained, of whom more than one hundred had gone to China with CIM.[13]

THE KESWICK INFLUENCE ON MISSIONS

The inaugural Keswick Convention, which arose out of the "holiness movement" and conferences such as those at Perth and Mildmay, occurred at the height of the impact of the London missions led by Moody in 1875. Held in the holiday season in a beautiful natural setting, this annual event became a demonstration of what has been called "pan-Evangelicalism." Meeting under the banner "All One in Christ Jesus," those attending were members of an Evangelicalism that transcended denominational boundaries, as had been the case in the CIM from its beginning.[14]

Among some Evangelicals, however, there was suspicion, if not outright opposition. There was justifiable concern that some preachers were promoting the requirement of a second conversion experience and that the doctrine of sinless perfection was implied in the teaching of others. An early sceptic was Rev. Handley Moule, principal of Ridley Hall, an Evangelical theological college in Cambridge. A "Holiness Convention" in Cambridge,

---

Christian imagination." See Austin, *China's Millions*, xi.

13. Taylor and Taylor, *Growth*, 57.
14. Evans and Paproth, *Evangelisation Society*, 19.

soon after the Moody evangelistic mission there (which Moule had supported wholeheartedly), had been led by several Keswick speakers, including Rev. Evan Hopkins. Moule wrote a series of anonymous articles, based on hearsay, in criticism of the convention. Later, having listened to Hopkins in another setting, he changed his position, offering wise counsel about the theological basis of their teaching. Hopkins was forever grateful to Moule for this, and in future years he was a frequent speaker at Keswick.[15]

Though from the beginning requests had been made for a missionary focus to be provided in the Keswick program, this had been refused, with similar reasoning to that given to Taylor in Perth in 1865. However, "unofficial" missionary meetings were held from about 1884, with Hudson Taylor addressing one such meeting at the end of the 1887 convention. The next year this type of meeting was part of the official program and it remained an integral part of it thereafter.[16]

CIM INFLUENCE GROWS

Though there was growing support, there was relative ignorance of the CIM among British Christians. This swiftly changed in 1885, when Hudson Taylor and the mission were catapulted into public awareness. This occurred because of the extraordinary publicity surrounding the departure of seven young Cambridge students as missionaries to China with the CIM.

That the "Cambridge Seven" were men from wealthy, aristocratic families was surprising enough. At a time when academic achievement appeared to take second place to sporting prowess, that one of them, Stanley Smith, was oarsman in the university rowing eight was astonishing. He had been converted at the Moody mission of 1874. That another was C. T. Studd, the youngest of three brothers from a famous cricketing family, seemed incomprehensible, because he was not just a Cambridge cricketing blue but regarded as the best current all-round cricketer in England. It soon became a talking point throughout the land, challenging many university students to consider missionary service.[17]

---

15. Pollock, *Keswick Story*, 68–71; Paproth, *Failure*, 29.

16. Stock, *History of CMS*, 3:288–89. There was fear that appeals for funds for missions would be made. Later, however, was enunciated "the great principle that 'Consecration and the Evangelization of the World ought to go together.'"

17. A. F. Walls, cited by Paproth, *Failure*, 40. "No event of the [nineteenth] century has done so much to arouse the minds of Christian men to the claims of the field, and the nobility of the missionary vocation." Stock, *History of CMS*, 3:284.

Quite apart from such a singular event, the combined influence of the spiritual impact of the Moody evangelistic missions, the growing missionary emphasis at Keswick-type conferences, and the peripatetic ministry of a dynamic mission leader such as Hudson Taylor, was undoubtedly responsible for an "explosion" in candidate numbers, and not just for China.[18]

A similar response occurred in North America, where Taylor took meetings during a prolonged visit in 1887. This included meetings at the annual Northfield Conference for student leaders, which had been started by Moody in 1886, inspired by the Cambridge Seven.

As a result, non-denominational Bible colleges sprang up on both sides of the Atlantic to provide training in a theologically conservative environment.[19]

C. H. NASH AT CAMBRIDGE

It was in the English autumn of 1885, in the same year as the departure of the Cambridge Seven, that Clifford Harris Nash, aged nineteen, went up to Cambridge University to begin studies at Corpus Christi College.

Corpus Christi's theological bias had varied through the years but was now firmly positioned in the Evangelical fold. Here Nash's personal spiritual commitment was cemented soon after his arrival in what he later described as a "conversion" experience. He became involved in the activities of CICCU (Cambridge Inter-Collegiate Christian Union) and came to share the missionary vision so recently awakened among its members.

Having completed his BA in 1888, Nash moved to Ridley Hall for one year, in the expectation of being ordained in the Church of England. The chair of Ridley's council was the first Bishop of Melbourne, Charles Perry, who had recently returned to England. Of its teachers noted for their scholarly instruction, the most spiritually influential for Nash was the aforementioned Rev. Handley Moule, later Bishop of Durham. Of him it was said that "he had a scholar's critical eye and a saint's loving insight."[20]

Throughout the Christian world, the 1880s were a time of great skepticism about the truth of the Scriptures. The implications of Darwinism and the approaches of historical criticism to the biblical texts were being widely espoused and had unsettled many Christians. It was not surprising

---

18. Though Moody was respectful and supportive of those involved in Keswick-type spiritual activities, he never personally promoted this approach, preferring to speak of "practical holiness." Pollock, *Keswick*, 66.

19. Bebbington, *Evangelicalism*, 225; Austin, *China's Millions*, 298.

20. Paproth, *Failure*, 17–18, 27–28.

that amongst those who held a very conservative view about the inspiration and infallibility of Scripture, a defensive, even more intensely dogmatic, response could be aroused.[21]

However, the environment in which Nash trained was balanced. His teachers at Ridley Hall were open and respectful in their examination of current scholarship, and were writing commentaries, especially on New Testament books, that gave fair treatment of the issues raised. So it was that Nash always valued scholarship and sought to express an "informed but critical conservatism."[22]

AUSTRALIAN CHRISTIANS AND CHINA

It was in Australia in 1889, only four years after the Cambridge Seven had left England for China and while Nash was still at Ridley Hall, that four ministers from Melbourne began to meet regularly to pray for the spread of the gospel in China. Their leader was Rev. H. B. Macartney, vicar of St. Mary's Anglican Church, Caulfield. The others were his curate, Rev. C. H. Parsons; Rev. Lockhart Morton, a Presbyterian minister; and Rev. Alfred Bird, a Baptist pastor. Macartney was known in Melbourne as an expository preacher and parish leader, and throughout colonial Australia for his advocacy of missionary work. He was to be a key person in the formation in 1892 of the Church Missionary Association (later the Church Missionary Society [CMS]) within the Church of England in Australia.[23]

When this ecumenical quartet began their regular prayer meetings, Australian interest in missionary work in China was limited. There had been an influx of Chinese people to Victoria at the time of the gold rush. Evangelistic activity among them by Chinese Christians from Hong Kong and China, as well as by Australians, had seen Chinese congregations formed.[24] But the Chinese had brought with them opium and gambling habits, and this did not increase their popularity in a society where there was already racial prejudice and that soon afterwards established the White Australia Policy in the Immigration Restriction Act of 1901.[25]

---

21. Piggin and Linder, *Fountain*, 385, 396, 400, 408; Lake, *Bible in Australia*, 168–69; Paproth, *Failure*, 16, 18.

22. Paproth, *Failure*, 20, 21.

23. Piggin and Linder, *Fountain*, 414; Evans and Paproth, *Evangelisation Society*, 29; Cole, "Macartney," 227; Evans and Paproth, *Evangelisation Society*, 29.

24. Lake, *Bible in Australia*, 127.

25. Lake, *Bible in Australia*, 238; Piggin and Linder, *Fountain*, 420.

A significant stimulus for the prayer group is likely to have come from the visit of Mr. George Nicoll, who had served with CIM in China for ten years. When he became ill in 1885, Hudson Taylor suggested a sea voyage to Australia to benefit his health. He stayed for nearly four years, speaking of the work in China at many meetings.[26]

THE AUSTRALIAN CIM COUNCIL FORMED

The first tangible outcome of the group's prayers was the discernment by C. H. Parsons of God's call for him to go to China. He left early in 1890, after Macartney had been given approval from Hudson Taylor to accept him for service.

Unbeknown to them, he was not the first CIM recruit from Australia. Mary Reed of Launceston had been living in London when she enlisted in 1888, and had traveled directly from London to the field. The next year, ill health brought her home to Tasmania, where she spoke widely of her concern for the spread of the gospel in China. Alfred Bird of the Melbourne prayer group, while visiting Launceston, was impressed by the degree of interest that she had stimulated. Mary Reed was invited to the mainland, where, in the churches and private homes of Melbourne and Sydney, her firsthand accounts of the work resulted in offers of service and monetary gifts.

Contact with Hudson Taylor had been established, and requests for a visit from him to capitalize on this interest were sent. While waiting for his response, Macartney called a meeting to form an interim committee. This was held in a room at the Collins St. Baptist Church on May 22, 1890. Nine men were present, including Rev. H. B. Macartney (Chair), Rev. Alfred Bird (Secretary), Mr. Philip Kitchen (Treasurer), and Rev. Lockhart Morton. A tenth person, Rev. Samuel Chapman (minister of Collins St. Baptist), was not present but had agreed to join the council. The cable from Hudson Taylor sanctioning their appointment as an Australasian Home Council had arrived the evening before.[27]

On that first day alone, they had eight offers of service to consider, and interest only intensified during a three-month visit later that year by Hudson Taylor himself. Accompanied by Montague Beauchamp, one of the Cambridge Seven, he addressed meetings in Darwin, Brisbane, Sydney, Melbourne, Hobart, and Adelaide. Three thousand people attended their

---

26. Loane, *Story of CIM*, 5.
27. CIM Australasia Council Minutes, MST Archives, May 22, 1890.

farewell meeting in the Melbourne Town Hall, and they returned to China accompanied by twelve new missionaries, eight women and four men.[28]

With the appointment of mission representatives in state capitals, reports from missionaries on leave, and a further visit from Hudson Taylor in 1899, missionary opportunity in China was consistently presented.[29] By September 1920, when MBI commenced, 211 Australian and New Zealanders had already been sent to China with CIM, fifty of them within five years of the council's formation.[30]

EVANGELICAL NETWORKS IN MELBOURNE

Concurrent with the growth of CIM interests in Australia was the development of meetings for the deepening of spiritual life, as had similarly occurred in Britain. Macartney had been present at the English Keswick Convention in 1878, when he had given addresses at the daily prayer meetings, and again in 1893.[31] At home, he accompanied the visiting Keswick missioner, George Grubb, to the first Geelong Convention in 1891, where they were both speakers, as was Alfred Bird. At least two other CIM council members were on the convention committee: its convenor, Rev. Samuel Chapman, and Rev. George Soltau.[32]

As in Britain, so in Australia, the impact of evangelistic campaigns, such as those of Torrey and Alexander in 1902 and that of Chapman and Alexander in 1909 and 1912, together with a strong focus on personal witness and missionary endeavor at these small Keswick-style conventions around Australia, resulted in the interest of more candidates for all missions.

TRAINING FOR CIM CANDIDATES

From the beginning in 1890, a major concern for the CIM council was the adequacy of applicants' preparation for a missionary assignment. More than spiritual passion was needed. Indeed, in the minutes of their first meeting, we read a recommendation that "Candidates needing training in Christian work and testing as to their general adaptation be placed under the care and

---

28. Loane, *Story of CIM*, 11.

29. The minutes of October 21, 1919 record that in one six-month period in 1919, 413 meetings with a total attendance of 28,464 had been held (MST Archives).

30. Loane, *Story of CIM*, 20, 21, 35, 49. Taylor and Taylor, *Growth*, 585.

31. Piggin and Linder, *Fountain*, 450; Renshaw, *Marvellous Melbourne*, 35.

32. Renshaw, *Marvellous Melbourne*, 35, 36.

direction of some of the city or suburban pastors for a few months as may afterwards be directed."[33]

At their monthly meetings, there were few occasions when there were no new applicants to meet or papers of applicants to examine. Comments about the suitability of candidates in regard to their sense of calling and spiritual maturity were minuted. Concern for some was expressed because they "had led sheltered lives and needed to be in contact with human nature on its darker side," so experience in "city mission work" was recommended. Repeatedly, however, the main reservations centered around their knowledge of Scripture. "Exceedingly deficient" or "abysmally ignorant" are some of the judgments recorded. Those sent to individual pastors for supervised training were expected to gain biblical knowledge. But there was no defined program and subjective judgments were used to assess progress.

In the thirty years before the opening of Melbourne Bible Institute, there were several semi-official training possibilities for CIM candidates, both men and women, in some instances shared with CMS. Mrs. Warren, wife of council member Dr. W. Warren, ran a training home for women candidates in Melbourne from 1892 to 1901.

It so happened that C. H. Nash, having been ordained as a Church of England minister in England, had arrived in Australia in 1895, becoming the vicar of St. Columb's Church of England, Hawthorn, Victoria in 1900. In that parish, in 1902, he commenced St. Hilda's College, the purpose of which was to train women as Church of England deaconesses. Also in 1902, Mr. and Mrs. James Griffiths, strong supporters of both CIM and CMS, had opened "Hiawatha" in Fitzroy for women candidates for CIM and CMS. In 1907, these two colleges amalgamated and continued to function in East Melbourne under the name St Hilda's.[34]

Rev. Lockhart Morton, another council member, moved to Adelaide in 1893, establishing a training home for men, with a facility for women commencing two years later. In 1915, Rev. C. Benson Barnett, a CIM missionary from 1894 to 1907 and now a council member, assisted Morton, who had been ill. Early in 1916, Barnett moved to Sydney, where he commenced what later became the "Sydney Missionary and Bible College" (SMBC). From its beginning, SMBC welcomed male CIM candidates, though it was independent of the mission. The college became open to women in 1928.[35]

---

33. CIM Minutes, MST Archives, May 22, 1890.
34. Paproth, *Failure*, 59–60; Piggin and Linder, *National Soul*, 133.
35. Brammall, *Out of Darkness*, 47–51, 81.

MELBOURNE BIBLE INSTITUTE COMMENCES

The CIM council minutes of January 24, 1919 record that St Hilda's was no longer considered suitable for their training needs. Then we read: "The suggestion was considered as to the possibility of training our own women candidates in which Mr. Nash—on the CIM council since 1916—would be willing to help."

The subject of training is not mentioned again in the minutes for more than eighteen months. In that interval, the conviction grew among individual council members that Nash's teaching gifts could be well used in the establishment of a Bible Institute for both men and women—something for which several had long prayed. This plan was reinforced as Nash led a series of weeknight Bible studies in the home of Dr. Kitchen, attended by other council members.[36] The CIM minutes for August 17, 1920 read: "It was reported that preliminary steps had been taken to found a Bible Institute to be called Melbourne Bible Institute with Rev. C. H. Nash as Principal." The first meeting of the MBI Committee occurred six days later, on 23 August.

Comparing the makeup at this time of the Australasian Council of CIM, the MBI council, and the Upwey Convention council (the latter constituted formally in 1922), several committed laymen were members of two, if not three, of these groups. Mr. Edwin Lee Neil, a highly respected Melbourne businessman, having been on the CIM council, became the first chairman of the MBI council.[37] Most notable was Dr. J. J. Kitchen, vice-chairman of the new MBI council and a member until 1950. His father, Philip Kitchen, had been the first treasurer for the Australasian CIM. Dr. Kitchen himself offered to serve in China in 1896 but for health reasons did not proceed.[38] He joined the council in 1897, visited China for two months in 1911, and in 1915 became the assistant director for Australasia and the director from 1922 to 1938. He was also vice-chairman of the Upwey Convention council at its formation, becoming the chairman from 1928 to 1947.[39]

A statement from the new council informing friends of the founding of MBI drew attention to the success of the Moody Bible Institute in Chicago and other such institutes and its intention to pursue similar goals. Assurance was given that the committee "is interdenominational in character and

---

36. Dr. Kitchen's "Life Memories," cited by Paproth, *Failure*, 93.

37. Neil had been a close friend of Nash since being appointed the organist at St. Columb's Church, Hawthorn, during Nash's ministry there.

38. Taylor, Personal letter to J. J. Kitchen.

39. Paproth, "Kitchen, John James," 205. J. J. Kitchen's son, Rev. Howard Kitchen, was a missionary in China with CIM from 1928 to 1950, after which he joined the lecturing staff of MBI.

consists of men who accept in the fullest sense the authority and inspiration of the Scriptures, and who hold firmly to the fundamentals of the faith."[40]

The MBI council remained alert to the growing influence of liberal theology within denominational colleges in Australia and worldwide. As members of the CIM council, they had endorsed the action of the China council of the mission in 1916 in withdrawing from the continuing committee of the Edinburgh World Missions Conference. This committee arose from the 1910 conference and had held great promise for global evangelism, but it quickly lost its Evangelical roots.[41]

Just as Hudson Taylor had desired to unlock the potential within people of limited education to become evangelists, so MBI had no required level of education for entry. Indeed, during the first three decades at least, it was rare for a student to have a university degree. The content of the curriculum was almost exclusively the study of the biblical text, with a strong devotional emphasis, alongside practical training in evangelism in open-air preaching, city mission work, hospital visiting, and religious education in schools.

MBI was never intended to be a training college solely for CIM candidates, though a significant proportion of the students went to China as missionaries. In the twenty-two years before Nash retired as principal in 1942, over one thousand students had been enrolled, of whom approximately two-thirds had proceeded into full-time Christian service at home or abroad. In that same period, 240 Australians and New Zealanders went to China with CIM, of whom at least eighty had trained at MBI.[42]

Students were regularly addressed by visiting mission and church leaders and by former students on leave from China and elsewhere. In the visitors' book commenced in 1923, the first entry is of Frank McCarthy, headmaster of the CIM Boys' School in Chefoo, China. In 1926, Dr. Howard and Mrs. Geraldine Taylor, son and daughter-in-law of Hudson Taylor, visited MBI, and Mrs. Taylor spoke at the annual public meeting for MBI supporters. Nash took a close and prayerful personal interest in all the former students wherever they were ministering. He made visits to overseas mission fields, including several weeks in China in 1936.

Strong links with the "holiness movement" were maintained, though Nash was careful to reject any hint of the excesses that this movement could encourage and tended to emphasize rather the necessity of "scriptural

---

40. C. H. Nash, "The Melbourne Bible Institute, Prahran, Victoria, August 27, 1920," MST Archives; Piggin and Linder, *National Soul*, 134.

41. CIM Minutes, MST Archives, November 21, 1916; Neill, *Christian Missions*, 418.

42. Loane, *Story of CIM*, 159–63. See also MBI records.

obedience" and the importance of discipleship.⁴³ He gave the Bible readings at Upwey Convention in his first year as the principal of MBI and did so again at many future gatherings. For more than fifty years there was a session at the convention devoted to the ministry of MBI as a missionary training center, thus strongly connecting it to the Keswick movement in Australia.⁴⁴

EVANGELICALISM IN MELBOURNE IN 1920

There is no doubt that in Evangelical Melbourne in the years leading up to 1920, the support given to foreign missions was seen as the truest indication of a person's commitment, "a barometer of spiritual fitness."⁴⁵ This quality, exhibited so prominently in the MBI culture, can be seen as an expression of the activism which Bebbington includes as one of the four characteristic features of Evangelicalism. MBI demonstrated their embrace of the other three characteristics just as surely, including their commitment to the authority of Scripture, to a crucicentric theology, and to the need for individual conversion to faith, all occurring within the spiritual fellowship of "pan-Evangelicalism."⁴⁶

In its fifty-five-year history, CIM had already demonstrated these characteristics, and in this time, it had also played a significant role, directly and indirectly, in the foundation of Bible colleges, especially in North America.⁴⁷ CIM's role in such strategic developments led Stanley to say: "The China Inland Mission, perhaps more than any other single organisation, was responsible for fashioning the international network of conservative Evangelicalism in the twentieth century."⁴⁸ Both the CIM under Hudson Taylor and his successors and MBI under C. H. Nash and his successors have been aligned wholeheartedly with orthodox Evangelicalism in a fellowship crossing denominational boundaries. A vital personal piety

---

43. Paproth, *Failure*, 124.
44. Renshaw, *Marvellous Melbourne*, 100.
45. Piggin and Linder, *Fountain*, 352, 431.
46. Bebbington, *Evangelicalism*, 3–4, 271; Evans and Paproth, *Evangelisation Society*, 19.
47. Austin, *China's Millions*, 298, 316. The founding of Toronto Bible Training School occurred in 1894 in a meeting of twelve members of the Canadian CIM council in a private home. It bore a marked similarity to circumstances in the foundation of MBI twenty-six years later.
48. Austin, *China's Millions*, xiv.

expressed in Keswick terms has been a significant added strand in its ongoing culture and strength.

Stanley also said, speaking elsewhere specifically of the Melbourne scene, "Through the Institute [MBI] and the Upwey Convention, the Australian counterpart of Keswick holiness revivalism shaped Melbourne Evangelicalism."[49]

BIBLIOGRAPHY

Austin, Alvyn. *China's Millions: The China Inland Mission and Late Qing Society, 1832–1905*. Grand Rapids, MI: William B. Eerdmans, 2007.

Bebbington, David. *Evangelicalism in the Modern World*. Grand Rapids, MI: Baker, 1989.

Brammall, Anthony C. *Out of Darkness*. Croydon, NSW: SMBC, 2016.

Cole, Keith. "Macartney, Hussey Burgh (Jr.)." In *The Australian Dictionary of Evangelical Biography*, edited by Brian Dickey, 227–28. Sydney Evangelical History Association, 1994.

Evans, Robert, and Darrell Paproth. *The Evangelisation Society of Australasia*. Hazelbrook, NSW: Robert Evans, 2010.

Lake, Meredith. *The Bible in Australia*. Sydney: Newsouth, 2018.

Loane, Marcus L. *The Story of the China Inland Mission in Australia and New Zealand 1890–1964*. Sydney: China Inland Mission, Overseas Missionary Fellowship, 1965.

Neill, Stephen. *A History of Christian Missions: Penguin History of the Church, vol. 6*. London: Penguin, 1986.

Paproth, Darrell. *Attending to the National Soul*. Melbourne: Monash University Press, 2019.

———. *Failure is not Final*. Sydney: Centre for the Study of Australian Christianity, 1997.

———. "Kitchen, John James." In *The Australian Dictionary of Evangelical Biography*, edited by Brian Dickey, 205. Sydney: Sydney Evangelical History Association, 1994.

Piggin, Stuart, and Robert D. Linder. *The Fountain of Public Prosperity*. Melbourne: Monash University Press, 2018.

Pollock, J. C. *Hudson Taylor and Maria*. Eastbourne: Kingsway, 1962.

———. *The Keswick Story*. London: Hodder and Stoughton, 1964.

———. *Moody: The Biography*. Chicago: Moody, 1983.

Renshaw, Will. *Marvellous Melbourne and Spiritual Power*. Melbourne: Acorn, 2004.

Stock, Eugene. *History of the Church Missionary Society*. London: Church Missionary Society, 1899.

Tan, Jin Huat. *Planting an Indigenous Church: The Case of the Borneo Evangelical Mission*. Eugene, Oregon: Wipf & Stock, 2011.

Taylor, Howard, and Taylor, Geraldine. *Hudson Taylor and the China Inland Mission: The Growth of a Work of God*. London: OMF, 1919.

Taylor, Hudson J. Personal letter to J. J. Kitchen. MST Archives, February 4, 1896.

---

49. Tan, *Planting an Indigenous Church*, ix.

2

The First Three Principals 1920–1970

Rowland S. Ward

THIS CHAPTER LOOKS AT the first fifty years of MBI/BCV/MST history. It reviews the origin of the Bible institute movement and notes the importance of significant businessmen who provided leadership support. The background of the three principals who served in the first fifty years is given attention at some length since each man brought to his task his previous experiences and their lessons. Each man was well educated and, with good sense and intelligence, stood for the Bible as the authoritative word of God. Each man suffered for his stand, but all made a major contribution to the missionary endeavor. The pattern established by the charismatic C. H. Nash was developed by the steady work of John W. Searle, while the farseeing Graham Miller sought to face up to the new circumstances of the 1960s. A path has been created for future principals to fulfill his vision.

What manner of men led MBI/BCV/MST in its first fifty years? This chapter seeks to understand the influences that shaped the three men who led MBI/BCV/MST as principals between 1920 and 1970.

C. H. NASH, PRINCIPAL 1920-1942

Clifford Harris Nash was born on December 16, 1866, the seventh of the eight children of Frederick and Ellen Nash. Frederick was a merchant in London, chiefly in the tea trade with the Levant. Cliff was educated at the Dames School in Hammersmith and was a boarder at the secondary school conducted by the Grocers' Company at Oundle, 125 kilometers north of London, from 1876 to 1885. In 1880 his father, with whom he did not have a close relationship, died, but scholarships from the Grocers' Company enabled him to stay on at Oundle. Cliff did well academically and in sport and was captain of the well-regarded private school in 1884 and 1885. He won a Classics scholarship to Corpus Christi College, Cambridge, and began there in October 1885 at the age of nineteen. Corpus Christi was then an Evangelical college led by the Rev. Henry Perowne. Nash had not shown any particular religious commitments other than the traditional Victorian Anglicanism of his early years. When he attended a Cambridge Inter-Collegiate Christian Union (CICCU) meeting in 1886 he found it distasteful,[1] but through an Australian student,[2] apparently himself recently converted, Cliff made a definite commitment of his life to Christ. CICCU meetings were now a pleasure and he soon began teaching a class of boys on Sunday afternoon in one of the local parish churches.

Religious tests had been removed from the English universities in 1871 even as improvements in theological education were advancing. Nash was significantly influenced by a trio of famous Cambridge scholars, B. F. Westcott, J. B. Lightfoot, and F. J. A. Hort. Lightfoot had left Cambridge in 1879 to become Bishop of Durham but deeply impacted the university he left behind by his thorough historical scholarship and work on reverent biblical commentaries with his friends Westcott and Hort. While the Cambridge Trio were not Evangelicals and somewhat accommodated to modern trends, they responded to rationalistic German criticism by an approach that committed to basic doctrines concerning the person of Christ and the reliability of the Bible. Most Evangelicals increasingly tended to rest the authority of the Bible in experience rather than the Scriptures themselves and coped well enough; others reacted into a more literalistic approach to Scripture associated with the rise of premillennial hermeneutics earlier in

---

1. Chambers, *Tempest Tost*, 14.

2. Arthur E. Bellingham (1858–1927) was the man (Paproth, *Failure*, 209, n. 29). He graduated with a BA from Corpus Christi in 1886 and spent from October 1886 to June 1887 in theological studies at Ridley Hall, Cambridge before beginning ministry in the Sydney diocese at the end of 1887; see *Cable Clerical Index*. On Bellingham and Nash, see Piggin and Linder, *Fountain*, 449.

the century. Nash remained loyal to the Church of England and avoided extremes. He graduated with a BA in 1888 (the MA was granted in the usual Cambridge way in 1890) and enrolled in October that year at Ridley Hall, Cambridge, for theological studies.

Ridley Hall had been founded in 1881 by Evangelicals led by Charles Perry (1807–1891), the first Bishop of Melbourne between 1847 and 1876, who had retired to England. The aim was to prepare men more adequately for ministry. There was a doctrinal test to ward off the twin errors of rationalism and ritualism. The principal from 1881 to 1899 was Handley G. C. Moule (1841–1920), whose influence in Cambridge was growing and whose likeminded brother Charles was a tutor at Corpus Christi in Nash's time. Nash's uncle, Rev. Thomas Nash, was also on the Ridley Council. These connections, as well as the example of his friend Arthur Bellingham, who had finished at Ridley the year before, would have led Nash to Ridley. Of Handley Moule, it was said that "he had a scholar's critical eye and a saint's loving insight," and his many books were popular. Moule concentrated on daily exposition of the Greek text to his forty or so students and was not interested in interacting polemically with higher critical theories. He associated with the Higher Life movement and spoke at the first Keswick Convention in 1875. Moule's influence on Nash was considerable. Nash graduated at a first-class level in the Preliminary Theological Examinations in June 1889 but was six months short of the minimum age for ordination of twenty-three.

Nash taught at Loretto School in Musselburgh, Edinburgh from October 1889 to April 1891. He taught Greek, Latin, English, and Divinity, preached on Sundays, and maintained a clear Evangelical witness despite the rather different and autocratic leadership of the school of one hundred students. Nash was ordained deacon by Bishop B. F. Westcott on June 1, 1890. He soon moved, at the invitation of Canon Joseph Bardsley, to be third curate at St. Peter's Huddersfield, an Evangelical parish where he was responsible for a branch church. Within three months there was an invitation from a friend from Cambridge days to go with him on a world tour, all expenses paid by his friend's wealthy father, manager of Barclay's Bank. It was not mere tourism but essentially a visit to Church Missionary Society stations. Against the wishes of Bardsley and his bishop, Nash resolved to go, setting off in February 1892. They traveled through Europe to India, Ceylon, Hong Kong, and Shanghai to reach Japan, where his friend's uncle was a CMS missionary, and then on to Canada and the United States, returning home in July 1892. The trip broadened Nash's vision so that the missionary cause remained close to his heart.

Nash resumed work in Huddersfield and was ordained there as a priest on February 26, 1893. The work was going well, and it seems that there was an "understanding" between him and Bardsley's daughter, Gertrude. She usually played the organ at the evening service in Nash's church and walked home with him after the service. One evening she could not go and sent her sister Ethel instead. Although only twenty-eight, Nash had the offer of a parish in Staffordshire and, in high spirits as he walked Ethel home, he impetuously sought to kiss her. She resisted, her parents were outraged; Canon Bardsley withdrew his support for the move to Staffordshire, and Nash, protesting, "It was only a kiss," apologized but resigned. It was, as Bardsley later wrote, an act of impropriety not of immorality; but it was to cast a long shadow.

Nash in Australia

A Cambridge friend, son of the second Bishop of Brisbane (1875–1885), invited Nash to accompany him to Australia and so in February 1895 they left for Tasmania. From October 1895 Nash was the superintendent of the short-lived social experiment for the unemployed known as the Southport Settlement. He also preached in the Church of England at Dover, twenty kilometers further south. Old Evangelical friends in Sydney spoke up for him, and Canon Bardsley also recommended him for work. In February 1897 he was welcomed to Sydney by Arthur Bellingham and granted a general license to officiate by Bishop Saumarez Smith. He was curate at St. Philip's, Church Hill, a notable Evangelical parish, but served the mission church at Ultimo with enthusiasm, including open-air preaching and evangelism. He became *locum tenens* of the busy working-class parish of St. Paul's, Redfern, on January 2, 1899, the minister being absent for the rest of the year. On January 31 he married Louise Mary Maude Pearse, the twenty-year-old niece of the rector of St. Philip's. The congregation grew, as Nash was an excellent and persuasive preacher, but an invitation came later in the year from a prominent congregation in Melbourne, which he accepted.

Nash was inducted into St. Columb's, Hawthorn, on January 19, 1899. St. Columb's had a strong Evangelical tradition and attracted congregations of around six hundred morning and evening. He was doing well. In 1904 Nash visited England with his wife (the three young children being left in the care of Hawthorn friends) and he renewed friendships there. His wider vision was reflected in the activities beyond St. Columb's in which he was increasingly involved both before and after his overseas trip. He lectured on Scripture at the newly established St. John's Anglican theological college in 1906. In that year, Christ Church Geelong was looking to find a replacement for its now eighty-five-year-old vicar, who had served fifty-one years in this

Evangelical parish. The position was offered to Nash, who accepted and was inducted on September 5, 1906.

However, a year later, rumors circulated in St. Columb's of alleged impropriety with a female servant in his own employ. It arose because Mrs. Nash, who had been used to a spoilt social life and who now had responsibility for six young children, felt that she was not getting the attention that she deserved from her busy husband. The marriage was not working well; and Mrs. Nash confided in a recently widowed lady in the congregation concerns that lost perspective in the telling or the hearing. Nash was not always as careful as he might have been; but there was no substance to the allegations, nor to rumors from Nash's past in England that were also raised. The archbishop since 1902, Lowther Clarke, was not an Evangelical and he handled the matter poorly.[3] Nash foolishly agreed to a procedure that was prejudicial to him, rashly promising to resign if the decision went against him. Accordingly, he resigned at the end of October 1907. Christ Church Geelong, and Evangelicals generally, were not happy with St. John's College (which became High Church in orientation) or with the treatment of Nash. The press sided with Nash too. His circumstances meant that Nash did not play a significant role in Ridley College, Parkville, which was founded in 1910 for training ordinands and future missionaries on an Evangelical basis.

The archbishop was under pressure and, during a visit to England soon after, had to acknowledge that there was nothing relevant in the rumors. Nash was granted a general license on August 11, 1908, but Clarke repeatedly refused to allow Nash to be renominated to Christ Church, Geelong. Nash resolved to accept the offer to be rector of St. Paul's, Sale, and was appointed to this rural parish on October 30, 1908. He was doing well, but a disturbing libel case was raised in 1909 and worked its way to a conclusion in June 1912. It was brought by Lowther Clarke against the scurrilous newspaper *Truth*, which had attributed malice to Clarke in handling the Nash case. The case was settled in Clarke's favor, although for a lesser sum than he had claimed, before he could be cross-examined by the newspaper's barristers. Allegations against Nash were publicized, and to some it seemed that Nash had been discredited. He felt he should resign from Sale as he did not wish to be a disintegrating force in the church that he had loyally served. He duly resigned on August 1, 1912.

For a time, Nash conducted a school in Kew, but in February 1915 resigned his ministry in the Church of England and was inducted to charge of the Prahran Congregational Church on May 31, 1915. Later that year

3. Paproth is highly critical of Clarke, see *Failure*, 67–77; Grant, *Episcopally Led*, 134–35, states rather unhelpfully: "Clarke had done what he thought was his duty and hardly deserved the approbrium directed towards him by Nash's friends and supporters."

he joined the Council of China Inland Mission, and in June 1917 offered to serve CIM in any capacity or sphere thought suitable, although nothing came of it at that time. From 1917 to 1919 Nash was also Classics master at Caulfield Grammar, supplementing his income in this way to support his large family. He gave Bible expositions at the first Upwey Convention in 1918 and regularly in subsequent years. Then in 1920, at age 53, he was appointed as the first principal of Melbourne Bible Institute.

Founding MBI 1920

The Melbourne Bible Institute began in 1920 to answer a particular need but it was not an isolated endeavor without precursors overseas and in Australia.

The Bible institute movement was an outgrowth of the missionary concern of Evangelicals in the second half of the nineteenth century. Notable is the conversion around 1855 of Dublin-born Henry Grattan Guinness (1835–1910) and his ordination in London as an independent evangelist two years later. Guinness, who belonged to the Guinness brewing family, had been brought up in the Methodist Church in Ireland and became one of many Protestant Christians who formed a spiritual network based on a common belief in the authority of the Scriptures, the centrality of Christ, the necessity of conversion, and the importance of the missionary task.[4] Keswick "Higher Life" teaching had impacted many of these people from 1875. With its emphasis on "complete surrender" and trusting God to supply one's needs, as exemplified by George Müller (1805–1898), one of the founders of the Christian Brethren, the contribution to the missionary effort of these evangelicals was to be vast.[5]

Guinness was early described as "an eloquent young preacher . . . said to be equal in power to preacher Spurgeon with more mental culture."[6] He traveled widely in his endeavor to advance the cause of world evangelization. In 1873 Guinness began the *East London Training Institute* (also known as *Harley College*), which provided missionaries for, among others, J. Hudson Taylor's fledgling *China Inland Mission* formed in 1865. In 1859, while ministering in Canada, Guinness was instrumental in the conversion of A. B. Simpson (1843–1919), who became a Presbyterian minister

---

4. These four points correspond more or less with the quadrilateral (biblicism, crucicentrism, conversionism, and activism) of David Bebbington, *Evangelicalism*, 2–17, but contrast with the fuller convictions of historic confessional bodies and even the brief statement of the Evangelical Alliance on its formation in 1846.

5. For a survey see Banks, "Influence."

6. *Western Times* (Exeter, UK), February 22, 1856, 5.

in 1865. In 1882 Simpson founded the *Missionary Training Institute* in New York—the first in the United States—and later founded what became the Christian and Missionary Alliance.

If cooperation between the like-minded in different denominations owed much to Evangelical optimism in an age of progress, there was also a note of urgency because, in a premillennarian context, which had become quite usual in the latter half of the nineteenth century, the time before Christ's return was viewed as very short, and the gospel had to be preached to all of the nations first (Matt 24:14). Training through denominational agencies could take six or seven years. Higher-critical views of the Bible based on anti-supernatural bias emerged in the 1860s and were commonplace in regular theological colleges by the 1890s. Besides, it was considered that a thorough knowledge of the Bible and practical training in the skills needed for missionary work such as outdoor ministry and door-to-door work were sufficient.

The Evangelicals who joined hands in Melbourne were led chiefly by prominent and devoted businessmen with a vision for evangelism at home and abroad.[7] In May 1890 an Australian Council for the China Inland Mission was formed in Melbourne at the request of Hudson Taylor, who made a visit to Australia from August to November 1890. Several efforts were made to provide missionary training in which the Bible would be the textbook supplemented by practical subjects. The Rev. W. Lockhart Morton (1851–1928), a Presbyterian, was providing such training in Adelaide from 1893 with the encouragement of Taylor and the backing of prominent evangelical Baptist pastoralist, politician, and philanthropist John Howard Angas (1823–1904).[8] In Victoria there was the Missionary Training Home at Kew opened by Baptist medical doctor William Warren from 1891 to 1901 to train women for CIM under his wife's supervision. It closed with the Warrens' departure for an extended visit to England. In 1901 C. H. Nash was behind opening *St. Hilda's* near St. Columb's Church as an institution for training deaconesses, while in 1902 James and Emily Griffiths of Griffith Bros., the well-known tea merchants, opened the *Hiawatha Training Home for Women* at 199 Victoria Road, Fitzroy. In effect it carried on the work of Dr. and Mrs. Warren but aimed to supply missionaries for CMS as well as

---

7. A popular introductory overview is Renshaw, *Marvellous Melbourne*. Darrell Paproth has written extensively in this area and made it his own, for example, "1888 Centennial Mission," 31–65.

8. Paproth, "Faith Missions." The *Angas College Trust Act*, assented to December 7, 1921, enabled the assets to be used outside South Australia and recounts some of the history. Angas assets were absorbed into MBI in 1932.

CIM,[9] since the Griffiths were loyal Anglicans and also part of the Evangelical network. The following year St. Hilda's and Hiawatha were united under the name *St. Hilda's Missionary Training Home* using the Fitzroy premises. The Griffiths funded both this and the building in East Melbourne to which it moved in 1907.[10]

However, St. Hilda's became more Anglican after the First World War, and CIM felt it was not providing the training needed for its missionaries who would serve overseas. On August 23, 1920 the council took the opportunity to offer Nash the position of founding principal of what would be known as the Melbourne Bible Institute. Lockhart Morton and William Gray[11] in Adelaide, and Benson Barnett[12] in Sydney, were sent information explaining the purpose of MBI.[13] Thus in no parochial way was MBI begun, and it soon became the premier institution of its kind in Australia.

The Chief

However he is assessed, Nash's background made him the ideal principal for MBI. Certainly, he could be impetuous, he lacked administrative ability and business sense, and he did not have a very supportive wife. But he was an English middle- or upper-middle-class gentleman, well-educated, a born teacher, an arresting preacher, and good with people, and he had learned from his troubles. He was deeply connected with the interdenominational Evangelical network. He did not read the Scriptures in the excessively literalistic way of premillennialists but could work positively with those of diverse background who agreed on the fundamentals without falling into separatist narrowness. His deficiencies were made up by a body of supportive lay Evangelicals, which included shrewd and very successful business

---

9. Paproth, *Failure*, 60.

10. Kuan, *Foundations*, 212; Chambers, *Tempest Tost*, 66–67.

11. The Rev. William Gray (1854–1937) was a Presbyterian and acted as principal of the short-lived Adelaide-based Chapman-Alexander Bible Institute between the principalship of the Rev. Dr. John H. Elliot (1914–1916) of the US and James F. Archer (1921–1922) of BTI, Glasgow.

12. Barnett was born in Tasmania of Congregational parents. He studied with Morton in 1893, and served CIM between 1894–1907; Latrobe, Don and Forth CU 1908–1910; Brunswick CU 1911–1914; Angas College 1915; thence foundation principal SMBC 1916–1937 for whose history see Brammall, *Out of Darkness*.

13. Paproth, *Failure*, 94. The report in the *Argus* (Melbourne), October 13, 1920, 9, gives the impression Morton was "the originator" but that was certainly not so. However, the report is evidence at that point that Morton envisaged some kind of partnership with MBI.

people such as Edwin Lee Neil (1872–1934), who was the managing director of Myer, the first president of MBI, and also Nash's closest friend, and Dr. John James Kitchen (1866–1952), the vice-president and driving figure behind the forming of the institute.

MBI began in August 1920 with one student in a room at the Prahran Church. Others were soon added and in 1921 Nash became the full-time principal. He was to lead MBI until 1942 and set his stamp on the institute, training some one thousand students, 553 of whom entered full-time service.[14] He was reconciled to the Church of England and relicensed in 1926 but was active widely in Evangelical ecumenism. As well as involvement with CMS, Nash was a regular speaker at the Upwey Convention (later Belgrave Heights) from its beginning in 1918. He was the first chairman (1923) of the newly organized Bible Union, which challenged modernist assumptions.[15] Nash was also first chairman of the Borneo Evangelical Mission, which originated at MBI in 1927. He taught the evening City Men's Bible Class from its beginning in 1929 to 1942—in effect a very well-patronized evening extension of MBI, and in 1936 Campaigners for Christ arose out of the impact on many who attended it.[16]

He had definite ideas of what the institute should be and embodied them as an example of godly living. There were strict rules on conduct with students of the opposite sex, which reflected an understanding common in the Keswick tradition, doubtless reinforced in Nash's mind from his own experience. First names were not used between the sexes and male and female students could not speak to each other except in limited circumstances and under supervision. At the commencement address on August 27, 1920 Nash stressed that the institute was for "training men and women in the knowledge of the Holy Scriptures for all manner of Christian service." He said that, "The Bible is the very Word of God, the repository and the Bulwark of Divine Truth." He affirmed that, "Our most powerful and persuasive arguments in anti-Christian writings come from so-called Christian scholarship." On the other hand, the book of God "will bear without loss the sincerest and most searching examination. Its genuineness will defy the acid as well as the sledge-hammer of criticism."[17] No other book for the study of

14. From the total eighty-six served in China, seventy-two among Australian Aborigines, sixty-two in the Pacific Islands, and fifty-eight in India. Renshaw, *Marvellous Melbourne*, 101.

15. Contrary to some accounts, the Bible Union was not initially literalist or a body with a separatist approach, nor even one having a uniform doctrine of Scripture. Its minutes were deposited in MBI archives by the author who located them in 2008.

16. Paproth, *Failure*, 125.

17. Quotations from Nash, "Statements."

the Bible was used except the Bible itself, and when teaching the New Testament, Nash taught in English directly from the Greek text.

The position of Christian orthodoxy was, and is, that the Scriptures are the revelation of God and therefore without mistake or error in all they intend to convey, but that sin blinds us to this reality. Accordingly, *saving* understanding of the message is the work of the Holy Spirit and the experience of the new birth was, and is, the vital issue for Evangelicals. In the last half of the nineteenth century the impact of higher criticism led many to give greater emphasis to experience, and for some the inspiration of Scripture was limited to matters related to salvation with the historic basis of the faith retained. With such Nash could join hands, as in the Bible Union referred to earlier, but while he considered scientific or historical errors could conceivably exist in the Bible, he had not found any. Nash did not give experience priority in the way liberals did yet he could also quote approvingly the liberal Archdeacon of Manchester, James Wilson, who taught that the bedrock of experience was that on which faith in the Bible as the word of God rests.[18] Nash's attitude was movingly summed up in 1922:

> The one thing criticism can never expunge from this Book, the Bible, is what we speak of as the GOSPEL—its continuous, coherent, self-attesting discovery to man of the mind of God concerning man himself; his sin, the guilt and ruin into which sin has plunged him; and over against that, the method of a Divine salvation, the outcome of a purpose of eternal love, wrought out in the ages of progressive revelation and culminating in the mission, life, death, atoning work, and resurrection of his Son, Jesus Christ, and in his gift of His Spirit to the Church and believers.[19]

Christian theology was not taught as a distinct subject since a clear distinction was made between a Bible institute and a theological college. Of course, "the Bible alone" is not the be-all and end-all: it is "the Bible correctly interpreted" that is the sound principle. The Christian faith involves theological and historical reflection if mistakes are to be avoided. Evangelical interdenominational cooperation in equipping Christian workers was a more modest but more suitable approach, Nash held. It met the great need for frontline missionaries, avoided the danger of an excessively academic

---

18. An address given by Nash in Melbourne Town Hall. Chambers, *Tempest Tost*, 175, 178, says it was in 1907 but Nash's address on July 30, 1907 related to the virgin birth (*The Age*, July 31, 1907, 8). Rather, it appears to be the address given at an interdenominational "Conference on the Foundations of Christianity" on December 4, 1922 and was so reported in the *Southern Cross* in January 1923; see also Parker, "Fundamentalism," 61, n. 87.

19. From the closing section of the 1922 address in Chambers, *Tempest Tost*, 181.

approach, while it could be a good preparation for college training for those of academic ability. Nash's good sense and his irenic nature ensured there were no serious doctrinal disputes during his time, other than in 1925. In that year, there was advocacy of Pentecostal views involving the then-normal two-stage theology (i.e. a distinct baptism of the Spirit separable from initial conversion). Nash stood against this and the council backed him. They were unable to dissuade the advocates, and to Nash's sorrow, eight of the then fifty-one students withdrew.[20]

Nash became known as "the Chief" as he continued in a steady path as teacher of a total of 440 men and 573 women until his retirement in 1942. He maintained a ministry at St. George's Battery Point in Hobart, and also in Sydney under Archbishop Mowll.

He retired to Belgrave in 1953 to read, pray, and counsel the many who came to see him, as well as to preach as opportunity arose. Nash died on September 27, 1958 at the age of 91 and, after a funeral in St. Paul's Cathedral, was buried in Dromana with the graveside service taken by his only surviving son, the Rev. Laurence Nash.

"In the life of C. H. Nash, failure had not been final."[21] The effective Bible-teaching ministry of this charismatic leader, his encouragement and involvement in many good works of Evangelical endeavor, and his overall balance ensured his influence to be hard to overestimate. He became the elder statesman of Melbourne Evangelicals.

JOHN WILLIAM SEARLE, PRINCIPAL 1944-1963

The second principal was a man who had studied at MBI himself and who had become vice-principal in 1942 and acting principal the following year. Council member, the Rev. W. R. McEwen of the Reformed Presbyterian Church in Mackinnon, recalled:

> I remember, when he was Vice Principal and Mr. Nash has just resigned as Principal, I immediately thought that Mr. Searle would be the natural and logical choice. Then I met Mr. Tregaskis, the Secretary of MBI, in Elizabeth Street, and asked him, "Have you appointed a new principal yet?" "It's hard to get anyone," he said, "to take the place of the Chief." I replied, "John Searle will make a far better Principal than Mr. Nash. I admire Mr. Nash as the founder of MBI, and he is a genius. Mr. Searle is not a genius. He had to gain his knowledge and experience the

20. Paproth, *Failure*, 102–3.
21. Paproth, *Failure*, 173.

hard way. But that will give him a greater understanding of the students and a sympathy with them."[22]

Who was this John Searle? He was the first of the three children of William Herbert Searle (1876–1951) and Susan Fyfe Searle née Johnston (1869–1959), and was born in the town of Normanby, then in the North Riding of Yorkshire, on March 29, 1905. John's father was recorded as an insurance agent at this time. Isabella was born in 1906 and Walter in 1908. Soon afterwards the family moved a short distance south-east to the small farming village of Commondale, where his father had employment as an ironstone getter.[23] Later he worked in the brickworks that were then flourishing. In both places there was a Methodist church and, as the family was devout and maintained family worship, it is likely they were involved there. In 1919 the family moved to Glasgow, where John's mother had been born. They were connected with the Sydney Place United Presbyterian Congregation in the East End. John worked in a stockbroker's office, was active in Christian circles beyond his own denomination,[24] and was interested in music. He became an accomplished violinist.

In the aftermath of the Great War economic conditions in Glasgow were difficult, and John and his brother Walter were accepted for an assisted passage to Australia. They arrived in Melbourne on the *Diogenes* on January 15, 1925. Offered a choice between two situations, he accepted a position at Wangaratta with Mr. and Mrs. Windsor who ran an orange orchard, because the employer references included one from the president of the YMCA (who he afterwards learned was also the president of MBI). The Windsors were Open Brethren, although they worshipped in the Baptist church. They had no family and their relationship with John was very positive. (In 1967 their substantial legacy to MBI became available.)

Walter had a position in Sydney, and the brothers were able to sponsor their parents and sister, who duly arrived in February 1926 and settled in Melbourne. Meanwhile, John was exercised on the subject of baptism and came to the Baptist position. He was baptized in the Wangaratta Baptist Church on February 27, 1927. He continued to be concerned about a call to missionary service and by April 1928 he determined on that course, although the road ahead seemed difficult compared to the bright prospects

---

22. Mercer, *Faithful Hands*, 94.

23. UK Census, 1911. The ironstone mines in the district had closed some years before (see https://www.nmrs.org.uk/mines-map/iron-mining-in-the-british-isles/cleveland-north-yorkshire-moors-iron-mining/) but perhaps there was an effort to salvage some material. Mercer refers only to work in the brickworks.

24. A great friend was J. Douglas McClymont (1903–1982), who trained for the Church of Scotland ministry in the 1920s.

otherwise available. His interest lay in medical missionary work in Africa, and several of the missionary societies to which he wrote indicated that he should do a two-year course at MBI. So after a memorable farewell from the Baptist church, he enrolled at MBI as student 353 in July 1928. Here he spent two happy and fruitful years, concluding in September 1930.

After completing the course, he spent some time with the Munro family on their property at Shelford, west of Geelong. Four of that missionary-minded family were students at MBI between 1927 and 1930. There seemed no opening for service in Africa, so New Guinea became an interest. In the meantime, John supplied various pulpits, including the Balranald–Moulamein Presbyterian parish from March 1931 to August 1932. This experience taught him important lessons concerning the difficulties of Christian ministry and the sufficiency of the Lord in the midst of them. The work was revived and soon attained sanctioned charge status, so was able to call its own minister. But Balranald remained in John's thoughts and prayers and all the more as he had lost his heart to Alice Lister of that place. They were duly engaged in March 1933, but it was not until December 19, 1939 that they could marry, as John's studies took priority (BA in 1937 and BD in 1939).

John commenced preliminary studies for acceptance as a candidate for the ministry of the Presbyterian Church of Victoria in September 1932, just as his brother was preparing to sail for missionary service in China with China Inland Mission. John's views of baptism now conformed to the Presbyterian Confession of Faith, although he did not major on this topic. At this point, Searle was appointed assistant to the Rev. J. A. Porter of Cheltenham parish. Searle's ministry was appreciated by the people and the elders, but Porter was liberal in theology along Social Gospel lines,[25] and this contributed to termination of his work at Cheltenham at the end of August 1933 and difficulties with the Theological Education Committee. This was chaired by the rather liberal Rev. Dr Borland of Scots' Church from 1928 to 1939, who sought, unsuccessfully, to move Searle from the authority of Scripture.[26] Eventually, Searle was able to commence the regular course for the BA degree at the University of Melbourne at the beginning of 1934, was president of the Evangelical Union in 1935 and duly received the degree in April 1937. The secretary of the Presbyterian Senatus was the Rev. Prof. John Gillies (1870–1952), the lone conservative in a liberal faculty.[27] There were about forty students, few of them orthodox. Gillies wrote a fine

---

25. He advocated a Socialist platform as that most consistent with Christianity.

26. On Borland see Ward, *Scots' Church*, 130–32, 135–36, 144; on Porter's and Borland's relationship with Searle see Mercer, *Faithful Hands*, 63–67.

27. On the faculty see Ward, *Presbyterians in Australia*, 247–48.

commendation of Searle's work in his subsequent theological studies, which included the Melbourne BD, at the conclusion of his studies in 1939.[28] He was licensed to preach the gospel by the Presbytery of Melbourne North on December 13, 1939. He married Alice Lister six days later, and they departed for his first appointment to Queenstown, Tasmania, early in February 1940.

Queenstown on the west coast was a mining town of five thousand, and about one hundred people were connected with the Presbyterian church. Searle was ordained and inducted there on February 21, 1940. He would conclude his service in December 1941, but in those two years he showed energy and perseverance and saw some growth despite the impact of the war. He had already made his mark among Evangelicals in Melbourne.

In March 1941, having been duly authorized to do so by the MBI council, the Rev. C. H. Nash wrote offering him the position of vice-principal of MBI. Searle accepted the offer, was released from his charge in December and took up residence in part of the newly purchased MBI premises at 117 Kooyong Road, Armadale, in January 1942.

Searle was a different man from Nash. He came from quite humble origins but was clearly a man with gifts developed by disciplined effort. Like Nash, he had faced opposition from those unsympathetic to the Evangelical faith but had not been embittered by it. In a theological education by a faculty largely unsympathetic to his position, he had emerged clear and mature in his grasp of the historic faith. While his denomination had drifted away from the Scriptures, he was not a separatist and he fitted into the Evangelical network well. His wife was very supportive.

His appointment as vice-principal and superintendent of men occurred at a particularly challenging time. The Japanese bombing of Pearl Harbor had occurred on December 7, 1941, Singapore fell on February 15, 1942, and the first of sixty-four bombing raids on Darwin occurred four days later. The MBI council had resolved to continue the institute unless government action prevented it, and the first term duly commenced on February 7, 1942 with twenty-eight women and twelve men enrolled. Searle commenced regular Lord's Day preaching in Presbyterian and other pulpits two months later. C. H. Nash retired on November 23, 1942, and John Searle became the acting principal. His formal appointment as principal occurred on March 31, 1944 when he had just passed his thirty-ninth birthday.

With the end of the war, student numbers expanded rapidly (68 in 1945 and 119 in 1946, of whom 82 were in residence). A home to accommodate fifty women students was secured nearby in 1945. No longer were visiting lecturers sufficient, and the Rev A. H. Hawley, BA, BD (Baptist),

---

28. Mercer, *Faithful* Hands, 68.

for many years a missionary in South America, and the Rev. Roy V. Merritt, BDSc (Presbyterian), who had served in the Solomon Islands and from 1936 in Tasmania,[29] were added to the staff in 1947. The years from 1947 to 1949 saw a disruptive influence from some who had embraced a spiritual perfection teaching as then taught by the Church of the Nazarene, and this was opposed by the principal with the support of the faculty.[30] The 1950s and 1960s saw further development of facilities.

John Searle's teaching approach followed very much in Nash's line. After a suitable hymn and a prayer, which invariably reflected the glory and majesty of Christ crucified and risen, Searle would proceed to expound the set passage of Scripture. His lectures on John's Gospel made a deep impression, but he covered a range of material from both Old and New Testaments. All the reports the present writer has heard speak of him as gracious, warm, godly, prayerful, and interested in and helpful to his students, who held him in some awe. He was a serious man, though with a definite sense of humor and a practical bent, who exemplified the high standards that he desired of others. His hobbies were gardening and golf. Searle continued Nash's strict rules governing relationships between men and women students to secure the utmost propriety. In common with most theological colleges of the time, students were not permitted to marry during their course.

Searle's involvement in Christian work beyond MBI was considerable, including lengthy periods on the CIM Council, as well as the Council of Missionary Aviation Fellowship, which was birthed in MBI in 1945, and Interdenominational Missionary Fellowship (Victoria). Among other involvements were his positive support for the forming of the Christian Leaders Training College in Papua New Guinea as an extension of MBI. It opened with nineteen students in 1965.

As a consequence of serious heart trouble in May 1962, Searle relinquished the principalship at the end of that year but continued to lecture. He had met the Rev. J. Graham Miller in the New Hebrides (Vanuatu) in 1948,[31] and Miller became Searle's successor in 1965. Between 1966 and 1969, Searle had the satisfaction of seeing his four sons married to Christian women. On July 7, 1969, Searle lectured on John chapter 12. That afternoon, while playing golf with Len Buck and the Rev. George Lazenby, he collapsed and died on the course from a heart attack, having completed the work the Lord had given him to do.

---

29. Merritt had given the solemn charge to Searle at his ordination in 1940.

30. Mercer, *Faithful Hands*, 107–8 and for Searle's later article on the subject, 196–201.

31. Mercer, *Faithful Hands*, 138–39.

As principal he had been the steady hand on the tiller, loyal to the vision of the founders and of Nash, his mentor. He was well suited by his background to head up the institute as it progressed in numbers and influence under his leadership. He was perhaps not the man to progress the changes that were increasingly necessary, constrained by his cautious nature, a conservative staff, and an influential council, but he was a fine leader whose memory is rightly cherished.

J. GRAHAM MILLER, PRINCIPAL 1965–1970

John Graham Miller, always known as Graham, was born on October 8, 1913 in the Presbyterian manse at Rangiora, New Zealand, where his father was minister and maintained a clear and definite Evangelical faith, which was quite rare among ministers in New Zealand at that time. Both parents had MA honors degrees from the University of Otago, and Graham was the second of seven children. It was a literary home that inculcated vital religion. Graham was converted at age fourteen through his father's faithful personal dealings with him. Graham had not shone academically but at age seventeen he secured a position with a legal firm in Dunedin, where his father, who was also chairman of the New Zealand Keswick Convention, was then ministering. Graham was active in the Evangelical Unions and became traveling secretary in New Zealand for InterVarsity Fellowship for part of 1938. Graham completed the final law degree subjects in 1938 on his second attempt.[32]

In 1938 Miller began the three-year course at Knox College training for what he hoped would be overseas missionary service. In 1940 an urgent need to fill a vacancy in the New Hebrides Mission meant his application was requested and accepted, together with that of his fiancée Flora McDonald, who was a trained nurse. A year was cut from his studies, the couple were married on March 15, 1941, Graham was ordained on March 27, 1941, and they reached the island of Tongoa the following month.

He ate with the local people, learned the local vernacular and, in nearly six years on Tongoa, saw considerable renewal of the church there and on other islands. A corporate body of elders (the session) appointed and made decisions rather than individual missionaries or elders as previously. He encouraged indigenous leadership and sought to prepare the people for

---

32. For what follows on Miller's personal history I draw on Murray, *Day's March*, compiled from extensive journals kept by Miller supplemented by the admittedly limited material in BCV archives and recollections of those who knew him, including myself.

independence. Miller's legal training had made him a disciplined thinker who stood out among the missionaries.

In April 1947 Miller took up appointment as principal of the Mission's Teacher Training Institute at Tangoa islet, off Espiritu Santo island.[33] The 1948 Mission Synod in July was not only the centenary of the founding of the Presbyterian Church in the New Hebrides but the occasion of the forming of the General Assembly of the Presbyterian Church as an independent church with regular sessions and presbyteries (regional bodies). At its first meeting in August, Miller was elected moderator at which, as promised the year before, he proposed a constitutional amendment, and it was passed with general support. This made the constitution state that the Scriptures *are* the word of God rather than that they *contain* the word of God, as the New Zealand Committee had required in 1948.

Family circumstances in 1952 led to the family's return to New Zealand, where Miller was inducted as minister of Papakura in the Auckland area on February 5, 1953. The parish prospered under Miller's ministry with its emphasis on the systematic teaching of Scriptures. There were numerous conversions, and two daughter congregations were established. Miller, then on furlough from the New Hebrides, had been appointed as president of the Westminster Fellowship, which had been established in 1950, on the motion of Miller's capable ministerial brother Robert.[34] There were about fifty at its inaugural meeting, and Graham Miller's address on that occasion was "Doctrine as Vital to Spiritual Life"—a constant conviction throughout his life. The aim of the fellowship was to further the recovery of sound teaching in the Presbyterian Church of New Zealand. Miller was also appointed chairman of the Rotorua Convention in 1953. This annual Keswick-style gathering was at a low ebb but steadily grew to several hundred participants. Miller's clear and effective Bible teaching led to an invitation to write *Bible Study Notes* for Scripture Union and then *Daily Notes*, and he continued this from 1956 to 1968.[35] There were also smaller booklets on practical subjects. In 1958 he led the Bible studies at the Belgrave Heights Easter Convention and at the Katoomba Convention in the 1959 to 1960 Christmas break. In early 1961, Miller spoke in various Indian cities at a series of meetings over ten weeks arranged by the Evangelical Fellowship of India, then at the Belgrave Heights Convention (1961–1962), and in 1963 he spoke at the English

33. Tangoa islet, just off the main island, is to be distinguished from Tongoa island well to the south.

34. Miller, *Robert Strang Miller*, 47. Robert's most substantial writing was *Misi Geddie: John Geddie, Pioneer Missionary to the New Hebrides* (Launceston, 1975).

35. In 1986, the Banner of Truth Trust published many of these under the title *The Treasury of His Promises*.

Keswick Convention and the Port Stewart Convention in Northern Ireland as well as other meetings during a six-week visit to the UK. Miller returned home via Israel. He was to speak at the Belgrave Heights Convention at Easter 1965, and again at Christmas (1965–1966), and Easter 1968.

He was now widely known as a very acceptable Bible expositor and teacher, and it was not surprising that there was interest from several quarters in his availability to become principal of a Bible college. He could not accept the Adelaide Bible Institute offer in 1962 as the statement of faith required premillennial belief, nor for other reasons the invitation to be inaugural principal of Christian Leaders Training College in Papua New Guinea. The president of the New Zealand Bible Training Institute, the notable classicist Prof. E. M. Blaiklock (1903–1983), was opposed to the Reformed theology espoused by Miller, and Miller's nomination as principal of NZBTI (now Laidlaw College) did not proceed.[36]

However, Miller did accept the invitation from MBI in August 1965. He arrived there in December after attending the World Congress on Evangelism in Berlin (October–November 1965).

C. H. Nash, the first principal, famously said: "Principals come and principals go, but principles remain the same." There is truth in the saying but it is not entirely right. MBI arose in a particular religious and cultural context, and a new context might necessitate significant change. From the 1960s there were a number of issues that needed to be addressed, but Searle was reluctant in the absence of unanimity. For example, there was pressure from some to change the rules on relations between the sexes, which, while not very different from those in a number of other institutions, did not sit well in a world where women were taking a larger part in public life as they had in work situations during the war. Miller introduced a change at the opening dinner of the 1966 session, when men and woman were seated together. While he had conferred with Len Buck, he had not obtained the reaction of the whole executive before making the change—not a wise decision under the circumstances.[37] It did not help relations with senior staff, who were attached to the earlier practice.

---

36. Murray, *Day's March*, 168.

37. Hollings, *Shaped*, 4, recounts something of the severity of the rules in her time as a student in 1968. On November 24, 1969 the council resolved: "Needless regimentation is to be avoided, and encouragement given to responsible Christian freedom. Use of first names between the sexes to be permitted, conversation without waste of time approved; Study not to be supervised, and students may opt to study in lecture halls, library or rooms. Quiet time in the morning will not be supervised." Even these changes did not command universal acceptance for some time.

More significantly, there was also a desire to raise the standard by adding a third year of study. This raised the old question of the nature of a Bible institute as distinct from the more academic training of a theological college. Searle recognized the need to raise the standard, but he was not happy about a proposal to use the LTh program of the Melbourne College of Divinity, since it would mean a reading list of a wider perspective than he felt fitting, while the focus on training for missionary service could be lost. These were issues that would need to be resolved—ones also faced elsewhere in the Bible institute movement as missionary societies pressed for higher standards.

Miller, conscious of the doctrinal decline in theological colleges, and mindful of the need for strong Christian churches at home to support missionary endeavor, was happy to admit those who were preparing for regular ministry in Australia, even if married. Student numbers grew strongly from 165 in 1966 to 209 full-time students in 1968, about 38 percent Baptist, 18 percent Presbyterian, 13 percent Methodist, and 10 percent Churches of Christ.[38] Between 1965 and 1967, the numbers doing the LTh or DipRE rose from 44 to 72. An additional Diploma of Theology was introduced in 1969. The Bible institute's conference in Brisbane proposed to explore a trans-institute advanced course in missions, but the delay involved was a barrier, and SMBC, MBI, and NZBTI developed their own courses. Thus in 1968, MBI ran six lectures a week at third-year level for one term with fourteen enrolled, and a fuller course in 1969. In May 1969 a Bible institutes' conference was held in Victor Harbor with SBMC, MBI, ABI, QBI, Illawarra Bible College, Tahlee Bible College, and NZBTI represented, and issues related to training were discussed. The great majority (70%) of students had an academic background below matriculation, with only about 5 percent having a degree, and this in an era where universities were expanding at a rapid rate, as Miller noted in the 49th Annual Report. Miller made the point that 1,007 MBI graduates had served overseas and 501 in Australia, and that 75 percent of those in home service had entered the ministry.[39]

If there were some changes in approach, a raising of standards and wider interaction with other bodies, there was also appreciation by students of the leadership Miller was giving with his effective teaching. Enrollments reached an all-time high in 1968.[40] However, there were undercurrents in the council and among the staff. The Rev. Roy Merritt, who had acted as principal

---

38. MBI, *48th Annual Report*.

39. Miller, "Relevance."

40. Len Pearce, the top student in 1969 and Hebrew tutor 1970–72, detected no dissatisfaction with Miller among the student body, *vide* personal conversation, May 19, 2020.

between Searle and Miller, retired at the end of 1968; the long-standing council treasurer, J. W. Fawckner (1900–1970), retired from that role in 1968 and was replaced by Will Renshaw; John Searle died in July 1969, at work lecturing until the day he died; while council chairman, Alfred Coombe (1892–1984), a Presbyterian layman and businessman, retired as president in 1970 after thirty-one years in the position. Ralph Davis (1912–1991), a Methodist layman and managing director of the vast Mayne Nickless Ltd. transport company, succeeded Coombe. The dynamics of Evangelical cooperation shifted, both among staff and on the lay-led council.[41]

Miller was a real leader, a gracious and prayerful gentleman of the old school. In his ministry in the New Hebrides, he had been early revered by the people as a godly man of ability and ideas who had the good of the local people at heart. The deference given him in that context had not transferred easily to the very different MBI context. Miller was farseeing and usually right; but it needs to be said that to some colleagues he came over as autocratic, as not giving enough consideration to their opinions. Even others who loved and respected him, whether fellow missionaries in the New Hebrides or Presbyterian colleagues in Australia, recognized that. Yet if in essence he held the theology of Martyn Lloyd-Jones, he was a man for peace like John Stott.[42]

In October 1969 the report of a committee commissioned by the council to review staffing, courses, and accommodation was received, and shortly afterwards Miller brought its recommendations to a meeting of staff to see how they felt. The recommendations were not Miller's, but four staff members openly opposed him, nevertheless. The report of this matter was considered by the MBI executive on January 29, 1970, at which meeting a further item of correspondence from staff member Rev. A. T. Stevens (1919–2012) was taken up.[43] Stevens had written directly to the council president suggesting that some were disturbed by Miller's "Calvinistic emphasis" and that Miller appeared to be projecting the image of a Reformed college rather than a Bible institute. Given that John Searle had very definitely been "Calvinistic," Miller was not unique in that respect, and his position had been very well known through his writing and convention ministry before he came to

---

41. Mercer, *Faithful Hands*, 173.

42. I owe the comparison to the Rev. Dr. Peter Barnes, current moderator of the General Assembly of the Presbyterian Church of Australia, who knew Miller well. The difference between these two men at the UK Keele Conference in 1966 is illustrative.

43. Stevens (1919–2012), an honorary lecturer for some years, had been appointed on Miller's recommendation to full-time staff on February 1, 1969 to head the New Testament department. Previously, Stevens had been the minister of Balaclava Presbyterian Church, which Miller had joined when he came to Melbourne.

MBI. Miller also recognized the need to accommodate differences among conservative Evangelicals. His recommendation of Stevens to staff appointment a year previously was evidence of that. The projection of "the image of a Reformed College" reflected the resurgence of Reformed theology taking place worldwide in the 1960s,[44] the impact of Miller's lectures on Romans, and Miller's push for academic standards to be raised. For some of Arminian persuasion in theology, and this included Stevens,[45] this was a matter of deep concern threatening the missionary focus of the institute. The very success of Miller's leadership now became a threat. Indeed, the incorrect claim had been advanced that under Miller's watch the proportion of those going to the overseas field had declined. The contrasting visions of Bible institute *vis à vis* theological college would continue to be aired in MBI well into the 1990s.[46]

Miller submitted his resignation on January 31, 1970 and was not willing to withdraw it when pressed to do so at a meeting with the chairman on 5 February.[47] It was accepted on February 12, and Miller was willing to stay until May 14, 1970 to finish up to the end of term. He withdrew without voicing complaint and with no other position lined up. It was MBI's loss. MBI faced some years of decline before it regained unity among leadership and staff and growth in student numbers.

Miller continued to be well regarded in Christian circles, and God had work for him to do. He went on to serve as the principal (1971–1973) of the newly formed Presbyterian Bible College at Tangoa, New Hebrides, which had replaced the earlier Teacher Training Institute.[48] At the 1973 General Assembly of the Presbyterian Church in the New Hebrides, he drafted a motion that expressed the goal of independence for the nation, which was realized in 1980. It was an influential decision, given that 50 percent of the population was affiliated with the Presbyterian Church. Dogged by bouts of malaria, he then returned to Australia. He served St. Giles' Presbyterian Church in Hurstville from 1974 to 1980.[49] He was preacher at Belgrave Heights at Christmas 1975 and Easter 1981. He mentored and influenced

---

44. The Banner of Truth Trust commenced in 1955 and its republication of Puritan and Reformed literature began in 1957.

45. Stevens, *Appraisal*.

46. Note Renshaw's working paper for MBI council, "Bible Colleges," with much based on C. H. Nash's writings.

47. MBI council minutes, February 12, 1970.

48. In 1986 the Bible college relocated to Espiritu Santo island as the Talua Theological Training Institute.

49. He received by mail an honorary DD in 1974 from a tiny private unaccredited school in the US and regularly used it. He deserved such an honor but from a more credible source.

many young ministers. Miller retired to rural Wangaratta and wrote seven volumes on the history of the church in Vanuatu as well as other books. His death on September 6, 2008 was a significant loss and was marked by a national day of mourning in Vanuatu.

Evangelicals have not always found it easy to adjust to new situations and sometimes, because of failure to perceive well-recognized points of difference, they have demonstrated a spirit that breaks down effective cooperation. While Miller's time at MBI was short compared with that of the principals who had preceded him, he had marked out the course that the institute would have to take to meet the needs of the changed context, even if the transition period was to be longer than might have been expected.

BIBLIOGRAPHY

Banks, Robert. "The Influence of the Keswick Movement on Christian Missions to China from the 1880s to the 1920s." *Lucas* 2, no. 9 (2015–16) 49–72.
Bebbington, David. *Evangelicalism in Modern Britain: A History from the 1730s to the 1980s.* London: Unwin Hyman, 1989.
Brammall, Anthony C. *Out of Darkness: 100 Years of Sydney Missionary and Bible College.* Croydon, NSW: SMBC, 2016.
Cable Clerical Index. http://anglicanhistory.org/aus/cci/.
Chambers, David. *Tempest Tost: The Life and Teaching of the Rev. C. H. Nash, MA.* Melbourne: Church, 1959.
Grant, James. *Episcopally Led and Synodically Governed: Anglicans in Victoria 1803–1997.* North Melbourne: Australian Scholarly, 2010.
Hollings, Kaye. *Shaped: Is Your Life Pear-Shaped or Purpose-Shaped?* Ark House: Mona Vale, 2017.
Kuan, Wei-Han. *Foundations of Anglican Evangelicalism in Victoria: Four Elements for Continuity 1847–1937.* Eugene, OR: Wipf & Stock, 2018.
MBI. *48th Annual Report.*
Mercer, John T. *In the Faithful Hands of Another: The Life and Ministry of the Rev. John William Searle.* St. Kilda: Onesimus, 1997.
Miller, J. G. "The Relevance of the Ministry and Sacraments for Bible Institutes." Unpublished, May 19, 1969.
Miller, Margaret Jane. *Robert Strang Miller—A Tribute by His Family.* Self-published: Melbourne, 1983.
Murray, Iain H., ed. *A Day's March Nearer Home: Autobiography of J. Graham Miller.* Edinburgh: Banner of Truth Trust, 2010.
Nash. C. H. *Statements Concerning the Objectives of the Melbourne Bible Institute.* Unpublished, August 27, 1920.
Northern Mine Research Society. "Cleveland and North Yorkshire Moors Iron Mining." https://www.nmrs.org.uk/mines-map/iron-mining-in-the-british-isles/cleveland-north-yorkshire-moors-iron-mining/.
Paproth, Darrell. *Failure Is Not Final: A Life of C. H. Nash.* Sydney: Centre for the Study of Australian Christianity, 1997.

———. "Faith Missions, Personality and Leadership: William Lockhart Morton and Angas College." *Lucas* 1, nos. 27–28 (2000) 64–89.

———. "The 1888 Centennial Mission in Victoria." *Lucas* 2, no. 1 (2009) 31–65.

Parker, David. *Fundamentalism and Conservative Protestantism in Australia, 1920–1980*. Unpublished PhD, University of Queensland, 1982.

Piggin, Stuart, and Robert D. Linder. *The Fountain of Public Prosperity*. Melbourne: Monash University Publishing, 2019.

Renshaw, Will. *Marvellous Melbourne and Spiritual Power*. Melbourne: Acorn, 2014.

Renshaw, William F. "Bible Colleges and Theological Colleges." MBI Council, October 1, 1996.

Southern Cross, January 1923.

Stevens, A. T. *An Appraisal of the So-Called "Five Points of Calvinism."* Victoria: Burning Bush Society, March 1994.

UK Census, 1911.

Ward, Rowland S. *Presbyterians in Australia: Origins, Conflicts and Progress, 1803–2018*. Wantirna: New Melbourne, 2018.

———. *The Scots' Church Melbourne: A Story of 175 Years, 1838–2013*. North Melbourne: Australian Scholarly, 2014.

Theological and Spiritual Approaches

3

The COVID-19 Pandemic

The Global Mental Health Crisis and a Reflection on the Human Condition

Michael T. H. Wong

THE COVID-19 PANDEMIC HAS precipitated a global mental health crisis. It reminds us of the reality of the human condition and brings us into close encounter with fundamental issues such as life and death, pain and suffering. This pandemic challenges the values and beliefs held in this secular age of science and technology about health, happiness, and meaning. The Christian narrative about who we are helps us go beyond the biopsychosocial discourse of humanity and provides a whole-person understanding of health and wellbeing.

THE COVID-19 PANDEMIC

A novel coronavirus (nCoV) was identified on January 7, 2020. It was temporarily named 2019-nCoV and subsequently COVID-19 virus. The World Health Organization (WHO) announced the COVID-19 outbreak as a pandemic on March 11, 2020.[1] More than seventeen million people

1. World Health Organization, "Timeline."

around the world have been diagnosed with this viral pneumonia, and among them more than 670,000 have died as of late July 2020.[2] Around the same time, many places around the world recorded an unexpected surge of new cases. The state of Victoria in Australia is one such location, and the premier announced a lockdown of the state.[3] In Hong Kong, where the author is based, the surge of new cases in locals who have no travel history and no contact with known diagnosed cases raises the alarm that the virus may have mutated and become more infectious.[4]

COVID-19 not only affects people physically but also psychologically and socially. Public health measures involve compulsory social distancing, restrictions on the size of social gatherings, wearing of face masks, suspension of schools, working from home, closure of public facilities and services, cancellation of public events, trade fairs and conferences, and even banning domestic and international travel for business and pleasure. The struggle to cope with COVID-19 at all levels of society and the collapse of public infrastructures and financial operations in many countries and communities has led to financial hardship, unemployment, social crisis, and even political unrest.[5]

GLOBAL MENTAL HEALTH CRISIS

WHO reported extreme concern in regard to the impact of COVID-19 pandemic on people's mental health. Social isolation, fear of contagion, and loss of family members are compounded by the distress caused by loss of income and often employment. A policy brief on COVID-19 and mental health issued by the United Nations highlights the urgent need to increase investment in services for mental health or risk a massive increase in mental health conditions in the coming months. Such crisis has already happened in a number of countries. One of them is Ethiopia, which in April 2020 reported a threefold increase in the prevalence of symptoms of depression compared to estimates from Ethiopia before the epidemic.[6] In Australia,

---

2. Worldometer, "COVID-19." The last pandemic was the swine flu outbreak. It was caused by a new strain of H1N1 that originated in Mexico in the spring of 2009 before spreading to the rest of the world. In one year, the virus infected as many as 1.4 billion people across the globe and killed between 151,700 and 575,400 people (Center for Disease Control and Prevention, "2009 H1N1 Pandemic").

3. Iorio, "Melbourne."
4. Hong Kong Government Geodata, "Latest Situation."
5. Kluth, "Social Revolutions."
6. United Nations, *Policy Brief*, 7.

an online survey recruited 13,829 residents aged eighteen or above between April 3 and May 2, 2020. The results showed that the prevalence of clinically significant depressive and generalized anxiety symptoms, thoughts of being better off dead or of self-harm, and irritability were at least twice as prevalent as before this pandemic.[7]

There are groups that are at particular risk of COVID-related psychological distress. Top of the list are those frontline health care workers who are faced with heavy workloads, life-and-death decisions, and risk of infection. In China, health care workers have reported high rates of depression (50%), anxiety (45%), and insomnia (34%). In Canada, 47 percent of health care workers have reported a need for psychological support. Another group is children and adolescents. In Italy and Spain, parents have reported that their children have had difficulties concentrating, as well as irritability, restlessness, and nervousness. Lockdown or stay-at-home measures can potentially increase the risk of children witnessing or suffering from violence and abuse. Children with disabilities, children in crowded settings, and those who live and work on the streets are particularly vulnerable. Other groups include women, especially those who have to juggle homeschooling, working from home, and household tasks, older persons, and people with preexisting mental health conditions. A study carried out among young people with a history of mental health needs living in the UK reports that 32 percent of them agreed that the pandemic had made their mental health much worse. A group non-specific observation is that there is an increased risk of alcohol misuse. Statistics from Canada report that 20 percent of those between fifteen and forty-nine years old have increased their alcohol consumption during the pandemic.[8]

Vindegaard and Benros reviewed forty-three studies that looked at psychiatric symptoms and morbidities associated with COVID-19.[9] Two studies focused on the mental health symptoms of patients with confirmed COVID-19 infection, and forty-one studies evaluated the indirect effect of the pandemic on people with preexisting mental health disorders (2 studies), on healthcare providers (20 studies), and on the population as a whole (19 studies). As predicted by the experience of the previous SARS epidemic in 2002 and 2003 that the epidemic affected mental health among patients who survived the disease and among the healthcare professionals treating them, the authors noticed that patients who survived severe COVID-19 symptoms exhibited high levels of post-traumatic stress symptoms and

---

7. Fisher et al., "Mental Health."
8. United Nations, *Policy Brief*, 11–13.
9. Vindegaard and Benros, "COVID-19 Pandemic."

significantly increased depressive symptoms after hospitalization. These symptoms might be the effect of the infection on the brain, either directly or through the induced immune response. Their review also suggests worsening of symptoms among people with preexisting psychiatric disorders and heightened levels of anxiety, depression, psychological distress, and poor sleep quality in health workers; while the general public experienced a drop in psychological well-being and an increase in anxiety and depression.

While there is an increase in need for psychosocial support and intervention, there is an interruption of access to physical and mental health services in many countries. In addition to the conversion of mental health facilities into care facilities for people with COVID-19, care systems have been affected by mental health staff being infected with the virus and the closing of face-to-face services. Community services, such as self-help groups for alcohol and drug dependence, have, in many countries, been unable to meet.[10]

It is critical that people living with mental health conditions have continued access to treatment. Changes in approaches to provision of mental health care and psychosocial support are showing signs of success in some countries. In Madrid, when more than 60 percent of mental health beds were converted to care for people with COVID-19, people with severe conditions were, where possible, moved to private clinics to ensure continuity of care. Local policy makers identified emergency psychiatry as an essential service to enable mental health care workers to continue outpatient services over the phone. Home visits were organized for the most serious cases. Teams from Egypt, Kenya, Nepal, Malaysia, and New Zealand, among others, have reported creating increased capacity of emergency telephone lines for mental health to reach people in need.[11]

Support for community actions that strengthen social cohesion and reduce loneliness, particularly for the most vulnerable, such as older people, has become indispensable. Such service is only feasible with support from government, local authorities, the private sector, and members of the general public, with initiatives such as provision of food parcels, regular phone check-ins with people living alone, and organization of online activities for intellectual and cognitive stimulation.

Dr. Tedros Adhanom Ghebreyesus, Director General of WHO, sees it as "crystal clear that mental health needs must be treated as a core element of our response to and recovery from the COVID-19 pandemic." For him this is the collective responsibility of governments and civil society, for a

---

10. Vindegaard and Benros, "COVID-19 Pandemic."
11. United Nations, *Policy Brief*, 9.

"failure to take people's emotional well-being seriously will lead to long-term social and economic costs to society."[12]

A CHRISTIAN REFLECTION

It is an understatement that the contemporary world, which thrives on unprecedented advances in science and technology, has been shocked by the COVID-19 pandemic. We are struggling to cope medically, socially, and politically, and at individual, community, and global levels. According to a survey released by the American Psychiatric Association, many people have significant anxiety and concerns related to coronavirus disease (COVID-19).[13] Nearly half of Americans (48%) are anxious about the possibility of contracting coronavirus. Nearly four in ten Americans (40%) are anxious about becoming seriously ill or dying from coronavirus. Far more Americans (62%) are anxious about the possibility of family and loved ones contracting coronavirus. One in four people who seek help for mental health concerns turn to faith leaders before they seek help from clinical professionals.[14]

COVID-19 brings us into close encounter with life and death. The pain and suffering of losing loved ones and going through quarantine and surviving the intensive care unit (ICU) is not something that most of us have even imagined would happen to us. We thought a pandemic was only an unfortunate tragedy in the Middle Ages. The fear of becoming infected and the anger over all those restrictive measures and mishandling of infection control seems to have spared no one. The repeated waves and surges of new cases despite all these restrictive measures further heightens the sense of sadness and helplessness.

People in lockdown, overwhelmed by social isolation, by increasing conflicts due to spending more time with family members, by losing loved ones or by losing income and employment, start to find themselves confronted by various doubts and questions that they have long forgotten, ignored, dismissed or simply taken for granted—health and illness, pain and suffering, life and death, family and friends, relationships and communication, work and wealth, leisure and happiness, hope and fear. In short, the COVID-19 pandemic confronts us with the fundamental questions of: "Who am I? What can I do? What should I do?" In other words, we are forced to reflect on the reality of the human condition.

12. World Health Organization, "Mental Health Crisis."
13. American Psychiatric Association, "New Poll."
14. Canady, "APA Poll."

This draws us to the Pauline notion of the "groaning creation" in Romans 8:18–39.[15] God made us in his image so that we would have the capacity to have fellowship with him in the garden of Eden. We are not programmed robots, and we can choose and have chosen against this fellowship; and we find ourselves now in paradise lost, experiencing pain and suffering (v. 22). Good can still come out of it (v. 28), however, as God's prayers (vv. 26–27) and love (vv. 31–39) through the atoning death and resurrection of Christ are with us and are available; but we need to have the will to take that on.

A poll[16] found most of the 1,002 respondents saw a deeper meaning in the pandemic that had killed nearly 87,000 Americans at the time of the study.[17] Some 63 percent of the believers surveyed said they thought God was telling humanity to change the way they were living. Evangelical Protestants are the most likely to believe that, compared to mainline Protestants and Catholics. The majority of respondents attributed the situation to either foreign governments or the US government (43% and 37%, respectively). Around 10 percent of the respondents directly attributed the pandemic to human sinfulness. More than 50 percent of those surveyed said they felt God would protect them from infection, though 9 percent said that God had abandoned humanity. The virus had prompted some of the respondents to reevaluate their beliefs. Most of them continued to believe in God, and the current pandemic had strengthened that faith for many, with 2 percent of respondents saying that they believed in God today but did not before the pandemic and fewer than 1 percent reporting that it had caused them to abandon their beliefs.

Nearly two-thirds of the respondents believed the COVID-19 pandemic is a message from God. They disagree, however, on what that message is, although they think that God is telling humanity to change the way we are living. As many religions have to account for why suffering exists, and

---

15. Rom 8:22–28: "We know that the whole creation has been groaning as in the pains of childbirth right up to the present time. Not only so, but we ourselves, who have the firstfruits of the Spirit, groan inwardly as we wait eagerly for our adoption to sonship, the redemption of our bodies. For in this hope we were saved. But hope that is seen is no hope at all. Who hopes for what they already have? But if we hope for what we do not yet have, we wait for it patiently. In the same way, the Spirit helps us in our weakness. We do not know what we ought to pray for, but the Spirit himself intercedes for us through wordless groans. And He who searches our hearts knows the mind of the Spirit, because the Spirit intercedes for God's people in accordance with the will of God. And we know that in all things God works for the good of those who love Him, who have been called according to His purpose."

16. University of Chicago Divinity School, "Religious Practice."

17. Pal, "Message from God."

why bad things happen even to good people, it is not surprising that people are trying to make sense of the COVID-19 pandemic by turning to their religions. The explanations that believers are *not* offering on this occasion are interesting, however. Only 11 percent of the respondents mentioned sin as a cause of the pandemic. Among all surveyed religious groups, those who identified as Evangelical Christians were the most supportive of that explanation, but even then, only a small number, 15 percent, identified human sinfulness as a cause. Scapegoating is another common way of making sense of this COVID-19 pandemic.[18] Incidents of harassment and violence against Asian-Americans have happened since the COVID-19 outbreak, and some conspiracy theories have surfaced on social media blaming the Chinese, Jews, and others for inventing and/or deliberately spreading the virus. In India and South Korea, minority religious groups have been accused of spreading the virus. That said, only 3 percent of respondents blamed members of minority religious groups and very few blamed climate change (7%) or immigrants (9%). While global trade (21%) and nature (28%) have been seen as culprits, most respondents blamed the actions of their own (37%) or foreign (43%) nations. Religious affiliation did have an effect on the response. White Evangelical Christians were much more likely to blame foreign governments (50%) as opposed to their own (20%). Believers in other faiths were in the middle, and non-believers tended to blame their own government (49%) more than foreign ones (41%). Political affiliation also had an effect on the response. Over three-quarters of Republicans surveyed did not think their own government was to be blamed for the current pandemic (as opposed to 22% who thought it was). Faith and politics therefore have an impact on how the COVID-19 pandemic is being dealt with. This again brings us back to the fundamental questions of how we should lead our life as an individual and as a member of the community in order that we can work together to deal with this COVID-19 pandemic and the associated global mental health crisis.

A very brief reflection on theological anthropology is in order here.[19] Who are we and how should we live? We are made in the image of God. We are not just a soul (premodern), a mind (early modern), a brain (late modern) or a constructed or deconstructed self (postmodern). We are a

---

18. During the Black Death's peak in Europe, from 1348 to 1351, more than two hundred Jewish communities were annihilated after their members were accused of intentionally spreading the disease by poisoning wells. When the Plague returned again in the sixteenth and seventeenth centuries, conspiracy theories circulated about doctors and health workers—including cleaners and gravediggers—who were said to be perpetuating the disease for self-interested gain.

19. Wong, "Theological Anthropology."

whole person, a bio-psycho-socio-spiritual being.[20] God wills us to have a blessed and full life.[21] We are capable of communicating and relating to God and other people in a loving and caring way.[22] And we are to share this good news of the true meaning of being human to people around us.[23] In short, as human beings we are to care and share an abundant and fulfilled life as individuals in an integrated community, free from personal fragmentation and interpersonal alienation. We cannot afford to lose sight of this Christian understanding of being human when dealing with the COVID-19 pandemic and its associated global mental health crisis.

Why is my faith not helping me to cope with anxiety and depression? How do I face the loss of income and my job? Where do I find the strength to cope with the grief for my loved ones who have passed away? How do I deal with communication and relationship breakdowns at home during lockdown? Am I able to make the most of solitude during lockdown? How can I be productive working from home? How can I be a source of blessing and encouragement to others during this pandemic and global mental health crisis?

The COVID-19 pandemic is real. It is not going away any time soon. The uncertainty about its course and cure and when a vaccine will be available adds further to the distress. Denial does not help. Minimizing the seriousness and risk of infection is dangerous. Avoiding social distancing, not wearing a face mask, and neglecting to attend to personal hygiene is not an act of Christian love. We as Christians know we are finite, fallible, and fallen beings. We know we do not own our bodies, which are a gift from our Lord, and we have to be good stewards of our health and well-being as well as other people's happiness and safety. We have to practice our faith. We have to accept our vulnerability and that we have no full control over COVID-19. We have to pray to tune into the wisdom and will of God so that we are empowered to develop resilience in God's way.

Live in the way we are meant to. Sleep well. Eat properly. Be positive and have hope. Relax and have faith to go beyond fear and worry. Exercise

---

20. Wong, *Third Discourse*.

21. John 10:10: "I have come that they may have life, and have it to the full."

22. Luke 2:52: "And Jesus grew in wisdom and stature, and in favor with God and men." Mark 12:30–31: "Love the Lord with all your heart and with all your soul and with all your mind and with all your strength. The second is this: 'Love your neighbor as yourself.' There is no commandment greater than these."

23. Matt 28:19–20: "Therefore go and make disciples of all nations, baptizing them in the name of the Father and of the Son and of the Holy Spirit, and teaching them to obey everything I have commanded you. And surely I am with you always, to the very end of the age."

to keep our bodies, the temple of God, in good shape with immunity and fitness. Love and respect those who are different from us but exercise assertiveness to them if they behave in ways that put people at risk of becoming infected with COVID-19.

Our resilience comes from the fact that God became man and suffered and died but rose again. Our Lord knows what pain, suffering, dying, and death are like. Others do not have the final say on our health and wellbeing. God is full of grace and mercy—he understands our pain and suffering with more empathy and compassion than any counsellor, psychologist or psychiatrist can give us. The COVID-19 pandemic and the global mental crisis can be an opportunity for change for the better. This unusual and strange episode in our history will let us understand the human condition better and experience the reality of God and his creation more deeply.

BIBLIOGRAPHY

American Psychiatric Association. "New Poll: COVID-19 Impacting Mental Well-Being: Americans Feeling Anxious, Especially for Loved Ones; Older Adults are Less Anxious" (March 25, 2020). https://www.psychiatry.org/newsroom/news-releases/new-poll-covid-19-impacting-mental-well-being-americans-feeling-anxious-especially-for-loved-ones-older-adults-are-less-anxious.

Canady, Valerie A. "APA Poll Finds Nearly Half Anxious About Getting COVID-19." *Mental Health Weekly* 30, no. 13 (March 27, 2020) 5.

Center for Disease Control and Prevention. "2009 H1N1 Pandemic (H1N1pdm09 virus)" (June 11, 2019). https://www.cdc.gov/flu/pandemic-resources/2009-h1n1-pandemic.html.

Fisher, Jane R. W., et al. "Mental Health of People in Australia in the First Month of COVID-19 Restrictions: A National Survey." *Medical Journal of Australia* (June 10, 2020). https://www.mja.com.au/journal/2020/mental-health-people-australia-first-month-covid-19-restrictions-national-survey.

Hong Kong Government Geodata. "Latest Situation of Coronavirus Disease (COVID-19) in Hong Kong." https://chp-dashboard.geodata.gov.hk/covid-19/en.html.

Iorio, Kelsie. "Melbourne Enters New Coronavirus Lockdown. Here Are the Key Points from Premier Daniel Andrews." *ABC News*, July 8, 2020. https://www.abc.net.au/news/2020-07-07/melbourne-lockdown-daniel-andrews-key-points/12431708.

Kluth, Andreas. "This Pandemic Will Lead to Social Revolutions." *Bloomberg*, April 11, 2020. https://www.bloomberg.com/opinion/articles/2020-04-11/coronavirus-this-pandemic-will-lead-to-social-revolutions.

Pal, Soumyadeep. "Two-Thirds of Religious Americans Believe Coronavirus Is a Message from God." *Q News Hub*, May 16, 2020. https://qnewshub.com/business/two-thirds-of-religious-americans-believe-coronavirus-is-a-message-from-god/?doing_wp_cron=1596092578.2392780780792236328125.

United Nations. *Policy Brief: COVID-19 and the Need for Action on Mental Health* (May 13, 2020).

The University of Chicago Divinity School and The Associated Press-NORC Center for Public Affairs Research. "Religious Practice in the Time of Coronavirus" (May 2020). https://apnorc.org/projects/religious-practice-in-the-time-of-coronavirus/.

Vindegaard, Nina, and Michael Eriksen Benros. "COVID-19 Pandemic and Mental Health Consequences: Systematic Review of the Current Evidence." *Brain, Behavior, and Immunity* (May 30, 2020). https://www.ncbi.nlm.nih.gov/pmc/articles/PMC7260522/.

Wong, M. T. H. *Ricoeur and the Third Discourse of the Person: From Philosophy and Neuroscience to Psychiatry and Theology*. London: Lexington, 2019.

———. "Theological Anthropology as Informed by the Changeux-Ricoeur Dialogue on Science, Philosophy and Religion." In *Paul Ricoeur: Poetics and Religion*, edited by J. Verheyden, P. Vandecasteele, and T. L. Hettema, 519–29. Leuven: Uitgeverij Peeters, 2011.

World Health Organization. "Substantial Investment Needed to Avert Mental Health Crisis" (May 14, 2020). https://www.who.int/news-room/detail/14-05-2020-substantial-investment-needed-to-avert-mental-health-crisis.

———. "Timeline of WHO's Response to COVID-19" (July 30, 2020). https://www.who.int/news-room/detail/29-06-2020-covidtimeline.

Worldometer. "COVID-19 Coronavirus Pandemic" (July 31, 2020). https://www.worldometers.info/coronavirus/.

4

"The Wound of Love" and the Pursuit of Holiness

Frances Young's Spirituality in a Broken World

Justin T. T. Tan

PROFESSOR FRANCES YOUNG EXPLORES a spirituality that embraces people with disabilities. Based on her personal life experience of living and caring for her profoundly disabled son, she leads us to a path of holiness that challenges the tenets of Christianity and yet is able to see the dark side of humanity in its brokenness in need of a generous and compassionate God. It is a journey through the desert of transformation, encountering with God, imitating Christ, and embracing the stranger, to an ongoing path to longing and fulfillment. Throughout the journey, nobody is excluded, all are called to the holiness that is never-ending joy.

One of the most unlikely arenas of theological reflection comes from people with disabilities. It is a perspective from a broken world that challenges the "usual" tenets of Christianity. There is the obvious attitude of compassion to consider, but also a concerted effort in tackling a spirituality of inclusion in a world of brokenness. Prominent Methodist theologian, Professor Frances Young, has embodied this deep spirituality in her life and writings. She is the mother of a seriously disabled child, Arthur. Being highly intellectual and a deeply committed Christian, she has struggled through the theological and spiritual implications of living in a broken world. Her spirituality is poignantly put in this way—contrary to the popular psychology, humans are not in control of their lives, but are mutually dependent and dependent on God. Nevertheless, vulnerability and mortality are essential to our being, therefore suffering is simply unavoidable, yet this is precisely the place where we are formed for the holy life. This chapter attempts to learn from her.

BRIEF BIOGRAPHY OF REVEREND PROFESSOR FRANCES YOUNG

The Reverend Professor Frances Young[1] taught theology at the University of Birmingham from 1971, becoming the Edward Cadbury Professor and head of the Department of Theology in 1986. During her time at the university, she also served as dean of the Faculty of Arts (1995–1997) and as pro-vice-chancellor (1997–2002). In 1984 she was ordained as a Methodist minister and has combined preaching in a local circuit with pursuing her academic career. She was made an OBE for her services to theology in 1998 and has written an extensive list of both academic books and more popular theological writings. In 2005 she retired from the university.

She and her husband cared for their son Arthur Thomas, born in 1967 with profound learning disabilities, until June 2012, when at forty-five years of age he finally left home for residential care. In 1985 she published *Face to Face*, an account of her son's life, development and education, her own struggle with faith, coming to terms with the situation, and her call to ordination. Since then she has frequently been asked to speak about theology and disability, and her journey of understanding has continued through Arthur's adulthood.

This throws up in broad relief the problem of suffering and evil and a good God. Frances Young looks at the issue of disability in a person with wide open eyes, as it is a reality that she has been facing every moment since Arthur's birth. Therefore, she will not face it with a naive sentimentality that refuses to admit it is an evil, much as though in all her being she wants to protest against it as cruel and unnecessary. The inevitable question is why a good and beautiful God would "inflict" upon his creations the so-called

---

1. This bibliography note is a combination of several sources, which are all available online, e.g. Wikipedia. Most of them give an accurate summary of Frances Young's life and work. I quote only the part that is relevant to this chapter. I had the privilege of having her as my PhD thesis examiner and of serving in the wider Methodist Church, being, as she is, a Methodist minister both in Hong Kong and Australia.

imperfection, denying them the possibility of fullness of life. Yet she sees through this veil of tears into the hope that is re-created in the cross and resurrection of Christ.

Frances Young's works on spirituality are very impressive, not least on the spirituality of brokenness from the perspective of her experience as the mother of Arthur. Because of this she has worked on the theological and ecumenical dimensions of the L'Arche communities with Jean Vanier, their founder. From the first account of her reflection on her life with Arthur in *Face to Face: A Narrative Essay in the Theology of Suffering* (1990) to *Brokenness and Blessing: Towards a Biblical Spirituality* (2007) and then the continuing story of Arthur in *Arthur's Call* (2014), they are full of deeply-felt reflections on the very central tenets of Christianity and Christian spirituality.

MISCONCEPTIONS AND THE REALITY ABOUT DISABILITY

In her reflection on the spirituality in the broken world, Frances Young first leads us into a world of discrimination, misconception, and fanciful promises.

Ancient societies looked upon disability as a menace and a curse to nature and society, especially from the perspective of the Greek notion of order, balance, and harmony. Diseases, malformation, and material misfortune were often seen as signs of the ill will of the gods.[2] With the advent of Christianity, there was a dramatic change in attitude that followed the example of Christ in strongly embracing the intrinsic value of human life. This value has become less and less tied to whether that life contributes to the public good, and thus "Christians' countercultural social practices paved the way for public institutions of charity for the socially excluded."[3]

However, Frances Young notes that when it comes to these types of questions, the answers will inevitably be ambivalent;[4] it is never easy when subjective feelings and reactions, and very personal ones at that, always intrude into rational theological reflections.

---

2. Caspary, "Patristic Era," 24. Caspary goes on to paint a very bleak picture of those born with disabilities: "The disfiguring conditions of monsters, as they were called (*pridigia* in Latin, *terata* in Greek), were largely ascribed to supernatural powers that needed to be exorcised and purified for the benefit of society as a whole. Often such monsters were seen as manifestations of supernatural powers foreboding danger for the community; divine signs, portents, or bad omens for their families and the polis at large" (25).

3. Caspary, "Patristic Era," 25.

4. Young, *Face to Face*.

Nevertheless, life must go on no matter how we try to rationalize it, she admits. "There had been a time when I could not break the hopeless mood which underlay the whole of life, even as we coped and joked and survived."[5]

From the moment of Arthur's birth, Frances has been constantly struggling to show affection and love. Breastfeeding became a problem as baby Arthur was not capable of normal suckling. The craving to show love and the feeling of rejection have persisted throughout their mother-son relationship.

The reality of Arthur's disability came as a shock: "When the full nature of his problems were revealed, shock, puzzlement and some anger were the first reactions. It all soon turned into a dreadful sense of failure."[6] But there was an even worse reality check awaiting her and her husband: "Consciously or unconsciously, all parents have dreams for their children. We had to accept we could dream no dreams."[7]

It was at this point that Frances Young, being an intellectual with high achievements, fought with all her breath to seek to reconcile this shocking reality with her Christian faith. She was not one to give up on her faith when the going was tough, but she was also realistic enough to expect a tougher battle of the mind and the soul, a life and death struggle with her whole self and her God. She would describe herself as the wrestling Jacob, seeking blessing even though in the end there was brokenness, but came away with blessing nonetheless, bringing along with her the suffering of the broken world.[8]

THE PURSUIT OF HOLINESS[9]

Frances Young defines the pursuit of holiness in terms of biblical spirituality that "challenges the culture we have assimilated, and its assumptions and values, while offering a realistic view of the human condition and the wonderful gift of grace which brings hope of transformation. It is the

---

5. Young, *Face to Face*, 29.
6. Young, *Face to Face*, 33.
7. Young, *Face to Face*, 34.
8. In a lecture at St. Martin-in-the Fields Autumn Programme, *The Alpha and the Omega, the First and the Last: The Bible Opened to All* (2010), entitled, "Being Biblical, Being Broken and Blessed."
9. Here I want to be true to her exposition on biblical spirituality as she articulated in her deeply touching Sarum Theological Lectures, published as *Brokenness and Blessings: Towards a Biblical Spirituality*. Her reflections there intersperse anecdotes of her life with Arthur. Here in my chapter, I have attempted to bring in more "flesh" from her other works.

conversion of heart which constitutes the purpose of Scripture, according to the Fathers."[10]

The obvious challenge of this formulation of authentic biblical spirituality is to the modern cultural environment that fosters a desire to assert the basic right of freedom from pain and suffering. Rather than viewing our human frailty and mortality as liabilities to be denied or overcome, biblical spirituality encourages us to place them at the very center of our being and our belief. This is because true biblical spirituality involves suffering and an acceptance of our own and others' brokenness and flaws.

Frances Young puts authentic spirituality in simple terms as the discovery of our limitations, wrestling, following, imitating, emptying, and longing. It is a journey of faith, hope and love, and above all, of longing to be whole again. And more specifically, it is the pursuit of holiness. She loosely categorizes it in five stages, each helping to build up the argument for the other, but there is still a logical progression from the first stage of accepting the present, to embracing the world of brokenness, and finally hope.

First Stage: Holiness as a Journey through the Desert

Frances Young never sees holiness as a static attribute; it is always a dynamic interaction with God and with the world. Part of the reason why she starts the contemplation of a life of holy living as a journey through the desert is because we need to begin at the beginning: a contemplation of who we are and where we are going. However, her experience with living with a severely disabled son creates a unique premise for her contemplation.

Drawing from the spirituality of the Desert Fathers, she, like them, also looks at the desert in metaphorical terms.[11] The desert is a place of trial and temptation. There we find our inner demons exposed: fear and insecurity, anger and violence, self-deception and self-hatred. Drawing from the example of Christ in the wilderness, the Desert Fathers saw temptation as inseparable from experience, and this was a good thing, enabling discernment of spirits and endurance. It produces freedom and a willingness to move on and venture into unknown territories. This is where Frances's experience comes in, forcing her to rethink her beliefs and what is meant by "normal."

The spirituality of disability will inevitably need to critique the ideology of normalcy. Being created in God's image and likeness can no longer be articulated in terms of how that image relates to the attributes of God. It demands a fresh understanding of the human condition that will expand

10. Young, *Brokenness and Blessing*, 8.
11. Young, *Brokenness and Blessing*, 14–22.

our definition of "normal": "Because many kinds of difference are feared and shunned, the disability experience has been a different experience . . . Variety is normal."[12] Perhaps Beldon Lane's observation is pointedly obvious and demands our change in attitude towards the disabled:

> Our culture substitutes the glamorous for the grotesque, denying this awkward vision of the *imago dei* . . . If we define a person exclusively in terms of rational ability and productivity, someone with Down syndrome will inevitably appear less than whole. The eccentric, the ugly, the abnormal lie beyond the measure of our society norms. We are left with a stylized and truncated humanity, dangerously imaging itself complete.[13]

There is in Christian theology the concept of God creating the world and humans in it with a moral purpose. Frances Young's experience of a profoundly disabled child would question that, as this would make the disabled child less than who he is, less than human even! She feels as if she is thrown into the desert of trial and temptation but also given the gift of venturing into new and unknown territory. She relates her desert journey thus:

> Indeed, my pilgrimage with Arthur has been a kind of Exodus, through the wilderness to the Promised Land. For years I found holding onto my faith profoundly difficult. God seemed absent . . . The need to let go of preoccupations and anxieties, to journey into the unknown, to accept the utter transcendence and incomprehensibility of God, allowed me a renewal of faith, and soon afterwards a sense of vocation in which Arthur became a central part of my ministry. Overall my journey has involved a profound shifting away from the questions of theodicy, from the anguished questioning of a Job, to a sense that through the wilderness of coping with Arthur I have had the privileged access to a deeper sense of meaning and value."[14]

Eventually Frances comes to understand humans as frail beings, as part of the natural order and therefore inevitably will face up to "what can go wrong." Accidents do indeed happen, and can happen even while an embryo is in the womb. This vulnerability and frailty is part of being human. And yet, to Frances, not all is gray and subjected to fate, it does in fact lead to the core of Christian belief.

---

12. Block, *Copious Hosting*, 85, quoting from Shaw, *Ragged Edge*, xii.

13. Quoted by Block, *Copious Hosting*, 86, from Lane, "Grace and the Grotesque," 109.

14. Young, *Brokenness and Blessing*, 27–28.

By "the deepest truths of Christianity" she means "the God-ness of God" and "the frailty of creation." She would explore the former in her second stage of her journey, but here the frailty of creation is absolutely crucial to her formulation of theological anthropology. It means that human beings are no longer defined in terms of "normalcy" but "frailty" in all its forms.[15] The very humanness of human beings is limited and vulnerable, prone to accidents, even in the womb. Disability is thus not an exception but in fact one manifestation of humanity!

She then relates her experience of the frailties of humans to the very heart of Christianity in Jesus Christ:

> It seems to me that one of the things that Christianity says is that strangely, and in a way that I find it difficult to understand, it was God's own self which in Jesus came and took responsibility for all the, what I call, " gone wrongness" in the creation. The fact that we do wicked things; that things go wrong; that there is suffering and hurt, and all kinds of the terrible things that happen. That somehow, in Jesus, God took responsibility for that and through that we can know that at heart, even though he dared not damage it by grabbing it like that butterfly, the whole world is in the hands of God.[16]

The desert way of life, or the first stage in our path to holiness, according to Frances, is the acceptance of human frailty and nonconformity with the values and the conventional "labeling" of the world.

Second Stage: Holiness as a Journey toward Encounter with God

Frances Young takes the biblical stories as a record of people encountering God, falling short of God's glory and finding salvation in all kinds of different ways.[17] She takes the story of Jacob wrestling at the Jabbok (meaning "wrestling") in Genesis 32:24–32 as the paradigm. The emphasis lies in the experience of Jacob being both blessed and disabled at the same time. It is revealing that Jacob called that place of encounter "*Penuel*," stating that, "I have seen the face of God and yet my life has been preserved."

The story has become a paradigm of human encounter with God, especially when Jacob was renamed "Israel." As one commentator puts it: "The history of the people of Israel was often to be a tale of just such encounter

---

15. Young, *Face to Face*, 189–93.
16. Young, "Being Biblical," 7.
17. Young, "Being Biblical," 1.

with God: a costly turbulent struggle in the darkness of tragedy, exile and persecution, but an authentic experience in which they came face to face with God."[18]

Frances Young then takes us on a journey of early Christian interpretations of the story, but confirms that "at the core is the idea of Jacob wrestling with God, a mysterious Being discerned in human form, and being disabled, blessed and given a new name through the contest."[19] What really caught her eyes and mind is, as expounded by St. Gregory of Nazianzus,[20] the mystical interpretation of the wrestling, and it is this interpretation that brought Frances face-to-face with the problem of suffering. She puts the exposition succinctly thus:

> For Gregory the story is about the human struggle to know God, and its ultimate failure because we are mere creatures. It's only because God accommodates the divine self to our human level, through the inevitably limited human language of Scripture, and above all by accepting the constraints of incarnation, that we have any chance of knowing anything about God.[21]

None of the human struggle is as acute as the problem of suffering. Frances speaks boldly and realistically from her own experience of her life with Arthur: "He became for me the symbol of all the 'gone-wrongness' that modernity has identified as a good reason for calling God in question."[22] The "gone-wrongness" is the presumption that humans are self-sufficient and should have the God-given right to demand things from God. We imagine we are in control; we make up our minds; we decide whether we would seek God or not; but the whole point is that we are mere limited creatures, vulnerable, far from in control. By wrestling with God, we may think to prevail, to be master, to accuse and to demand, only to discover that we are the ones to be marked by the struggle, and yet given a new name. In the end it is not that we judge God, rather we are judged by God; and that implies a need to reconfigure our concept of God.[23]

So the spiritual struggle at this second stage of the journey to holiness is not the attempt to find answers to theodicy but to seek to know God as God is. Sometimes, life experience becomes the truest critique of the theology that we hold dear. Theologians like Karl Rahner and David Tracy

18. Davidson, *Genesis 12–50*, 186.
19. Young, "Being Biblical," 6–7.
20. Gregory Nazianzen, "Second Theological Oration."
21. Young, *Brokenness and Blessing*, 44.
22. Young, "Being Biblical," 8.
23. Young, "Being Biblical," 8.

have both advocated that for any theological investigation to be relevant, it must engage two principle sources: the Christian texts and common human experience and language.[24] This is when theology and spirituality meet and inform each other.

She relates one such experience. Out of the constant burden of having to take care of Arthur, in her tiredness and desperation, she began to waver a little in her once staunch belief. "How could I go on believing in a good God when something had gone so wrong in the very act of creating a new human being? How could I go on believing that God had a purpose for everyone, to become saints, when here was someone who would apparently never be capable of any independent moral choice?" This was her Jabbok wrestling. And as the Jacob story implies, there came the experience of reconfiguration of her concept of God. As she was going into the kitchen, she suddenly had a "loud thought": "It makes no difference to me whether you believe in me or not!"[25] It dawned on her that if God is who he is, he has the power of "existing absolutely in virtue of himself, requiring no cause, no other justification for his existence except that his very nature is to exist."[26]

However, the place of doubt cannot be denied, because truth, honesty, and integrity belong to spirituality. Jesus's agony in the garden can be read as facing the sense of abandonment by God, a "wrestling" of the soul, in the face of suffering and inexplicable destruction. Yet with this cry of agony came the blessing of obedience as Jesus prayed, "Thy will not Mine!" His agony is also his blessing!

Frances eventually came to realize that from her son Arthur she received much blessing. Instead of seeing herself as his carer, she began to see that Arthur was ministering to her. She found the fruit of the Spirit bearing in her as she saw it from the perspective of the powerless speaking to the one who thought she was holding the power over someone else. She can now say with much conviction:

> So I would say that after all those years of struggling with the questions, I discovered that through Arthur I have been given privileged access to the deepest truths of Christianity. I stand alongside him as a vulnerable creature, disabled and mortal, knowing my creaturely limitations and my lack of knowledge, especially of God. I know my need of God and my resistance to God's grace, the inner demons like self-pity that so easily take

---

24. As summarized by Block, *Copious Hosting*, 11–12.

25. Young, "Being Biblical," 8.

26. Young refers favorably from Merton, *Elected Silence*, 139; see her *Brokenness and Blessing*, 28, 46–47.

over my interior life. Yet again I find myself lamed and blessed. I discern signs of God's presence, I meet God in human form, I discover glimpses of Christ, in the face of some of the most damaged and disabled human persons.[27]

She quotes with much approval Charles Wesley's rendition of the wrestling Jacob:[28]

> Come, O Thou Traveller Unknown, Whom still I hold, but cannot see!
> My company before is gone, And I am left alone with Thee;
> With Thee all night I mean to stay, And wrestle till the break of day.
>
> I need not tell Thee who I am, My misery and sin declare;
> Thyself hast called me by my name; Look on Thy hands, and read it there:
> But who, I ask Thee, who art Thou? Tell me Thy name, and tell me now.
>
> Content now upon my thigh I halt, till life's short journey end;
> All helplessness, all weakness, I on Thee alone for strength depend;
> Nor have I power from Thee to move: Thy nature and Thy name is Love.
>
> Lame as I am, I take the prey, Hell, earth and sin with ease o'ercome;
> I leap for joy, pursue my way, And as a bounding hart fly home,
> Through all eternity to prove, Thy nature and Thy name is Love.

Third Stage: Holiness as Imitatio Christi

By the grace of God, the gift of struggling with God is the self-emptying of Christ. Frances Young starts this leg of the journey with a famous hymn[29] that recapitulates the theme of *Imitatio Christi*[30]:

> My song is love unknown,
> My Savior's love to me,
> Love to the loveless shown,
> That they might lovely be.

27. Young, "Being Biblical," 10.
28. Wesley, "Come O Thou Traveller Unknown," 386–87, stanzas 1, 2, 7, 14.
29. Samuel Crossman, "My Song is Love Unknown." See Hawn, "My Song."
30. Young, *Brokenness and Blessing*, 59.

> O who am I,
> That for my sake
> My Lord should take
> Frail flesh, and die?

The theme of the way of Jesus is simple enough: trust and *kenosis*; but Frances gives them a fuller meaning in light of her own experience. She herself as a theologian has been involved in the so-called "Quest for the Historical Jesus,"[31] but finds it tedious and lifeless now. Rather, more truthful and life-giving is the hymn's emphasis on the love of Christ, who for our sake, came to us to bridge the gulf between God's "Otherness" and our creatureliness by self-emptying (*kenosis*) in the incarnation.[32] This is God accommodating himself to the human level for our sake. This holds the key to biblical spirituality.[33]

The concept of self-emptying is poignantly true when we look at it from the perspective of the relationship of people with disabilities and their carers. The carer will need to see as Christ does that the people whom she assists are also fully human, having their own way of relating with the Divine. Just as Christ's self-emptying love shows his total disregard of the state of the humanity that he came to serve, the carer's self-emptying service needs to recognize this and allow God to relate to them in God's own way.

Amos Yong,[34] speaking from a Pentecostal perspective, having a younger brother with Down syndrome, redefines the *ordo salutis* of traditional soteriology, preferring to state it in terms of *via solitis*, as a dynamic process, agreeing with the theologian John Swinton. He says:

> Rather than asking whether people with intellectual disability are religiously conscious or responsible, he enquires into how they become religiously engaged. If human beings are multidimensional, dynamic, and relational through and through, then with regard to people with intellectual disabilities, relational criteria comes into play that are not exhaustively determined or constricted to the intellect. There can be a genuine affective apprehension of and even conversion to God for those with profound cognitive disabilities whereby their existence in loving relationships mediates real saving experiences of God.[35]

---

31. Young, *Brokenness and Blessing*, 59.
32. Young, *Brokenness and Blessing*, 59.
33. Young, *Brokenness and Blessing*, 68–69.
34. Yong, *Theology and Down Syndrome*.
35. Yong, *Theology and Down Syndrome*, 237.

Frances Young sees the dynamism being played out between the disabled and carer. We need:

> a reorientation which can face and accommodate the challenge that the handicapped present . . . to our ideology of what is human. . . . It is not the handicapped who need community care. It's US. To learn from the handicapped requires a new heart and a new spirit within us, but if we are prepared to learn, it will produce the new heart and new spirit and we will be immensely enriched—indeed, it will be our salvation. We shall discover what it really means to be human.[36]

Amos Yong adds:

> As importantly, I suggest, our conversion facilitates their own, so that what emerges is a new community consisting of us and them, beyond us versus them.[37]

The relationship is played out in terms of self-emptying and trust, and it goes both ways. The reliance of the disabled manifests the emptying of oneself and simple trust in the carer; the service of the carer is a manifestation of self-emptying and willingness to learn from the simple trust of the disabled. The disabled see a Christ-figure in the carer in her service, and the carer sees a Christ-figure in the disabled in their trust. This is life-giving and life-transforming: "I come so that they may have life and have it more abundantly." And that is *kenosis* in the true sense of the word.

Frances relates an episode in the Othona community, where she was invited to speak, taking Arthur with her for the week.[38] Silence was required throughout the prayer session. As usual, it was impossible to keep Arthur quiet, so with Arthur present, silence could not be kept in the usual way. So the leader suggested that they create silence by singing Psalms. The Othona community's version of Psalm 131 brought tears and silence of the soul to all present:

> I am too little, Lord, to look down on others.
> I've not chased great affairs, nor matters beyond me.
> I've tamed my wild desires and settled my soul.
> My soul's new-fed child at rest on the breast.
> My brothers seek the Lord, both now and for ever.[39]

---

36. Yong, *Theology and Down Syndrome*, 177, 183.
37. Yong, *Theology and Down Syndrome*, 238.
38. Young, *Brokenness and Blessing*, 79.
39. Young, *Brokenness and Blessing*, 80.

Frances exclaims: "Suddenly Arthur became the Christ-figure in our midst." What Arthur had done was to make us more than what we were.

Fourth Stage: Holiness as Resident Alien

It follows that recognizing the Christ-figure in people will inevitably lead to embracing humanity as they are. Frances Young proposes that welcoming "difference" lies at the heart of the gospel and deepens spirituality and the experience of worship. She puts it succinctly: "It is being open to meeting the strangeness—welcoming the difference—of others, which allows us glimpses of God's Otherness."

The idea of resident alien is never far from the core of biblical theology. It is at the very core of the identity of ancient Israel:

> He defends the cause of the fatherless and the widow, and loves the foreigner residing among you, giving them food and clothing. And you are to love those who are foreigners, for you yourselves were foreigners in Egypt. (Deut 10:18–19, NIV)

Therefore, the person who is the "other" is a sign of what Israel truly is, i.e., gēr (resident alien), whose status and condition cannot be changed. But God is no respecter of persons and loves the alien who lives among them. In the New Testament, Christians may be ethnically related to their pagan neighbors, but they have become different—aliens and exiles, sojourners, resident aliens (cf. 1 Pet 2:11–12).

For people with a disability, they are more often than not being looked at as strangers or resident aliens,[40] sometimes even by their carer. Frances Young relates the times of alienation with Arthur. At times, despair set in. She was forced to accept: "Little by little he got weaker. It is impossible to know what to do for the best! At least I don't get guilty any more—whatever you do is wrong anyway!"[41] Frances is honest enough to call her life with Arthur "a battle of love." She puts it in a very stark and raw emotional outburst:

> The worst feature of it was that when he was distressed, there would be gradual build up of distress in me, until I could no longer contain my feelings. It was his rejection of love and care that hurt; it was the distress for his distress which undermined

---

40. Frances Young draws heavily on the work of a paper read by Ian Cohen, later collected and reproduced in a private publication (see Pattison, *Mental Handicap*). Young, *Face to Face*, 135, n. 4.

41. Young, *Face to Face*, 27.

> my ability to cope. There seemed no point in his life. If you put an animal out of his misery on compassionate grounds, why not Arthur?[42]

She concludes her outburst by saying: "How could we justify [Arthur's] continued misery when the future held nothing for him?"[43]

This is what Ian Cohen termed "the strange belonging yet not belonging of the 'alien' child in the family, the strange child who is different, though 'bone of my bone, flesh of my flesh.'"[44] Frances confesses that, "As a parent myself, I have to acknowledge having the powerful conflicting emotions about my son, who is flesh of my flesh but not like me, not at all like his adult younger brothers . . . It is no good pretending there is no difference."[45]

It is precisely by the recognition of this difference and the discovery of "letting go" that love can return. Frances went through it this way. At first she tried every which way to "remedy" Arthur, but eventually she had to admit that they did more harm than good, and indeed a lot of permanent damage to Arthur's physique. It all seemed to ease her self-accusation of not trying hard enough. The release ironically came in the form of realizing her own possessiveness, a form of self-centered love. Then came the healing idea of letting go.

> It is only when we can let go, become detached that we really love the other person for himself, allowing him to be himself and do his own thing without the binding cords of possessiveness. And this is when the relationship, paradoxically, deepens.[46]

So if we are to welcome difference, to affirm the "other" and embrace the stranger, we have to acknowledge first that there is a difference. Then new life can be found in being open to meeting the strangeness, welcoming difference, which allows us glimpses of God's Otherness.[47] Welcoming God's difference in fact deepens spirituality. Welcoming the difference of others deepens the experience of worship. This indeed is a path to holiness.

---

42. Young, *Face to Face*, 39.
43. Young, *Face to Face*, 42.
44. Young, *Brokenness and Blessing*, 90.
45. Young, *Brokenness and Blessing*, 94.
46. Young, *Face to Face*, 47.
47. Young, *Brokenness and Blessing*, 101.

Fifth Stage: Holiness as Longing and Fulfillment

Is there hope for the broken world? The path of the pursuit of holiness inevitably leads us to the future, where expectations and fulfillment of our longing can be realized, otherwise the journey would be in vain. Yet according to Frances Young, "People in contact with the handicapped have to learn to accept disappointment."[48] She calls this the dark side of hope, which becomes the birth pangs of the new creation!

The experience of Frances Young's gradual realization of the insight above has been played out throughout Arthur's life till now, when he is forty-five years of age. There is always a parent's longing and expectation for her son to grow at least to an acceptably normal adult. Frances had to acknowledge early in Arthur's life that it was not to be. When longing became a false hope, it came crashing down on her, increasing her sense of "failure" and creating unnecessary "guilt" and feelings of inadequacy.[49]

In her desperation earlier in Arthur's life, Frances went through the so-called "I will do anything" syndrome, hoping against hope by trying every remedy that was available to stimulate Arthur to achieve progressive response and mobility. She soon realized that this approach would be unhealthy. "The mother's singlemindedness really can become an obsession, to the exclusion of any other care that might be needed in the family as a whole. It would only lead to breakups and maybe delinquency in other siblings."[50]

What can you do when a child stays practically on one spot of development and no progress is in sight?[51] The acceptance of the fact, ironically enough, is "progress" in itself, both for the carer and the child. For the carer it is a "progress" in coping with failure. "Our ideology is so 'success-oriented,' and 'success' defined in terms of constant little bits of 'progress' towards 'normalcy,' that the reality of non-progress is far too demoralizing to admit . . . what matters far more is trust and respect, a relationship in which love can flourish because it is relaxed and accepting."[52] For the child it is a "progress" in terms of the switch in the carer to "force" or "foster" a change in

---

48. Young, *Face to Face*, 196.
49. Young, *Face to Face*, 196–97.
50. Young, *Face to Face*, 3–37.
51. Young, *Face to Face*, 199: "He remained in the same class for years, and the same school until he left at eighteen. Effectively teachers were struggling with the same self-help skills when he finished as when he started —notably feeding and toileting. The reality is that at twenty-one he is still in nappies and still has to be fed, and you could say that no progress was made at all over all those years."
52. Young, *Face to Face*, 200, 201.

him, albeit with very good intentions. Frances's words have a strong ring of truth: "But I do think that Arthur's progress has to a large extent been 'inbuilt,' and a lot of our efforts to force it have in fact created more problems for him and us."[53] It is this that finally brought Frances to formulate her very brand of a theology of hope. She starts, as she always does, with biblical wisdom and her own experience. We can summarize it thus.[54]

1. Human beings are dust and to dust they will return. In the field of handicap, it is usual to recognize that no complete cure is possible and that learning to accept the situation is only realism. True, we should not give up finding ways to alleviate the situation, but we need to accept the limits of human competence.

2. It is the power of God that keeps one in being; all life is a privilege, not a right.

3. Life is a miracle, and resurrection a miraculous renewal of life by God. Thus, there is no expectation that humans can create Utopia or solve all problems or reach perfection by their own strength or wisdom. For this to happen, it has to be a miraculous re-creation.

4. There is a mutuality in all humans: we share the same need, we have the same instinctive desire for life (even for the profoundly disabled), the same ultimate end in death, the same frailty, and the same vulnerability.

5. Yet there is the inauguration of hope when Jesus came announcing the kingdom of God, the "now" and the "not yet" of God's dealing with the world: on one hand, believers are already justified, sanctified, adopted as children of God, and heirs of the kingdom; on the other hand, they have to become what they already are.

6. Despite all the doom and gloom of the present world, human life is shot through with miracles of grace, genuine change, and real hope at the penultimate level.

7. This is realistic hope: the dark side of hope is the pain and judgment involved in the world's labor to give birth to God's new creation, a hope for the ultimate new creation guaranteed by anticipations now.

The theology of hope has given rise to a reflection on the fifth stage of the pursuit of holiness. Frances Young uses the term "desire frustrated and fulfilled" to describe the paradox of hope. She explores the various ways in

---

53. Young, *Face to Face*, 201.
54. Young, *Face to Face*, 206–15.

which the early fathers interpret the Song of Songs, and comes to see Gregory of Nyssa's language of *epektasis* as the most appropriate of this paradox of hope. Gregory's idea was first formulated in his spiritual interpretation of *The Life of Moses* and then elaborated in his spiritual commentary of the Song of Songs. Essentially, Gregory saw "desire" in a positive light. The longing of the soul for God creates a desire to follow him and reach beyond the boundary of its own capacity into the incomprehensible. This is an endless quest, because no created being can ever fully grasp the infinite God. Nevertheless, the desire to pursue is created by God, giving glimpses of his glory and beauty; but it is also a "frustrated" journey as it is always beyond our reach. It is not all negative, however, as the frustration induces further desire to pursue.[55]

In terms of our spiritual journey in a broken world, glimpses of God's goodness and glory will invigorate our desire to experience more of it. It becomes a perpetual spiraling quest from frustration to fulfillment, but all the while in ascending order, till we meet him face-to-face in perfect love.

Thus, Frances Young comes back full circle to her Methodist spiritual roots and concludes her vision of the pursuit of holiness with Charles Wesley's best-known hymn:[56]

> Love divine, all loves excelling,
> Joy of heaven to earth come down.
> Fix in us Thy humble dwelling,
> All Thy faithful mercies crown.
> Jesus, Thou art all compassion,
> Pure, unbounded love Thou art;
> Visit us with Thy salvation
> Enter every trembling heart.
>
> Finish then Thy new creation,
> Pure and spotless let us be;
> Let us see Thy great salvation,
> Perfectly restored in Thee;
> Changed from glory into glory,
> Till in heaven we take our place,
> Till we cast our crowns before Thee,
> Lost in wonder, love and praise!

We conclude this contemplation of the holy life with Frances Young's words:

---

55. See my unpublished PhD thesis: Tan, "Gregory of Nyssa."
56. Charles Wesley, "Love Divine, All Loves Excelling."

Disability is the condition of blessing. Humankind has overreached itself, forgotten its essential creatureliness and its role in creation's ecology, and put itself in God's place. The rediscovery that God is beyond us, and yet reaches out to us in Christ to grasp our hands in the midst of the struggle, even to wound us with his arrow of love, might enable us, both individually and as the body of Christ on earth, to live the way of love and true humility in following Jesus, this would make us the best witness to the Gospel in the pluralist global village of the twenty-first century.[57]

BIBLIOGRAPHY

Block, Jennie Weiss. *Copious Hosting: A Theology of Access for People with Disabilities.* NY: Continuum, 2002.

Caspary, Almut. "The Patristic Era: Early Christian Attitudes toward the Disfigured Outcast." In *Disability in the Christian Tradition: A Reader,* edited by Brian Brock and John Swinton, 24–64. Grand Rapids: Eerdmans, 2012.

Davidson, Robert. *Genesis 12–50.* Cambridge: Cambridge University Press, 1979.

Gregory Nazianzen. "Second Theological Oration." *New Advent.* https://www.newadvent.org/fathers/310228.htm.

Hawn, C. Michael. "My Song is Love Unknown." *History of Hymns.* Discipleship Ministries of The United Methodist Church. https://www.umcdiscipleship.org/resources/history-of-hymns-my-song-is-love-unknown.

Lane, Beldon. "Grace and the Grotesque." *Christian Century* 107, no. 33 (November 14, 1990) 109.

Merton, Thomas. *Elected Silence: The Autobiography of Thomas Merton.* London: Hollis and Carter, 1949.

Pattison, Stephen, ed. *Mental Handicap, Theology and Pastoral Care.* Birmingham: University of Birmingham, Department of Theology, 1987a.

Shaw, Barrett, ed. *The Ragged Edge: The Disability Experience from the Pages of the First Fifteen Years of the Disability Rag.* Louisville: Avocado, 1994.

Tan, Justin. "Gregory of Nyssa's Mystical Anthropology in His Homilies on the Song of Songs." PhD diss., King's College, London University, 1995.

Wesley, Charles. "Come O Thou Traveller Unknown." In *The United Methodist Hymnal.* Nashville, TN: United Methodist, 1989.

Yong, Amos. *Theology and Down Syndrome: Reimagining Disability in Late Modernity* Waco: Baylor University Press, 2007.

Young, Frances. "Being Biblical, Being Broken and Blessed." Lecture at St. Martin-in-the Fields Autumn Programme, *The Alpha and the Omega, the First and the Last: The Bible Opened to All* (2010).

———. *Brokenness and Blessings: Towards a Biblical Spirituality.* London: Darton, Longman and Todd Ltd., 2007.

———. *Face to Face: A Narrative Essay in the Theology of Suffering.* Edinburgh: T. & T. Clark, 1990.

---

57. Young, *Brokenness and Blessing,* 126.

5

Transformation through Contemplation

Reflective Liturgies that Transform Us

Thomas Kimber

JAMES JOYCE INTRODUCES US to a character named Mr. Duffy, who illustrates an insulated existence completely disconnected from his physical and spiritual worlds. Yet, as spiritual beings, humans were created for contemplation. This chapter considers, first, that God is our homeland and the source of our identity. Second, we are created with the capacity to be contemplative. Third, we are most fully ourselves in community with others. And lastly, we will consider four contemplative liturgies that transform us.

INTRODUCTION

In his short story *A Painful Case*, James Joyce introduces us to Mr. Duffy, a man who lives a routine, machinelike existence. Mr. Duffy inhabits a town that is rich with symbols and metaphors of a fulfilling life, yet he purposefully and intentionally creates for himself an insulated existence that would protect him from the possibility of introspection. Indeed, his only course in life was to follow religiously the routine he had set for himself. He was, as Joyce so pointedly describes him, a man "who lived a little distance from his body."[1] He was, like so many other people, a man who lived disconnected from his physical and spiritual worlds. Wrapped in the carefully constructed cocoon of his ordered existence, he presented to his world the facade of a man of culture. Mr. Duffy has created for himself a life routine as a response to all his fears, thereby protecting himself from the fear of being hurt by others or the fear of looking within himself. His machinelike routine also insulates him from ever experiencing emotion; ultimately it insulates him from the possibility of experiencing love. In truth, Mr. Duffy not only lived a little distance from his own body, he lived a great distance from all others as well.

Mr. Duffy is such a painful caricature of so many who carefully order the liturgies of their lives as a protective means of avoiding the very thing that would give their lives meaning and purpose. His nonidentity becomes his identity. His nonexistence becomes the whole point of his existence. Oddly enough, though, Mr. Duffy is a man of liturgy. He is a man of carefully ordered cultural practices that have formed him into a certain kind of man. "Liturgy," as James K. A. Smith defines it, "is a shorthand term for those rituals that are loaded with an ultimate Story about who we are and what we're for."[2]

I suggest that as humans, we are created for certain types of liturgies. These would be the liturgies of the soul, which require silence, solitude, and a renewed perspective on community. As humans, we were created for contemplation, though in our disconnected world, each of us, like Mr. Duffy, lives a little distance from ourselves. Through the spiritual discipline of contemplation, we close the distance between ourselves and God, thereby reestablishing the identity for which we were created. We will consider, first, that God himself is our homeland, which is the context of our identity. Second, we must understand that as humans we were created for contemplation. Third, we will consider some thoughts about the contemplative community, which reorients our understanding of relationships. And finally, we will look at four contemplative liturgies that transform us.

GOD IS OUR HOMELAND: THE CONTEXT OF OUR IDENTITY

In *The City of God*, Augustine makes the observation that "We must fly to our beloved fatherland. There is the Father, there our all."[3] Augustine's words take us, of course, to the observation Moses made in Psalm 90, "Lord, you

---

1. Joyce, "Painful Case," 96.
2. Smith, *You Are What You Love*, 46.
3. Augustine of Hippo, *City of God*, 296.

have been our dwelling place in all generations." We think of dwelling places as physical residences, with addresses and postal codes. The children of Israel longed for a promised land, where they would no longer be nomads or slaves. We find our identity in national origins and countries of citizenship. But Moses, who led these wanderers from slavery, through the wilderness, and into the promised land, reminds these people that our deeper identity is not in the place but in God himself. "You, Lord, are our dwelling place." So, Augustine asks the obvious question, "God is love: Why do we go forth and run to the heights of the heavens and the lowest parts of the earth, seeking Him who is within us, if we wish to be with Him?"[4]

David asks, "Where shall I go from your Spirit? Or where shall I flee from your presence?" (Ps 139:7). No matter where I go, there you are, before me and behind me, beside me, and within me. Jesus puts it even more intimately: "In that day, you will know that I am in my Father, and you in me, and I in you" (John 14:20). And Paul reminds us that "we are a dwelling place for God by the Spirit" (Eph 2:22).

To be fully human, we must understand that our ultimate home and dwelling place is not in a physical residence, but in God himself. By the power of the Spirit, God himself dwells within us. He is, indeed, our fatherland. He is our dwelling place. And, as Paul reminds us, we are his dwelling place. Apart from God, we have no ability to form any sense of true identity. To shift the metaphor a bit, Genesis 1:27 tells us that we are created in God's image. An image has meaning only in relation to the original. Apart from the original, the image has no substance, no form, no identity. Ours is a derived identity, not an original one. Apart from God, we have no ability to form a true and lasting identity. In the same manner, apart from a homeland, we have no citizenship. Any attempts, as an image, to create an identity apart from God as our original will be a false attempt leading ultimately to futility.

> I cannot ground my own existence, for I am made for love. . . . The answer to our question, "who am I?" is simply this: "I am one who is loved by God, by the Spirit who created my spirit, who indwells my very spirit, who is in union with me at the core, despite my ability or inability to be conscious of this." Here I discover what my self is all about—a self made to be inhabited by another self in love.[5]

---

4. Augustine of Hippo, "On the Trinity," 784.
5. Coe and Hall, *Psychology in the Spirit*, 265.

WE WERE CREATED FOR CONTEMPLATION: WE BECOME LIKE THE ONE WE WORSHIP

The question, then, is how do we realize this identity? In truth, it happens more in silence than in noise. The liturgies of our world so often are designed to keep us from the very activity that will close this distance between us and God, and between us and ourselves. The whispers of God are best heard in silence.

Diarmaid MacCulloch observes, "Above all, Yahweh himself is a communicator."[6] This is why when Samuel writes, "And the word of the Lord was rare in those days" (1 Sam 3:1) we are meant to understand that God's silence is unusual. Throughout Scripture we are confronted with the truth that God speaks.

But not only that, God has created us with the capacity to hear him. Paul reminds us that "the Spirit bears witness with our spirit" (Rom 8:16). Jesus says, "My sheep hear my voice" (John 1:27). The psalmist encourages us to engage our senses, to "taste and see that the Lord is good" (Ps 34:8). "What can this mean," asks Tozer, "except that we have in our hearts organs by means of which we can know God as certainly as we know material things through our familiar five senses?"[7]

To be fully human, we must understand that not only does God make his home within us and has created us for relationship with himself, but that he has also created us with the capacity to hear him when he speaks. We were created for contemplation. We are not merely rational beings who think about God with our intellectual and cognitive abilities; we are spiritual beings who have the capacity for communion with God in the depths of the soul. But this requires silence and stillness. It requires a change in our liturgy.

Elijah reminds us that God often speaks in a still, small voice. Indeed, he often communicates without words. And the message conveyed cannot be described in words. This is the true depth of contemplation: the gaze of the soul on the beauty of God. And such beauty often leaves us speechless. St. John of the Cross attempts to describe this experience: "There is no way to catch in words the sublime things of God that take place in these souls. The appropriate language for the persons receiving these favors is that they understand them, experience them within themselves, enjoy them, and be silent."[8]

---

6. MacCulloch, *Silence*, 16.
7. Tozer, *Pursuit of God*, 49.
8. John of the Cross, "Living Flame of Love," 665.

But in this place of silent contemplation we not only commune with God but we are transformed more into his image. Psalm 115 sets the principle in a negative context. The passage describes false idols that cannot speak, cannot hear, cannot see, cannot smell, cannot feel, and cannot walk. In other words, they have none of the capacities of either humans or God. But the real lesson is that "those who make them become like them" (v. 8). Not only are they less than God, they are less than human. Conversely, Paul says that "we all with unveiled face, beholding the glory of the Lord, are being transformed into the same image from one degree of glory to another" (2 Cor 3:18). We become like the object we worship.

John of the Cross describes a spirituality that leads us more deeply into a fuller experience of our relationship with God, not only because we know him more fully, but because in that experience we come to know ourselves more fully. A contemplative knowledge of God "brings with it knowledge of our true selves transformed into the likeness of Christ."[9] In this experience, we find our true selves. Both knowledge of God and knowledge of self are indispensable and integrated in our journey toward discovering our identity.

THE CONTEMPLATIVE COMMUNITY: WE ARE MOST OURSELVES WITH OTHERS

The contemplative life is life in community. We were created for relationship, not only with God but with others. The contemplative life not only restores our relationship with God and our identity in Christ, it restores our relationships with others in a manner that God intends for us. The early church used the image of a wheel to describe the experience of this.

> The hub of the wheel is God; we are the spokes. Out on the rim of the wheel the spokes are furthest from one another; but at the center, the hub, the spokes are most united to each other. They are a single meeting in the one hub. The image was used in the early church to say something important about that level of life at which we are one with each other and one with God. The more we journey towards the Center the closer we are both to God and to each other. . . . The personal journey into God is simultaneously ecclesial and all-embracing.[10]

---

9. Tillyer, *Union with God*, 19.
10. Laird, *Into the Silent Land*, 12.

In this we are reminded that the goal of our personal spiritual formation is a relational goal. In the experience of God's love, we can finally "come out of hiding and open to one another in love and need. . . . As I come to trust others more, having been loved in the truth of myself, this experience may be used by the Spirit to encourage me in prayer to trust that God cares and loves me as well."[11]

This experience of love, both of God and others, allows me to experience fellowship in deeper and much more profound ways. In true fellowship, we are reminded not only that Christ is in me, but Christ is in us—as a body, as a people, as a church. And in that truth, we are all collectively and individually open to the presence of Jesus in our midst. We reaffirm and celebrate our collective identity as the people of God.

Within the contemplative community we have the opportunity and experience of deeper fellowship with one another as we acknowledge Jesus in our midst. As we break bread together and enjoy fellowship around the table, we invite the presence of Jesus, collectively opening our hearts to him as both our welcomed guest and the founder of our feast. In genuine fellowship we strengthen one another's bodies in the sharing of food—imitating Jesus in breaking and giving bread. In fellowship we strengthen one another's souls as we share life and love and beauty. In fellowship we strengthen one another's spirits as we collectively invite Jesus's presence and welcome his ministry to each of us. In fellowship we deepen our identity as the *familia dei*—the family of God—the children who bear the family likeness of our heavenly father. This, too, is a journey back to our homeland, back to God, where brothers and sisters dwell together in unity. It is in this collective experience that we finally experience the *shalom* God desires for us.

CONTEMPLATIVE LITURGIES THAT TRANSFORM US

Unlike James Joyce's Mr. Duffy, the Desert Fathers refused to allow themselves to be passively shaped by society. They believed that simply to "let oneself drift along, passively accepting the tenets and values of what they knew as society, was purely and simply a disaster."[12] Liturgies serve an important purpose to restore order and meaning to a world that would otherwise descend into disorder and chaos. Rightly understood, liturgies are a form of rites of intensification,[13] which restore a sense of rhythm and order

---

11. Coe and Hall, *Psychology*, 268.

12. Nouwen, *Way of the Heart*, 9.

13. The theory of rites of intensification was developed by Chapple and Coon, *Principles of Anthropology*.

to life, recognizing the tendency to devolve into disorder, disintegration, and even chaos. These rites, which can be both individual as well as corporate, preserve equilibrium, reinforce our deepest values, and strengthen the relationships of a group. Even something as simple as a family meal reinforces the importance of fellowship, relationship, and the restoration of family equilibrium. The regular practice of these rites, or liturgies, helps to sustain and even deepen our conditioned responses toward God, others, our world, and even ourselves. Religious services, spiritual disciplines, holidays and festivals, Lent and Advent all use symbols and rituals to intensify our deepest relationships and beliefs. As rites of intensification, liturgies are meant to reinforce our deepest values and aspirations and restore a sense of order, meaning, and identity.

With that in mind, I would suggest four contemplative liturgies that transform us as individuals and as a community.

Liturgy of Solitude and Silence

In the liturgy of solitude, we enter into the experience of Jesus, who was "led up by the Spirit into the wilderness" (Matt 4:1). In solitude, we take up Jesus's invitation to "come away by yourselves to a desolate place and rest a while" (Mark 6:31). But in taking that invitation, we must realize that this is not a solitude of aloneness; it is a solitude with Jesus. It is a place of refinement and transformation. The wilderness of solitude is the place where my hidden self, and the many false selves I have created suddenly fall away and I sit completely still and open before God.

Solitude, in our society, can be a frightening thing. Alone with my God and my thoughts. Perhaps the greater challenge is the message in our world that solitude is unproductive, a waste of time. But solitude reminds us, again, of the ultimate Story—God's story—of who we are and why we are here. It reorients us from the daily liturgies of this life that would reshape us into another image. In solitude, we open to God and discover, as Augustine says, "that He is closer to me than I am to myself." In solitude, we discover over again who we truly are, that our life is hidden with Christ in God (Col 3:3).

Solitude removes us from the distractions and the compulsions of the world, where we can sit silently without distraction and face the truth of who we are. "Only in the context of grace can we face our sin. Only in this place of healing can we dare to show our wounds; only with a single-minded attention to Christ can we give up our clinging fears and face our own true nature."[14] This is where we come to realize that it is not we who live but

14. Nouwen, *Way of the Heart*, 17.

Christ who lives within us. He is our true self. And suddenly this place of solitude is not a frightening place but a welcome place. It is not a lonely place, but one filled with the presence and beauty of God. The place of solitude is our homeland, where God welcomes and receives us.

Henri Nouwen reminds us that silence completes and intensifies solitude. In silence we not only remove ourselves from the noise of the world, but we quiet the inner static of noise in our souls.

We are too often addicted to words. But we also find that words are inadequate and incomplete. Words can only convey part of a message. And we take that craving for words into our expectations of God. We ask him to speak, and we listen for a word. But often God's most profound messages are wordless. And our deepest prayers are prayers without words. The Spirit intercedes for us in groans too deep for words (Rom 8:26). And God responds in answers beyond words. Silence is the atmosphere of the abiding heart, content only with the presence of God. The liturgy of silence learns to deaden the sounds of distraction and listen intently to the still small blowing of God within. It is where we wean ourselves from our addiction to words, and with the Spirit we are content to groan, or laugh, or sigh, and to let those breaths carry our prayers to God. And he groans, and laughs, and sighs with us. And in that silence we hear Jesus's words, "I know what it feels like." And he sympathizes with us in our weakness and our temptation (Heb 4:15).

Liturgy of Service

We are too deeply steeped in the liturgies of consumerism. We have been formed and shaped by cravings and gluttonies of greed. Our world is filled with the liturgies of advertisers and shopping centers that have formed us into a certain image. But the liturgy of service shatters that image. In service, I must set aside my selfish desires in order to care for another person. I look for the image of God stamped on every human soul, even the one buried beneath the grime of fallenness. It is that image of God which not only moves me to compassion but ultimately to serve another person in their need. Service frees us from the bondage of self and imitates Jesus, who came to serve and not to be served.

"I was hungry and you gave me food, I was thirsty and you gave me drink, I was a stranger and you welcomed me." And Jesus reminds us that "as you did it to one of the least of these . . . you did it to me" (Matt 25:35, 40). In order to serve I must look for the image of God in a fellow human, and my soul gazes on the beauty of that image and serves out of love. All humans, both the redeemed and the unredeemed, bear the image of God. And it is this image that gives each human unique value and demands our love and respect. Calvin says that even if we say someone is "contemptible and worthless, the Lord shows him to be one to whom He has deigned to give the beauty of His image." Even if someone has done evil, contemplating upon the image of God enables us to look beyond the "intention but look upon the image of God in them, which cancels and effaces their transgressions, and with its beauty and dignity allures us to love and embrace them."[15] The liturgy of service opens my soul to God in a way that will imitate him. Gazing on the beauty of God's image stamped on every human soul enables me, like Jesus, even to wash the feet of my enemy, my betrayer.

The liturgy of service releases me from the bondage of liturgies of consumerism and self-absorption, and looks for the beauty of God in the soul of everyone created in his image.

Liturgy of Lament

The book of Psalms is our guide for liturgies of lament. The psalms express lament more than any other emotion. They remind us of the brokenness of this world and that we individually and universally experience the pain of that brokenness. Exercising the liturgy of lament, we admit with God that the chaos, hurt, and disorder we experience are not the way life is supposed to be. Lament begins with an inward contemplation of my own brokenness, sadness, hurt, and understanding why this is wrong. As we discern our own perceptions of our sadness, anger, and hopelessness, we bring them full of emotion to the only one who can carry the sadness, anger, and hopelessness with us and for us. Genuine lament must turn outward to God. It is only when we truly know God and feel safe with him that we can fully lament. Lament may often look and even feel like a crisis of faith, but in reality, it is an expression of a deep and secure faith that looks into the heart of God with a pleading brokenness. True lament is being honest with oneself and with God, courageously opening to the truth of what lies deep in one's soul. "Help me, for I cannot help myself" is the deepest cry of the sorrowful lamenter. In lament, our soul gazes deeply, fully, reflectively on the loving and just character of God and pours out its cry. Only God can save me, help me, and relieve me.

True lament opens the way for redemption. Redemptive contemplation embraces the vision of all things redeemed through the finished work of Jesus. It dares to envision the end of all things—a picture of shalom. Isaiah

15. Calvin, *Institutes*, 3.7.6.

lamented the adulterous spirituality of his people, but out of that came the shalomic vision of the lion lying down with the lamb and a small child leading them. As a prisoner in a concentration camp, Olivier Messiaen lamented the inhumanity of war. And from his lament emerged the *Quartet for the End of Time*, which captures in rhythm, melody, and harmony the beauty of the redemption of Jesus rising from the ashes of destruction.

True lament begins with an understanding of my soul's deepest brokenness, my greatest longing, and ultimate trust in God's ability to redeem all things through the blood of Jesus's cross.

Liturgies of Morning and Evening

Mornings and evenings set the boundaries of our day. By attending to the ways in which we begin and end our days, we restore and reaffirm meaning and order in a world that threatens to descend into disorder and chaos. Waking in the morning, we set the course of our day. David's liturgy of waking is summed up in the words, "I awake, and I am still with you" (Ps 139:18). As the day begins, I set my soul to reflect on the presence of God before anything else. In the liturgy of the morning, we open our souls to God in a way that enables us to experience his presence and to live this day in him. Morning liturgies have the power of shaping our way of being in the world. What vision of the good life is my morning liturgy forming in me? Morning liturgies of sitting in silence and stillness before God, even before I get out of bed, opens my soul to him and invites me to ponder and reflect on the active presence of God. I am reminded that I am not alone. I awake, and he is with me. In those first moments of the day, I set the sails of my soul to catch the wind of the Spirit and to move me along through this day in his ways and in his timing.

Likewise, evening liturgies allow us to reflect back on the day to be reminded of God's presence with us throughout the day. The prayer of examen invites us to ask him: When did I most sense your love today? When did I least sense your presence? Examen awakens us to the presence of God in unsuspected moments. In our evening liturgies, we finish the day as we began, with our hearts open to God. Even as we sleep, we ask that God's Spirit will commune with our spirit, and that we will sleep soundly in his presence and in his company. The ancient church prayed that even while our bodies are deep in sleep that God would keep our hearts awake and aware of his presence.[16] Even in our sleep, our souls rest in the hands of God. We are reminded that God gives to his beloved even as they sleep.

---

16. Bonhoeffer, *Life Together*, 75.

CONCLUSION

The contemplative life is the life for which we were created. It is the life of dwelling fully in our homeland, in God. This is where we are truly found, truly at rest, and most fully our true selves. Our contemplative liturgies are the path back to this homeland, living fully, moment by moment, in the presence of God, gazing on the beauty of God. This is where I am most at home, most alive, most in fellowship with others, most myself, resting in the shalom of God.

BIBLIOGRAPHY

Augustine of Hippo. *The City of God*. Translated by Marcus Dods. New York: The Modern Library, 1950.

———. "On the Trinity." In *Basic Writings of Saint Augustine Vol. 2.*, edited by Whitney J. Oates, 667–878. Grand Rapids, MI: Baker, 1948.

Bonhoeffer, Dietrich. *Life Together*. New York: HarperCollins, 1954.

Calvin, John. *Institutes of the Christian Religion*. Edited by John T. McNeill. Philadelphia: Westminster, 1960.

Chapple, Eliot Dismore, and Carleton Stevens Coon. *Principles of Anthropology*. New York: Henry Holt and Company, 1942.

Coe, John, and Todd W. Hall. *Psychology in the Spirit: Contours of a Transformational Psychology*. Downers Grove: IVP Academic, 2010.

John of the Cross. "The Living Flame of Love." In *The Collected Works of St. John of the Cross*. Translated by Kieran Kavanaugh and Otilio Rodriguez, 633–718. Washington, DC: Institute of Carmelite Studies, 1975.

Joyce, James. "A Painful Case." In *The Dubliners*, 95–104. New York: Bantam, 1990.

Laird, Martin. *Into the Silent Land: The Practice of Contemplation*. London: Darton, Longman and Todd, 2006.

MacCulloch, Diarmaid. *Silence: A Christian History*. New York: Viking, 2013.

Nouwen, Henri J. M. *The Way of the Heart*. New York: Ballantine, 1981.

Smith, James K. A. *You Are What You Love: The Spiritual Power of Habit*. Grand Rapids: Brazos, 2016.

Tillyer, Desmond B. *Union with God: The Teachings of St. John of the Cross*. London: Mowbray, 1984.

Tozer, A. W. *The Pursuit of God: The Human Thirst for the Divine*. Camp Hill: Wing Spread, 2006.

6

Challenge, Critique, and Celebration

The Role of Humor in Proclaiming the Gospel and Engaging the World

Brian Edgar

THIS CHAPTER EXAMINES THE importance of laughter for mission, the gospel, and the nature of God, especially as seen in the Gospel of Luke. The church has traditionally had more to say about sacrifice and suffering than about laughter and lightness of being, but it is argued here that the gospel should not only be accompanied by laughter but that the essence of the gospel itself involves playfulness and laughter. The Gospel of Luke uses humor and laughter to challenge people to make a decision, to critique those who make the wrong decision and as a way of celebrating God. Joy and laughter ought to be normal parts of the Christian life, and mission and evangelism should be undertaken with great joy. Laughter is at the heart of one's relationship with God because as Repplier says, "we cannot really love anybody with whom we never laugh."[1]

"Proclaiming the Gospel and Engaging the World" is a serious theme that reflects the *raison d'être* of the MBI-BCV-MST community. Consequently, discussing humor or observing that the gospel is so important that

---

1. Martin, *Between Heaven and Mirth*, loc. 3941, Kindle.

"it is a matter of laugh or death" runs the risk of being seen as trivializing the subject. But humor can be serious; indeed, Johann Huizinga argues that play and humor are of a higher order than seriousness, and that *only* a playful way of living does justice to the seriousness of life.[2] The aim here is to explore the importance of laughter for mission, the gospel, and our understanding of the nature of God, especially as it is seen in the Gospel of Luke.[3]

This project stands in contrast to the fact that the church has traditionally had much more to say about sorrow, sadness, sacrifice, and suffering than about laughter, levity, ludicity, and lightness of being. This is so despite the fact that the gospel message, as when presented in preaching, is frequently accompanied by humor. But this is typically a utilitarian use of humor as a pedagogical aid that lightens a serious topic and enhances attention. This is not the same as asserting the theological and spiritual importance of laughter itself. The argument here is not that the gospel ought to be *accompanied by* laughter but rather that *the essence of* the gospel itself involves playfulness and laughter. Laughter is the sound of joy and both are at the heart of the gospel.

The connection between laughter and the *missio dei* begins with the Abrahamic covenant, wherein God promises to create "a great nation" of his people (Gen 12:2) starting with the birth of a child to Sarah. But the beginning is inauspicious as both Abraham (17:17) and Sarah (18:10–12) laugh at God's promise of a child for Sarah! This laughter, however, intentionally stands in contrast to the divinely given laughter that comes when God accomplishes what has been promised. Sarah becomes pregnant and a child is born, who is named Isaac, which means "he laughs." In the end Sarah can say, "God has brought me laughter, and everyone who hears about this will laugh with me" (21:6). Skeptical laughter is thus replaced with joyful, believing, faithful, covenant laughter, a motif that continues throughout the life of Isaac, fulfilling an important theological purpose with laughter as a faithful human response to the grace of God.[4]

Theologically significant laughter continues in the new covenant established in Christ. Unfortunately, this theme has been both neglected and negated, such that the seriousness of the gospel has made laughter morally suspect. By the third century the early church had developed the view that laughter was intrinsically problematic and ought to be treated with great caution because it was dangerous to one's spiritual life. There was particular

---

2. Huizinga, *Homo Ludens*, 211–12.

3. While exploring new material on the role of humor in the Gospel of Luke this chapter also draws on my previous work in *The God Who Plays* and *Grace of God*.

4. See Edgar, *Grace of God*, 57–68.

opposition to laughter among those most committed to seeking spiritual perfection, that is, among those within the earliest monastic movements. The Essenes imposed a penance of thirty days on those who laughed foolishly; the rule of Pachomius forbade joking and, according to the teaching of Ephraim the Syrian, "laughter is the beginning of the destruction of the soul."[5] For Clement of Alexandria (ca. 150–215 AD), humor, which is typically ridiculous or absurd, was an indication of a mind that was in need of control.[6] Basil (ca. 330–379 AD) wrote that "raucous laughter and uncontrollable shaking of the body are not indications of a well-regulated soul, or of personal dignity, or of self-mastery."[7] The tenth step to humility of the Rule of St. Benedict notes that "only a fool raises his voice in laughter," and the eleventh step essentially repeats the admonition by saying that a monk speaks gently, seriously, quietly, briefly, reasonably, modestly—and without laughter.[8] John Chrysostom (ca. 347–407 AD) warned people about the dangers of any delight or pleasure because of the possibility that "somewhere in the depth of the pleasure some iniquity should lie enveloped" and so one should "search closely, and if thou discoverest it, hasten away!" The disciple of Christ should therefore not only avoid those things that are sinful but also those things that are indifferent, that is, not sin in themselves, but which are "yet apt to make us stumble against sin. For example; to laugh, to speak jocosely, does not seem an acknowledged sin, but it leads to acknowledged sin." Some versions of his teaching includes further advice that makes the situation very clear: "avoid not merely foul words, and foul deeds, or blows, and wounds, and murders, but unseasonable laughter itself, and the very language of raillery; since these things have proved the root of subsequent evils. Therefore, Paul saith. 'Let no foolish talking nor jesting proceed out of thy mouth.' For although this seems to be a small thing in itself, it becomes, however, the cause of much mischief to us."[9] In this ascetic version of the spiritual life, even what is good can become a source of evil.

In the (post) modern era humor is a more acceptable trait for Christian believers, and yet it is still rarely given its central place as a specifically theological and spiritual good in itself. It is simply seen as a useful, practical, healthy, natural human trait. Congregations today are less likely to make the kind of change that was made to some versions of William Kethe's hymn "All people that on earth do dwell," which has as the second line "Sing to

---

5. Morreall, "Philosophy and Religion," 216.
6. Clement of Alexandria, "*Paedogogus*," chap. 5.
7. Morreall, "Philosophy and Religion," 216.
8. Benedict of Nursia, *Rule of St. Benedict*, 61 and 162.
9. John Chrysostom, "Homilies," XV, 7 and 11.

the Lord with cheerful voice." Some twentieth-century editions allowed that happy line to stand but changed the third line from "Him serve with *mirth*, His praise forth tell" to a more theologically acceptable "Him serve with *fear*, His praise forth tell."[10]

Generally speaking, the Evangelical tradition in which MBI-BCV-MST stands certainly has had elements of mission focus and a certain seriousness that has tended to mitigate against there being too much laughter, at least in spiritual, theological contexts. In truth, laughter has never been the spiritual problem that early asceticism reckoned it to be. Nonetheless, the seriousness of the gospel message of salvation for those in danger of being lost to Christ meant that the *missio dei* was not to be taken lightly. This was, at least in part, precisely a result of the sheer effectiveness of the Evangelical tradition. In *The Call to Seriousness: The Evangelical Impact on the Victorians*, Ian Bradley analyzes Evangelical influence on nineteenth-century Victorian England. He shows how its serious and high-minded Evangelical activism brought about positive social change. This serious, dedicated approach to ministry and mission was the approach of C. H. Nash and the early ethos of MBI-BCV. However, general observations such as that should not be seen as producing inflexible stereotypes. While Evangelicals were generally "serious" about mission in the sense of being committed to it, not all evangelicals were so "serious" about it that they avoided levity. Being committed to mission certainly means being sincere, earnest and hardworking, but this does not exclude laughter, light-heartedness, and joy. Indeed, anyone who studies the Scriptures cannot fail to notice the connection between the gospel and joy.

In this regard there is a sense in which the origins of this article lie in lectures given in the 1970s when I commenced study at MBI. It is not usual for me to be able to remember the specific content and the particular effect of individual lectures; but I recall a certain surprise in the first of a course of lectures on evangelism given by an adjunct lecturer, the Reverend Norman Allchin (1935–1983). This was a course taken by all first-year students in addition to the usual introductory courses in Bible and church history, and its presence is an indication of the priorities of the college. The first lecture focused on the first chapters of the Gospel of Luke, the birth of Christ and, especially, the joyful angelic proclamation that the birth of Christ was "good news of great joy" (2:10). My understanding of evangelism to that date had been exclusively focused on the significance of the death of Christ and on the seriousness and solemnity of this sacrifice overcoming the effect of human sin, rather than on the matters surrounding his birth. These other

---

10. It appears, for example, in this form in the Harvard Classics compilation of *Hymns of the Christian Church* published in 1909–1914.

themes were not, of course, seen as unimportant, but the initial, emphatic point was that the whole life of Christ was involved in redemption and that it is a fundamentally joyful message that the church bears to the world. The good news of the coming of Christ is about life, joy, and Christ, not simply about death, solemnity, and the problem of sin. The gospel begins and ends in joy and laughter.

The notion of "the angelic gospel of joy" establishes a theme for the rest of the Luke's Gospel. From incarnation to resurrection it is a gospel of joy. Jesus's birth in a stable leads the angel to declare that this is "good news that will cause great joy for all the people" (2:10). And the gospel ends with the ascension of Christ which led to "great joy" and the disciples "stayed continually at the temple, praising God" (24:52–53). The one whose "spirit rejoices in God my Saviour" (1:47) knows and experiences the will, the purposes, and the nature of God in a new way and anticipates the final coming of Christ with joy and laughter. This is what Karl Rahner calls "redeeming laughter,"[11] which is essentially the deepest praise of God.

With this foundation in place it is possible to see in the remainder of Luke's Gospel that laughter has three related functions. It is used to:

- challenge people to consider carefully the choices they make concerning their relationship with Christ
- critique those who have decided on a way that is contrary to God's will and purposes, and to
- celebrate with God and all those committed to serve him.

HUMOR IN LUKE AS CHALLENGE, CRITIQUE, AND CELEBRATION

The most extensive use of humor in the Gospel of Luke is found in the way Jesus challenges people to consider the choices they make concerning their response to God's calling and their relationship with Christ. Some think that teaching that challenges people morally and existentially must necessarily be solemn in order to reflect the gravity of the situation. But apparently Jesus did not think this. He appears to think that the graver the choice involved the greater the need to lighten people's hearts.

The simplest and most common form of humor in his teaching involves his description of various comical characters and situations. This may involve hyperbole, as in "Why do you look at the speck in your brother's eye

---

11. Rahner, *Content of Faith*, 150.

and pay no attention to the plank in your own?" (Luke 6:41), a visual image used as a criticism of hypocritical behavior; or absurdity, as when he asked the disciples, "Can the blind lead the blind? Will they not both fall into a pit?" (6:39); or when he spoke of the foolishness of the person who lights a lamp only to put it under a bed or in the cellar (8:16; 11:33). These are not earth-shatteringly funny but the lightness and playfulness in Jesus's teaching is obvious. There is the builder who builds without foundations (6:46–49), and the king who does not plan his battles (14:31), as well as the builder who does not think ahead and so can't afford to finish the building (14:28–30). Then there is the banquet guest who takes a place of honor only to end up being humiliated (14:8–11), and the father who gives his son a snake instead of a fish or a scorpion instead of an egg (11:11–13). These comic situations point, in a very gentle way, to the plight of those who make foolish choices, especially those most serious and important choices concerning discipleship, serving Christ and honoring God. They are reminders that disciples of Christ should consider the long-term cost before beginning their journey, know that humility is better than pride, and that God blesses his children like a good father.

One of the problems in interpreting biblical humor is that familiarity can blunt one's awareness of the humor. This is a real problem, as Dorothy Sayers commented: "If we did not know all His retorts by heart, if we had not taken the sting out of them by incessant repetition . . . we should reckon Him among the greatest wits of all time."[12] The mental image of a blind person trying to lead another blind person or of a lamp placed not-so-strategically under a bed may not be hilarious but these mental pictures can be amusing and they make the teaching more memorable.

The more extended parables typically deal with matters of critical importance, and a failure to make the right choice is typically characterized as nothing less than disaster and personal tragedy; yet they frequently contain humor. It is possible, of course, to make *any* story funny by adding or distorting elements; but here the humor can be found in the original. In some cases, the original verbal form is important. The parable of the great banquet (14:15–24) has a number of the hallmarks of humor and, in this case, a certain level of innuendo. Three men invited to a banquet give various excuses for not attending (the need to attend to new property, new oxen, and a new wife) and there are at least three elements of the parable that deliberately lead the reader to expect humor. The first is the literary pattern with identical terminology in the accounts of the three men who come with excuses. There is, in each case (a) a statement about a new acquisition (land

---

12. Sayers, *Born to Be King*, 26.

or oxen), followed by (b) an expression of a desire to see it or try it out, and then (c) the same, repeated apologetic conclusion, "I cannot come." A pattern is established that is reminiscent in other cultures of immediately recognizable forms of humor (as in, "Three men walk into a pub . . ." or "There was an Englishman, an Irishman, and a Scotsman . . ."). The structure tells the listener that something is afoot and that they should be ready to be surprised. In addition to that, the wording is identical in each case, except for one deliberate variation in the third account, which is emphatic precisely because it is different.

The second clue towards the parable's humorous intent is found in the nature of the excuses provided by the first two to decline the invitation. The first man buys a property: is it the case that he only then goes to look at it? That would be unusual; and if he did see it before buying it, then is it necessary for his second look to take place at the very same time as the banquet? The second man buys an ox and has to go and examine it. Again, most people do that before they buy. And if he had already checked it prior to purchase, then why the rush to do it again now and miss the banquet? One wonders whether these excuses arise from the fact that they really don't want to be at the meal. Do they have something against the man giving the banquet? The third situation is somewhat different. Although the excuse is initially phrased in exactly the same form of words, the second part of the response is omitted so that there is simply a statement of acquisition ("I have just married") followed by the apologetic conclusion ("I cannot come"). There is nothing that parallels the excuses, ("I want to see it" or "I want to test it"). Although it is possible that in the original oral tradition the anticipated explanation that would parallel the other two situations could well have been included in the form of a pregnant pause, allowing the audience to figure out for themselves exactly what it is that the newly married man wants to go and see or try out. (Perhaps as in something like, "I am sorry, I have just got married and so I need to go and . . . oh, never mind, I just can't come.")[13] And so, with that, although Jesus may not be described as laughing himself, he certainly has his listeners smiling—and perhaps also wondering whether this marriage (or the other acquisitions) is something that has genuinely arisen recently or whether it is simply an excuse to avoid an invitation the guest does not want. All of this creates a situation where the amused audience is now in a better position to be challenged

---

13. As Bruce Longenecker says, we should not think that "this involves an eagerness to taste the wife's cooking or assess her cleaning skills . . . or to discover her intellectual acumen by discussing current events with her. Clearly the third invitee is eager simply to enjoy the sexual delights of married life with his new wife." Longenecker, "Humorous Jesus?," 188–89.

by the unexpected conclusion: in the end none of his neighbors came and the wealthy farmer was angry, and so he went into town and invited all the homeless and poor people he could find. "None of those who were invited need bother turning up," he declared, "they will never get anything from me." Suddenly the humor has a purpose, a challenging one for anyone saying that he or she is ready to accept Jesus's invitation to discipleship. This becomes very clear when one considers the words of Jesus immediately following. There is the cryptic and challenging statement about followers needing to "hate father and mother, wife and children" if they wish to be his disciple, the warning implicit in the stories of the builder and the king who do not count the cost before commencing either to build or to wage war, and the statement about salt that eventually loses its saltiness and thus is fit for nothing. This is challenging teaching and, as Jesus concludes, "Whoever has ears to hear, let him hear."

Humor has an important function in challenging people to make the right choice. It can make clear the potentially disastrous consequences of making the wrong choice, and yet it does so without an air of gloom and doom. Even more importantly, the humor points to the nature of the choice as a moral rather than an intellectual issue. That is, if this were a hard choice to make, where weighing up the merit of the various possible outcomes were difficult, where it would be quite possible for one to make the wrong choice, then levity would be less appropriate. But the levity makes the point that the choice that ought to be made is so blindingly obvious that one is not going to make the wrong choice accidentally. The one who does not make the right choice is deliberately acting against God. He or she is grossly foolish and not merely mistaken. The failure to choose the right is culpable and not accidental. The humor makes it clear that there is a moral, rather than an intellectual, choice to be made.

HUMOR AS CRITIQUE

While the first function of humor in the teaching of Jesus is to *challenge* people to make a decision, the second is to *critique* those who make the wrong decision. This shifts the humor from being a simple description of a comic situation toward more satirical and ironic observations involving an implied criticism of certain choices. Sometimes there is a further shift beyond satire to outright mockery and scorn of those who deliberately choose the wrong way, and thus humor becomes more of a critique of the foolish and a warning to others considering doing the same. This form is found in the Magnificat (1:46–55), which echoes the teaching of the Psalms concerning the divine laughter of Yahweh, who derides the wicked (Psalm 2:4–9). Many of those who lived under Roman rule and who heard Mary's hymn would have laughed at the welcome thought that proud rulers would be brought down from their thrones and the humble lifted high.

But not only rulers can be scorned. In the parable of the rich fool (12:16–21), a man who plans a life of leisure based on an accumulation of wealth is derided because he cannot control the length of his life. "You fool! This very night your life will be demanded from you. Then who will get what you have prepared for yourself?" More commonly it is the Pharisees who are the butt of Jesus's derisive humor. The contrast between the Pharisee and the tax collector at prayer (18:9–14) does not go well for the Pharisee, yet this is a mild criticism compared to the scathing character assessment provided in the parable of the tenants (20:9–19). Wicked tenants withhold the owner's share of the farm produce, then kill his son; they are then themselves killed by the owner. The Pharisees well understood this as an attack on them and they immediately looked for a way to arrest Jesus "because they knew He had spoken the parable against them." Elsewhere these Pharisees are variously compared to ridiculous people who clean the outside of their cup and dish while leaving the inside dirty (i.e., inside they are "full of greed and wickedness," 11:39); and like unmarked graves, which people walk over without knowing it (thus becoming unclean themselves) (11:44). These are strong, stunning charges laid against those responsible for leading the community in religion and morality and they angered the scribes and many others also (11:45). But the graphic images of wicked tenants, dirty cups, and unmarked graves would have been amusing to those who, like Jesus, saw the very real problems of hypocrisy, ostentatious religiosity, corrupt community leadership, and the abuse of widows. There would have been a receptive audience willing to laugh at Jesus's mocking humor.

An appreciation for scorn and mockery requires a robust understanding of the role of humor. For some mockery does not seem to be humorous at all, yet it is one of the classic forms of humor. Mockery is connected with innocent humor in that both are responses to the presence of a perceived incongruity. Some incongruities (whether a funny nose or a confused understanding of the situation) produce laughter while others (the presence of foolishness or wickedness where there ought to be love and justice) result in scorn. They are, in a sense, two sides of the one coin. Innocent laughter provides relief and refreshment, while scorn and derision reveal the wickedness of certain actions and imply that such behavior will not triumph in the end (there would be no place for laughter if it were believed that wickedness would ultimately triumph).

HUMOR AS CELEBRATION

After *challenge* and *critique*, the third function of humor in Luke's account of mission is *celebration*. Note the inverted sayings: the warning "Woe to you who laugh now, for you will weep" and the promise "Blessed are you who weep now, for you will laugh" (Luke 6:21, 25). While there may be trauma in the present, in the end there will be laughter and joyful celebration. This eschatological dimension of joy reflects the common saying, "He who laughs last laughs loudest." This is seen in the three parables (15:1–32) of a lost sheep, a lost coin, and a lost son. In all three the emphasis is upon the joy that there is at finding what is lost. The first two have exactly the same conclusion: "He [she] calls his [her] friends and neighbors together and says, 'Rejoice with me; I have found my lost sheep [coin].'" There is a universal sense of joy at finding something valuable that has been lost. But the third parable makes the point that if there is such joy and celebration, feasting and laughter in these situations, then there will be more joy in heaven in finding people who have been spiritually lost: "I tell you that in the same way there will be more rejoicing in heaven over one sinner who repents than over ninety-nine righteous persons who do not need to repent" (15:7). True joy in heaven cannot be without laughter any more than the celebrations on earth for the sheep, the coin, and the son that were found could have been without laughter! The eschatological nature of joy and laughter in the Gospels is consistent with the various accounts of Jesus eating and drinking—and laughing—with tax collectors and sinners, which is not merely evidence of his good nature but is a sign in itself, an anticipatory foretaste of the joy and laughter of the heavenly banquet. Jesus's joy is grounded in his delight in God and in the way that sinners can share in the kingdom of God (Luke 15:7).

THE THEOLOGICAL IMPLICATIONS OF HUMOR

Having collated this material, we now take the final step of drawing out some of the theological implications. The most obvious is that under normal circumstances each believer ought to be a visible expression of joy. Yet there have been many times when the tradition of the church has been more sober than it deserves and less attuned to joy and laughter than it could have been, given that the gospel message is fundamentally one of joy. The Reverend Alex Stevens (1919–2012) taught New Testament at MBI-BCV and, although a man of considerable decorum, he had a quietly subversive sense of humor. He was, for example, well able to address gently the perception that the ethos of his own Presbyterian denomination was not typically that of ecstatic enthusiasm.

Each year, in the same lecture, he told the story of the preaching class where, after observing a number of sermons, the somewhat exasperated lecturer advised his students, "When preaching about the joys of heaven, please smile a little. When preaching about the terrors of hell, your usual expression will do." Joy and laughter ought to be normal parts of the Christian life.

The second point to make is that this is a matter for whole communities as well as individuals. It is important for theological institutions such as MBI-BCV-MST to continue to develop forms of corporate life that engender a spirituality of laughter and joy. This involves a form of happiness that is based on holiness rather than self-centeredness. There is, unfortunately, contemporary evidence that there have been some Christian training institutions that have not been conducive to the development of healthy, joyful, loving people. Abusive institutions will never be joyful places. The presence of genuine joy and laughter is evidence of a healthy community.[14]

In doing this, it is important to note, as a third point, that the church needs an active and developed theology of joy and laughter as much as it needs a theology of sacrifice, sin, and pain. It is not unusual in teaching institutions for the emphasis in a particular discipline to drift towards pathological forms. That is, what is normal, routine, and healthy is not presented or taught as much as the deviant, the defective, and the diseased. This is typically because the former do not seem as interesting or as urgent as the latter. This can happen in fields as diverse as politics, psychology, philosophy, and theology. Some years ago, the teaching of psychology in many institutions was criticized for teaching that neglected (without completely ignoring) the psychology of health in favor of a focus on mental illness and downplayed the positive in favor of the study of maladaptive behaviors. Abnormal psychology became, ironically, the norm. What became known as "positive psychology" was a direct reaction to this. It very rightly encouraged a renewed emphasis on happiness, wellbeing, positivity, and the good life.[15] Theology can also focus too much on the negative and the pathological, and this can happen in various ways. There is a need for a theology of joy as much as a theology of service, for aesthetics as well as ascetics, and for a focus on positive holiness as much as on heresy. The resurrection and the glory of eternal life are as important as the cross, and laughter is important as the expression of joy. Incidentally, while it is not for me to determine the program, the proposed development of a center for theology and psychology at MST presents many

---

14. None of these suggestions, or anything else in this chapter, should be taken as implying a criticism of MBI-BCV-MST at any time. Indeed, I hope it is clear that my understanding of this topic benefited from my experience of the college. Nonetheless, these are themes that need to be remembered and lived out in every era.

15. Al Taher, 5 *Founding Fathers*.

opportunities for an exploration of the positive dimensions of the spiritual life of the believer, including joy and laughter.

Fourthly, it should be noted that it is Christology that really determines the shape of theology. Unfortunately, there is sometimes more of a tendency to agree with John Chrysostom, who insisted on focusing on a theology of tears on the basis that Scripture does not speak of Christ, Paul or the other apostles as laughing but as weeping. This present life, he argued, is not the theater for laughter.[16] However, the Lord Jesus did not only weep, he laughed. Indeed, his teaching reveals him as something of a laugh-maker, and this needs to be recognized. "Jesus Laughing and Loving" is a collection of original, multicultural works of art, all of which portray the Lord Jesus "loving and laughing." It is accessible online. Pictured here, for example, is *Behold the Joy of Jesus* by Lindena Robb.[17] Together these works of art explore a dimension of the life of Christ too often neglected.

Lindena Robb, *Behold the Joy of Jesus*. Copyright P. Wallace, used by permission.

16. John Chrysostom, *Homilies*, Homily VI.6.
17. Robb, "Behold the Joy," 6.

Fifthly, a developed theology of humor is important because it is closely related not only to joy but also to faith and hope. Laughter is a part of the life of Christ and the nature of God, and thus it is part of the relationship that God wants with us. Humor is not merely a human good but an essential part of the life of the kingdom.

Finally, mission and evangelism should be undertaken with great joy. The news of the coming of Christ is, as the angels noted, a matter of great joy. The gospel is good news for the world. It is not inappropriate for laughter to accompany the proclamation of the gospel. In so doing, in a positive sense, it demonstrates the nature of the God who loves and laughs, and, in a negative sense, laughter has the ability to uncover hypocrisy and injustice. Christ has overcome evil and death and laughter demonstrates the faith of the believer who trusts in God who is ultimately over all. In this way laughter is, in a sense, one of the weapons of the Spirit, demolishing pretentiousness, pride, and the belief that the evil one could eventually prevail.

In all of this, laughter is not merely a technique to be used; it is not, as mentioned earlier, merely an accompaniment to the gospel that makes the message more tolerable; it is actually intrinsic to the nature of the gospel and of God. There is a sense in which it is rightly said that the medium is the message. Of course, the most fundamental connection lies in the relationship between laughter and the love of God. Laughter is at the heart of it because, as Agnes Repplier says, "We cannot really love anybody with whom we never laugh."[18]

BIBLIOGRAPHY

Al Taher, Reham. *The 5 Founding Fathers and A History of Positive Psychology*. https://positivepsychology.com/founding-fathers/.

Benedict of Nursia. *The Rule of St. Benedict*. London: SPCK, 1931.

Clement of Alexandria. "*Paedogogus*." In *The Ante-Nicene Fathers*, vol. 2, edited by Alexander Roberts, James Donaldson and A. Cleveland Coxe. Buffalo, NY: Christian Literature, 1885.

Edgar, Brian. *The God Who Plays: A Playful Approach to Theology and Spirituality*. Eugene, Oregon: Cascade, 2017.

———. *Laughter and the Grace of God: Restoring Laughter to its Central Role in Christian Spirituality and Theology*. Eugene, Oregon: Cascade, 2019.

Huizinga, Johan. *Homo Ludens: A Study of the Play Element in Culture*. Boston: Beacon, 1955.

John Chrysostom. "Homilies on the Gospel of St Matthew." In *A Select Library of the Nicene and Post-Nicene Fathers*, vol. 6, edited by Philip Schaff. Grand Rapids, MI: William Eerdmans, 1988.

---

18. Martin, *Between Heaven and Mirth*, loc. 3941, Kindle.

Longenecker, Bruce. "A Humorous Jesus? Orality, Structure and Characterisation in Luke 14:15–24, and Beyond." *Biblical Interpretation* 16, no. 2 (April 2008) 179–204.

Martin, James. *Between Heaven and Mirth: Why Joy, Humor and Laughter are at the Heart of the Spiritual Life*. New York: Harper One, 2011.

Morreall, John. "Philosophy and Religion." In *The Primer of Humor Research*, edited by Victor Raskin. Berlin: De Gruyter Mouton, 2008.

Rahner, Karl. *The Content of Faith: The Best of Karl Rahner's Theological Writings*. New York: Crossroad, 1993.

Robb, Lindena. "Behold the Joy of Jesus." *Jesus Laughing and Loving*. Major Issues and Theology Foundation, 2012. https://www.miat.org.au/jesus-laughing-ex/Jesus%20Laughing%20and%20Loving%20-%20Web%20Copy.pdf.

Sayers, Dorothy. *The Man Born to be King: A Play Cycle on the Life of our Lord and Saviour Jesus Chris*. Eugene, Oregon: Wipf and Stock, 2011.

7

Sanctified Reason

Exploring the Why of a Christian Liberal Arts Education

Christopher Green

> *He made good proficiency in all the arts and sciences,*
> *and had an uncommon taste for natural philosophy,*
> *which he cultivated to the end of his life,*
> *with that justness and accuracy of thought which was peculiar to him.*[1]
>
> SAMUEL HOPKINS (ON JONATHAN EDWARDS)

CHRISTIAN LIBERAL ARTS EDUCATIONAL institutions such as Eastern College Australia can provide a service to the Christian community by placing reason in a strategic environment for sanctification. Faith focuses the work of reason in three conceptual environments: the created world, the Christian life, and the church community. Each of these domains can be closely associated with the appropriations of the three members of the

---

1. Marsden, *Jonathan Edwards*, 67.

Trinity. Sanctified reason extols the creative work of the Father, abandons prejudice in conformity with the death and resurrection of the Son, and apprehends a united-yet-pluriform breadth of perspectives in the Spirit. Faith teaches reason to "open the door" to the real world in these particular ways. A Christian learning community responds to the triune God by undertaking its work with gratitude and joy, which enables reason to welcome the truth, and is the only fitting attitude for seeing the world through redeemed spectacles.

INTRODUCTION

It is almost a truism that Christian liberal arts educational institutions—institutions such as Eastern College, recently joined together with Melbourne School of Theology—aim to equip people for faith, life, and leadership in the world. But *why* should they seek to do this? My answer, in brief, goes like this: this mission exemplifies Christian faith by situating reason in a strategic hotbed for sanctification. In seeking to help Christians along their way in a modern, technologically advanced society, they need to be encouraged to relearn the world through redeemed spectacles. Whether one pursues an education in a broadly classical, practical or "vocational" manner, this pursuit only validates the extension of God's kingdom if it takes place alongside Christian sanctification. This movement is not a natural or quantifiable progression, but a striving of the Christian mind, directed by the Holy Spirit; it is not grounded in self-gratifying curiosity or fascination—which are forms of learning that do not call the self to die with Christ—but rather, by a deep-seated expression of faith, a "faith seeking understanding" that is coextensive with Christian sanctification.

Broad questions regarding the relationship between the liberal arts and theology often settle into two familiar domains—the objective and subjective. On the objective side, there are several ways to account for the relationship theology might have with the realities that the various disciplines investigate. Theology's now-shunned role in the university has a long lingering past of slow decline, as it once was the "queen of the sciences." Now the university is eclipsed by a fickle demand for utilitarian knowledge.[2] The story of theology's previous place of supereminence, its lamentable decline as the "uni-" in "university," and the hope of its resurgence is an important cause for our time.[3] With regard to the "objective" status of theology

---

2. Cf., for example, Sommerville, *Decline of the Secular*.

3. One example of this resurgence would be the post-postmodern and Platonic "radical orthodox" approach; note Long's summary, "Radical Orthodoxy."

amongst the disciplines, I am presupposing John Webster's exposition in his essay *Regina artium: Theology and the Humanities*.[4] However, my focus in this (mostly reflective and descriptive) chapter is on the subjective side of that relationship. Christian theology needs to account for *how* the knower is an involved self, a person in the process of sanctification, and is also invested in being studious and grasping at created realities. This means that I will not focus *exclusively* on the academic disciplines as an environment for knowing but will aim to provide a brief account of how reason is sanctified by the triune God *with a view to* the real, without regard to the particular situation in which learning and discovery take place. What change does God's Spirit bring about for the reasoning of the Christian mind? My contention is that reason undergoes a process of redemption that takes place by grace, in Christian community, and it is in this environment that it learns to strive to do what Esther Meek calls "inviting the real."[5]

This chapter is meant to be an outline for a theological basis for the sanctification of Christian reason with a view to learning about objective reality. I describe an embarking of Christian reason on the journey of sanctification as having a three-sided shape, matching the appropriations of the three members of the Trinity.[6] These are distinct dimensions of reason's threefold pathway or commerce with the economy of redemption. With regard to the Father, *fallen* reason faces an inevitable temptation to misconstruct the Creator-creature distinction. This is a crucial aspect of the captivity of reason apart from Christ, which leads to numerous epistemic failures. So, setting reason back on course to full sanctification satisfies reason's doxological orientation, which finds rest in, and gives all glory to, the Father. Second, reason's sanctification takes place through what John Calvin describes as *mortification* and *vivification*, through the dying and rising of the self, which takes place in Christ. This process of death and resurrection expels reason's old paradigms and perspectives and revitalizes the spiritual life around the resurrected presence and power of Christ, our Teacher. Third, reason's transformation takes place in the context of a Christian community, according to the Holy Spirit's form of action, which creates a diversity of

---

4. Webster, "Regina artium." "Theology is about everything; but it is not about everything about everything, but about everything in relation to God." Webster, "Intellectual Life," 85.

5. Meek, *Loving to Know*, 425–68.

6. Since this chapter is more about spelling out my beliefs and assumptions, it is not so much about justification: "The word *Trinity* does not appear in the pages of the Bible because *Trinity* is not a theory the Bible puts forward about God. *Trinity* names the language of the Bible. The Bible speaks fluent trinitarianism the way I speak fluent English—naturally and without preamble or justification." English, *Theology Remixed*, 101.

hearing faith and obedience in response to the word of God. Altogether, this work of reason's sanctification acknowledges the larger providential and creational order of things and this transformation leads reason to a point of grateful activity that sees the world, as 1 Corinthians 13:12 says, "in part."

THE TRINITY AS THE BASIS OF REASON'S SANCTIFICATION

Christian reason is shaped by and operates in response to God's triune mode of action. God's creative work establishes and sustains the existence of reason. Further, God's redemptive action works eschatologically to liberate reason from its bondage to sin and all rebellious and oppressive powers. The redemption of reason also orients it to its Christian purpose: to fulfill a calling that is shaped by the same economy of grace that sustains, governs, and perfects the surrounding world. Reason is not freed, then, for the exercise of a neutral and generic "human rationality." Reason is not "free" if it only exercises its own natural capacity. Rather, the grace of redemption sends reason back to its original path, established in creation, to be returned to the triune God. Redemption has its effect by resituating reason into the world with a new orientation, a new *telos*. This means that "free" reason seeks an understanding of the world as it is established, sustained, and brought to perfection in and through the triune God's economy of grace.

In order to describe this reorientation with some depth, we must turn to a discussion of the triune appropriations. I am not making an argument here that reason is a natural organ with "three parts." Rather, reason has a redemptive interplay with the triune God, and so the appropriations, the mysteriously united—yet unique—distinctions in action that enable us to identify the triune persons, these are the surrounding theater for the dramatic sanctification of human reason. So, I will unpack this relationship between the triune God and reason's sanctification with a conscious glance at each of the three members of the Trinity.

First, we should briefly discuss God as triune. The God of the Bible is the God of the Christian faith, the eternal and triune life of Father, Son, and Holy Spirit. God's identity is not isolated or aloof as mere transcendence. This God is no "prisoner of his own eternity"[7] but rather chooses to extend his light, life, and love to others.[8] True to form, God acts as a Trinity in all of his gracious, creative, and redemptive works, which encompass all things.

---

7. Barth, *Church Dogmatics* II/2, 183–84; IV/2, 92.
8. "The Father shares his light, life and love in the Son, through the Spirit." Vanhoozer, *Faith Speaking Understanding*, 75.

As the One and perfect, Trinitarian life unfolds a providential plan across the whole of creation, God operates in and through what Irenaeus calls his "two hands," his Word and Spirit.[9] God's actions express his character, and so they are always gracious. In the context of creation and providence, God establishes and maintains our created capacities. In the context of redemption, God saves. Both of these works are expressions of divine grace, and they "map" all of God's external works onto his benevolent character.

EXTOLLING THE FATHER

In response to the love of the Father, sanctified reason has a vertical focus. That is, human reason has a doxological *telos*, which is to adore and hallow the name of the Father, acknowledging God as the Creator and Sustainer of all things. This acknowledgement comes at the price of humility—to eulogize the Father is to acknowledge one's poverty to sustain life in the face of God's sheer majesty. In doxology, reason recognizes its inability in the face of the incomprehensible—that God is not another "thing" to be grasped and is not available unless he makes himself known. Doxological reason abandons "*the* lie," the comprehensive deception that exchanges the Creator for the creature (Rom 1:25). A doxological stance also finds freedom in this: that knowing God cannot be accomplished by sheer volitional or intellectual exertion. True knowledge of the God of all creation is not an available commodity but only arises as sheer gift. Consider the awe that Paul exhibits in his descriptions of redemption, which frequently result in doxological outbursts (Gal 1:5; Rom 11:33–36; Eph 3:20–21; Phil 4:20; 1 Tim 1:17). These are moments in which Paul ascribes all glory to the Father as a grateful response to the grace of an incomprehensible salvation.

This doxological orientation of reason keeps it humble, and it is exemplified again in the creation account. In the garden, it is made obvious to Adam that he did not create himself.[10] When reason abandons praise and gratitude, it denies this clear dependence. Subsequently, reason begins an oppressive process of self-grounding, and the surrounding world is subjected to the demands of instrumentalization and curiosity.[11] After the entrance of sin into the world, Adam and Eve begin to *use* creation for self-serving purposes. They pluck the leaves of the trees in the garden *for* embroidery (Gen 3:7). In their sin, they use the garden's forest as a *means* for hiding from God "among the trees of the garden" (Gen 3:8). To say it plainly, this ingratitude is

---

9. Irenaeus, *Against Heresies*, 4.20.1.
10. Blocher, *In the Beginning*, 79–94.
11. Webster, "Curiosity."

echoed in our everyday modern practice in our use of reason, which is a sign of reason's bondage to the powers of sin and death. Our modern, consumer economy coaxes us into a visceral use of reason that only acts volitionally— "you want it, you buy it." As Edward Farley argues, "The more our cognitive undertakings move toward the technical [. . .] and toward the uses of knowledge in pursuit of power, the more indifferent they become to questions of reality."[12] This truncates the full life of human reason by removing its *telos* and in practice uses it as if it were merely a transient organ.

By way of contrast, doxological reason sees the thing-ish aspect of the world—the objective appearance of created things—as it stands in a position of service to the providential Lord as part of a larger and deeper composition. God's Word and Spirit symphonically draw together all things unto the praise of the Father.[13]

DYING AND RISING WITH THE SON

Second, reason has an outward focus that interfaces with the work of the Son as the only begotten of the Father, his eternal self-expression through which the world was created and to which it will someday return (Col 1:15–20). This focus describes reason's vocation to undertake a faithful performance in the world, to follow the cruciform way of the Son, as Karl Barth said it, "into the far country."[14] This is perhaps best described with the language of John Calvin's use of *mortificatio* and *vivificatio* in his doctrine of sanctification.[15] Reason dies and rises with the whole of the old and new selves in the Christian life. The old pretensions, skewed values, and self-serving constructs of reason are put to death in Christ. Rising again, reason names the world correctly, as it should be seen from the standpoint of its *telos* in the new creation, exemplified by the transformed and risen body of Christ.

Importantly, reason does not "imitate" Christ through an autonomous performance or exemplification but is first grounded in the gift of redemption—which is anterior to sanctification. This alleviates the anxiety that so often characterizes Christian experience, aiming to secure good standing with God, or with others, with some sort of accomplishment. Mortification

---

12. Farley, *Fragility of Knowledge*, 23.

13. Barth frequently appealed to the highs and lows of Mozart's music as his favorite illustration for the ups and downs of divine providence: "This is the point which I wish to make" in his own doctrine of providence. *CD* III/3, 299.

14. Barth, *CD* IV/1, 157–210; cf. Noll's "Jesus Christ: Guidance for Serious Learning," in *Jesus Christ*, 43–64.

15. Leith, *John Calvin's Doctrine*, 65–82; Zachman, *John Calvin*, 94–96.

and vivification are not simply expressions of Christian virtue—they find their impetus in God. Regeneration, as the gift of God, is not established in a static sense but awaits completion in and through Christian living.[16] This *theologia crucis* orients reason toward an accurate perception of self, the world, and others in the present. Calvin finds that the process of mortification, on which he focuses the most in his discussion, helps God's children to not be tied to the things of earth.[17] Further, vivification reorients the Christian to see the present life in the light of the life to come. That is, repentance loosens the ties that bind us *too closely* to the present and enable us to enjoy what is in the here and now in the light of what is to come.

> The life, therefore, which we attain by faith is not visible to the bodily eye, but is inwardly perceived in the conscience by the power of the Spirit, so that the bodily life does not prevent us from enjoying, by faith, a heavenly life [. . .] Paul's writings are full of similar assertions that while we live in the world, we at the same time live in heaven, not only because our Head is there, but because, in virtue of union, we enjoy a life in communion with him (John 14:23).[18]

The mortification of reason reminds us that the accuracy with which we see the world is *sola gratia*. Mike Higton's insightful description of a theology of higher education looks to Peter's betrayal of Jesus in Mark to depict the dying and rising that takes place on the pathway of learning. When Peter denies Christ,

> The problem is not, of course, that Peter is lying. The problem is that he is speaking quite truthfully when he says, "I do not know this man." Even at this point, when he has seen and heard and—yes—learnt so much, he has as yet failed to grasp the shape into which all the pieces of his new knowledge fit. He only begins to learn, truly to learn, in the moment when he breaks down and weeps.[19]

Higton illustrates here that knowledge has not been successful apart from the *mortificatio* that must take place in the Christian life in order for reason to achieve some level of success. This is not unlike Paul, who thanks God for his limitations after wrestling with the thorn in his flesh (e.g., 2 Cor 12:10). Adam also recognizes, after many failed attempts at finding a

---

16. Webster, "Communion with Christ," 125.
17. *Corpus Reformatorum*, 26:629–30; Leith, *John Calvin's Doctrine*, 78.
18. *Corpus Reformatorum*, 50:199; Leith, *John Calvin's Doctrine*, 81.
19. Higton, *Higher Education*, 157.

"helper" and after his long sleep (e.g., his *mortificatio*), that his companion has been found in Eve (Gen 2:21–23). There is no method or science that can establish reason into a sanctified position as these are "put to death" in the old self. Philosophical constructs, political ideologies, and scientific methods may find points of alignment with sanctified reason. However, they can never completely distract Christian reason because the presence of the spirit of God in the life of the mind safeguards the outcome of reason's sanctification, "guaranteeing what is to come" (2 Cor 1:22).

The *vivification* of reason reminds us that reason's victory only operates in the train of the risen Christ, the firstfruits of the new creation. Fortunate and accurate exercises of reason do not merely refer back to its mere existence as a transient capacity. Rather, reason does not accomplish its task apart from the economy of grace. This is true regardless of whether one is speaking of practical or theoretical matters. Seeing creation according to Christ is a seeing of the whole in the light of the *telos* of all things (Col 1:20). Due to God's economy of gracious action and this aspect of Christian sanctification, the Christian mind is able to name the self, the world, and others as they are.

Jeremy Begbie provides us with a helpful depiction of *vivification* in Calvin's theology with his comments on the Eucharist. Begbie reminds us that, despite the accusations that are often made against the Reformed tradition for denigrating materiality (and with that would go the arts and sciences), Calvin's position on the Eucharist makes room for the Christian's redeemed involvement in seeking and striving to know the thing-ish aspect of world on account of Christ's risen victory. The new creation includes the knower *within it* by the Spirit, who, then, invites the knower to explore this world: "The Holy Spirit plays a leading role, so that the entire eucharistic action becomes a means through which the church encounters and shares in the ascended reality of Jesus Christ, as a foretaste of the fullness of eschatological life to come." Begbie describes this version of reality as being a dynamic, "Spirit-driven frame of reference," which helpfully describes a Reformed outlook on the investigation of the liberal arts and sciences.[20]

The result of the vivification of reason brings both *joy* and *love* into the process of knowing the real world. Esther Meek sets up her reiteration of Michael Polanyi's personalist philosophy of science by spelling out how the knower must *invite the real* in the process of knowing. This invitation is undertaken in love for the other and what is known; this makes personal investment, or *love*, into a central factor, love instead of what she calls "longing."

---

20. Begbie, "Future of Theology," 162. This reading of Calvin finds support in Canlis's account, *Calvin's Ladder*.

Longing would be the passive, love the active. Longing calls for the other to give; love actively gives oneself for the sake of the other. Together as passive and active, longing and love in a way say it all. If knowing is, as covenant epistemology proposes, interpersonal covenantal relationship, then (as the Beatles sang) love is all you need [. . .] no difference exists between inviting the real and knowing itself.[21]

The Heidelberg Catechism confirms that this affective stance, which repositions the knower, is a gift, taking place through the "mortification of the old and the quickening of the new" (Q88). When we are raised to life in vivification, this brings about *love and joy*: "Q: What is the coming to life of the new nature? A: It is a heartfelt joy in God through Christ, and a love and delight to live according to the will of God in all good works" (Q90).

COMMUNING WITH CREATION IN THE SPIRIT

Thirdly, reason is inherently dependent on the Holy Spirit for attaining its goals in the present. Reason needs God's immanent presence, which brings about its growth and fulfillment unto Christian maturity. Self-exaltation distorts reason's results, like the mangled results that arise from the misuse of a practical tool. When sanctified reason sees the world through the ministry of *this* God, it apprehends his mystery, majesty, and sheer immensity. The Holy Spirit is the only one who gives us the grace to negotiate this mystery in active fidelity to the Son, the Word in the world, and then again, to adore the Father freely.

Sanctification "liberates" or "frees" human knowledge from the personal encumbrances that unsettle the knower's ability to *see, hear, sense* or *grasp* the reality in question. The Spirit *effects* the grace that liberates nature from its bondage to sin, which in this case rears its ugly head as misplaced anxiety, folly, arrogance, and sloth. All of these, as well as other vices, distort our process of learning what is new. Rather, by applying the benefits of our salvation in Christ, the Spirit encourages the mind to apprehend our created, fallen reality in the light of Christian hope, looking forward to its transformation and its return to God. Again, I return to Calvin:

> Our mind is too rude to be able to grasp the spiritual wisdom from God which is revealed to us through faith; and our hearts are too prone to distrust or to perverse confidence in ourselves or other creatures to rest of their own accord in God. But the

---

21. Meek, *Loving to Know*, 428.

Holy Spirit by his illumination makes us capable of understanding those things which would otherwise far exceed our grasp, and brings us to a sure persuasion by sealing the promises in our hearts.[22]

This third dimension of reason means that it has a social aspect. From a Christian and theological point of view, the word is brought to fruition by the "Lord of hearing," who is the Spirit.[23] The Christian's hearing of the word of God is wholly given by God, but this giving calls for the Christian to hear that word. It is the gracious work of the Holy Spirit that this hearing should take place in the context of its proper setting, the church community.[24] The hearing community is a key sign that is given to Christian reason, enabling it to see that our hope for the future is not in vain, that transformation is taking place in the present.

This preliminary statement about the setting of the church is required because of the shape of God's action as triune. The completion of God's spoken word is the renewal of creation, and the Spirit brings about a diversity of hearing in the present, in a community called the church, which is the beginning of the new creation. The Spirit fashions and forms this hearing of the saints as he carves out a properly human space for the reception of the word. In the Spirit, God effectively calls and redeems believers and he reshapes their minds according to the image of Christ. This fashioning of the Christian takes place in the context of the missional community, which is established by God's grace. Dietrich Bonhoeffer's writing on the church reminds us that this fellowship is rooted in the mystery of the triune relation between the word and Spirit: "Tying the Spirit to the word means that the Spirit aims at a plurality of hearers [. . .] the word [. . .] is qualified by being the very word of Christ; it is effectively brought to the heart of the hearers by the Spirit."[25]

Keith Johnson sketches the implications of what Bonhoeffer's view might mean for a Christian learning community:

> Bonhoeffer would argue that every single member of the body of Christ has a responsibility to see the world through the lens of the crucifixion and resurrection, to live in intrinsic connection to the church's being and mission, and to go out into the world and then return to the church to equip and challenge it to see the world as it is. The Christian academy is just one member

---

22. Calvin, *Calvin Theological Treatises*, 105. Cf. Partee, "Calvin and Reason."
23. Barth, *CD* I/1, 182.
24. See Higton, *Higher Education*, 158–61.
25. Bonhoeffer, *Sanctorum Communio*, 158.

doing what the entire body should be doing [. . .] Not everyone is in a position to instruct the church about its interpretation of Scripture or its worship, but every single believer, if he or she is obeying Christ's command to go out in the world, has the responsibility of keeping the church accountable to the reality of the world so it can truly live for the sake of the world.[26]

There are several implications to this work of the Spirit in the sanctification of reason. First, Christian inquiry cannot be subsumed under a secular category—"open-ended inquiry"—that focuses on reason's individuality and uninhibited natural capacity. This approach detaches reason from the communal shape of God's generosity. Further, the social character of inquiry is its *churchly* character in which the renewal of the Christian takes place. This ensures that reason learns to describe God's world within the context of the redeemed community around the church's worship, preaching of the word and the administration of the sacraments.

Second, Calvin mentions above that we grasp the "things which would otherwise far exceed our grasp." The renewal of intellectual life means that capacities that were dormant in the self's bondage to sin come alive. New growth takes place as the believer takes on "the mind of Christ" (1 Cor 2:16). This means that the location of the knower, with all of its historical and situational limits, is not seen as a hindrance to enquiry but is instead embraced as an asset. The capacities for, and limitations to, study, when the individual is seen in the light of a larger community, are given by the spirit of God.

> Intellectual dispositions that had fallen asleep are awakened at the Spirit's approach; powers that had ebbed away and dissipated are restored and concentrated; desires that had scattered into chaos are directed to what is good and holy. And so the intellect begins once again to move, and by the breath of the Spirit there arises a new intellectual *life* corresponding to the new intellectual nature.[27]

Third, there are the things "themselves". That is, with the endowment of the fruit of the Spirit, reason is given a patience with the "other" (e.g., materiality, language, and culture) that enables the mind to apprehend creation in an appropriate way, without attempting to reach beyond the temporal-historical contours in which a reality gives itself to be known (Gal 5:22–23). As Paul says, there is "no law" against the fruitful and *patient*

---

26. Johnson, "Bonhoeffer," 170.
27. Webster, "Intellectual Life," 111.

teachableness that aims to see the world, oneself, and others in the light of the Creator, Redeemer, and Sanctifier.

CONCLUSION: FAITH SEEKING UNDERSTANDING

Overall, the whole triune God is the One who brings about this sanctification of reason within the context of a faith seeking understanding. This means that faith is a primary, contextual and spiritual determinant for our use of reason. Reason expresses the faith that it has in these contexts for the Christian: creation, the Christian life, and the church community. The movement of the Christian to extol the Father and conform to the life of the Son in the Spirit creates an epistemic centrifugal force. Faith is not content in an isolated position, apart from community; and faith knows that it must "take up" its cross and look to creation in the hope of its renewal. Finally, faith sees creation as part of a larger, symphonic, and providential whole, which is meant to be returned to God in worship. Since those of us who are "in the know" participate in this process of knowing in and through the new creation established in Christ, we undertake this task with deep thankfulness and joy, grateful to take on new questions and to learn about the world that surrounds us.

BIBLIOGRAPHY

Barth, Karl. *Church Dogmatics*. Edited and translated by G. W. Bromiley and T. F. Torrance. 4 vols. in 13 parts. Edinburgh: T. & T. Clark, 1956–75.
Begbie, Jeremy. "The Future of Theology Amid the Arts: Some Reformed Reflections." In *Christ Across the Disciplines: Past, Present and Future*, edited by Roger Lundin. Grand Rapids: Wm. B. Eerdmans, 2014.
Blocher, Henri. *In the Beginning: The Opening Chapters of Genesis*. Leicester: InterVarsity, 1984.
Bonhoeffer, Dietrich. *Sanctorum Communio*. Minneapolis: Fortress, 2009.
Calvin, John. *Calvin Theological Treatises*. Translated by J. K. S. Reid. Philadelphia: Westminster, 1954.
Canlis, Julie. *Calvin's Ladder: A Spiritual Theology of Ascent and Ascension*. Grand Rapids: Wm. B. Eerdmans, 2010.
Corpus Reformatorum: Joannis Calvini Opera Quae Supersunt Omnia, vols. 26, 50. Edited by Guilielmus Baum, Eduardus Cunitz, and Eduardus Reuss. Brunswick, CA: Schwetschke et Filium, 1863–1897.
English, Adam. *Theology Remixed: Christianity as Story, Language, Game and Culture*. IVP Academic, 2010.
Farley, Edward. *The Fragility of Knowledge: Theological Education in the Church and University*. Minneapolis: Fortress, 1988.
Higton, Mike. *A Theology of Higher Education*. Oxford: Oxford University Press, 2012.

Irenaeus. *Against Heresies*. In *The Ante-Nicene Fathers: The Writings of the Fathers Down to A.D. 325*, vol. 1, edited by Alexander Roberts. New York: Cosimo Classics, 2007.

Johnson, Keith L. "Bonhoeffer and the End of the Christian Academy." In *Bonhoeffer: Christ and Culture*, edited by Keith L. Johnson and Timothy Larsen, 153–73. Downers Grove, IL: IVP Academic, 2013.

Leith, John H. *John Calvin's Doctrine of the Christian Life*. Louisville: Westminster John Knox, 1989.

Long, D. Stephen. "Radical Orthodoxy." In *Cambridge Companion to Postmodern Theology*, edited by Kevin J. Vanhoozer, 126–45. Cambridge: Cambridge University Press, 2003.

Marsden, George. *Jonathan Edwards: A Life*. New Haven: Yale University Press, 2004.

Meek, Esther L. *Loving to Know: Covenant Epistemology*. Eugene: Cascade, 2011.

Noll, Mark. *Jesus Christ and the Life of the Mind*. Grand Rapids: Wm. B. Eerdmans, 2011.

Partee, Charles. "Calvin and Reason." In *The Theology of John Calvin*, 304–30. Louisville: Westminster John Knox, 2008.

Sommerville, C. John. *The Decline of the Secular University: Why the Academy Needs Religion*. New York: Oxford University Press, 2006.

Vanhoozer, Kevin J. *Faith Speaking Understanding: Performing the Drama of Doctrine*. Louisville: Westminster John Knox, 2014.

Webster, John B. "Communion with Christ: Mortification and Vivification." In *Sanctified by Grace: A Theology of the Christian Life*, edited by Kent Eilers and Kyle C. Strobel, 121–38. London: Bloomsbury, 2014.

———. "Curiosity." In *The Domain of the Word: Scripture and Theological Reason*, 193–202. London: T. & T. Clark, 2012.

———. "On the Theology of the Intellectual Life." In *Christ Across the Disciplines: Past, Present and Future*, edited by Roger Lundin, 100–16. Grand Rapids: Eerdmans, 2013.

———. "Regina artium: Theology and the Humanities." In *The Domain of the Word: Scripture and Theological Reason*, 171–92. London: T. & T. Clark, 2012.

Zachman, Randall C. *John Calvin as Teacher, Pastor and Theologian*. Grand Rapids: Baker Academic, 2006.

8

We Have to Change

New Strategies for Theology in Australia

Michael Bräutigam[1]

THEOLOGY AS A SUBJECT in academia is in a deep crisis. Around the globe—and in particular in the West—theology departments are either shrinking or closing their doors altogether. Once lauded as the "queen of sciences," theology has been suffering an unprecedented decline. Yet the voice of theology is desperately needed today, more than ever. In a climate of profound confusion about ethical norms and values, theology can point the way, humbly yet confidently. The time to act and to change is now. In this chapter, I suggest six strategies that I hope will help theology not only survive but thrive in academia. Theology, and, of course, theologians and those involved in theological education and governance, are to *serve effectively, listen carefully, communicate eloquently, integrate strategically, engage publicly*, and *live authentically*. Australia, strategically placed in the Asia-Pacific region where Christianity is on the rise, finds itself with the unique opportunity to explore new pathways towards a resuscitation of this most crucial discipline.

---

1. I am indebted to Rosemary Wong, Eric Oldenburg, Christopher Green, Ernie Laskaris, and Richard Shumack for very helpful comments on an earlier draft of this essay.

THEOLOGY IN CRISIS: CHALLENGES AND HOPES

Theology is facing a crisis, and to a large degree, this is its own fault.[2] Theology, and many theologians, have failed to spot new, significant trends and developments, often retreating to the safe haven of the ivory tower. Only now do they seem to be waking up to the surprising news that the tower is not as safe as once presumed.

Over the last decades, theology has experienced an unprecedented demise. "In the *university*," writes Lieven Boeve, "theology's place as first among the academic disciplines is either already abolished long ago or reduced almost completely to mere tradition."[3] One by one, theology departments around the globe are being swallowed up by philosophy or religious studies departments,[4] or they are disappearing from university campuses altogether.[5] London's Heythrop College, for instance, founded over four hundred years ago, had to close its doors due to a lack of students and funding just earlier last year.[6]

Pushed to the margins of academic life, theology languishes in the basement of the modern university—eking out a meagre existence only in theological seminaries. Ridiculed by new atheists such as Richard Dawkins, who tweeted, "*Theology* is not a subject at all and has no place in our universities,"[7] theologians have retreated behind locked doors (provided they still have an office with a door to lock). If not ridiculed, theology has been challenged by other disciplines, such as economics or physics, for instance, regarding its *raison d'être*. Graham Tomlin, Bishop of Kensington, captures the charge that is again and again thrown at theology: Theologians, he writes, don't "produce anything useful, scientifically verifiable or economically profitable."[8] Of course, once pragmatism and profitability determine the rules of the game, theology is forced into checkmate (which,

---

2. When referring to "theology" and "the theologian" in this chapter, I adopt a rather wide definition. Theology, and the theologian pursuing his or her task, involves here the whole range of biblical studies, languages, dogmatics/systematic theology, practical theology, historical theology, and analytical theology.

3. Boeve, *Theology at the Crossroads*, 5 (emphasis original).

4. On the consequences of this development, see Boersma, "Relevance of Theology," 3–4.

5. The subject of church history, for instance, is now basically nonexistent in South African campuses. Pillay, "Historical Theology."

6. https://london.ac.uk/heythrop-college-closes-its-doors; https://en.wikipedia.org/wiki/Heythrop_College,_University_of_London.

7. https://twitter.com/richarddawkins/status/509361532254556161.

8. https://www.london.anglican.org/articles/the-future-of-theology-yale-divinity-school/.

however, would also be true of philosophy and history). Something needs to be done. And we need to be quick. Theology needs to change its strategy, or it will soon be game over.

In early 2019, the British Academy published a report that rings alarm bells: "Theology and Religious Studies disciplines must confront significant challenges, or risk 'disappearing from our universities' at a time when they have never been more needed."[9]

This is far away in Europe, one might say; but the same applies for us here in Australia.[10] Perhaps it is even more so here, since due to our special history of legislation, theology has had its difficulties in gaining a foothold (and recognition) in the university.[11] Of course, the Bible has been "intricately bound up with the way contemporary Australian society has taken shape," writes Meredith Lake. "It has had social, cultural and institutional impacts that we continue to live with today."[12] That was yesterday—but what about tomorrow?

There is a glimmer of hope, though, for theology and the theologian are needed today more than ever. Confronted by the cacophony of materialism, relativism, and individualism, people desire new direction and meaning. Indeed, theology is still strategically placed within an environment that desperately needs the work of the theologian. As Boeve points out, theology "is pushed to the margin in the domains of the university, church and society, while, on the other [hand], theology finds itself at the crossroads of academy, church, and society—precisely at the place where these three domains meet each other."[13] This is our opportunity.

In what follows I will address central starting points where we could take up the challenge at the intersection of "academy, church, and society." I think it is about time for a combined effort to rethink, reconsider, reform, and rejuvenate the task of theology at the outset of a new millennium. It is my hope that the following six principles will stimulate our discussion and lead to a fruitful conversation. Theology ought to *serve effectively*, *listen*

---

9. https://www.thebritishacademy.ac.uk/news/theology-and-religious-studies-risk-disappearing-our-universities-says-british-academy.

10. For some insights into the specifics of theology in Australia, see Piggin, *Evangelical Christianity*; Lake, *Bible in Australia*.

11. Although things have changed considerably in the recent past, Stuart Piggin writes in the early 1990s that "[t]heology and theological education are now accorded the same status as other disciplines in the universities and will do much to remove the prejudice against theological study endemic to Australia." Piggin, *Evangelical Christianity*, 180.

12. Lake, *Bible in Australia*, 365.

13. Boeve, *Theology at the Crossroads*, 54.

carefully, communicate eloquently, integrate strategically, engage publicly, and *live authentically.*

SERVE EFFECTIVELY

First of all, theology ought to turn its attention again to its core task: serving the church. Karl Barth reminds us in his *Church Dogmatics* that theology is "a function of the church" (*Theologie ist aber eine Funktion der Kirche*).[14] Theology's primary task is not to churn out ever more theology professors but to educate and equip faithful servants of the church: pastors, youth ministers, chaplains, counsellors, cross-cultural workers, and so many more.

Kevin Vanhoozer's definition of theology is helpful for our purposes here: "Theology serves the church by directing the people of God in ways of speaking and acting that embody the love of God, the reconciliation won by Jesus Christ, and the fellowship of the Holy Spirit. Theology not only articulates beliefs but suggests *designs for living.*"[15]

I think we can work with that: we pursue "designs for living" from a theology that exists at the intersection of academia, church, and society.[16] This would require us, of course, to be relevant in each of these domains, especially with a view to church and society. But are we?

This question deserves a more careful exploration, for in the past few decades, we have witnessed a portentous decoupling between academia and the church.

On one hand, we have watched how the ivory tower spiraled all too often into the lofty heights of theoretical speculation. At times, it seems theology has lost touch with the reality of the concerns and needs of the church. I remember vividly the occasion some years ago when I listened to a highly complex paper in dogmatics at a theological conference in Edinburgh. After the presentation, my courageous Peruvian friend, Apolos, stood up and complained that this paper was so far removed from the church and our Christian experience that it was simply superfluous. His lament was delivered with an intense mix of anger and sadness that I have never forgotten.

Of course, foundational research in theology is vital. This is not in question. But I am talking about something else here. I am referring to a subspecies of theologian who lives in the labyrinthine corridors of the hallowed halls of the university and pursues theology for theology's sake,

---

14. Karl Barth, *KD I/1*, 1.

15. Vanhoozer, "Reader's Guide," 7 (emphasis original).

16. Vanhoozer reminds us of theology's important cross-links with everyday life, church life, and life in society. Vanhoozer, "Reader's Guide," 7.

drafting papers in which perhaps only four people in the world are interested, and that, of these four, only two might actually read and use. The theology department must never be a playground for abstract speculation detached from the questions, concerns, and needs of the church.

Theologians are never mere theoreticians. Yes, of course, we conduct thorough research and strive for academic excellence. But we never lose sight of what is going on around us. Some years ago, Hans Bayer, Professor of New Testament at Covenant Theological Seminary, delivered a talk in Edinburgh's Rutherford House where he referred to himself as a "recovering theoretician." I would like to emulate his example.

On the other hand, largely due to the mentioned excesses, one observes a sometimes latent, sometimes more prominent anti-intellectualism in some corners of the church.[17] Both the topic of theology and the activity of the theologian are at times regarded with suspicion and—as a consequence—many churches and movements have decided to set up their own training institutions, independent of (confessional) seminaries and colleges. This is a tragic development; and the task of restoring confidence in *academic* theology falls to us.

Relevance is key. Only relevant theology serves the faith community effectively. Recovering theoreticians pursue relevant theology. Now when I say relevant, I do not mean pragmatic. The challenge is to be relevant without succumbing to pragmatism. Relevant theology, however, is the contemporary interpretation and appropriation of timeless truths in the context of church, academia, and society.

Relevant theology is profound yet applicable and accessible. When preparing lectures, curricula or essays, we constantly ask "so what?" questions.[18] Is what I intend to do relevant to my students, colleagues, and pastors? Would I be benefiting from sitting in my own seminar? From reading my own paper? How is God glorified in what I am doing?

We notice: rather than talking about the subject of "theology," we might need to focus more on the person of the theologian. And in this context, recent proposals that promote the role of the theologian as pastor (and vice versa, the pastor as theologian) are both stimulating and highly promising. Two important contributions deserve to be mentioned here. They are both collaborative projects (we return to the importance of collaboration later). The first is John Piper and D. A. Carson, *The Pastor as Scholar and the Scholar as Pastor: Reflections on Life and Ministry*. The second, more with

---

17. Noll, *Scandal of the Evangelical Mind*; Trueman, *Real Scandal*.

18. I am grateful to Rosemary Wong, who constantly reminds me of this important point.

a view to the church, is Todd A. Wilson and Gerald Hiestand, *Becoming a Pastor Theologian: New Possibilities for Church Leadership*.[19] Careful reflection on this topic has just begun, and we surely need many more elaborate contributions here. My own strategy so far has been to emulate the scholar-pastors I have experienced myself in my own personal history.

My friend and teacher, Scottish theologian Donald Macleod, was dubbed the "people's theologian."[20] Donald truly is a theologian for the people: in his lectures he communicates the most profound truths with uncanny ease and simplicity, always with an attitude of reverence and worship. I intentionally aim to follow in Donald's footsteps in this respect. Recently, one of my students told me, "Michael, you treat the theological classroom as a cathedral." I took it as a confirmation that I am on the right path. The classroom really *is* the theologian's cathedral. Here, we are called to explore *and* admire the truths laid out before us in Scripture and are moved to worship our God. If done in this way, in this spirit, I think, theology and the theologian take a step closer towards serving both academy and the church—and, through the church, serving society more faithfully and effectively. Next, in order to serve well, I think it is essential that we learn to listen (before we speak).

LISTEN CAREFULLY

Secondly, theology and the theologian need to listen with care.[21] Too often, we turn James's slogan on its head: we are quick to speak and slow to hear, rather than "quick to hear, slow to speak" (Jas 1:19). If we want to communicate well—and we will turn our attention to our speech act below—we first need to learn how to listen well.

To listen well is a virtue to which we all aspire. One of the *12 Rules for Life* that Canadian psychologist Jordan B. Peterson lists is this one: "Assume that the person you are listening to might know something you don't" (rule 9).[22] This is certainly helpful advice. We don't know everything, and there might be theologians, philosophers, and perhaps even psychologists and sociologists out there who have a lot to contribute to the theological debate today—both here and abroad—but we are somewhat selectively deaf.

---

19. Piper et al., *Pastor as Scholar*; Wilson and Hiestand, *Becoming a Pastor Theologian*.
20. Campbell and Maclean, *People's Theologian*.
21. Ulrich Lincoln examines the relationship between theology and the aspect of hearing: Lincoln, *Die Theologie*.
22. Peterson, *12 Rules for Life*, 233.

My colleague Thomas Kimber recently made the case that our "theological conversation . . . [is] virtually all one-sided."[23] Even though the majority of Christians, Thomas argues, live in Africa and Asia, the (white male) Westerners still dominate the theological conversation.[24] It is about time that we watched and learned, listened and heard what the themes, topics, concerns, and trajectories of the majority of our brothers and sisters in the world are. Of course, Western theology offers a rich tradition ranging from Augustine through the Reformers to modern theologians that provides a substantial foundation for our brothers and sisters in the majority world as they "do" theology.[25] Still, while they have been very good at listening and learning, we have seen it predominantly as a one-way street. There is a subtle but important difference between, "I hear you" and, "I listen to you." Theology in Australia actually finds itself in an ideal geographical location for this enterprise. Establishing essential "listening-links" with theologians in Asia will enable us to contribute to a new flourishing of theology in the Asia-Pacific region.

How do we learn to listen well? Good listeners carefully study their surrounding culture. They patiently learn how to read trends and how to understand current church cultures and societal developments.[26] Martin Luther was unquestionably a genius in this respect. When he was working on his translation of the New Testament, hiding in the Wartburg, he regularly dressed up as "Juncker Jörg" (there was a bounty on his head) and went to the marketplace, listening to the way people spoke, so that he could offer a translation that worked, that ordinary people could understand. He coined the dictum "to watch the gob" ("*auff das maul sehen*").[27] This is as important today as it was then. Theologians are translators who listen first before they speak. Translating and speaking God's timeless message into the contemporary cultural context first requires careful patient listening.

Once we have relearned how to listen well, we are in the position to engage in the speech act.

---

23. Kimber, "Virtue of Docility," 143.
24. Kimber, "Virtue of Docility," 143.
25. I am grateful to Richard Shumack for reminding me of this important point.
26. See Vanhoozer et al., *Everyday Theology*.
27. Luther, *Sendbrief vom Dolmetschen*, in WA 30/2: 637, lines 17–22 (". . . den man mus nicht die buchstaben inn der lateinischen sprachen fragen, wie man sol Deutsch reden, wie diese esel thun, sondern, man mus die mutter jhm hause, die kinder auff der gassen, den gemeinen man auff dem marckt drumb fragen, und den selbigen auff das maul sehen, wie sie reden, und darnach dolmetzschen, so verstehen sie es den und mercken, das man Deutsch mit jn redet.")

COMMUNICATE ELOQUENTLY

"Theology often does not read well," laments David F. Ford, and I think we have all experienced this phenomenon.[28] If theology wants to survive, it needs to learn how to speak clearly and communicate eloquently.

I am the first to admit that I have had to (and still have to) unlearn a few habits and develop some others. As a young psychology student in Germany, I quickly noticed a stark difference between our German textbooks and those found in North America. Although the American textbooks were, of course, written in English—and I was still learning the psychological lingo at that stage—they were often much easier to understand than their counterparts written in my native language.

In German there seems to exist the unwritten rule that the more complex the sentence sounds, the more profound the truth it communicates. Nothing could be further from the truth. Clarity and precision of expression and accessibility are all vital—*especially* when it comes to communicating profound truths. Yes, of course, we are dealing with the most complex themes, such as the Trinity, but complex themes do not need to be cumbersome. I am still learning the art of communicating the most profound, eternal truths with as much clarity and simplicity as possible.

This challenge, of course, is not merely ours. All the disciplines at an academic level have some serious room for improvement here. A research team in Sweden recently studied the accessibility of academic writing and came to the following conclusion: "Modern scientific texts are more impenetrable than they were over a century ago."[29] According to their findings, readability has steadily declined since 1881.[30] And it seems that our students are imitating us. One of the most common comments I write in the margins of my students' essays is: "How could you express this idea in a more accessible way? How could you make this less cumbersome?"

It is about time to change. This is a wake-up call, in particular for theology. We have the most precious message of all university departments—the gospel of Jesus Christ—so of course we are most interested in articulating this truth in all its beauty, profundity, and accessibility.

So, what can we do about it? Well, we can get to work. One way to start might be to hold rhetoric and writing workshops for theologians, where we learn how to declutter our sentences and throw out empty jargon. Studying

---

28. Ford, *Future of Christian Theology*, 20.

29. https://www.nature.com/news/it-s-not-just-you-science-papers-are-getting-harder-to-read-1.21751.

30. https://www.nature.com/news/it-s-not-just-you-science-papers-are-getting-harder-to-read-1.21751.

the art of crafting beautiful sentences needs to become an important part of our task. We could learn from good books,[31] and, of course, from one another, in this area. Others are far more gifted than I am in this respect, and I am more than happy to learn from them.[32] Collegial collaboration is key. "Even within academic theology," writes David F. Ford, "wider dissemination than within a small circle of specialists is often better achieved by collaboration with a colleague who is a better writer."[33]

Once our content is actually accessible and usable, we might want to think about selling it more effectively. There is too much good and actually well-written theology rotting away in dusty journals in the basements of our libraries, simply because we do not care enough about selling it.

Titles of theology papers and books are amongst the most boring and cumbersome one can imagine.

There is much we can learn from other disciplines that are selling their findings far more creatively and effectively. Here are a few of my favorite examples:[34] from medicine, "miR miR on the wall, who's the most malignant medulloblastoma miR of them all?"[35]; from psychology: "You probably think this paper's about you: narcissists' perceptions of their personality and reputation"[36]; or from biology/chemistry, "Carbon monoxide: to boldly go where NO has gone before." Oh, and here's one more: "The effect of having Christmas dinner with in-laws on gut microbiota composition."[37] (One can only hope that the content actually mirrors the eloquence and wit of the titles.)

When theologians are not writing, they are teaching, lecturing or engaging in some other form of public speaking. And here, too, we might want to think about improving our skill set. In terms of delivery, there is much to be learned from TED talks, where the challenge is to communicate complex themes in an accessible manner to an audience alien to the subject (in a short amount of time). It makes some of us blush that we cannot even

---

31. I have learned a great deal from William Zinsser and Howard S. Becker in this respect; Zinsser, *On Writing Well*; Becker and Richards, *Writing for Social Scientists*.

32. I am very grateful to my colleague Gillian Asquith, who again and again patiently lifts the level of my English expression in my essays.

33. Ford, *Future of Christian Theology*, 20.

34. Found elsewhere and here: https://www.sciencealert.com/scientists-sharing-their-best-pun-filled-paper-titles-has-us-in-stitches.

35. https://www.ncbi.nlm.nih.gov/pubmed/28575493.

36. https://www.ncbi.nlm.nih.gov/pubmed/21604895. Carlson et al., "You Probably Think."

37. https://www.sciencedirect.com/science/article/pii/S2452231719300090.

describe what we did in our PhD studies in a few understandable sentences (Gillian Asquith might be the only exception here).[38]

Theology conferences, in my view, also need to lift their game here. These conferences have increasingly become a source of frustration to me over the last few years. More than once I have found myself in a small auditorium that, unbeknownst to me, was actually an echo chamber for a small area of highly specialized theologians. The task of theology becomes futile when it is aimed to serve only a very small, finely selected elite.

It is, in fact, the declared goal of the Paradosis conference to offer something different. Since its inception in 2016, the Paradosis conference at Melbourne School of Theology has sought to promote a theology that is profound, relevant, and accessible. So far, we have covered Christology (2016), ethics (2018), and theological anthropology (2019). It remains for others to decide whether we have been successful in our attempt to "communicate eloquently," but at least I want to highlight the goal to which we are all aspiring.

Communicating eloquently goes hand in hand with communicating humbly, winsomely, and graciously. Theology is often perceived as a moralizing voice in Australia (and probably elsewhere, too) and that has drowned out the full message of what theology really wants to convey. Unfortunately, what raises the public's attention are often cases where (self-proclaimed) Christians speak from a position of self-righteousness and judgmentalism. Divisive and sectarian voices often attract much attention and undermine the credibility of Christianity even more. Communicating clearly and eloquently, yet also gently, is now more vital than ever.

INTEGRATE STRATEGICALLY

In academia, Karl Jasper reminds us that our task is "to seek the truth as a community of scholars and students" (*die Wahrheit in der Gemeinschaft von Forschern und Schülern zu suchen*).[39] "Community" is the important word here. It implies that we are working *together*.

Too often, though, theologians are isolated, insular warriors working independently from the general activities at the research university. Many are highly specialized in their area of expertise—the same applies to other scholars in the humanities, too, of course—and they rarely think outside their own boxes.

---

38. Gillian was awarded runner-up in the Australian Catholic University Three-Minute Thesis (3MT™) competition in 2019.

39. Jaspers, *Die Idee Der Universität*, 9.

The way forward for theology in an academic context is a more intentional pursuit of integration—both within the subject of theology itself (internal integration) and in interdisciplinary endeavors with the other disciplines in the university setting.

First, with a view to internal integration, there lies much promise in internal conversation and collaboration. By encouraging systematicians, church historians, biblical studies scholars, and practical theologians to talk with one another, and perhaps to collaborate in a more intentional way, new insights, angles, and approaches will evolve to the benefit of all. Whenever and wherever possible, we avoid hiding in our offices; rather, we get up and knock on our colleagues' doors, enquiring about possible avenues of collaboration. Theology is a communal project.

Yet we also seek external integration. We pursue cross-disciplinary dialogue on a larger scale. This is, in fact, part and parcel of the missional nature of theology. Robert Cummings Neville writes: "Too often in the last century theology, at least in [North] America, has tried to make itself into a profession, in which theologians read only other theologians."[40] Neville is right, and if we do not intervene, this will probably continue until the last theological college in the West has closed its doors. So, what do we do? Neville recommends the following: "Theology needs to transform itself so as to work out explicit connections with disciplines from which it might learn. It needs to internali[z]e the work of sociology, anthropology, cognitive science, psychology, the imaginative arts, literature, jurisprudence, and so forth."[41]

"Internalize" is a big word that presents us with a serious challenge because it highlights that it is simply not enough if the theologian now goes out for a coffee with the sociologist or finally picks up that book about theology and the arts. Internalizing, the way I understand Neville, refers to a sincere, intentional appropriation. It means, for instance, that we are prepared to learn the basic vocabulary of the other discipline's language, its key premises and tools. This will enrich, equip, and prepare us to become more relevant and ready to serve our constituencies well.

An internalizing approach to integration is what we are trying to pursue here at Melbourne School of Theology with our various centers of excellence (Arthur Jeffery Centre for the Study of Islam, The Chinese Centre for the Study of Chinese Christianity, and the Centre for Theology and Psychology); and with our unique partnership with Eastern College Australia, a Christian higher education provider that trains Christian

---

40. Neville, "Theological and Religious Studies," 130-31.
41. Neville, "Theological and Religious Studies," 130.

teachers, chaplains, and counsellors. But there is so much more work to do, for instance, in terms of an effective faith-work integration (our friends at Morling and Ridley have something to contribute here) and a more intentional and strategic approach to networking with important Christian grassroots movements (such as, for instance, the Institute for Civil Society). This brings us to our next point.

ENGAGE PUBLICLY

"No area of life," Dutch politician and theologian Abraham Kuyper said, "remains alien to the Christian!"[42] If theology wants to survive, it needs to take this statement seriously and engage more intentionally and fruitfully with the public sphere.[43] The pursuit of theology is not restricted to a stimulating in-house debate but calls for an active engagement at the marketplace of ideas. This necessarily involves moving beyond the cozy confines of our small seminaries and colleges.[44]

We have already pointed to theology's critical place at the "crossroads of academy, church, and society" (Boeve). The question is now whether theology stands at the crossroads like a scarecrow trying to chase away those who threaten to take its place at the university, or whether it aims to serve as a humble but confident, faithful and wise conversation partner, as Lady Wisdom at the intersection of academy, church, and society. "Does not wisdom call? Does not understanding raise her voice? On the heights beside the way, at the crossroads she takes her stand" (Prov 8:1–2). As Oliver O'Donovan frames it: "What wisdom demands is a response to the goodness of God's world, which is to say, to know it and to love it, to realise ourselves in engagement with it."[45] This is spot on. Engagement is key.

Over twenty years ago, David G. Kamitsuka issued the following warning:

> [Theology] must continue to develop as a fully critical discourse on Christian witness, taking its proper place in the public intellectual realm. It must continue to insist on the ethical mandate for solidarity with the oppressed who are marginalized from dominant culture. Without these values, theology becomes either an antiquated practice of an intellectual elite, unable to

---

42. Bratt, *Abraham Kuyper*, 58.

43. On public theology, see Kim, *Companion to Public Theology*; Williams, *Faith in the Public Square*.

44. See Davies et al., *Transformation Theology*.

45. O'Donovan, *Finding and Seeking*, 48.

convey the existential and social power of the Christian story to the world; or so absorbed in the thick description of Christian beliefs and practices that it loses all sense of accountability to critical public dialogue.[46]

This is a timely message. I see two main points that concern us in this context: first, a more effective positioning and involvement in the public sphere, and second, a more confident and effective implementation of theology's ethical mandate in our society today.

First, then, more in a general sense, theology needs to raise its voice and make itself heard at the marketplace of ideas.

This is what public theology does. Sebastian Kim defines public theology as such: "Public theology is Christians engaging in dialogue with those outside church circles on various issues of common interest. It involves urging Christians to take the opportunity to participate in the public domain in modern secular democracies and to converse with other citizens on issues wider than religious matters."[47] Yet how effectively do we engage in such dialogue?

Other disciplines and movements have very effective mouthpieces; we have already mentioned Richard Dawkins as the megaphone of the new atheism. Psychology has Jordan B. Peterson, physics has Prof. Brian Cox, and philosophy Jostein Gaarder. Yet where is the eloquent theologian who represents us in the public domain?

The way forward is probably to start small. Since we are already marginalized, we might as well start working from the margins. This is what Lieven Boeve suggests: "Theology must guard against reacting to this marginalization by either retreating out of or moving exclusively inside of one domain. Rather than abandoning the crossroads, it should learn to re-examine its place and contribution precisely *from the margin*."[48]

We begin to engage carefully and thoughtfully in the public discussion; we write small opinion papers for the local newspaper; we make ourselves available for radio interviews; we produce podcasts and YouTube videos about current issues. The means to engagement are endless. And having listened carefully (as mentioned earlier), we know what's on people's minds. What does theology have to say about the Fridays for Future movement? What do we say about gender dysphoria or euthanasia? And, of course, what about those who are really marginalized? Theology does have—and actually does say—something about these important issues. The challenge,

---

46. Kamitsuka, *Theology and Contemporary Culture*, 4.
47. Kim, *Theology in the Public Sphere*, 3.
48. Boeve, *Theology at the Crossroads*, 9.

though, is to hold this debate in a more public space (rather than an in-house discussion).

This brings us to our second point. Theology has a special mandate when it comes to voicing the concerns of those whose voice is scarcely heard. In face of eye-watering injustice, elitism, corruption, and economic exploitation, theologians take a stand for the less advantaged and articulate their concerns. The word of God clearly contains a significant concern for the disadvantaged, such as the mandate of "remembering the poor" (Gal 2:10), or of caring for the widows and orphans (Deut 10:18; 1 Tim 5:3; Jas 1:27). How do we fulfill this mandate faithfully?

The above-mentioned Abraham Kuyper might be able to lead the way for us here.[49] Over a hundred years ago, he combined in his own person many of the aspects on which we have touched so far. As a journalist, Kuyper authored over twenty thousand newspaper articles (often directing public attention to the needs of the less advantaged).[50] He was the cofounder of the Free University in Amsterdam (Vrije Universiteit, 1880), where he also taught as theology professor. He helped found a new denomination. And he was the leader of a political party for forty years, at one point also serving as prime minister of the Netherlands (from 1901 to 1905). We might not want to emulate *everything* he did, because this would soon lead to burnout (as it did, several times, in Kuyper's case).[51] But perhaps we can adopt his "big picture" approach to life and theology, namely the intention to see everything somehow related to the word and work of God and to play our own part. We can adopt his vision that the theologian is not to "shut himself up in his office," to paraphrase Kuyper, "and abandon the world to its fate." Rather, we want to follow our "high calling," that works to uphold "in the midst of so much painful corruption, everything that is honorable, lovely, and of good report among men."[52]

"Throughout almost two hundred years the mission of Australian evangelical Christianity has been to preserve society by reforming it along

---

49. For Kuyper's influence on theological colleges in Australia, see Piggin, *Evangelical Christianity*, 138–39.

50. Biographical information on Kuyper is based on my reading of Bratt, *Abraham Kuyper*.

51. Bratt, *Abraham Kuyper*, ix, 21, 38, 87ff.

52. The full quote goes like this: "The Calvinist cannot shut himself up in *his* church and abandon the world to its fate. He feels, rather, in his high calling to push the development of this world to an even higher stage, and to do this in constant accordance with God's ordinance, for the sake of God, upholding, in the midst of so much painful corruption, everything that is honorable, lovely, and of good report among men." Kuyper, *Lectures on Calvinism*, 73.

iblical lines," writes Stuart Piggin in the early 1990s.[53] We live in 2020 now and we need a new generation of theologians who, with creativity, courage, and conviction engage in the public sphere for the common good. I do not pretend to have all the answers, but I hope to inspire the conversation. Perhaps the way to start begins right at our doorstep, with ourselves, the persons of the theologians. And now to this final point.

LIVE AUTHENTICALLY

We all strive for authenticity. Or perhaps we should rather call it "Christothenticity," since it is Jesus Christ who authenticates our existence and experience. Living a Christothentic life is marked by the desire to be transformed, step by step, into the image of Jesus Christ (2 Cor 3:18). Personal transformation is therefore at the forefront of the theologian's mind. It is number one on our agenda and comes long before any desire for intellectual satisfaction or achievement (although there is not necessarily a contradiction between the two).

However, personal transformation is an item that is often absent on our agenda. I once heard someone say about a young and promising theologian: "Oh, yes, he has been making quite a name for himself recently." And that was meant entirely positively and respectfully. However, I cannot but wonder whether this is really an achievement that deserves to be desired or applauded. It rather feeds our vices. And a career in academia carries with it the risk of vanity; more so, I would say, than other career paths, since everything here is linked with our name. It is one's own name that is on any influential essay and one's own opinion that is asked at a panel. "Vanity, definitely my favorite sin," Al Pacino's devilish character says in the 1997 movie *The Devil's Advocate*.

There is clearly the temptation in academia to acquiesce to self-centered pursuit, and in theology it often leads to theology for theology's sake (and/or one's career's sake). Theology for God's sake, however, looks different. Bishop Graham Tomlin puts the idea in the following words: "There is a kind of theology which is conceptual clarification, a philosophical clearing of the ground, but constructive theology proper, *theologia*, involves the whole person in the quest. It does not just have God in view, but God as he relates to us—how life is to be lived under the rule of God."[54]

---

53. Piggin, *Evangelical Christianity*, 222.

54. https://www.london.anglican.org/articles/the-future-of-theology-yale-divinity-school/.

On a more personal note, I am very grateful to our principal, Tim Meyers, who in his regular chapel messages again and again directs our attention to the importance of "watching our own hearts," as he calls it. His catchphrase is: "We do not simply want to spread information, but we seek transformation." I have also learned a great deal from Swiss theologian Adolf Schlatter (1852–1938). Schlatter was a highly gifted scholar—his expertise ranged from archaeology to New Testament exposition, dogmatics, and ethics. At the same time, he was keenly aware that if this knowledge did not impact him personally, the one doing the study, and, of course, those whom he was called to teach, then it was all useless. He always emphasized that in addition to what he called the New Testament seeing act (*Sehakt*) and dogmatic thinking act (*Denkakt*), there needs to be the existential life act (*Lebensakt*), where the theologian implements and lives out the gained insights.[55]

In fact, in Schlatter's view, some things went awry after the Protestant Reformation. Post-Reformation theology, he argued, overemphasized knowledge at the expense of living out the truth in real life.[56] One could say, using Schlatter's language, the thinking act overshadowed the life act here. Schlatter writes in his *Christian Dogmatics* (*Christliches Dogma*): "Pivotal for our Christian life is not how rich our thoughts about God's works are, but whether we adhere to him and preserve the truth we have perceived, be it large or small."[57]

Unlike in other disciplines, the theologian is existentially bound up with his or her subject. There is a vital link between *doing* theology and *living* as theolog*ians*. Not many people care what a professor of chemistry, mathematics or English literature does outside her office hours. Yet the theologian is always in the role of the theologian, bound by an ethical imperative, to practice what he or she preaches, aspiring to an authentic overlap between orthodoxy and orthopraxy. This, of course, is not new. Long ago the Desert Fathers provided wisdom in this regard: "An elder said: 'There is nothing more poverty-stricken than a mind philosophizing about God remote from God. For one who teaches, whether in church or in a cell, he must first himself perform what he says and teaches.'"[58]

Deep and honest concern about our own sanctification is key. Of course, this is a lifelong and serious fight. Martin Luther saw that very clearly. He made the case that only when we are actually engaged in this

---

55. Schlatter, *Das Christliche Dogma*, 343–44.
56. Schlatter, *Das Christliche Dogma*, 495.
57. Schlatter, *Das Christliche Dogma*, 496.
58. Wortley, *"Anonymous" Sayings*, 591.

fight, neck and crop, that we might call ourselves "theologians": "It is by living—no, not living, but by dying and giving ourselves up to hell that we become theologians, not by understanding, reading, and speculating."[59]

This kind of living, or dying, as Luther put it, involves a new dedication to the spiritual disciplines in the theologian's life. It is through these personal encounters with Jesus Christ, in silence and solitude, in quiet reading, reflection, prayer, contemplation and meditation, that growth occurs.[60] "And we all, with unveiled face, beholding the glory of the Lord, are being transformed into the same image from one degree of glory to another. For this comes from the Lord who is the Spirit" (2 Cor 3:18).

CONCLUSION

Theology's crisis is real; but there is hope, especially for those of us who are doing theology here in Australia. Evangelical Christianity, as Stuart Piggin and Robert D. Linder recently argued, "has been a strong and pervasive influence on the shaping, not only of the heart and soul of the Australian nation, but also of its body."[61] And today we are tasked with the challenge to "attend to the Australian soul," they claim, as we seek to "strengthen its moral energy, inform its consciousness, and fire its imagination with a vision for the future."[62] At the forefront of this endeavor stands, in my view, the theologian who gives shape to such a vision. Australia enjoys the strategic advantage that it is relatively free from the centuries-old tradition of "doing theology" in a particular way. We are far more flexible and able to adapt to the current *Zeitgeist* than our European and North American friends. Circumstances are changing quickly, and Australia could show the way forward. I am not the only one who thinks so.

David F. Ford writes:

> The grip of certain sorts of [North] American theology on Evangelicals and Pentecostals elsewhere in the world (partly enabled by the Americans' capacity to fund those they agree with) now seems to be loosening due to a double pressure. On the one hand, within America there is a blossoming of new theologies within these churches; on the other hand, there is a new

---

59. Martin Luther, quoted in Bayer, *Theology the Lutheran Way*, 61.
60. Jonathan Edwards has much to say about this. See my essay, Bräutigam, "Jonathan Edwards."
61. Piggin and Linder, *National Soul*, 559.
62. Piggin and Linder, *National Soul*, 566.

theological confidence elsewhere, especially in Asia, Africa, and South America.[63]

One observes indeed a "new theological confidence" in the Asia-Pacific region. With our stimulating, multicultural, multilingual setting, we can move forward and contribute in creative ways to the flourishing of theology in our region and perhaps even beyond.

We only have these two options: engage effectively or retreat gracefully. If theology wants not simply to survive but to thrive, we have to awaken from our slumber. We have to act now if we do not want to disappear into the oblivion of irrelevance.

What I have suggested here is not rocket science. It is all quite straightforward: serve effectively, listen carefully, communicate eloquently, integrate strategically, engage publicly, and live authentically. I don't want simply to leave you with these active slogans. This would fall short of the bigger picture. The bigger picture is that Jesus Christ is doing all this in our world today—and we are invited to participate in his redeeming action. Jesus has always served effectively; let us follow him here. He always listened very carefully, especially to the marginalized. He certainly communicated eloquently—think of the Sermon of the Mount. He integrated strategically, engaged publicly, and lived authentically. These points are not more than a few guidelines towards rescuing theology. Our goal is much bigger than this. It means becoming more like Jesus Christ. And it is here that theology comes to life!

There are many reasons why *I* should not have been writing this chapter. I am the prototype of a theology of the past: a white, privileged male from Europe, a dying breed. However, we all know that when the grain of wheat dies, it bears much fruit (John 12:24). I'm happy to shovel my own grave if it leads to new life in theology.

BIBLIOGRAPHY

Barth, Karl. *Kirchliche Dogmatik*, vol. I. Die Lehre vom Wort Gottes: Prolegomena zur kirchlichen Dogmatik, part 1. Zürich: Evangelischer Verlag, 1964.

Bayer, Oswald. *Theology the Lutheran Way*. Translated by Jeffrey G. Silcock and Mark C. Mattes. Edited by Paul Rorem. Lutheran Quarterly Books. Grand Rapids: Eerdmans, 2007.

Becker, Howard Saul, and Pamela Richards. *Writing for Social Scientists: How to Start and Finish Your Thesis, Book, or Article*. Chicago Guides to Writing, Editing, and Publishing. 3rd ed. Chicago: University of Chicago Press, 2020.

---

63. Ford, *Future of Christian Theology*, 9.

Boersma, Hans. "The Relevance of Theology and Worldview in a Postmodern Context." In *Living in the Lamblight: Christianity and Contemporary Challenges to the Gospel*, edited by Hans Boersma, 1–14. Vanvouver, BC: Regent College, 2001.

Boeve, Lieven. *Theology at the Crossroads of University, Church and Society: Dialogue, Difference and Catholic Identity*. London: Bloomsbury T. & T. Clark, 2016.

Bratt, James D. *Abraham Kuyper: Modern Calvinist, Christian Democrat*. Library of Religious Biography. Grand Rapids, MI: W. B. Eerdmans, 2013.

Bräutigam, Michael. "Jonathan Edwards on Contemplating the Beauty of Christ." In *Engaging Ethically in a Strange New World: Some Perspectives from Australia*, edited by Michael Bräutigam and Gillian Asquith, 50–67. Eugene, OR: Wipf & Stock, 2019.

Campbell, Iain D., and Malcom Maclean, eds. *The People's Theologian: Writings in Honour of Donald Macleod*. Geanies House: Christian Focus, 2011.

Carlson, Erika N., et al. "You Probably Think This Paper's About You: Narcissists' Perceptions of Their Personality and Reputation." *Journal of Personality and Social Psychology* 103, no. 2 (2012) 379.

Davies, Oliver, et al. *Transformation Theology: Church in the World*. London: T. & T. Clark, 2007.

Ford, David. *The Future of Christian Theology*. Blackwell Manifestos. Oxford: Wiley-Blackwell, 2011.

Jaspers, Karl. *Die Idee der Universität*. Berlin: Springer, 1946.

Kamitsuka, David G. *Theology and Contemporary Culture: Liberation, Postliberal and Revisionary Perspectives*. Cambridge: Cambridge University Press, 1999.

Kim, Sebastian. *Theology in the Public Sphere: Public Theology as a Catalyst for Open Debate*. London: SCM, 2011.

Kim, Sebastian C. H. *A Companion to Public Theology*. Brill's Companions to Modern Theology. Leiden: Brill, 2017.

Kimber, Thomas. "The Virtue of Docility in Global Theological Conversation." In *Engaging Ethically in a Strange New World: A View from Down Under*, edited by Michael Bräutigam and Gillian Asquith, 141–48. Eugene, OR: Wipf & Stock, 2019.

Kuyper, Abraham. *Lectures on Calvinism*. Grand Rapids: Wm. B. Eerdmans, 1931.

Lake, Meredith. *The Bible in Australia: A Cultural History*. Sydney, NSW: NewSouth, 2018.

Luther, Martin. *Sendbrief vom Dolmetschen (1530)*. In *D. Martin Luthers Werke, Kritische Gesamtausgabe*, vol. 30, part II, 626–46. Weimar: Hermann Böhlau, 1902.

Lincoln, Ulrich. *Die Theologie und das Hören. Hermeneutische Untersuchungen Zur Theologie*. Tübingen: Mohr Siebeck, 2014.

Neville, Robert Cummings. "Theological and Religious Studies in the United States." In *Evangelische Theologie an Staatlichen Universitäten: Konzepte und Konstellationen Evangelischer Theologie und Religionsforschung*, edited by Stefan Alkier and Hans-Günter Heimbrock, 123–34. Göttingen: Vandenhoeck & Ruprecht, 2011.

Noll, Mark A. *The Scandal of the Evangelical Mind*. Grand Rapids, MI: Wm. B. Eerdmans, 1994.

O'Donovan, Oliver. *Finding and Seeking*. Ethics as Theology, vol. 2. Grand Rapids, MI: Wm. B. Eerdmans, 2014.

Peterson, Jordan B. *12 Rules for Life: An Antidote to Chaos*. Toronto: Random House Canada, 2018.

Piggin, Stuart. *Evangelical Christianity in Australia: Spirit, Word, and World*. Melbourne: Oxford University Press, 1996.

Piggin, Stuart, and Robert D. Linder. *Attending the National Soul: Evangelical Christians in Australian History 1914–2014*. The Fountain of Public Prosperity, vol. 2. Clayton, VIC: Monash University Publishing, 2020.

Pillay, Jerry. "Historical Theology at Public Universities Matter." *HTS Teologiese Studies/Theological Studies* 73, no. 1 (2017). https://doi.org/10.4102/hts.v73i1.4807.

Piper, John, et al. *The Pastor as Scholar and the Scholar as Pastor: Reflections on Life and Ministry*. Wheaton, IL: Crossway, 2011.

Schlatter, Adolf. *Das Christliche Dogma*. 2nd ed. Stuttgart: Calwer, 1923.

Trueman, Carl R. *The Real Scandal of the Evangelical Mind*. Chicago: Moody, 2011.

Vanhoozer, Kevin J. "A Reader's Guide: How to Use This Book." In *Everyday Theology: How to Read Cultural Texts and Interpret Trends*, edited by Kevin J. Vanhoozer, Charles A. Anderson and Michael J. Sleasman, 7–12. Grand Rapids, MI: Baker Academic, 2007.

Vanhoozer, Kevin J., et al. *Everyday Theology: How to Read Cultural Texts and Interpret Trends*. Cultural Exegesis. Grand Rapids, MI: Baker Academic, 2007.

Williams, Rowan. *Faith in the Public Square*. London: Bloomsbury, 2012.

Wilson, Todd A., and Gerald Hiestand. *Becoming a Pastor Theologian: New Possibilities for Church Leadership*. Downers Grove, IL: InterVarsity, 2016.

Wortley, John. *The "Anonymous" Sayings of the Desert Fathers: A Select Edition and Complete English Translation*. New York: Cambridge University Press, 2013.

Zinsser, William. *On Writing Well: The Classic Guide to Writing Nonfiction*. 30th anniversary ed. New York: HarperCollins, 2006.

9

To What Extent Does Theological College Contribute to a Deepened Sense of Spirituality?

Delle Matthews

A QUICK SEARCH THROUGH the websites of theological colleges within the Australian College of Theology (ACT) shows that most colleges claim the experience of theological study will be transforming. Indeed, one of the learning outcomes of all ACT courses is that students will demonstrate the capacity for independent reflection and learning to sustain personal and professional development in Christian, professional, and vocational life and ministry suggesting that there is an expectation for more than knowledge-based outcomes for students. This chapter seeks to answer the question of whether, for ACT students, spiritual transformation and personal development is achieved through the experience of theological study and in what ways. Results of a survey of students from across the consortium of ACT colleges will be discussed.

INTRODUCTION

The Australian College of Theology (ACT), a consortium of eighteen theological colleges scattered around Australia, claims as a learning outcome of its courses that students will:

> Demonstrate a capacity for independent reflection and learning to sustain personal and professional development . . .

To that end, the ACT has been proactive in discussing how its member colleges can best support students in their personal spiritual development as one aspect of personal development, sponsoring professional development conferences on the topic of personal spiritual formation or development.[1]

ACT member colleges also promise students an outcome of spiritual development through the experience of studying at their college. The expectation communicated on a number of college websites is that the student experience at theological college will be personally transformational.

> MST exists to equip God's people with transformational theology, biblical depth, and a missional heart, to effectively communicate the Gospel of Christ to a diverse and changing world.[2]
> Morling College values the gospel, people, and education that transforms you . . .[3]
> SMBC is . . . underpinned by a commitment to learning and being transformed in the context of caring community.[4]

Students also expect to experience spiritual development through theological study. In a survey of all ACT coursework students conducted in 2016, 79.7 percent of respondents reported that, when they commenced theological studies, commitment to their own spiritual formation was strong. This is compared to 69.8 percent of respondents who had a strong commitment to train for ordination or to train for a ministry.[5] So, although training for ministry was important to ACT students, a greater proportion of students indicated strong motivation for their own spiritual formation.

The question is whether or not the promise of transformation made by colleges and students' own expectations were met, and if so, how. This chapter reports on the responses ACT students gave to an open question,

---

1. Professional Development Conference, Christ College, 2015; Professional Development Conference, Ridley College, December 4–6, 2019.
2. https://www.mst.edu.au/about-us-2/.
3. https://www.morling.edu.au/.
4. https://www.smbc.edu.au/about/about-smbc.
5. Matthews, "Attrition and Retention," 167.

"To what extent did your studies contribute to a deepened sense of spirituality?" Both Maas and McGrath warn that theological study does not guarantee spiritual development in a positive direction or even an experience of God.[6] There is no guarantee that the claims of colleges and expectations of students for their spiritual development have been realized or that their spiritual formation has not been impacted negatively.

A commonly held belief often heard is that students who have dropped out of theological study and not completed their qualification did so as a result of disappointment with their lack of spiritual growth or even due to a faith crisis as a result of their studies. Given there is no guarantee that students' experience in theological study will be a positive one, this chapter will also explore the question of whether students who withdraw from their studies do so as a result of disappointment in their own spiritual formation.

SPIRITUALITY

As Sheldrake points out, definitions of spirituality tend to be "fuzzy" and spirituality could be understood in a number of ways.[7] The term has also found its way into contemporary culture, adding further fuzziness. In contemporary culture it often refers to a search for meaning and purpose through the spiritual rather than the physical and is not expected to be associated with religion.[8] Although spirituality is seen by many to be an alternative to religion, the term did originate with Christianity.[9]

Definitions put forward by Christian theologians tend to include reference to values and meaning that shape the experience of the Christian life.[10] It cannot be dissociated from the practical outworking of faith and touches the whole of life. Spirituality also suggests an understanding of God and relationship with him.[11] The knowledge of Christian beliefs is foundational to the lived experience of the Christian life, the spirituality of the believer. Transformation of the mind is an essential starting point for spiritual formation (Rom 8:5–8; 12:1–2)[12] and transformation and change in the believer is to be expected and comes as a result of the work of the Spirit.[13]

---

6. Maas and O'Donnell, *Spiritual Traditions*, 11–12; McGrath, *Christian Spirituality*, 6.
7. Sheldrake, *Brief History*, 1–2.
8. Raiter, *Stirrings of the Soul*, 40.
9. Holt, *Thirsty for God*, 3.
10. Sheldrake, *Brief History*, 2; McGrath, *Christian Spirituality*, 2.
11. Wilhoit, *Spiritual Formation*, 23; Sheldrake, *Brief History*, 2.
12. Raiter, *Stirrings of the Soul*, 203.
13. Holt, *Thirsty for God*, 7; Raiter, *Stirrings of the Soul*, 200; Sheldrake, *Brief History*,

McGrath drew many of these elements together and spoke of spirituality as beliefs, values, and the outworking of those in all of life. Spirituality is the means by which Christians deepen their relationship with God. His definition of Christian spirituality, although it makes no reference to the role of the Spirit, does draw together the knowledge and practice that emphasize the whole of life experience of spirituality. His definition will be used in this chapter to discuss students' experience, suggesting a dynamic process including both knowledge of and the lived experience of the Christian faith:

> Christian spirituality concerns the quest for a fulfilled and authentic Christian existence, involving the bringing together of the fundamental ideas of Christianity and the whole experience of living on the basis of and within the scope of the Christian faith.[14]

If spiritual formation comes from God and is the work of the Spirit and must impact the lived experience of the Christian, what is the role of the theological college, an academic institution, in the spiritual formation of its students? Although theological colleges can be simply institutions that study the historical and theological issues of spirituality they also have the possibility of shaping beliefs and values, helping students apply these to their lives as theological lecturers work in cooperation with the Spirit's work.[15] The shaping of beliefs through knowledge of the mind becomes the role of the theological college in spiritual formation. This chapter explores the extent to which the possibility of spiritual formation is a reality for students of the ACT.

METHOD

In 2016 all students enrolled in a coursework award of the ACT between 2013 and 2015 were surveyed. Six hundred and fifty-nine responded to the open question on the extent to which theological study had deepened their sense of spirituality. The question was answered by a cross section of students, including those who had discontinued their studies, and 659 responses is a large enough sample to give insight into the experience of Australian theological students on a scale that has not been studied before. The research took a mixed-methods approach. The questions this chapter is concerned with were analyzed qualitatively using NVivo and results compared quantitatively with the frequencies of other factors identifying students.

2, 3; Wilhoit, *Spiritual Formation*, 23.

14. McGrath, *Christian Spirituality*, 2.

15. Maas and O'Donnell, *Spiritual Traditions*, 18; Ochs, "Functional Absence," 7.

RESULTS AND DISCUSSION

Extent of Spiritual Formation

Although the language used by students to describe the extent that theological studies had deepened their sense of spirituality varied, results indicate that theological study for most students does contribute to their spiritual formation. Overwhelmingly, respondents (72.9%) reported that their studies had contributed positively to a deepened sense of spirituality. Many students used superlative language or referred to a deepening of some aspect of their faith.

> Greatly. Both from the course material studied and the lived example of staff and students.
> Significantly increased my spiritual maturity.
> Very deep extent. Always seems to be perfectly timed according to private journey with the Lord, church friends, unbelieving neighbors, and prayer time.
> Massively helpful and greatly affected my relationship with God.

A further 11.3 percent reported some limited but still positive impact of studies on their spiritual formation. Those who did elaborate on the reasons for limited formation mostly spoke of the pressures of study or the academic nature of study detracting from spiritual formation.

> Somewhat improved my sense of spirituality. Knowing God better though my studies and being surrounded by a Christian community reminds me of what is really important in life.
> A small amount, most subjects were theological so as a part-time student didn't get to deepen personal spiritual aspects as much.
> To a moderate extent. There is a deepening but that has to be held in tension with the grind of producing assessments etc. which means that mostly there is not time to stop and integrate.

Only 4.8 percent of students reported no impact or a negative impact of studies on their sense of spirituality. Again, the academic nature of studies was the most common reason reported for this.

> Left disappointed.
> To be honest my experience has been somewhat negative in this regard. My enthusiasm for Scripture and delight in the gospel was (surprisingly) more pronounced before formal study.
> It hasn't. I find that it is all academic and my personal prayer life and devotional time has suffered.

Eleven percent of answers were unclear; either the students did not know whether their spirituality had been impacted or their answer was unclear. Some expressed enjoyment in theological study but did not respond to the question directly.

Willard made the point that to be transformed spiritually, a person should have an intention to be transformed.[16] It is likely that students' high commitment to their own spiritual formation at the commencement of theological study resulted in their determined effort to achieve formation. However, despite reporting similar intentions not all subgroups in this research experienced formation equally.

Women were more likely to report positively and were less likely to report minimal or negative impact on their spirituality. There was also a difference between the age-groups in reporting the impact of theological study on their spirituality. Students under twenty-four years of age and over forty-four years of age were more likely to report positive impact compared to students in the 25 to 44-year age bracket. Students enrolled at diploma level were more likely to report positive impact of college on their spirituality compared to other course levels. These three factors may be related, as the majority of students enrolled in a diploma course were more likely to be doing so as a gap year after completing secondary education or to be returning to study when they were older and no longer encumbered by other responsibilities such as childcare or paid work. Women tended to be in the latter category. When it came to a commitment to their own spiritual formation, there was no difference found between students enrolled in different courses, between different age-groups or between men and women.

There was a statistically significant difference between the proportion of students studying online and on campus. Students studying online were less likely to report positively and more likely than on-campus students to report negative impact. However, although a couple of students claimed part-time study was the reason they experienced minimal impact on their spirituality, there was no statistically significant difference between full-time and part-time students in response to the extent to which their spirituality had been impacted.

Hussey reported other research also undertaken at one of the ACT colleges in support of the findings of this research that the majority of students were satisfied with their spiritual formation and identified the contribution of college to that formation. The difference reported by part-time

---

16. Willard, *Renovation of the Heart*, 62.

and full-time students was also minimal, suggesting that even when study is not the first priority in a student's life, spiritual gains can be made.[17]

Spiritual Development and Course Withdrawal

Respondents who had withdrawn or taken leave from theological study prior to 2016 were more likely to report negatively when asked about the impact of studies on their sense of spirituality compared to students who maintained enrollment or graduated. They were also less likely to report positively and if positively, to report a limited or minimal growth. It is not possible to determine whether disappointment in their lack of spiritual development was the cause of withdrawal but it certainly may have contributed for some students. However, it should be noted that 62.8 percent of respondents who had discontinued their studies reported a positive spiritual impact and only 10.7 percent reported a negative impact. While disappointment in their lack of spiritual growth may have contributed to some respondents discontinuing their studies, it was not the case for the majority of students who had withdrawn or taken leave.

This does not answer the question of whether theological students withdraw from studies due to a faith crisis or disappointment in their spiritual formation. However, students who had discontinued their studies were asked the reason why. The two most common reasons were work/life/study balance and demands of paid work. None reported that disappointment in their spiritual formation was the reason for leaving.[18] Of course, it is possible that such students did not respond to the survey in the first place.

Type of Impact

This research offered no definition of spirituality to students nor did it seek one from students. Many students did not elaborate on the nature of the impact of theological study on their spirituality and, therefore, offered no clue as to how they understood spirituality. Nevertheless, of those that did, many echoed the themes of some of the common definitions of spirituality, including that of McGrath.

In this research, the most commonly reported type of impact was deepened knowledge and understanding of the "fundamental ideas of Christianity." According to McGrath, theology or the basic Christian beliefs

---

17. Hussey, "Contributors to Spiritual Formation."
18. Matthews, "Attrition and Retention," 186.

form the framework within which spirituality fits as it impacts the lived experience of the believer.[19] One hundred and thirty-six students indicated that their understanding of Scripture and Christian beliefs had improved. This is not surprising, given the nature of theological study and that the learning outcomes of every subject taught are firstly knowledge based.

> Enormous, enhanced my understanding of the Christian faith.
> Huge—understanding biblical theology has provided useful tools in understanding the Scriptures.
> Extensive. Greater confidence due to a tested understanding of the core beliefs and testimony of the Bible.
> College has deepened my understanding of the word of God in a huge way, I know my Bible a lot better since doing Bible college.

Beyond knowledge of Christian beliefs, eighty respondents said their understanding and experience of who God is had deepened, impacting their lived experience of the Christian faith, and fifty-three referred to an improved relationship with God. Some students related a deepened understanding of God to their growing understanding of Scripture. Although it is possible to remain detached from God due to the academic nature of theological study, relationship with God is important in order to be transformed.[20]

> A deeper sense of who God is.
> Each subject brings a deeper layer to my relationship with God.
> I have continued to gain a better understanding of who God is, what he is all about and how deep his love and mercy is. Each subject brings me closer to him. I have more and more love and desire for him.
> I have learned more of God and that brings me to be humble and call on his name for all that I do.
> Deepened my relationship with God by growing and sharing life with other students and God working through the things we studied [to] sharpen, shape and change me.

Holt says that since the 1960s Protestants have understood the term "spirituality" to begin with the lived experience of the Christian.[21] When theology shapes core values and worldview, these in turn determine behaviors. Thirty-two students referred directly to the positive impact on their lived experience of the faith.

---

19. McGrath, *Christian Spirituality*, 28–29; see also Holt, *Thirsty for God*, 4.
20. McGrath, *Christian Spirituality*, 28, 32.
21. Holt, *Thirsty for God*, 8.

> How that applies to my life as a Christian. I feel that I wouldn't have grown to the same extent if I hadn't made the choice to study at college.
> A great deal! It is not simply an academic exercise but impacts all areas of life.
> Each task or assignment has led me to think deeply about my spiritual life, and how to apply what I am learning.

Willard claims that transformation as a Christian is possible with surrender to Christ and denial of self.[22] The experience of theological study had such an impact on thirty-six respondents that they reported personal transformation, suggesting a profound impact on the lived experience of the Christian faith.

> Participating in college as a student and as a person has been transformational in the way I view myself in God's kingdom.
> I think it safe to say I have changed, more likely have had added benefits to my understanding and application of scriptural and spiritual matters as a person.
> A very deep sense—my time at college has been life-changing for sure.
> One hundred percent. Thanks to my theological studies I was transformed!
> Studying at Bible college has completely transformed my way of thinking, reading, researching, and living. Faith affects all we do and who we are, thus, I feel I have a deeper sense of spirituality in that life and faith are interchangeable.

Holm[23] suggested that spiritual transformation only occurs through praxis and that theological education undertaken in the context of ministry rather than in preparation for ministry has greater potential for student growth. Transformation really only occurs when reflection results in action rather than through reflection on ministry alone. For some students in this research theological study was undertaken in preparation for ministry, but for others, mostly studying part-time, theological study was professional development done in conjunction with their ministry. Fifty-one responses related a deepening sense of spirituality to ministry formation or suggested that personal spiritual formation gave them confidence to communicate their faith.

> Has helped develop a framework of life and think critically about all aspects of my spiritual life in order to serve in the church.
> Helps provide framework and knowledge for ministry.

22. Willard, *Renovation of the Heart*, 53, 57.
23. Holm, "Analysis of 'Soul,'" 67–68.

> It has helped me to discern my areas of gifts and weaknesses and led me to apply for ordination and try out new areas such as prison ministry.
>
> Great extent, understanding who God is, and what he has done for me in Christ by the Spirit, as well as my ministry skills/confidence.

Forming Students

Some research, although very limited, suggests that intervention strategies can benefit students' spiritual formation and have a positive impact on other aspects of life.[24] It is possible that respondents experienced a deepened sense of spirituality from simply participating in theological study. However, as reported above, spiritual formation is not guaranteed for all from theological study.

In the Hussey research, students identified research and writing essays, private reading related to study, discussion in class, informal discussion with faculty and other students, learning guide content, and particular units as contributing to spiritual gains rather than other activities targeted at spiritual formation or through praxis in the context of ministry. As Hussey pointed out, ACT colleges could make better use of other activities to enhance spiritual formation, since students are not currently attributing spiritual growth to them.[25]

As discussed above, spiritual formation is the work of the Holy Spirit in the life of the believer.[26] Although some students expressed thankfulness in understanding the role of the Holy Spirit, only two suggested that their spiritual formation while studying was in part due to the work of the Spirit. That does not exclude the work of the Spirit in the lives of the rest of the students, of course.

> Immensely. The Spirit has used study to mature me in my walk with God, in my understanding of his plan and my part in it.
>
> To a fair extent. The material (including readings, as well as researching for assignments) oftentimes challenged or encouraged me, allowing the Holy Spirit to teach me/change attitudes, etc.

---

24. Oemig Dwosky et al., "Winding Road"; Capeheart-Meningall, "Role of Spirituality," 33; Kuh and Gonyea, "Exploring the Relationships," 7.

25. Hussey, "Contributors to Spiritual Formation," 246–52.

26. Wilhoit, *Spiritual Formation*, 23; Raiter, *Stirrings of the Soul*, 197. See also Ochs, "Functional Absence," 7.

Some authors claim that spiritual formation can only happen in the context of relationships with others, in community.[27] Bowman found that the support of faculty and mixing with others who held similar views resulted in spiritual growth for students in US colleges.[28] Forty-one respondents of this research reported that was also true for them. The experience of studying within a Christian community, having fellowship with other Christians and observing the life of fellow students and staff contributed to their spiritual formation. The challenges in creating community through online study may be the reason why online students were less likely to report positively to a deepened sense of spirituality.

> The fellowship with other students like listening to their stories.
> Greatly. Both from the course material studied and the lived example of staff and students.
> Massive. Learnt about the importance of being formed for community, in the context of community and practice the awareness of God for the sake of the world.
> Not sure. As a distance student, I am not sure how well the college can really do that though. It is something that needs to be done in relationship.

McGrath suggests that although there are a number of positive impacts of theology on spirituality, there is a danger that the academic nature of theology can lead to a loss of the relational aspect of faith.[29] He refers to the tension between the relational aspects of spirituality and the detached approach typical of academia. In this research, all of the students who gave a reason for no or limited spiritual growth through theological study suggested that the reason was the academic nature of study and assessments. McGrath suggests that the study of theology is intellectual while spirituality is relational, and while the two can and should enhance each other, the focus on a detached academic approach to theology can draw attention away from the relational outworking of theology in faith, which was the experience of these students.

Some students in this research suggested that the problem for them was that assessments left little time for the reflection needed for spiritual growth, which may also be related to the challenges of maintaining study/life balance, the most common reason given for withdrawing from study.

---

27. Holt, *Thirsty for God*, 8; Ochs, "Functional Absence," 6; Wilhoit, *Spiritual Formation*, 23; Raiter, *Stirrings of the Soul*, 214.

28. Bowman and Small, "College Students," 610.

29. McGrath, *Christian Spirituality*, 32.

Mezirow[30] suggests that critical reflection is essential for transformative learning in adults. As students reflect on their studies the opportunity comes for either affirming preexisting assumptions or in the adoption of new interpretations of past experiences. For some students in this research, the busyness of study and the academic nature of study robbed them of the personal reflection necessary to validate new ideas and be transformed spiritually.

CONCLUSION

For the majority of students, theological study does contribute positively to a deepened sense of spirituality. For most students that meant an increased understanding of the word of God, the Christian faith, and the nature of God, which most definitions of spirituality would include as only one aspect. It is not necessary to complete a qualification in order to make gains in spiritual formation. However, although disappointment with spiritual growth was not the major reason reported for dropping out of theological study, a small proportion of students who did withdraw from theological study also reported no or limited spiritual growth. The major reasons ACT students give for dropping out may be contributing to the lack of growth spiritually. Addressing the academic nature of college, student work/life balance and overall study workload may help to improve the spiritual formation of students.

Since an overwhelming majority of responses indicated that theological study deepened their understanding of the Christian faith and Scriptures, there does appear to be a strong tendency for ACT students to associate theological study with increased knowledge before, or rather than, the lived experience of the faith. The predominant mode of delivery, the lecture, and the academic nature of theological study communicated primarily through the type of assessments may imply to students the importance of knowledge over experience. A question for theological institutions to consider is what aspects of spirituality are most important and how they are best communicated. Theological education can play a positive role in the spiritual formation of students in cooperation with the work of the Spirit in their lives. The goal of a deepened relationship with God that results in a transformation of all aspects of life is one of which theological education should not lose sight.

---

30. Mezirow, *Transformative Dimensions*, 11.

BIBLIOGRAPHY

Bowman, Nicholas, and Jenny L. Small. "Do College Students Who Identify with a Privileged Religion Experience Greater Spiritual Development? Exploring Individual and Institutional Dynamics." *Research in Higher Education* 51, no. 7 (2010) 595–614.
Capeheart-Meningall, Jennifer. "Role of Spirituality and Spiritual Development in Student Life Outside the Classroom." *New Directions for Teaching and Learning* 104 (Winter 2005) 31–36.
Holm, Neil. "An Analysis of 'Soul' as the Central Construct in Dirkx's and Ruether's Transformative Learning Theory." In *Learning and Teaching Theology: Some Ways Ahead*, edited by L. Ball and J. R. Harrison, 62–68. Melbourne: Morning Star, 2014.
Holt, Bradley P. *Thirsty for God: A Brief History of Christian Spirituality.* 2nd ed. Minneapolis: Fortress, 2005.
Hussey, Ian. "The Contributors to Spiritual Formation in Theological Education: What the Students Say." In *Theological Education: Foundations, Practices, and Future Directions*, edited by Andrew M. Bain and Ian Hussey, 241–56. Australian College of Theology Monograph Series. Eugene, OR: Wipf & Stock, 2018.
Kuh, George D. and Robert M. Gonyea. "Exploring the Relationships between Spirituality, Liberal Learning, and College Student Engagement." Bloomington: Center for Postsecondary Research, 2005.
Maas, Robin, and Gabriel O'Donnell. *Spiritual Traditions for the Contemporary Church.* Nashville: Abingdon, 1990.
Matthews, Delle. "Attrition and Retention in Theological Colleges: Why Do Theological Students Discontinue Their Studies and How as Christians Do They Make that Decision." Australian College of Theology, 2019.
McGrath, Alister E. *Christian Spirituality: An Introduction.* Malden, MA: Blackwell, 1999.
Mezirow, Jack. *Transformative Dimensions of Adult Learning.* San Francisco: Jossey-Bass, 1991.
Ochs, Christoph. "The Functional Absence of God in Theological Education." *The Theological Educator* 7 (2014) 1–8.
Oemig Dwosky, Carmen K., et al. "Winding Road: Preliminary Support for Spiritually Interated Intervention Addressing College Students' Spiritual Struggles." *Research in the Social Scientific Study of Religion* 24 (2013) 309–39.
Raiter, Michael. *Stirrings of the Soul: Evangelicals and the New Spirituality.* Kingsford, NSW: Matthias Media, 2003.
Sheldrake, Philip. *A Brief History of Spirituality.* Oxford, UK: Blackwell, 2007.
Wilhoit, James. C. *Spiritual Formation as if the Church Mattered: Growing in Christ through Community.* Grand Rapids, MI: Baker Academic, 2008.
Willard, Dallas. *Renovation of the Heart: Putting on the Character of Christ.* Leicester, England: Inter-Varsity, 2002.

10

Between Two Worlds

The Gospel and the ANZAC Myth

Michael Raiter

ARGUABLY THE MOST RESPECTED and cherished day in the Australian calendar is Anzac Day. Australians from all backgrounds, faiths, and walks of life stop to honor the sacrifices of the brave men and women of all our armed services but particularly those who fought at Gallipoli from April 25, 1915 to January 9, 1916. However, over the decades Anzac Day has grown from a day of remembrance to become an event resonant with religious significance. Since rejecting Christianity, Australia is a nation in search of a faith or civil religion. We are in search of a "metanarrative," the one great story that explains us. In the Anzac myth we have found our origin as a nation (Australia was born on the beaches of Gallipoli), our values, our sense of unity, and a faith in something spiritual and transcendent. This chapter examines how, as "prophetic preachers," we can respond to the current "sacralization" of an esteemed national day.

INTRODUCTION: THE PREACHER'S TWO WORLDS

It has often been noted that Christian preachers inhabit two worlds.

The first world is the world of the Bible. It's the Bible that gives meaning and sense to everything around us. The Bible is the one big story that explains all other stories. It explains our personal, individual stories. It tells us why we crave love and relationship. It explains why we long for meaning in life and why, deep down, we long to live forever. The Bible tells us why our lives are so often full of frustration, disappointment, shame, illness, and heartbreak. Our larger, cultural stories find their proper analysis and understanding in the Bible. The preacher, therefore, spends much of his or her time in the Scriptures.

Secondly, there is the world we have just been describing; the world in which we live. In 1982 John Stott wrote a contemporary classic on preaching. It was called *I Believe in Preaching*.[1] However, the American edition was entitled *Between Two Worlds*. In other words, the sermon is a dialogue between the Bible and contemporary culture.

My first work as a preacher is to exegete the primary text, the Bible. I can't understand my world and speak words of truth into my world unless I understand the Bible. But I must also exegete my world, and my world is twenty-first-century Australia. I need to understand and expose the dreams, aspirations, fears, gods, attitudes, and worldviews of the culture to which I am speaking. I can be sure that, to varying degrees, the people in my church have been shaped in their thinking, feeling, and behaving by the culture, or cultures, in which they are immersed.

My more particular work is to coach and train preachers. I work mainly with pastors, helping them to improve in their preaching. Generally speaking, most are competent at exegeting the Bible. This isn't surprising, since most have completed theological studies. Where we are weaker and less confident is in understanding our cultural context and applying the Bible to that context. We may be aware that there is a spiritual dimension to many of the attitudes, behaviors, events, and festivals of our culture, but identifying and rightly responding to these spiritual realities is much more difficult.

RETHINKING ANZAC DAY

This book is a celebration of a centenary of service by the Melbourne Bible Institute/Bible College of Victoria/Melbourne School of Theology. The college opened its doors for the first time just after the end of the Great War. In this contribution commemorating the college, I want to think about how a preacher of the gospel might understand and respond to what is arguably Australian's chief icon. Anzac Day is now the most celebrated and respected

1. Stott, *I Believe in Preaching*.

of all public holidays. While the whole nation enjoys a holiday at Christmas and Easter, it would not be true to say that the nation "celebrates" these holidays in that they respect and pay homage to their true meaning. Anzac Day is the one day that is nationally honored.

Every year news media send their journalists to Anzac Cove to cover the dawn service. This has traditionally been a day of remembrance, but it has become more than that. It is now an avowedly religious celebration. It has become a profoundly sacred day with all the resonance that accompanies the word "sacred." Therefore, it is an important Australian cultural icon that demands Christian analysis.

It must be recognized that this is a difficult topic for Christians to analyze and critique. It is right and proper to acknowledge the sacrifice that thousands of Australian men and women have made to protect their country. We may have grave misgivings about the rightness of some of the wars in which we have participated, but we can still pay tribute to those who suffered and died.

In this chapter I want to examine the metamorphosis of Anzac Day from a day of remembrance into a day of religious significance, and then think about how we might respond to Anzac Day as those committed to the proclamation of the Christian gospel.

The Facts about Gallipoli

The Gallipoli campaign lasted eight months, from April 25, 1915 to January 9, 1916, when the last soldier was evacuated. The defeat was a costly one. An estimated 27,000 French troops were killed or wounded, and there were 115,000 British and dominion (Australia, New Zealand, India, and Newfoundland) casualties. Of these, 18,500 Australians were wounded or missing and 7,500 killed. Turkish casualties are estimated to have been 109,042 wounded or missing and 57,084 killed.

By the way, it's worth remembering that Turkey expected more than 2.5 million Turks to visit Gallipoli for the 2015 centenary of the campaign. The government portrayed its victory in 1915 as the successful defense of Islam.[2] This is a further reminder to us that it was a major military disaster.

The total number of Australians killed in World War I is reckoned at 62,300, out of a total contribution of 308,000. However, what is often forgotten is that, of those who survived, one half were discharged medically unfit. Of the rest, 60 percent applied for pension help after the war. In

---

2. McKenna, "Patriot Act," 3, 14–15, 16.

other words, of those who survived the war four out of five were, in some way, damaged or disabled.[3]

The Development of the Anzac Myth

The main focus of this chapter is not an analysis of the sobering facts of the high cost that Australians (and many others) paid to fight the Gallipoli campaign, but the later and more recent development of our thinking and reflection upon this campaign. It is the growth of what has been called the Anzac *myth* or *legend* or *saga*.

I was in Sydney on April 25, 2015, the centenary of the Gallipoli landing. There was a dawn service at Coogee Beach. Randwick Council were expecting five thousand people, but twenty thousand turned up. The guest of honor was Major General Andrew Bottrell, who acknowledged that, "There is no doubt that as time has gone by, the legends surrounding our soldiers have become a little bolder."[4] I suspect the word "legend" was deliberately chosen. The facts of the Gallipoli campaign are becoming less and less important. Today, it's what Anzac Day represents more than what it was.

It is fascinating to follow the development of the Anzac myth over the past seventy years.

The First Anzac Day

In this chapter I'm not suggesting that Anzac Day has always been devoid of religious significance. Far from it. The origins of Anzac Day were essentially religious.[5] Within weeks of the landing at Gallipoli the first memorial service for those who died at Gallipoli was held at St John's Cathedral in Brisbane on June 10, 1915. Moses persuasively argues that, "Anzac Day was conceived and organized in a liturgical sense."[6] In fact, the Anzac Day Commemoration Committee, which finally succeeded in the passing of federal legislation in 1930 institutionalizing Anzac Day as a national day of commemoration, was composed predominantly of leading clergy.[7]

---

3. For further statistics, see https://encyclopedia.1914-1918-online.net/article/war_losses_australia.
4. Thompson, "Anzac Day 2015."
5. Moses, "Civil Religion," 26.
6. Moses, "Civil Religion," 32.
7. Moses, "Civil Religion," 24.

The 1950s—A Time of Apathy

Mark McKenna has written a series of articles tracking the sacralization of Anzac Day. He notes that in the 1950s Australians showed almost no interest in visiting Anzac Cove. He writes that, "in 1956, the hills were 'deserted as ever, and packs of wolves still appear[ed] from time to time.'" The war cemeteries were tended by an old Australian soldier, Major Millington, and a handful of Turkish stonemasons and gardeners. Apart from organized tours, there were as few as half a dozen visitors each year.[8] Of course, there may be good reasons for explaining this apathy—if that's the right word. Air travel back then was uncommon and expensive. And spare money was scarce in the years following the Second World War. Further, one can understand why soldiers, weary after fighting two great wars, might not be in a hurry to return to battlegrounds.

The 1960s—The Decade of Cynicism

In 1960 Alan Seymour wrote a powerful and provocative anti-war play, *The One Day of the Year*. It tells the story of Hughie, the rebellious, working-class, university-educated son of Alf and Dot Cook, who damns Gallipoli as an expensive shambles that resulted in men wasting their lives. He labels Anzac Day as just an excuse for a grog-up. "It's just a lot of old has-beens getting into the RSL and saying, 'Well boys, you all know what we are here for, we're here to honour our mates that didn't come back.' And they all feel sad and have another six or seven beers." The play was banned by the Adelaide Arts Festival. It reflected the cynicism of the 60s and 70s against the background of the Vietnam War.

The 1980s—Rediscovering Gallipoli

The 1980s saw dramatic changes in attitudes and popularity towards Anzac Day. The antiwar sentiments fueled by the Vietnam War were disappearing. Australian governments were promoting a sense of national pride. By this time more and more people, especially young people, began to attend Anzac Day celebrations.

In 1981 Peter Weir's film, *Gallipoli*, was released. I remember seeing the film in the cinema and I vividly recall the powerful last shot as Archy Hamilton, one of the two main characters, is killed charging from the

---

8. McKenna, "Lest We Inflate."

trench. The camera freeze-framed the last picture. He flung his arms back as bullets shattered his young body. I recall the cinema audience sat there quiet and stunned. Then everyone slowly and almost reverently left the theater.

In 1985 Channel 9 aired the five-part miniseries, *Anzacs*. It was at this time that we began to debate whether Anzac Day should replace Australia Day as our national day. Given the growing controversy over the appropriateness of celebrating January 26 as our national day,[9] a case could be made that our *de facto* national day is Anzac Day.

The 1990s—The Politicization of Anzac Day

In 1996 John Howard became the twenty-fifth Prime Minister of Australia. From that point on, Anzac Day was given a prominence and meaning that it hadn't had before. Not surprisingly, the debate about the development of the Anzac myth has been heavily politicized. I've no intention of taking sides in this political stoush. Howard's critics on the left argue that Howard rather crassly used Anzac Day as a political tool to garner support for, and stifle criticism of, the invasion of Iraq in 2003. Howard's supporters just see him as appropriately recognizing the sacrifice of those brave diggers who died to safeguard our freedoms. I suspect there's truth in both sides. I've little doubt that Howard was utterly sincere in his sentiments about the Anzacs. However, it's also clear that the Anzac myth was appealed to for support for modern military conflicts like Iraq.

In a speech on Anzac Day 2004 at Baghdad airport, Howard said:

> You are seeking to bring to the people of Iraq, who have suffered so much for so long, the hope of liberty and the hope of freedom, and your example, your behaviour, your values, belong to that great and long tradition that was forged on the beaches of Gallipoli in 1915.[10]

Interviewed by radio presenter Neil Mitchell in 2003, Federal Treasurer Peter Costello said,

> There are problems in the world today, just as there were in 1915. You can't turn your back on them . . . and young Australians, even today, are serving in the Middle East because they want to make a difference, they want to address some of

---

9. January 26 marks the official colonization, and some would say "invasion," of Australia.

10. ABC News, "PM Commemorates."

these problems. And you think back how their grandfathers and great-grandfathers would have felt the same in 1915.[11]

The Sacralization of Anzac Day

The 2015 centenary of Anzac Day saw record attendances at dawn services. At the War Memorial in Canberra, 120,000 attended the service, 85,000 flocked to Melbourne's Shrine of Remembrance, and 30,000 came to the service at Martin Place.

But my interest is in how this event has been clothed with religious significance. Here's my contention: since rejecting Christianity Australia has been a nation in search of a faith, a civil religion. We're in search of a story, what theologians like to call "a metanarrative." We are looking for the one great story or myth that explains us. We seek a story that:

- explains our *origin*—where we came from.
- gives us our *values*—what is it about Aussies that makes us distinctive; that tells us who we are and how to live?
- gives us a sense of *unity*—for all our amazing cultural and ethnic diversity, what gives us a sense of cohesion and a national identity?
- gives us a *faith*—we seek a story which transcends us, which is spiritual and that we can turn to and believe in and use to find strength and courage in times of need. Further, we want "gods," our larger-than-life men (and the Anzacs are men) of whom we can speak in hushed voices of deep respect and somber reverence.

I want to suggest that we've found the answer to all of these spiritual cravings in something that we've created: the Anzac legend.

Our Origins

In an article in *The Sydney Morning Herald*, writer historian Meredith Lake wrote,

> The observation that Gallipoli was a military disaster is beside the point. Anzac serves as Australia's creation story: in proving

---

11. McKenna, "Anzac Myth."

their manhood, Australian men proved our nationhood—a nation was born on that day of death. So, the legend ran.[12]

Similarly, academic Martin Crotty wrote on Anzac Day, 2015:

> Anzac Day is Australia's most commemorated national occasion, and Australia's experience of war, particularly the First World War, has assumed a quasi-religious status in Australian collective memory. Anzac constitutes an almost biblical creation story for Australia, a national equivalent of the Book of Genesis.[13]

It is now recognized that Australia wasn't born on January 26, 1788, when the land was taken from its original owners.[14] The nation of Australia was born on a beach in Turkey where the Aussies proved their mettle. The Anzacs proved that we could stand tall beside the others who fought and died in the trenches of Europe.

Our Values

On the shores of Gallipoli, our values were forged. One "pilgrim" recalled:

> ... the feeling one gets at Gallipoli, of patriotism and pride that these people gave their lives so that we could have the country we have today. They gave us the birth of the individual ... what it is to be Australian ... carefree, hard-working, mates that give anything for (their) friends, that sense of mateship in adversity.

Other pilgrims spoke of how they now "appreciated what it was to be Australian." Many of our cherished Australian values are seen to find their finest expression in the spirit of the Anzac. Values such as "mateship," "a sense of humor," "an irreverence for authority, but doing the right thing," "the ability to do great things for fellow Australians," "perseverance," and the ability to do "what your country asked, even to die for your country." John Hannaford and Janice Newton have described the Anzac spirit as, "a practical sort of Christianity, without pomp and ritual."[15]

---

12. Lake, "Fight Free of Anzac."

13. Crotty, "Birth of a Nation?" Cf. Moses, "Civil Religion," 34, which claims: "the legend has become our very own *origin myth*" (italics his).

14. As I write this chapter the movement to amend the wording of our national anthem is growing. It is argued that the words "for we are *young* and free" should be replaced by "for we are *one* and free."

15. Hannaford and Newton, "Sacrifice, Grief and the Sacred."

In May 2015 Director of the Australian War Memorial, Brendan Nelson, said that young people are "increasingly looking for and finding meaning . . . in the qualities they perceive to find or do find in these men and women." Nelson observed that the example of those who gave their lives "informs in many ways who we are and if you think about . . . what makes us Australians . . . (it) is our values and beliefs and the way we relate to one another and how we see our place in the world."[16]

Probably no one has done more to encourage this sacralization of the Anzac myth than John Howard. He described it as "a creed to which we can all aspire." It is "a great tradition which has shaped the character and the destiny of this country more than any other tradition or influence," and one that occupies "the eternal place in the Australian soul."[17]

The walls of the War Memorial are replete with stained glass windows (which one normally associates with churches and cathedrals). There are fifteen panels of members of our fighting forces. Each window represents an Anzac value. For example, the five windows on the south side represent personal qualities:

- Resource: an airman. These images represent the Australian quality of finding creative and bold solutions to difficult problems.
- Candor: a signalman. This refers to the frank way Australian servicemen and women express themselves.
- Devotion: a nurse. She bears a red cross, the symbol of self-sacrificial love.
- Curiosity: an infantryman. This expresses the reward of knowledge stemming from enquiry.
- Independence: a naval captain. This expresses national steadfastness in the face of war.

The other panels display different servicemen and women who reflect the values of comradeship, ancestry, patriotism, chivalry, loyalty, coolness, control, audacity, endurance, and decision.[18]

---

16. Daley, "Australian War Memorial." Cf. Moses, "Civil Religion," 34: "Anzac Day has become, on the surface at least, Australia's moral compass."

17. McKenna, "Patriot Act."

18. The Australian War Memorial. "Hall of Memory—Stained-Glass Windows." Author, https://www.awm.gov.au/visit/visitor-information/features/hall-of-memory/windows

Our Unity

Australia is one of the most multicultural countries in the world. What gives us a sense of national unity? To some degree it is the Anzac values and the myth that enshrines them. It is interesting to read the testimonies of those who have made the annual pilgrimage to Anzac Cove. They describe "the sense of oneness the group experiences with other pilgrims." They testified to "a breakdown of social differentiation." Age, gender, and ethnic background seemed unimportant because all came together for a common purpose.[19]

Our Faith

We have already described the visit to Anzac Cove as a "pilgrimage." Both the visitors and the media regularly describe it in such terms. People who visit Anzac Cove don't describe themselves as tourists. They testify that they've gone there "to better understand [sic] and experience their most cherished values." One person said, "I was a tourist in Istanbul but the moment we got anywhere near the site we were pilgrims."[20]

John Hannaford has defined a pilgrimage as "a non-local physical journey to a historically and or mythically significant site or shrine that embodies the centre of a person's most valued ideals. These ideals may or may not be theistic but must be portrayed within the limits of the culture."[21] The journey is often associated with some difficulty or hardship. The greater the hardship, the more intense the spiritual experience. Interestingly, some of the pilgrims to Anzac Cove made a point of enduring special physical feats such as climbing up to Lone Pine through Shrapnel Gully.

Many who visited Anzac Cove described it as "a spiritual phenomenon." One pilgrim said, "I feel I could go there every year of my life. It is a time to give myself a moment, just like going to church." Another said, "You get a sense of awe and spirituality about the place."[22]

Observers of the Anzac phenomenon are recognizing—rightly, I believe—that as we jettison traditional forms of religion then we need to replace them with new forms. In Anzac Day we've been given, with the support, approval and financing of the government, a new kind of civil religion.

And, being a religion, the Anzac myth has its cathedral: the War Memorial in Canberra. Paul Daley noted that in 2014 the War Memorial was

---

19. Hannaford and Newton, "Sacrifice, Grief and the Sacred."
20. Hannaford and Newton, "Sacrifice, Grief and the Sacred."
21. Hannaford, "Two Australian Pilgrimages."
22. Hannaford and Newton, "Sacrifice, Grief and the Sacred."

named by *Trip Advisor* as Australia's top landmark, coming in ahead of the Opera House and Uluru. Indeed, it came in at number seventeen worldwide (just ahead of the pyramids, which were ranked at eighteen).[23] The Federal Government has spent more than $330 million on the memorial, and there is now a daily "service" in the memorial to honor the dead.

Finally, because Anzac Day is our national faith, then any taking of its name in vain is blasphemy. The Protection of Word "Anzac" Regulations on the website of the Department of Veteran Affairs warns:

> No person may use the word "Anzac," or any word resembling it, in connection with any trade, business, calling or profession or in connection with any entertainment or any lottery or art union or as the name or part of a name of any private residence, boat, vehicle of charitable or other institution, or other institution, or any building without the authority of the Minister for Veterans' Affairs.

And, as our new creed, it is almost above criticism. Criticizing Anzac Day is tantamount to criticizing Australia. Mark McKenna, one of the few voices that have been raised in alarm, wrote: "It has become an article of national faith and communion, a sacred parable we dare not question."[24]

THE MYTH OF ANZAC DAY

We saw earlier that Major General Bottrell spoke of the "legends surrounding our soldiers," and others speak of the "Anzac myth." It is important to remember that some of the stories of what happened at Gallipoli are based on fabrication.

One famous example will suffice. No one better embodies the Anzac spirit than Private John Simpson and his donkey. He is portrayed as a tough, stoic, fearless, and selfless soldier who, at the cost of his own life, saved the lives of many.[25] He exemplified the finest qualities of mateship and heroism. His deeds have inspired, and been celebrated by, generations of young Australians. His image has graced banknotes, coins, and postage stamps. His story has been told and retold in books, movies, and plays. He's been "deified" (not my word) in paintings and sculptures.

His name was John Simpson Kirkpatrick. Actually, he dropped the "Kirkpatrick" to hide the fact that he was a deserter from the merchant navy.

---

23. Daley, "Australian War Memorial."
24. McKenna, "Anzac Myth," 337.
25. Baker, "Taken for a Ride."

He landed at Gallipoli on April 25, 1915 as a stretcher-bearer with the 3rd Field Ambulance. Just twenty-four days later he was shot through the heart carrying a wounded soldier on the back of a donkey.

The *Sydney Morning Herald* in March 2013 reported on a year-long enquiry by a government tribunal into the Simpson story to see if he deserved the Victoria Cross. The tribunal flatly rejected the claim, concluding "they were unable to find any witness accounts of a specific act of valour ... which could single out Simpson's bravery from other stretcher-bearers in the Field Ambulance."[26] There is no evidence of any lives that he saved. He was a stretcher-bearer, as were many others, and nothing at all distinguished him from the rest.

While researching records, the tribunal heard startling evidence that much of the legend of the man with the donkey had been built on false or faulty evidence. Over the years the facts have been richly embellished and turned into hagiography. Graham Wilson, an official in the awards branch of the Defense Department, has written extensively about Simpson over many years. In a sixty-page private submission he said:

> Just about every word that has ever been written or spoken about Simpson, apart from the bare facts of his civilian life and his basic military service, is a lie.[27]

The historian Les Carlyon, who wrote the highly acclaimed *Gallipoli*, agrees:

> The myths are stronger, and more numerous, than the facts. Simpson became the legendary figure of Gallipoli, not on the peninsula itself, but in Australian and British newspapers months after his death. He was beatified, then canonised.[28]

THE PROPHETIC PREACHER

As "prophetic preachers," how do we respond to the current "sacralization" of an esteemed national day?

---

26. Baker, "Taken for a Ride."
27. Baker, "Taken for a Ride."
28. Baker, "Taken for a Ride."

Anzac Day and the Gospel of the Cross

Many pastors are given the opportunity to speak at Anzac Day services. Some host an Anzac Day service in their church. Anzac Day provides an opportunity to preach the gospel. Anzac Day tells the story of men who gave their lives so we could live and be free. It's entirely appropriate, then, to speak of another man who willingly surrendered his life so others could be free.

Of course, one needs to remember that, in this act of self-sacrifice, there is nothing distinctive in what the Anzacs did. Many others, including the Turks, paid the same ultimate price. Their nation was being invaded. We know that Churchill's goal was the capture of Constantinople, and 57,000 Turks died to defend their nation. But we do see on the shores and hills of Gallipoli, on both sides, remarkable acts of courage and self-sacrifice. In that respect, Gallipoli does point us to the cross.

However, the death of the Lord Jesus Christ on the cross is not just the story of a man who gave his life that we may be free. Here was a man who gave his life that his enemies might be free. Further, Jesus gave his life and won a great victory without raising a hand in anger. Indeed, Jesus raised his arms in glad surrender to the Father's will. The only blood shed that day on the hill of Golgotha was his own.

Exposing the Myth

One of the responsibilities of Christian preachers is to expose our nation's myths. We must unmask our nation's gods for the false gods they are.

Chapters 17 and 19 of Acts record Paul's ministry in Athens and Ephesus in the mid-first century. Both cities were famous as centers for idolatry. It was said that there were more gods in Athens than in the entire country, and Ephesus was the world center for the worship of the goddess Artemis. It seems that Paul's approach was to confront the emptiness of these idols. In Athens he pointed to their statue marked "to the unknown god" (Acts 17:23). I wonder if, in our preaching, we can say this to people: "As I was walking around the Australian War Memorial in Canberra, I saw a monument there to the Unknown Soldier. He is the nameless, brave soldier who gave his life for others. This morning what you respect as 'unknown,' I proclaim to you. There was a man whose name was Jesus and he gave his life that we might live forever."

Of course, there is a risk in that kind of approach. People might think you're being disrespectful. There could be a backlash, as there was in

Ephesus, when there was a riot in the city. But it seems to me that we have a duty to tell our people that the Aussie emperor whom people now worship has no clothes. We are to remind people that our civil religion is based, to a significant degree, on myths and fabrications.

Yes, we must honor those who gave their lives for this country. A day of remembrance is an important day in our national calendar. Moments of silence are appropriate, respectful acknowledgements of the great debt that we owe to these men and women. But, then, we remind them that there is another story. We speak of the "true creation story." It is a story that begins with men and women together in Eden. One of the problems with the Anzac creation myth is that it's a thoroughly man-centered story; women are virtually absent in the myth that gave birth to our nation.

The real story gives us true, universal values, which are much more life-enhancing than the rather facile "mateship," "a sense of humor," and "an irreverence for authority." This is a story that can give us real and lasting unity because it brings together people from every tribe, nation, and tongue. It is a faith that is based solidly on truth.

The Search for the Spiritual

We need to understand the "spiritual" power and appeal of the Anzac myth.

In 2003 I wrote a book called *Stirrings of the Soul*.[29] It was an investigation into spirituality in Australia. At the time, Australia was undergoing a "spirituality revolution." Still today people speak of "being spiritual" and experiencing the sacred. However, if you ask them what they mean by such terms, they become vague. Indeed, it's claimed that, if you try to define the "spiritual," then you've lost it. It's intangible and beyond words. Nevertheless, for almost all human beings, it's real. People believe in the spiritual, not necessarily a world of other beings like gods and angels, but people have a sense of the transcendent, that we are part of something much bigger than ourselves.

While there may be an objective basis, contemporary spirituality is at its heart subjective. The fact is that 7,500 men died on the shores of Gallipoli. But the significance of the event transcends the facts. So what if Simpson wasn't all that history has cracked him up to be? So what if it was a senseless slaughter based on a strategically flawed plan? So what if we were invading another country? What is experienced by the Anzac pilgrims when they visit Anzac Cove is real and, for some, life-transforming.

---

29. Raiter, *Stirrings of the Soul*.

And once you've had that spiritual experience it does two things for you. First, it gives you a sense of connection with others around you who've had a similar encounter. You are "one" with the other pilgrims. Secondly, it helps you to understand your place in the world. You now know what it means to be Australian and you can go home with a more profound sense of your national identity.

This is contemporary spirituality. This is the appeal of the Anzac myth.

CONCLUSION

Let me end with three brief concluding thoughts.

First, I've found the whole Anzac Day phenomenon quite remarkable. It bears out what the Bible tells us. We are made in the image of God and, therefore, made to relate to God. So there is a spiritual vacuum in every person, and no person can live in a vacuum. The question is not "Will you live your life with a spiritual vacuum?" but "What will you find to fill your spiritual vacuum?"

Second, and following on from the first point, to what or whom will you give glory and honor? A nation needs a god, something or someone to worship. Historically, we create gods in our own image, in the image of a mortal human being.[30] And that's what we've done with Anzac Day. While we don't see the diggers as divine, they are our nation's saviors. Therefore, we construct a "dawn service" with hymns, readings, and eulogies in their honor and memory.

Third, our calling, like the prophets of old, is to expose our myths and icons. Of course, it's more complicated and nuanced for us. The Anzacs aren't Baal or Zeus or Hermes. They are confessedly mortal men and we can genuinely admire their courage and acts of self-sacrifice. But as preachers who live "between two worlds," we need, through the lens of Scripture, to exegete, critique, and challenge our society. Then we must turn their eyes to the true Savior of men and women, the one who saves us from the greater enemies of sin, Satan, and death.

BIBLIOGRAPHY

ABC News. "PM Commemorates Anzac Day in Iraq." *ABC News*, April 25, 2004. https://www.abc.net.au/news/2004-04-25/pm-commemorates-anzac-day-in-iraq/175550.

Baker, Mark. "Taken for a Ride." *The Sydney Morning Herald*, March 7, 2013.

---

30. Rom 1:23.

Crotty, Martin. "The Birth of a Nation? Gallipoli, Trial and Trauma." *ABC News*, April 24, 2020. https://www.abc.net.au/religion/the-birth-of-a-nation-gallipoli-trial-and-trauma/10094786.
Daley, Paul. "Australian War Memorial: The Remarkable Rise and Rise of the Nation's Secular Shrine." *The Guardian*, May 19, 2015.
Hannaford, John. "Two Australian Pilgrimages." MPhil diss., Australian Catholic University, 2001. https://pdfs.semanticscholar.org/b8e3/f4c8ff4ea9dfccbef21dd8a17d2af7f915ad.pdf.
Hannaford, John, and Janice Newton. "Sacrifice, Grief and the Sacred at the Contemporary 'Secular' Pilgrimage to Gallipoli." *Borderlands E Journal* 7, no. 1 (2008). www.borderlands.net.au>vol7no1_2008> hannafordnewton_gallipoli.
Lake, Meredith. "Fight Free of Anzac, Lest We Forget Other Stories." *The Sydney Morning Herald*, April 23, 2009.
McKenna, Mark. "The Anzac Myth." *The Australian Literary Review* (June 2007). In *The Best Political Writing*, edited by Maxine McKew, 1–16. Melbourne: Melbourne University Press.
———. "Lest We Inflate: Why Do Australians Lust for Heroic War Stories?" *The Monthly*, December 2012. https://www.themonthly.com.au/issue/2012/december/1363672450/mark-mckenna/lest-we-inflate.
———. "Patriot Act." *Australian Literary Review* 2, no. 5 (June 2007) 3, 14–16.
Moses, John A. "Anzac Day as Australia's 'Civil Religion.'" *St Mark's Review* 231 (April 2015) 23–29.
Raiter, Michael. *Stirrings of the Soul: Evangelicals and the New Spirituality*. Sydney: Matthias Media, 2003.
Stott, John. *I Believe in Preaching*. London: Hodder and Stoughton, 1982.
Thompson, Sean. "Anzac Day 2015: Sydney Remembers Centenary of Gallipoli Landing at Dawn Services Across the City." *Daily Telegraph*, April 25, 2015. https://www.dailytelegraph.com.au/newslocal/anzac-day-2015-sydney-remembers-centenary-of-gallipoli-landing-at-dawn-services-across-the-city/news-story/294c2704d45b5f8e8ea01627d328bc15.

Biblical Perspectives

11

What Does "Mission" in Acts Mean in Relation to the "Powers that Be"?[1]

Steve Walton

THE EARLIEST CHRISTIANS CARRIED out their mission in a world dominated by the Roman Empire. This essay explores the opportunities and problems presented from that context by studying how the book of Acts portrays mission in relation to the "powers that be." Mission is a divine activity leading ultimately to all things being restored. The earliest Christians' engagement with the authorities see Jesus's promises of help fulfilled (Luke 12:12; 21:14–15), and this is seen in Peter and John's appearance before the Jewish authorities (Acts 4:5–22), Paul's engagement with the local magistrates in Philippi (Acts 16:16–40), Paul's speech in Athens (Acts 17:16–34), and in Paul's appearance before Governor Felix in Caesarea (Acts 23–24). These encounters show the early believers testifying to Jesus, challenging the

---

1. This chapter was originally published as a paper in *JETS* 55 (2012) 537–56, and is reproduced here by kind permission of the editor of *JETS*. A shorter version of this paper was presented at the Luke-Acts section of the Evangelical Theological Society in San Francisco in November 2011. I am grateful to the steering committee for their kind invitation to contribute this paper for this purpose.

powers when they acted unjustly, and calling the powers to act rightly when they failed to do so.

My wife and I have recently worked our way through all seven seasons of *The West Wing* on DVD and greatly enjoyed the experience. This is a fascinating series which portrays a devout Christian president of the United States and his staff engaging in the world of politics. One incident caught my attention recently in reflecting on our topic today—for those interested, it is in episode eleven of season four, called "Holy Night," set just before Christmas at the end of President Bartlet's first term of office. A new character, Will Bailey, has been introduced to the West Wing world, and he is now helping Toby Ziegler, the White House Director of Communications, with the president's second inaugural address, presently as a temporary appointment for three months. Bailey is cautious of power and has been working in a hotel and meeting Ziegler in the lobby of the White House to discuss drafts of the inaugural which they are preparing. This is frustrating for Ziegler, and early in the episode Ziegler moves Bailey to the office next to his. They have given the president a draft of a section of the inaugural and get three notes back from the president on this section, for review; what Bailey doesn't know is that one of these notes is deliberately mistaken and is there as a test of whether he will notice it is wrong and say so to the president. Bailey raises his concerns about this "bad note" to Ziegler, but when Bailey has two opportunities to mention his concerns to the president—one alone with the president, and one with the president, Toby Ziegler, and Leo McGarry (the president's chief of staff)—he does not do so. This conversation follows during the second occasion, in the Oval Office:

> "In his defense," Ziegler tells McGarry in front of Bailey, "he caught the bad note. He came to me, he made it important . . . He wasn't distracted by the fact that his office was filled with bicycles."
>
> "Excuse me?" Bailey interrupts. "You said that I caught the bad note?"
>
> "Yeah, that was planted there to see how you'd do telling truth to power," Ziegler tells Bailey.
>
> "Not very well so far," the president muses.
>
> "I have no difficulty, Sir, telling truth to power."
>
> "Okay, except when I asked you to come into the Oval Office," the president says (referring to a previous opportunity), "You said, 'No. No, no. No, no, no, no.'"
>
> "And I was firm in my convictions . . ."
>
> Leo McGarry interrupts. "Can we get back to why you think . . ." And finally Bailey makes his point. "Maybe,"

McGarry says. "But I'm not convinced and that's 'cause you haven't convinced me. This isn't Tillman at the Stanford Club or the California 47th. This is big-boy school, Mr. Bailey. You understand?"

"Yes, sir, I do."

One of the hardest things to do in political life—and in life in general—is to tell the truth to power, especially when the person with power has the power to affect your own life and career. And yet what politicians need around them as advisers is not people who are "yes" men and women, but people who will tell them the truth, however unpalatable. I want to suggest to you that the essence of the way Luke portrays the earliest Christians' engagement with the "powers" of their day is *speaking truth to power*.

Recent study of the New Testament has increasingly engaged with questions of politics, notably how the earliest Christians engaged (or not) with the Roman Empire in its various manifestations, and (more broadly) the human "powers" and authorities in the ancient world.[2] In this chapter, we shall consider the specific question of what we mean when we speak of "mission" in relation to these human powers and authorities.

To ask this question is necessarily to ask what we mean by "mission," both in general and in the book of Acts, and our first task will be to seek a working definition, so that we know what we are looking for. Our question also requires consideration of the range of "powers that be" which are found in Acts, and our second task will be to consider the variety of people and institutions which come under this umbrella. We shall then be in a position to sample some encounters between the earliest Christians and these powers, before drawing some interim conclusions. Our conclusions will necessarily be provisional, as a fuller study would be required to provide a comprehensive answer to our question; hopefully, we shall have considered sufficiently typical examples to enable us to come to interim conclusions which will stand up to further scrutiny.

WHAT IS "MISSION" IN ACTS?

In thinking about constructing a New Testament understanding of "mission," the passages which come most quickly to mind are not in Luke's corpus: they are Matthew 28:18–20 and John 20:21–23. Both include statements by the risen Jesus in which he sends his followers with a task: in

---

2. For examples see Alexander, *Images of Empire*; Allen, *Political History*; Bryan, *Render to Caesar*; Carter, *Roman Empire*; Cassidy and Scharper, *Political Issues*; Rhoads et al., *Luke-Acts and Empire*; Yamazaki-Ransom, *Roman Empire*; Rowe, *World Upside Down*.

Matthew, the task is to make disciples (the imperative μαθητεύσατε is the main verb of the command); in John, the task involves bringing and declaring forgiveness of sins.

Acts 1:8 is sometimes understood to be a similar statement, but it is worth noticing a significant difference from the Matthean and Johannine passages, namely that Acts 1:8 contains no explicit command. Rather, it is a statement by the risen Jesus of what will happen: there is no imperative verb; there is no statement that the disciples are being sent. The same applies to Luke 24:47-49: the verbs there are indicatives, not imperatives—Jesus does not command the disciples to go out, but tells them that they are witnesses of the crucial events of his suffering, death, and resurrection. Let us explore Acts 1:8 further.

Acts 1:8

Several Isaianic echoes reverberate through Acts 1:7-8.[3] Luke reads Isa 32:15 LXX ἕως ἂν ἐπέλθῃ ἐφ᾽ ὑμᾶς πνεῦμα ἀφ᾽ ὑψηλοῦ "until a spirit from on high comes upon you," which is located in a passage about Israel's new exodus restoration, in terms of the Spirit's coming to empower for witness. Isa 43:10-12 sits in a passage about the role of God's servant, Israel (43:1), and proclaims "you are my witnesses."[4] Isa 49:6 speaks of the role of God's servant not only as restoring Israel, but also as "a light to the nations, that my salvation may reach to the end of the earth."[5] Isa 49:6 LXX is echoed in Acts 1:8 and will be directly quoted in Acts 13:47, in the context of the mission turning toward gentiles. These Isaianic echoes signal that the disciples are to take part in God's restoration of Israel (which is the Isaianic servant's ministry) in order to bring light to the nations, in conjunction with Jesus the Messiah (cf. Acts 3:19-21). In this task they are to follow Jesus's example and lead.[6] Empowered by the Spirit, they will reach beyond and through the restored Israel to the world—a servant ministry in which Paul, too, will participate.[7]

Jesus's response here thus reshapes the disciples' assumptions in their question, "Are you at this time restoring the kingdom to Israel?" (v. 6). There is an eschatological hope of Israel's restoration, but the restoration's shape will not be Israel *ruling over* the nations, but *incorporation of* the nations

---

3. Turner, *Power from on High*, 300-301; Pao, *Acts*, 91-96; Mallen, *Reading*, 78-84; Moore, "End of the Earth"; Johnson, "Jesus," 346-49.
4. MT: LXX has "be [γένεσθε] my witnesses"; cf. also 44:8.
5. LXX ἕως ἐσχάτου τῆς γῆς, echoed precisely in Acts 1:8.
6. Luke 2:32; Mallen, *Reading*, 81-82.
7. Mallen, *Reading*, 84-93.

into Israel's hope through Israel's Messiah—the restored and reshaped Israel will *serve* the nations as light-bringer, rather than rule them.[8] It is not, however, that the disciples' Spirit-empowered witness "to the end of the earth" is the substance of the restoration of Israel, but rather that this witness is the means by which the way is prepared for what will become ἀποκαταστάσεως πάντων ("the restoration *of all things*," 3:21).[9] Verse 7 clarifies (in similar vein to 3:20–21) that the timing of this (final) restoration is in the Father's hands. The need for witness "to the end of the earth" implies that the promised return of Jesus (v. 11) will not be immediate.[10]

By contrast (ἀλλά "but," v. 8) with the lack of clarity over the timing of restoration, Jesus expresses confidence over what will happen next: the Spirit will come and bring power for witness throughout the world. Luke signals that the purpose of the Spirit's coming (a coming expressed in the subordinate genitive absolute clause ἐπελθόντος τοῦ ἁγίου πνεύματος "the Holy Spirit having come") is that the disciples will receive power (main clause: λήμψεσθε δύναμιν) for witness. This is the heart of Luke's understanding of the Spirit's role, although it is not the *only* facet of the Spirit's work in Acts.[11]

The disciples' vocation as witnesses flows from the coming of the Spirit: ἔσεσθε is indicative "you shall be" rather than imperative "be!"[12] Jesus makes a promise that the disciples shall be witnesses as a result of divine enabling, rather than giving a direct exhortation to witness.[13] For Luke's readers this saying certainly signals that the heartbeat of the believing community is witness to the gospel, and also that with this great responsibility comes the promise of great power by divine enabling: to this extent Jesus's words contain (as Haenchen puts it well) "at once gift and obligation."[14]

---

8. Cf. Bauckham, "Restoration," 435–87, 477. Buzzard, "Acts 1:6," esp. 203–14 rightly highlights that the disciples' question is a natural one, but does not recognize how much the scriptural hope of Israel's restoration is reshaped in Acts.

9. Bauckham, "Restoration," 476–77; Turner, *Power*, 299–300.

10. Carroll, *Response*, 124 notes that the parallel questions in Luke 19:11 (implied) and 21:7 receive a similar answer which suggests a period of time before the end.

11. Agreeing with what Menzies affirms (Menzies, *Empowered for Witness*) but rejecting what he denies (with Turner, *Power*, esp. 431–33).

12. *Contra* Schnabel, *Early Christian Mission*, 1:371, n. 240, who treats the future as having "imperatival meaning."

13. See the excellent summary, with references, in Turner, *Power*, 92–103. That the Spirit enables inspired speech is a commonplace in Jewish expectation of this period.

14. Haenchen, *Acts*, 144.

Luke stresses the boldness of the believers' testimony at a number of points,[15] identifying their boldness as stemming from divine empowerment (Acts 2:4, 14; cf. 8:29; 10:19; 11:12; 13:2, 4; 16:6–7). Thus Peter confidently announces to the Jerusalemites that they were responsible for killing Jesus (2:29)—hardly the way to win friends and influence people. Peter and John speak boldly to the Sanhedrin (4:9–10, 13). Barnabas and Paul speak boldly in Antioch and Iconium (13:47; 14:3). Paul speaks boldly in the synagogue in Ephesus (19:8), before Agrippa (26:26), and while under house arrest in Rome (28:31).

μου μάρτυρες ("my witnesses") portrays the group both as witnesses who belong to Jesus (and are thus sent and authorized by him) and as witnesses whose testimony concerns Jesus—we need not torture the genitive μου to choose one or other alternative.[16] This phrase suggests that Lesslie Newbigin (in an otherwise helpful article) overstates when he writes, "It is the Holy Spirit who is the Witness, and the Witness of the Apostles (words and 'signs') is subordinate,"[17] for *the disciples are the witnesses*—empowered, for sure, by the Spirit. "Witness" is a judicial term, used metaphorically concerning testimony which these disciples will offer in order to persuade people to come to the right verdict concerning Jesus. The word group is widespread in Acts: the noun μάρτυς "witness" is found at 1:8, 22; 2:32; 3:15; 5:32; 6:13; 7:58; 10:39, 41; 13:31; 22:15, 20; 26:16; the nouns μαρτυρία and μαρτύριον "testimony" at 4:33; 7:44; 22:18; the verb μαρτυρέω "I testify" at 6:3; 10:22, 43; 13:22; 14:3; 15:8; 16:2; 22:5, 12; 23:11; 26:5; and the verb μαρτύρομαι "I testify" at 20:26; 26:22.[18] There are a number of courtroom or quasi-judicial scenes in Acts where such testimony takes place,[19] but "witness" terminology is not restricted to these places.[20] This term's use signals Luke's wider purpose of providing apostolic testimony in writing Acts:[21] Luke does not use "witness" language of the believing community at large, but uses it predominantly as a semi-technical term for ear- and eye-witness testimony to Jesus by people qualified to offer such testimony, principally the apostles (2:32; 3:15; 4:33; 5:32; 10:39, 41; 13:31), but also

---

15. Using παρρησία and παρρησιάζομαι; see Trites, *Concept*, 151–53.
16. Cf. the same *double entendre* in Isa 43:12.
17. Newbigin, "Witness," 82, citing Acts 1:6–8; 5:32.
18. See Trites, *Concept*, 128; Bolt, "Mission and Witness." See 192–94 for helpful analysis of this word group.
19. Acts 4:5–22; 5:27–41; 6:12–7:60; 16:16–40; 17:6–9; 18:12–17; 21:27–26:32; cf. Luke 12:9–12; 21:12–15; see Trites, "Importance"; Johnson, "Jesus," 347–48.
20. Trites, *Concept*, chap. 9.
21. Cf. Trites, *Concept*, 140.

Paul (13:30; 22:15; 26:16) and Stephen (22:20).[22] Hence, the qualifications for the replacement for Judas include the experience which will allow them to give eyewitness testimony (1:21-22), and the preface to Luke's Gospel signals the importance of eyewitness testimony, clearly referring to the apostolic band (Luke 1:1-4). However, Jesus's commission in Luke 24:44-49 does not distinguish between the apostles and those with them.[23] Further, the group being addressed here in Acts, mentioned rather vaguely in verse 6 as οἱ . . . συνελθόντες "those who had come together," may include the larger group mentioned in verses 14 and 21.[24]

Trites helpfully identifies that their testimony in Acts concerns Jesus in at least three senses.[25] They witness to: (i) the facts of Jesus's ministry (1:21-22; 2:22-24; 10:36-42); (ii) Jesus's character of holiness and righteousness which gave rise to his deeds of power and healing (3:14; 10:38); (iii) the Christian faith, in the sense that their testimony calls for a verdict of repentance and trust in Jesus (2:38; 3:22-23; 10:43). Their witness to Jesus is also interpreted in Acts as witness to the kingdom of God (28:23) in continuity with the gospel (cf. 1:3).[26] However they do not "take on Jesus' mantle" in the way that Elisha did after Elijah—the apostles are Jesus's witnesses, not his successors.[27]

The testimony will spread in a series of growing circles which are widely understood to signal the structure of Acts.[28] First, they will testify in Jerusalem (chaps. 1-7); then persecution will drive them into Judaea and Samaria (chap. 8), before the call of the key witness who will go to the end of the earth, Saul (chap. 9), and the beginnings of including gentiles (10:1-11:18).[29] However, Acts does not follow such a structure tidily, since it returns on several occasions to Jerusalem (9:26-30; 11:2-18; 15:4-29; 19:21; 21:15—23:24). This statement, rather, reorders the disciples' perception of

---

22. Bolt, "Witness," esp. 196-210.

23. αὐτῶν (second use), αὐτοῖς and αὐτούς "them" in vv. 36 and 44 include "the eleven and their companions" and the two who walked to Emmaus, v. 33; see Nolland, *Luke*, 3:1220.

24. Haenchen, *Acts*, 142-43; contra Estrada, *Followers*, 47, who maintains that Acts 1 has an exclusive focus on the apostles. For fuller critique of Bolt's view, see Mallen, *Reading*, 191-93.

25. Trites, *Concept*, 144.

26. Del Agua, "Evangelization," 655.

27. Contra Estrada, *Followers*, 96.

28. E.g. Conzelmann, *Acts*, 7; Dunn, *Beginning*, 145.

29. It is noticeable that it is not those present who mainly accomplish the later parts of the mission, to Gentiles. Biguzzi, "Witnessing," 3-6.

space,[30] for the land of Israel—and Jerusalem, and its temple in particular—is no longer central to God's ordering of the world: instead, the whole of the inhabited world becomes "sacred space," for God meets people in the whole world, and Jesus sends his disciples into the whole world.

In sum, this verse clarifies the nature of the restoration of Israel which the disciples ask about (v. 6) by highlighting two features: the restoration will be empowered by the Holy Spirit who will shortly come upon the disciples; and the route to the final restoration of all things will be the Spirit-empowered witness of the disciples. For Luke's readers, there is an implicit call to participate in this task, but (to repeat) there is no call to "go" or sending vocabulary here. Luke's Jesus simply identifies that the disciples will be witnesses to, for, and of Jesus. Thus our central question, about the nature of the early believers' *mission* in the sphere of earthly power, can now be rephrased and clarified as a question about the nature of their *witness* in this sphere.

Luke's "Mission" Vocabulary

All that said, Luke does speak of people as "sent," and he includes commands to "go" and to "speak" at a number of places. Let us explore how those terms contribute to our study.

The theme of being "sent" is fairly common in Luke-Acts.[31] Frequently, *God* is the sender, whether of angels (Luke 1:19, 26; Acts 12:11), Jesus himself (Luke 4:18 [quoting Isa 61:1–2], 43; 9:48; 10:16; Acts 3:26[32]), John the baptizer (Luke 7:27, echoing Mal 3:1), or biblical prophets and Moses (Luke 4:26; 13:34; Acts 7:34, 35[33]). In Luke's Gospel, *Jesus* sends disciples, in the missions of the twelve (9:2), those going ahead of him as he traveled to Jerusalem (9:52), and the seventy (10:1–3). *Jesus, God or the Spirit* sends in Acts: the exalted Jesus sends Ananias to Saul (9:17); Cornelius's messengers are sent by God at the angel's instigation (10:8, 17, 20, 22, 29, 32, 33; 11:13); Barnabas and Saul are sent out by the Spirit (13:4); Paul is sent by Jesus to Jews and gentiles (22:21; 26:17, both in accounts of his Damacus road experience); and the gospel message itself can be described as "sent"

---

30. Sleeman, *Geography*, 70–72.

31. The key terms used are πέμπω and compounds, ἀποστέλλω, ἐξαποστέλλω, ἀπολύω.

32. And, implicitly, in the parable of the wicked tenants, where Jesus is the son (Luke 20:9–19).

33. Cf. again the parable of the wicked tenants, where the servants are surely the prophets (Luke 20:9–19).

by God (10:36; 13:26). In addition, Jesus sends the Spirit on the disciples to empower them for the task of witness (Luke 24:48–49), and Jesus himself will be sent at his return (Acts 3:20).

In addition, Luke's Gospel contains commands to "go," notably in the mission of the seventy (Luke 10:3). In Acts, Philip is told to "go" to a place where he meets the Ethiopian eunuch (Acts 8:26,[34] 29), and Peter is told to "go down" to Cornelius's messengers (10:20)—both are rather specific commands, as opposed to general calls to "go." Paul is told to keep speaking for Jesus (18:9), and Paul's retellings of the Damascus road story include clear statements that Paul has an assigned task (22:10, 21; 26:16). Paul's task of testimony[35] must be carried out in both Jerusalem and Rome, the Lord assures him (23:11).

Luke's use of "sending" and "go" language provides evidence that the mission of testimony is both initiated and empowered by God, Jesus, and the Spirit; it is not a human initiative—rather, as I have argued elsewhere, the believers are frequently playing catch-up with the divine driver who expands the mission beyond the circles and circumstances in which the believers are comfortable.[36]

Summary

Let us draw breath and review the point we have reached. The "mission" in Acts is a divine mission, which will ultimately result in the restoration of all things. It is a mission which will ultimately go to "the end of the earth" (Acts 1:8), a phrase which echoes Isaiah 49:6 and Jesus's statement that the disciples will go to "all nations" (πάντα τὰ ἔθνη, Luke 24:47), and signals the universality of the mission.[37] Such a claim is implicitly critical of the claims of the Roman Empire to govern the world, exemplified in Augustus's claim that he had subjected "the whole world" (*orbem terrarum*) to the Romans (Preface, *Res. gest. divi Aug.*), or Ovid's statement, "The land of other nations has a fixed boundary: the circuit of Rome is the circuit of the world" (*Fasti* 2.684, LCL).[38] What form did the testimony take, then, when it encountered the "powers that be," whether Roman or other "powers" subordinate

---

34. Luke echoes the imperatives ἀνάστηθι καὶ πορεύου "get up and go" (8:26) precisely in Philip's ready obedience: καὶ ἀναστὰς ἐπορεύθη (v. 27).

35. Using διαμαρτύρομαι, a "witness" verb, which incidentally shows that it is not only the eyewitnesses who can testify to Jesus.

36. See Walton, "Acts—of God?"; Walton, "Acts, Book of."

37. See a helpful summary of discussion of this phrase in Schnabel, *Mission*, 1:372.

38. Cf. Acts 10:36; Walton, "State," 26–28; Romm, *Edges of the Earth*, 121–27.

to Rome, such as the Jewish authorities or local officials in cities around the empire? To this question we turn.

THE "POWERS THAT BE" IN ACTS

To speak of the "powers that be" is to throw together into a bucket category a variety of different "powers," and so it is worthwhile first to distinguish these different authorities and their different realms and ranges of authority.[39]

The Roman Empire

At the top of the pile in the first century AD was Rome, focused in the emperor.[40] He, in conjunction with the Imperial Senate, led the Roman Empire, which dominated its territory. In the first century the empire was divided into provinces, some under direct imperial authority and some under senatorial control. In charge of each province was a governor, normally of senatorial rank, supported by a (usually very small) staff under his immediate control. Only in frontier or troublesome provinces, such as Judaea, were significant numbers of Roman troops present, in order to preserve Roman control and political stability. A key member of the governor's staff was the procurator, whose duties could include the collection of taxes, as well as looking after the emperor's interests.[41]

Within a province there would be a number of communities with "city" (πόλις) status, and the nature of this status could vary considerably from one community to another.[42] Among its inhabitants, some were citizens of the city, and a smaller group (often much smaller) were Roman citizens. Philippi, Corinth, and Pisidian Antioch were Roman colonies, all of whose citizens were Roman citizens—many were former soldiers granted citizenship on their retirement from the army.[43] Athens, by contrast, retained the

---

39. Cf. the helpful overview of trials and authorities in the ancient world in Skinner, *Trial*, 13–32.

40. For fuller accounts of Roman administration, see the following: Reynolds, "Cities"; Millar, *Roman Empire*; Gill, "Context"; Gill and Gempf, *Book of Acts*; Lintott, *Imperium Romanum*, esp. chaps. 3–4, 8; Jones, *Greek City*, esp. chaps 4, 8, and 11; Macro, "Cities of Asia Minor." Helpful collections of sources in English translation can be found in: Lacey and Wilson, *Res Publica*; Shelton, *Romans*, esp. sections 10 and 12.

41. Judaea and Egypt were exceptions to this structure in NT times, not having their own governor, but rather a procurator or prefect of equestrian rank: Schürer et al., *History*, 1:358.

42. See Reynolds, "Cities," 23 for a helpful taxonomy.

43. Gill, "Macedonia," 411–13.

feel of a Greek city with the Areopagus as its ruling council.[44] In this case, the Romans had taken an established Greek city and permitted its own civic structures to continue, but now overseen by the governor of the province of Achaia and his staff. As long as the city ran smoothly and peacefully, and Roman taxes were paid promptly, the governor would not be likely to interfere.

Typically, a πόλις in the eastern empire would consist of an urban center which controlled a surrounding territory, usually containing villages under the center's jurisdiction—thus, to think of a modern "city" does not give quite the right picture. When the emperor granted the status of πόλις to an existing place, he would allow the people to appoint (or, in the case of an established city, to continue to appoint) a council (βουλή) which could pass local laws, and to elect their own magistrates annually,[45] who dispensed justice in many matters and had their own subordinate officials.[46] Cities usually had a citizen assembly (ἐκκλησία), but under the Romans it was increasingly subject to the council, which tended to consist of members of the wealthy social elite.[47] Magistrates were frequently appointed from the council members, and on appointment were required to contribute financially to the city's affairs,[48] further limiting those who could afford to be candidates for office.

The powers of these local magistrates, councils, and assemblies were circumscribed by those of the governor. Hence the Ephesian town clerk warns the citizens that the city is in danger of being charged with rioting (Acts 19:40), which could lead to the governor disbanding the citizen assembly, punishing city officials or taking away privileges already granted to the city.[49]

More specifically, cases which could result in death or exile were reserved for the governor's judgment, as well as cases involving Roman citizens,[50] and some cases involving commercial questions or public or-

---

44. Gill, "Achaia," 441–43, 447.

45. Luke gets the designation and jurisdiction of these officials right in place after place; see Hemer, *Book of Acts*, 115 (on 16:22), 119 (on 17:34), 121 (on 19:31), 122 (on 19:35), 123 (on 19:38), 153 with n. 152 (on 28:7).

46. Cicero, *Att.* VI.1.15 (written ca. 50 BC) says that he allowed Greeks to try cases between provincials under their own laws. Methods of election varied considerably across the empire: Reynolds, "Cities," 26–27.

47. Millar, *Empire*, 87.

48. Reynolds, "Cities," 36.

49. Trebilco, "Asia," 344–45 (where examples are given).

50. Macro, "Cities of Asia Minor," 671. Hence the Philippian magistrates are taken aback when they realize they have beaten Roman citizens, thus acting in a case over

der.⁵¹ The governor would travel annually to various cities within his province to try such cases, and others which the local magistrates could not resolve.⁵² In Achaia, Luke records Gallio hearing the Jews' case against Paul in Corinth, the governor's seat (Acts 18:12-17).⁵³ In Judaea, this comports well with John's assertion that the Jews were not allowed to "put anyone to death" (John 18:31).⁵⁴

It is within this setting that the Acts accounts of encounter between the Christians and the "powers that be" should be seen. This limits the number of *direct* contacts between the Christians and the Roman Empire.⁵⁵ Specifically, Paul encounters the proconsuls Sergius Paulus in Cyprus (13:4-12) and Gallio in Corinth (18:12-17), the tribune Claudius Lysias in Jerusalem (22:26-30; 23:16-30), the governors Felix (23:33-24:26) and Festus (24:27-25:12).

In terms of more local officials, we also encounter the magistrates in Philippi (16:16-40), the politarchs in Thessalonica (17:1-15), the Areopagus in Athens (17:16-34),⁵⁶ the Asiarchs and the town clerk in Ephesus (19:23-41),⁵⁷ the client king Agrippa in Caesarea (25:13-26:32), and the first man of the island in Malta (28:7).

Judaea

A particular question is the role of the Sanhedrin in Judaea, presented in the NT as "the Jewish supreme court of justice."⁵⁸ The believers have several encounters with this body in Acts (4:5-22; 5:17-41; 6:12-7:60; 22:30—23:10; 24:20), and its powers seem to have been considerable, although in the first century it was not allowed to administer the death penalty (John 18:31; cf.

---

which they have no jurisdiction (Acts 16:37-39).

51. Winter, *Welfare*, 107-8.

52. See Burton, "Proconsuls," for a careful description of the system of traveling assizes.

53. Most governors had at least one legal advisor among their personal staff (cf. Acts 25:12), whereas Gallio, a noted jurist, gives his own judgment without consulting advisors.

54. Supported by Josephus, *J.W.* 2.8.1 §117. See discussion (and further references) in Beasley-Murray, *John*, 308-10; Carson, *Gospel*, 590-92.

55. See the study of the three most direct Pauline encounters with imperial representatives: Walton, "Trying Paul."

56. See Winter, "Introducing Gods," 75-80, for the role of the Areopagus.

57. As well as the offstage proconsuls, v. 38.

58. Schürer et al., *History*, 2:206; Twelftree, "Sanhedrin," 1063. See Schürer et al., *History*, 2:199-226 and Twelftree, "Sanhedrin" for the debate over the nature of the Sanhedrin(s) and its (their) authority.

Josephus, *J.W.* 2.17.1 §405; *y. Sanh.* 18a, 24b; *b. Sanh.* 41a).[59] The high priest presided over its meetings and, under the Romans, this body seems to have had considerable powers over Judaea, but not other provinces within Palestine (and this may explain why they did not act against Jesus until he came to Judaea[60]). However, Luke presents the high priest as having sufficient authority (perhaps moral rather than judicial) to write letters authorizing Saul to arrest believers in Damascus (Acts 9:1-2). Thus the appearances of believers before the Sanhedrin were significant occasions on which the Jewish judiciary sought to quash the Jesus movement in its infancy, as they had sought to suppress Jesus himself.

Political or Religious?

A key point to recognize is that in all of these levels of power within the Roman Empire, the two categories which we today distinguish, religion and politics, were inextricably intertwined.

Roman officials regularly functioned as priests, offering sacrifice to the gods in order to seek their favor. What Westerners today would consider "political" decisions were taken in the light of auguries, haruspicy, necromancy, and omens. Leaders were expected—nay required—not only to participate in cultic activities, including imperial cultic activities, but also to preside over them.[61]

In a different way, the same was true of the Jewish Sanhedrin. All of its members were significant people within Judaism and their decision-making was governed by the legal framework provided by Scripture and "religious" oral tradition.

---

59. The murder of Stephen in what appears to be a Sanhedrin meeting looks more like a lynching than a judicial execution (Acts 7:54-60). The inscriptions in Latin and Greek in the Jerusalem temple at the edge of the Court of the Women that any gentile who crossed that line was liable to be killed looks, similarly, like a warning against mob action (*CIJ* 1400 n. 85; cf. Josephus, *J.W.* 5.5.2 §§193-94).

60. Twelftree, "Sanhedrin," 1064.

61. E.g. Fishwick, *Imperial Cult*, 360 notes three elements in imperial religion: "dedications to the gods on behalf of the emperor's *salus*, sacrifice to the gods performed by the emperor himself, rites to the emperor modelled on the cult of the gods." Winter in *Divine Honours*, chap. 3 exemplifies these three elements in one inscription from Sardis, *IGR* IV 1756 lines 6-21; I am grateful to Dr. Winter for sharing this material and references with me. Beard et al., *Religions of Rome* document priesthoods and offices as augur held by emperors and senators, including the emperor's role as *pontifex maximus*, intermediary between the people and the gods (1:186-96), and the roles of priestly figures who were magistrates in haruspicy (interpreting prodigies) and augury (establishing the gods' will through various techniques) (1:19-24).

This means that to try to distinguish and separate "political" and "religious" authorities and spheres in the ancient world is to make a category error. The ancient world had them joined inextricably together, and we should not seek to put them asunder. Peter Oakes provides a helpful example in considering a (reconstructed) family who were bakers in Philippi.[62] Half their bread is sold to three well-off families from the social elite as a regular order; the rest is sold from their shop. Simias, the father of the family, is a member of a burial club which provides for its members to have a good burial, paid for by a regular subscription. At club meetings, Simias meets other bakers and these contacts are very helpful if they get a big order and he suddenly needs extra oven space. The burial club meets for meals on the anniversaries of the death of former members, eats together at the former member's tomb, and prays to the gods for their dead friend. What would it mean for such a family to become Jesus-believers? Simias would either withdraw from the burial club or miss meetings on anniversaries of death, since he would no longer be willing to participate in prayer to the gods. This would damage his friendship with others in the club, and that alone might lead to some of his regular customers withdrawing their trade and buying their bread elsewhere. It would also mean that fellow bakers refused to help him when he needed extra oven space for a big order, so he would lose trade. Problems would arise at the shop, too. Simias and Ianthe, his wife, would remove the shrine of the god popular among bakers from the counter of their baker's shop, and this would rapidly be noticed by their customers and people would mutter that they were dishonoring the gods. The effect would be that people would assume the baker's family were now being disloyal to the city of Philippi—for they were disloyal to a town god—and thus people would stop buying bread in their shop, probably including at least one of the three elite families who are their biggest customers. In addition, their regular supplier of flour would stop supplying them so that they had to buy from another supplier at about 10 percent extra cost. Oakes's example is more extended, but this gives you the picture that for this family to become Jesus-believers would be costly, both economically and socially, precisely because the "religious" and "political" spheres were so intertwined in a city like Philippi.

THE BELIEVERS ENCOUNTERING THE "POWERS THAT BE"

We turn, then, to sample encounters between the believers and the authorities. After noting Lukan promises of help by the Spirit or Jesus when the

---

62. Oakes, *Philippians*, 89–93.

disciples encounter the powers, we shall briefly consider key features of engagement with Jewish authorities (Peter and John before the Sanhedrin), city authorities (Paul before the Areopagus and in Philippi), and imperial representatives (Paul before Felix), before drawing together some key features which emerge from these stories.

The Promises of Jesus in Luke's Gospel[63]

Luke's Jesus twice promises his disciples help when they are in front of the powers, in Luke 12:12 and 21:15.

Luke 12:12 appears in teaching about the importance of public confession of Jesus (12:8-10) and particularly in the context of trials before the authorities (12:11a). This teaching is addressed in the first instance to his disciples (12:1a) with the crowd overhearing (12:1b). In that setting, Jesus assures his disciples that the Spirit will teach them what to say (12:12) and thus that they need not worry in advance about how to defend themselves (12:11b).

There are parallels to Luke 12:12 in the other Synoptic Gospels (Matt 10:19-20; Mark 13:11) and Luke himself has an interesting parallel (21:12-15; cf. Matt 24:9-13). There are clear similarities and differences among these four passages: (i) all are placed in a context of trial, although there is considerable variation in the specified authorities; (ii) structurally, Luke 12, Matthew 10, and Mark 13 begin with a generalizing ὅταν ("whenever") clause, whereas Luke 21 does not, for this seems to refer to a *specific* time of trials; (iii) Jesus calls his disciples not to worry (μὴ μεριμνήσητε/προμεριμνᾶτε) in advance in Luke 12, Mark 13, and Matthew 10, whereas Luke 21 simply specifies that the disciples must not prepare (μὴ προμελετᾶν) in advance; (iv) Luke 12, Matthew 10, and Mark 13 mention the Spirit as the one who will give the disciples words to say (although Matthew alone specifies that it is the Father's Spirit), whereas Luke 21 says that Jesus himself will give them words to speak; (v) Luke alone (in 12:11 and 21:14) uses the language of "defense" (ἀπολογέομαι), a word found only in these passages in Luke and only here in the Gospels, although it is also used in Acts in forensic contexts.[64]

The Lukan promises are specific to the situation of judicial trial before authorities (Luke 12:11; 21:12), and thus stand alone among the promises of the Spirit to the disciples in the Synoptic Gospels in being situation specific. Other Spirit promises (granted that there are not many) are more

---

63. See a fuller discussion of these promises in Walton, "Whose Spirit?"

64. Acts 19:33; 24:10; 25:8; 26:1-2, 24; the only other NT uses are Rom 2:15 and 2 Cor 12:19.

general, concerning the role of the Spirit in equipping the disciples as witnesses to Jesus (notably Luke 24:49). Jesus's assurance of the Spirit's help in judicial trials prepares for the trials of believers in Acts, where Luke draws attention to the Spirit filling Peter and John when they respond to the charges against them in the Sanhedrin (Acts 4:8), and also Stephen on trial (Acts 7:51, 55; cf. 6:9-10).[65]

The parallel promises in Luke 12:12 and 21:14-15 are suggestive, too, for the relationship of Jesus and the Spirit. Both relate the promise of aid during trials to the instruction not to prepare a defense in advance, both use the rare ἀπολογέομαι ("I defend"), and both explain the basis of this statement with a γάρ ("for") clause. However, the one providing the aid in 12:12 is the Spirit, whereas in 21:15 it is Jesus himself (emphatic ἐγώ, "I myself"). This theme develops and expands in Acts, for while often it is the Spirit who empowers and leads the disciples in witness (Acts 4:8-12; 6:10; 8:29; 10:19; 13:2-4), sometimes it is Jesus (Acts 7:55-56; 9:4-5, 10-16; 18:9-10; 22:7-10, 17-21; 23:11; 26:14-18).[66] It is thus hard to agree with Green, if his implication is that it is *exclusively* by the Spirit that Jesus will be present to his disciples, when he writes:

> ... Jesus thus portends his continual presence with the disciples even as they face the tribunal, following his death; only with the onset of Acts we understand fully that he will be present to the community of his followers by means of the Holy Spirit poured out among them.[67]

Buckwalter points to an interesting parallel: in the OT, action by YHWH from heaven is described in similar terms to action by the Spirit, and YHWH is not limited to appearing on earth *as or by* the Spirit; in Luke-Acts, action by *the exalted Jesus* from heaven is described in similar terms to action by the Spirit, and again, Jesus is not limited to appearing on earth *as or by* the

---

65. Both Fitzmyer (*Luke*, 2:966) and Bock (*Luke*, 2:1144) draw attention to the immediacy of the promise (ἐν αὐτῇ τῇ ὥρᾳ "in that very hour," v. 12) and compare Philo's retelling of the angel's instruction to Balaam: "Go on in the journey in which you have set out, for you shall do no good to those who have sent for you, and you must say what I prompt you, without any thoughts of your own, finding utterance, as I will guide the organs of your speech in the way that shall be just and expedient, for I will direct your words, predicting all that shall happen through the agency of your tongue, though you yourself understand nothing of it" (*Moses* 1:274). Philo goes on to tell how "the prophetic spirit entered" Balaam (προφητικοῦ πνεύματος ἐπιφοιτήσαντος, 1:277) with the result that he prophesied (θεσπίζει, 1:278). However, this is not strictly parallel, since it is about prophetic inspiration, rather than inspiration when on trial.

66. See discussion, Buckwalter, *Character*, 197-204.

67. Green, *Gospel of Luke*, 737.

Spirit.[68] It is thus plausible that the parallel actions of Jesus and the Spirit in empowering and enabling speech when the disciples are on trial (in Luke 12 and 21) entail a relationship of Jesus in relation to the Spirit which is similar to that of YHWH and the Spirit.[69] Not only that, but the ability of the exalted Jesus to be present with disciples in different times and places when they are on trial shows Jesus (and the Spirit) to have the same multi-locational ability as YHWH.[70]

Peter and John Before the Jewish Authorities (Acts 4:5–22)

Peter and John appear before the Sanhedrin in Acts 4:5–22 as a result of the healing of the man at the Beautiful Gate (3:1–10). The question put to them is, "By what power or by what name did you do this?" Luke then records the Spirit's enabling to do this before they respond (v. 8). The Sanhedrin's question both invites and enables them to focus on witness directly about Jesus in their response. They address the Sanhedrin respectfully, as "Rulers of the people and elders,"[71] and then assert that it is through Jesus that the man has been healed. Not only that, but they boldly identify the Sanhedrin's part in Jesus's death, "whom *you* (emphatic ὑμεῖς) crucified." Jack T. Sanders mistakenly understands this as placing responsibility for Jesus's death on the Jewish people as a whole,[72] whereas verses 5–6 make it clear that it is the Jewish leaders in Jerusalem who are in view here.[73] The greatness of their error is highlighted by the contrasting divine verdict: God raised Jesus from the dead. Peter calls on Ps 117:21 LXX (MT 118:22) as witness to the crucial place which Jesus now has, as "head of the corner," after being rejected by "*you* builders"—the insertion of ὑμῶν into the biblical citation hammers the contrast of verdicts home.

The evident boldness of Peter and John causes comment (v. 13), and clearly comes from their sense of compulsion to speak (v. 20). Verse 29 will further clarify that such boldness is a divine gift flowing from being filled with the Spirit (v. 31). This boldness stops the Sanhedrin in its tracks, and they go into private session to decide what to do. Their discussion is striking

---

68. Buckwalter, *Character*, chap. 8.

69. Buckwalter, *Character*, 203–4.

70. Stein, *Luke*, 518–19. He goes on to suggest that we should therefore "describe Jesus as possessing an *essence* different from others" (519, his italics).

71. This phrase functions as a *captatio benvolentiae* and is respectful without being fawning. Soards, *Speeches*, 45.

72. Sanders, *Jews*, 238–39.

73. See also Weatherly, *Jewish Responsibility*, 69; Skinner, *Trial*, 111.

for its lack of mention or consideration of God and God's purposes, by contrast with the bold speech of Peter and John. They cannot even bring themselves to mention the name of Jesus: they use "that name" (v. 18) instead.

By contrast with the Sanhedrin's failure to speak about God, Peter and John identify the issue as being what God wants (v. 19). Thus the apostles turn the tables on the Sanhedrin by speaking truth to power: they have Peter and John on trial, but the apostolic κρίνατε ("you judge!") puts the Sanhedrin on trial concerning their assessment of Jesus. The issue is not just their assessment of Jesus, but also their impotence in the face of what God is now doing: they lack any legal ground to punish the apostles and their verdict is at variance with the people's (v. 21). The apostles are those who speak for God, rather than the Sanhedrin. Haenchen rightly notes that Luke wishes to bring

> . . . home to the reader the justice and obligation of preaching Christ, and showing from the example of the apostles . . . how the Christian, certain of divine assistance, should fearlessly bear witness for his Lord, unquelled by police, arrest or official interdict.[74]

Philippi: Engagement with Local Magistrates (Acts 16:16-40)

By contrast with the plain speaking of Peter and John in Jerusalem, Paul and Silas are silent in what passes for a trial in Philippi. Here, they are attacked because of the economic consequences of Paul's deliverance of the slave girl who has a "python spirit" (Acts 16:16-19). The owners of the slave girl have lost their source of income because she can no longer do divination for fees, and their (carefully chosen) claim against Paul and Silas is that they are advocating Jewish customs which Roman law prohibits (vv. 20-21). In the midst of what seems to be a disorderly crowd situation (v. 22a), Luke does not record any speech by Paul and Silas—after addressing the spirit to deliver the girl (v. 18), their next words in the story are to sing hymns to God (v. 25), not to address any human audience. After they receive a flogging, Paul and Silas are put in the innermost part of the prison (v. 24), presumably for security. However, God acts in an earthquake which opens the doors, and we next hear Paul and Silas speak in response to the jailer's question, "What must I do to be saved?," in response to which they lead him to faith in Jesus and baptize him and his household.

74. Haenchen, *Acts*, 223-24.

Verse 40 suggests that Paul and Silas return to prison after eating at the jailer's home; it is there, on the next morning, that the magistrates (οἱ στρατηγοί) seek to have them leave quietly. They send the lictors (ῥαβδοῦχος, v. 35) as messengers, and the jailer relays the message to them (v. 36). It is at this point that Paul engages the magistrates and sends a message back to them to the effect that they have acted unlawfully in beating Roman citizens without proper trial and imprisoning them, and that he is not now willing to leave quietly (v. 38). What is going on here? Why does Paul now seem to stand on his dignity, rather than earlier in this story? It may be partly that the earlier "trial" moved so speedily that it was not possible to object, but it is more significant that it is only following the earthquake that the magistrates decide to free Paul and Silas, and their desire to send them away quietly is designed to avoid the embarrassment of admitting that divine action by Paul and Silas's god had persuaded them that they should release the two men—at this point, they do not know that Paul and Silas are Roman citizens. Thus Paul wants to insist that the earthquake demonstrated that God has vindicated him and Silas against the city authorities, and plays the card of Roman citizenship to force the authorities to come and apologize. Here is speaking truth to power which is double-edged. There is a delicious irony in this about-turn, for the charge against Paul and Silas was anti-Roman behavior (vv. 20–21) and the authorities have to apologize for *their* anti-Roman behavior (vv. 38–39).

Paul and Silas thus insist on the claims of God and the name of Jesus not being marginalized by the city authorities; these believers are prepared to require the authorities to act justly, and this should be seen as much a part of Paul and Silas's testimony to Jesus as Paul's deliverance of the slave girl "in the name of Jesus the Messiah" (v. 18).

Athens: Paul Before the Areopagus (Acts 17:16–34)

The powers of the Areopagus in Athens as the "standing committee" of the citizen assembly (the *Demos*) were considerable and included jurisdiction over the introduction of new gods into the city and therefore over the construction of new temples. In an important article, Bruce Winter argues that this power is a key context for Paul's speech to the council.[75] Paul, Winter argues, would have been perceived as seeking to introduce new gods into the city: "He seems to be a proclaimer of foreign deities" (Acts 17:18), and it may be that he was seen as proclaiming Jesus and Anastasis as two gods. The Athenians took Paul to the Areopagus, and the council there stated that they

---

75. Winter, "Gods," citing Garland, *Introducing*.

had the legal right (δυνάμεθα = "we have the power") to decide (γνῶναι = "to form a judgment") (v. 19). They go on in verse 20 to say that they wish to make a judgment on what is being claimed by Paul. This is a polite enquiry, not a prosecution.[76] The council is concerned whether Paul's new gods could be acceptable to join the Athenian pantheon. Were the Areopagus to accept Paul's gods—or recommend to the *Demos* that they do so—Paul would be expected to purchase land, build a sacrificial altar, defray the costs at least of an annual dinner in the god's honor, and probably also of cultic officials.

Paul's speech in Athens takes on a new light in responding to their question if understood this way, for he declares that he is not introducing new gods, but one they already worship, albeit as "unknown" (v. 23). There was no requirement to acquire land for this god, for Israel's God was the creator of all land (v. 24a)—indeed, this god did not live in handmade temples (v. 24b), and so it was pointless to consider building a new temple for him. Paul thus undercuts the assumptions of the council and denies that there is any need for further evidence for them to honor this god among their pantheon, for this god provides for all and does not need human attendants (v. 25). The quest for more gods to add to the statues in Athens was a mistake (v. 29).

Paul turns the tables on his interlocutors, for he asserts that the resurrection of Jesus—ironically—shows that the council, rather than making judgments *about* gods, faces judgment *from* the one true God through Jesus (vv. 30–31).

Luke thus presents Paul as undermining the worldview of his hearers and offering them a replacement worldview drawn from Jewish monotheism re-understood in the light of Jesus's resurrection. Thus witness to Jesus in Athens in front of the Areopagus, a political body, involves speaking truth to power in the form of argument about worldview, including engagement with and critique of the council's assumptions. The speech is apologetic, but not as we often think of apologetics in today's world and situations, for it does not involve argument about Jesus and his identity—those things are assumed and asserted, rather than argued.

Paul Before the Governor Felix in Caesarea[77]

Felix enters the story of Acts as governor (technically, procurator) of Palestine who meets Paul after his arrest in Jerusalem. The tribune Claudius

---

76. Winter, "Gods," 83.
77. See fuller discussion in Walton, "Trying," 132–36.

Lysias sends a letter to brief Felix on Paul's case (Acts 23:26–30)—a letter which is rather economical with the truth, although it does make clear that the tribune regards the issue as an intra-Jewish matter which does not merit any serious penalty being applied to Paul (v. 29).

What we know of Felix from extra-biblical sources suggests that he could be a harsh governor who did not hesitate to use military means to keep the peace, and who was willing to cooperate with the *sicarii* terrorists to have the high priest killed.[78] However, Tertullus's positive introduction that seeks Felix's goodwill and attention (*captatio benevolentiae*, 24:2b–3[79]) is neither mere flattery nor simply disingenuous. Ananias, the high priest who led the delegation to Felix (24:1), and Ananias's predecessor Jonathan had pressed Claudius to appoint Felix as procurator.[80] It was an unusual appointment for a mere freedman rather than someone of equestrian rank.[81] The Jewish delegation was thus compelled to support Felix's administration. Further, not long before this, Felix had brought peace following a rebellion led by an Egyptian.[82] Tertullus's comments (24:2) may allude to this incident.

Luke presents Felix as acting properly, at least initially, in handling Paul's case. First, he establishes whether Paul falls under his jurisdiction by enquiring which province he comes from (23:34). Cilicia was probably at this time under the legate of Syria, Felix's line manager. So for Felix to fail to hear the case and pass it on to the legate of Syria would be to risk appearing to waste the legate's time with a minor matter[83]—even though the transfer of an accused person to his own province was optional at this time.[84]

Second, Felix wishes to hear firsthand from Paul's accusers (23:35a; cf. 25:16), as was normal in Roman law.[85] Paul's defense speech (24:10–21) initially focuses on the charges made against him and denies that they are valid (vv. 12–13). Paul then turns to testify to his faith as a valid form of

---

78. Respectively, Josephus, *Ant.* 20.8.7 §§173–78; *J.W.* 2.13.7 §§266–70 and *Ant.* 20.8.5 §162; *J.W.* 2.13.3. §§254–57. See the helpful brief treatments in Rapske, "Roman Governors," 982–83; *ABD* 2:783 and, more fully, Gill, "Roman Policy"; 21–26.

79. Winter, "Importance."

80. Tacitus, *Ann.* 12.54; Winter, "Importance," 515–16; Bruce, *New Testament*, 325.

81. Claudius Lysias and Tertullus address Felix as "most excellent" (κράτιστος, 23:26; 24:3), a title undoubtedly used for those of equestrian rank, but not exclusively for such people (Alexander, *Preface*, 133; Foakes Jackson and Lake, *Beginnings*, 2:505–7).

82. Josephus, *J.W.* 2.13.5. §§261–63; Acts 21:38.

83. Sherwin-White, *Society*, 55–57; Rapske, *Book of Acts*, 155. Cilicia was probably not formally a province at this time, but this distinction does not affect the point noted.

84. Sherwin-White, *Society*, 55.

85. Sherwin-White, *Society*, 17; Tajra, *Trial*, 115.

Judaism, worshipping the God of the Jewish ancestors and holding to the Jewish Scriptures (v. 14), and a faith which entails resurrection hope (v. 15). Paul makes the point that at least some of the accusers are not present (24:19), thus implying that the charges were invalid.[86] Their absence is reflected in the reduced claims that Tertullus makes, asserting only that Paul "attempted" to profane the temple (ἐπείρασεν, 24:6), whereas the missing Asian Jews had claimed that Paul "had defiled" the temple (κεκοίνωκεν, 21:28).

Felix then acts within his powers in deciding to await testimony from the tribune Lysias (24:22), since he needs advice to help him decide between the two contradictory testimonies he has heard.[87] Luke does not tell us whether Felix was able to consult Lysias or whether a consultation took place but was inconclusive. Whatever the case, Paul remained in custody at Governor Felix's pleasure (as the British judicial system charmingly puts it). In the situation of waiting for Lysias's testimony, Felix can afford to relax Paul's conditions of detention, and so he does (24:23).[88]

Strikingly, Paul's confinement does not prevent him from testifying to the gospel, for Felix wishes to hear him on the subject on numerous occasions (24:24–26), thus partially fulfilling the Lord's word to Paul (23:11). As Skinner notes, this situation gives Paul access to some of the most powerful people in Judaea.[89] Thus Paul the prisoner is Paul the *missionary*-prisoner.[90]

Paul persists in being Jesus's witness with Felix, speaking about "faith in Jesus the Messiah" (24:24), but the deal breaker for Felix seems to be the moral demands of Paul's testimony. Felix becomes fearful at Paul's talk "concerning righteousness and self-control and judgment to come" (24:25) and therefore sends Paul away. These qualities imply a call to repent, a key feature of evangelistic proclamation in Acts.[91] However, they may be particularly apposite for Felix as a governor who should act with righteousness and self-control, but had deceptively drawn Drusilla away from her former husband into his arms.[92] Self-control (ἐγκράτεια) may thus focus here on *sexual* self-control.[93] In this light, "judgment to come" would be an unwelcome thought to Felix if his conscience was at all sensitive to what Paul said. Paul is portrayed here as "turning the tables" on Felix, his judge,

---

86. Johnson, *Acts*, 417; Fitzmyer, *Acts*, 737.
87. Sherwin-White, *Society*, 53.
88. On the possible nature of the relaxation of conditions, see Rapske, *Book*, 167–72.
89. Skinner, *Locating Paul*, 137–38.
90. The expression is from Rapske, *Book*, e.g. 429–36.
91. E.g. 2:38; 3:19; 5:31; 11:18; 17:30; 20:21; 26:20.
92. Josephus, *Ant.* 20.7.1 §§141–44; Schneider, *Die Apostelgeschichte*, 2:351–52.
93. BDAG 274 s.v.

by speaking to Felix of the values which (ironically) should be guiding his judgment.[94] Testimony to Jesus involves speaking uncomfortable truth to power at times.

Not only that, but testimony to Jesus involves rejecting underhand ways out, for Felix hoped for a bribe from Paul, and not just on one occasion, but repeatedly (24:26).[95] This was not uncommon among judges in the Roman Empire,[96] although illegal under the *Lex Iulia de Repetundis*.[97] Luke takes a dim view of it,[98] for it results in Paul continuing to be held even though the tribune Lysias had written to Felix that Paul had not committed any crime worthy of death or imprisonment (23:29). As is often the case in Luke-Acts, how possessions are handled is an index of a person's standing with God,[99] and on that index Paul's stock is high and Felix's is low.

Summarizing What We Have Seen

We have seen the earliest believers engaging in a variety of contexts with the powers-that-be. Of necessity, we have sampled rather than attempted to be exhaustive, but some themes come through consistently and clearly concerning the shape which speaking truth to power—witness to and for Jesus—takes in these encounters.

First, testimony about Jesus himself is normally present, usually including some key moments from the gospel story being told or mentioned, notably Jesus's death, resurrection, understood as vindication by God, and his coming again to judge.

Secondly, believers speaking truth to power can involve direct attribution of responsibility for Jesus's death, as Peter and John do in Jerusalem.[100] The believers' testimony to the powers involves telling the powers when

---

94. Cf. Cassidy, *Society*, 106.

95. Although πυκνότερον is formally a comparative form, the lack of anything to compare suggests a superlative sense, meaning "very often" (with MHT, 3:30; Barrett, *Critical*, 2:1116; *pace* BDF §244[1], who assert it to be ambiguous).

96. E.g. Albinus, as reported by Josephus, *J.W.* 2.14.1 §§272–73. Rapske, *Book*, 65–67 lays out the evidence for such corruption in the judicial system.

97. Introduced in 59 BC to prevent corruption of this kind in the provinces; see Tajra, *Trial*, 131.

98. Gaventa, *Acts*, 330 suggests that Felix is portrayed in the image of the unjust judge of the parable (Luke 18:1–8).

99. For discussion of this theme in Luke, see Johnson, *Literary Function*, 144–58.

100. Note the shift from "you" bearing this responsibility when speaking in Jerusalem (Acts 4:10–11) to speaking of "them"—the Jerusalemites and their rulers—as hearing that responsibility when speaking in Antioch (Acts 13:27–29).

they have committed sin, and in this case sin of enormous magnitude. We have suggested that a similar theme is present in the scenes in Athens and with Felix.

Thirdly, testimony to Jesus can involve calling the powers to act justly when they fail to do so, as Paul does with the magistrates in Philippi and with Felix in Caesarea. This is not only because to get them to act justly will (as we might say) open more doors for the gospel, but also (I suggest) because justice itself is part of the gospel the believers proclaim, for it is a key feature of the Christian God's character and a key Christian hope for the world to come; by contrast, injustice, in the sense of distinguishing between citizens and non-citizens, between elite and non-elite, was just the way the world was.

BIBLIOGRAPHY

Alexander, Loveday. *The Preface to Luke's Gospel: Literary Convention and Social Context in Luke 1.1-4 and Acts 1.1.* SNTSMS 78. Cambridge: Cambridge University Press, 1993.

Alexander, Loveday, ed. *Images of Empire.* JSOTSup 122. Sheffield: JSOT, 1991.

Allen, Brent. *A Political History of Early Christianity.* London: T. & T. Clark, 2009.

Barrett, C. K. *A Critical and Exegetical Commentary on the Acts of the Apostles.* ICC. 2 vols. Edinburgh: T. & T. Clark, 1998.

Bauckham, Richard. "The Restoration of Israel in Luke-Acts." In *Restoration: Old Testament, Jewish and Christian Perspectives,* edited by James M. Scott, 435–87. JSJSup 72. Leiden: Brill, 2001.

Beard, Mary, et al. *Religions of Rome.* 2 vols. Cambridge: Cambridge University Press, 1998.

Beasley-Murray, George R. *John.* WBC 36. Dallas, TX: Word, 1987.

Biguzzi, Giancarlo. "Witnessing Two by Two in the Acts of the Apostles." *Biblica* 92 (2011) 1–20.

Bock, Darrell L. *Luke.* IVPNTC. Downers Grove: IVP, 1994.

Bolt, Peter. "Mission and Witness." In *Witness to the Gospel: The Theology of Acts,* edited by I. Howard Marshall and David Peterson, 191–214. Grand Rapids: Eerdmans, 1998.

Bruce, F. F. *New Testament History.* London: Oliphants, 1977.

Bryan, Christopher. *Render to Caesar: Jesus, the Early Church, and the Roman Superpower.* Oxford: Oxford University Press, 2005.

Buckwalter, Douglas. *The Character and Purpose of Luke's Christology.* SNTSMS 89. Cambridge: Cambridge University Press, 1996.

Burton, G. P. "Proconsuls, Assizes and the Administration of Justice under the Empire." *Journal of Roman Studies* 65 (1975) 92–106.

Buzzard, Anthony. "Acts 1:6 and the Eclipse of the Biblical Kingdom." *Evangelical Quarterly* 66 (1994) 197–215.

Carroll, John T. *Response to the End of History: Eschatology and Situation in Luke-Acts.* SBLDS 92. Atlanta, GA: Scholars, 1988.

Carson, D. A. *The Gospel According to John*. Leicester: IVP, 1991.
Carter, Warren. *The Roman Empire and the New Testament*. Abingdon Essential Guides. Nashville, TN: Abingdon, 2006.
Cassidy, Richard J. *Society and Politics in the Acts of the Apostles*. Maryknoll, NY: Orbis, 1987.
Cassidy, Richard J., and Philip J. Scharper, eds. *Political Issues in Luke-Acts*. Maryknoll, NY: Orbis, 1983.
Conzelmann, Hans. *Acts of the Apostles*. Hermeneia. Philadelphia: Fortress, 1987.
Del Agua, Augustín. "The Evangelization of the Kingdom of God." In *The Unity of Luke-Acts*, edited by J. Verheyden, 639–61. BETL 142. Leuven: Peeters, 1999.
Dunn, James D. G. *Beginning from Jerusalem*. Cambridge: Eerdmans, 2009.
Estrada, Nelson P. *From Followers to Leaders: The Apostles in the Ritual of Status Transformation in Acts 1–2*. JSNTSup 255. London: T. & T. Clark, 2004.
Fishwick, Duncan. *The Imperial Cult in the Latin West, Vol. 3, Part 3: Provincial Cult*. RGRW 147. Leiden: Brill, 2004.
Fitzmyer, Joseph B. *The Acts of the Apostles: A New Translation and Commentary*. AB 31. New York: Doubleday, 1998.
———. *Luke*. AB 28A–B. 2 vols. Garden City, NY: Doubleday, 1985.
Foakes Jackson, F. J., and K. Lake, eds. *The Beginnings of Christianity, Part I: The Acts of the Apostles*. 5 vols. London: Macmillan, 1920–33.
Garland, Robert. *Introducing New Gods: The Politics of Athenia Religion*. London: Duckworth, 1992.
Gaventa, Beverly R. *Acts*. ANTC. Nashville: Abingdon, 2003.
Gill, David W. J. "Achaia." In *The Book of Acts in its Graeco-Roman Setting*, edited by David W. J. Gill and Conrad H. Gempf, 433–53. BAFCS 2. Carlisle: Paternoster, 1994.
———. "Acts and Roman Policy in Judaea." In *The Book of Acts in its Palestinian Setting*, edited by Richard Bauckham, 15–26. BAFCS 4. Grand Rapids: Eerdmans, 1995.
———. "Macedonia." In *The Book of Acts in its Graeco-Roman Setting*, edited by David W. J. Gill and Conrad H. Gempf, 397–417. BAFCS 2. Carlisle: Paternoster, 1994.
———. "The Roman Empire as a Context for the New Testament." In *Handbook to Exegesis of the New Testament*, edited by Stanley E. Porter, 389–406. NT Tools and Studies XXV. Leiden: Brill, 1997.
Gill, David, W. J., and Conrad H. Gempf, eds. *The Book of Acts in its Graeco-Roman Setting*. BAFCS 2. Carlisle: Paternoster, 1994.
Green, Joel B. *The Gospel of Luke*. NICNT. Grand Rapids: Eerdmans, 1997.
Haenchen, Ernst. *The Acts of the Apostles*. Oxford: Blackwell, 1971.
Hemer, Colin J. *The Book of Acts in the Setting of Hellenistic History*. WUNT 49. Tübingen: J. C. B. Mohr (Paul Siebeck), 1989.
Johnson, D. E. "Jesus against the Idols: The Use of Isaianic Servant Songs in the Missiology of Acts." *Westminster Theological Journal* 52 (1990) 343–53.
Johnson, Luke T. *The Acts of the Apostles*. Sacra Pagina 5. Collegeville: Liturgical, 1992.
———. *The Literary Function of Possessions in Luke-Acts*. SBLDS 39. Missoula: Scholars, 1977.
Jones, A. H. M. *The Greek City from Alexander to Justinian*. Oxford: Clarendon, 1940.
Josephus, Flavius. *Josephus*. Translated by Henry St. J. Thackeray et al. 10 vols. LCL. Cambridge: Harvard University Press, 1926–1965.

Lacey, W. K., and B. W. J. G. Wilson. *Res Publica: Roman Politics and Society According to Cicero.* London: Oxford University Press, 1970.

Lintott, Andrew. *Imperium Romanum: Politics and Administration.* London/New York: Routledge, 1993.

Macro, Anthony D. "The Cities of Asia Minor Under the Roman Imperium." *ANRW* II.7.2 (1980) 658–97.

Mallen, Peter. *The Reading and Transformation of Isaiah in Luke-Acts.* LNTS 367. London: T. & T. Clark, 2007.

Menzies, Robert P. *Empowered for Witness: The Spirit in Luke-Acts.* JPTSup 6. Sheffield: Sheffield Academic, 1994.

Millar, Fergus. *The Roman Empire and its Neighbours.* 2nd ed. London: Duckworth, 1981.

Moore, Thomas S. "'To the End of the Earth': The Geographic and Ethnic Universalism of Acts 1:8 in Light of Isaianic Influence on Luke." *Journal of the Evangelical Theological Society* 40 (1997) 389–99.

Newbigin, Lesslie. "Witness in a Biblical Perspective." *Mission Studies* 3 (1986) 80–84.

Nolland, John. *Luke.* WBC 35A–C. 3 vols. Dallas, TX: Word, 1989–93.

Oakes, Peter. *Philippians: From People to Letter.* SNTSMS 110. Cambridge: Cambridge University Press, 2000.

Pao, David W. *Acts and the Isaianic New Exodus.* BSL. Grand Rapids: Baker Academic, 2002.

Rapske, Brian M. *The Book of Acts and Paul in Roman Custody.* BAFCS 3. Carlisle: Paternoster, 1994.

———. "Roman Governors of Palestine." In *Dictionary of the Later New Testament and its Developments*, edited by Ralph P. Martin and Peter H. Davids, 979–84. Downers Grove: IVP, 1997.

Reynolds, Joyce. "Cities." In *The Administration of the Roman Empire 241 BC–AD 193*, edited by David C. Braund, 15–51. Exeter Studies in History 18. Exeter: University of Exeter, 1988.

Rhoads, David, et al., eds. *Luke-Acts and Empire: Essays in Honor of Robert L. Brawley.* Princeton Theological Monographs 151. Eugene, OR: Pickwick, 2011.

Romm, James S. *The Edges of the Earth in Ancient Thought: Geography, Exploration, and Fiction.* Princeton, NJ: Princeton University Press, 1992.

Rowe, C. Kavin. *World Upside Down: Reading Acts in the Graeco-Roman Age.* Oxford/New York: Oxford University Press, 2009.

Sanders, Jack T. *The Jews in Luke-Acts.* London: SCM, 1987.

Schnabel, Eckhard J. *Early Christian Mission.* 2 vols. Downers Grove: IVP, 2004.

Schneider, Gerhard. *Die Apostelgeschichte.* HThKNT. 2 vols. Freiburg: Herder, 1982.

Schürer, Emil, et al. *The History of the Jewish People in the Age of Jesus Christ (175 BC–AD 135).* Rev. ed. 4 vols. Edinburgh: T. & T. Clark, 1973–86.

Shelton, Jo-Ann. *As the Romans Did: A Sourcebook in Roman Social History.* 2nd ed. Oxford: Oxford University Press, 1998.

Sherwin-White, A. N. *Roman Society and Roman Law in the New Testament.* Grand Rapids: Baker, 1981.

Skinner, Matthew L. *Locating Paul: Places of Custody as Narrative Settings in Acts 21–28.* Academia Biblica 13. Atlanta, GA: SBL, 2003.

———. *The Trial Narratives: Conflict, Power, and Identity in the New Testament.* Louisville: Westminster John Knox, 2010.

Sleeman, Matthew. *Geography and the Ascension Narrative in Acts*. SNTSMS 146. Cambridge: Cambridge University Press, 2009.

Soards, Marion L. *The Speeches in Acts: Their Content, Context, and Concerns*. Louisville, Kentucky: Westminster John Knox, 1994.

Stein, Robert H. *Luke*. NAC 24. Nashville: Broadman, 1992.

Tacitus. *The Histories and The Annals*. Translated by Clifford H. Moore and John Jackson. 4 vols. LCL. Cambridge: Harvard University Press, 1937.

Tajra, Harry W. *The Trial of St Paul: A Juridical Exegesis of the Second Half of the Acts of the Apostles*. WUNT 2:35. Tübingen: Mohr Siebeck, 1989.

Trebilco, Paul R. "Asia." In *The Book of Acts in its Graeco-Roman Setting*, edited by David W. J. Gill and Conrad H. Gempf, 291–362. BAFCS 2. Carlisle: Paternoster, 1994.

Trites, Allison A. "The Importance of Legal Scenes and Language in the Book of Acts." *Novum Testamentum* 16 (1974) 278–84.

———. *The New Testament Concept of Witness*. SNTSMS 31. Cambridge: Cambridge University Press, 1977.

Turner, Max. *Power from on High: The Spirit in Israel's Restoration and Witness in Luke-Acts*. JPTSup 9. Sheffield: Sheffield Academic, 1996.

Twelftree, Graham H. "Sanhedrin." In *Dictionary of New Testament Background*, edited by Craig A. Evans and Stanley E. Porter, 1061–65. Downers Grove: IVP, 2000.

Walton, Steve. "Acts, Book of." In *Dictionary for Theological Interpretation of the Bible*, edited by Kevin J. Vanhoozer, Craig G. Bartholomew, Daniel J. Treier, and N. T. Wright, 27–31. London: SPCK, 2005.

———. "The Acts—of God? What is the 'Acts of the Apostles' All About?" *Evangelical Quarterly* 80 (2008) 291–306.

———. "The State They Were In: Luke's View of the Roman Empire." In *Rome in the Bible and the Early Church*, edited by Peter Oakes, 1–41. Carlisle: Paternoster, 2002.

———. "Trying Paul or Trying Rome? Judges and Accused in the Roman Trials of Paul in Acts." In *Luke-Acts and Empire: Essays in Honor of Robert L. Brawley*, edited by David Rhoads, David Esterline, and Jae Won Lee, 122–41. Princeton Theological Monographs 151. Eugene, OR: Pickwick, 2011.

———. "Whose Spirit? The Promise and the Promiser in Luke 12:12." In *The Spirit and Christ in the New Testament in Christian Theology*, edited by I. Howard Marshall, Volker Rabens, and Cornelis Bennema, 35–51. Grand Rapids: Eerdmans, 2012.

Weatherly, Jon A. *Jewish Responsibility for the Death of Jesus in Luke-Acts*. JSNTSup 106. Sheffield: Sheffield Academic, 1994.

Winter, Bruce W. *Divine Honours for the Caesars: The First Christians' Challenge*. Grand Rapids: Eerdmans, 2015.

———. "The Importance of the *Captatio Benevolentiae* in the Speeches of Tertullus and Paul in Acts 24:1–21." *Journal of Theological Studies* 42 (1991) 505–31.

———. "On Introducing Gods to Athens: An Alternative Reading of Acts 17:18–20." *Tyndale Bulletin* 47 (1996) 71–90.

———. *Seek the Welfare of the City: Christians as Benefactors and Citizens*. First-Century Christians in the Graeco-Roman World. Carlisle: Paternoster, 1994.

Yamazaki-Ransom, Kazuhiko. *The Roman Empire in Luke's Narrative*. LNTS 404. London: T. & T. Clark, 2010.

12

Paul as Pastor in Romans

Theological Foundations

Colin Kruse

PAUL'S PASTORAL MINISTRY, AS it is reflected in his letter to the Romans, flows out of and employs his theological understanding of what God has done in Christ for the salvation of humankind, and the implications of that for believers. It is described as "the priestly ministry of the gospel," empowered by the work of the Holy Spirit, and aims to sanctify people so they become and continue to be acceptable "living sacrifices" well-pleasing to God. For Paul, this ministry was not just something he did *for* Christ, but also something that Christ did *through* him. It is significant that Paul's exhortations and encouragements are based on the solid foundation of the theology of the gospel, something we need to recognize and apply in our own ministries. This is not to deny the importance of Christian counselling, but to ensure that we do not shortchange people by failing to draw their attention to what God has done and continues to do for them, especially through the ministry of the indwelling Holy Spirit.

INTRODUCTION

Our access to information about the way Paul functioned as a pastor is available chiefly through the letters he wrote to churches. There is a sense in which all Paul's letters reflect his pastoral concerns and practice. This, it may be argued, is also true of his letter to the Romans despite views such as Melanchthon's that it is essentially a compendium of his theology, or Manson's that it is a theological manifesto,[1] or Bornkamm's that it is his "last will and testament."[2] Romans is certainly the clearest and most thorough exposition we have of Paul's gospel but this exposition was not written simply to outline his theology. Like all of Paul's other letters it was written with important pastoral aims and for a specific Christian community.

An understanding of Paul as pastor in Romans, therefore, needs to be sought against the background of what may be gleaned concerning his purpose in writing, and this in turn requires an understanding of Paul's own situation and that of his audience at the time of writing.

PAUL'S SITUATION WHEN HE WROTE ROMANS

The apostle wrote this letter at the conclusion of his mission in the northeastern Mediterranean during which he evangelized major cities in the Roman provinces of Galatia, Macedonia, Achaia, and Asia.

His ambition, in line with his determination to preach where the name of Christ was not known, was then to take the gospel to the western extremity of the Mediterranean, to Spain. It was his intention to visit the believers in Rome on his way to Spain (5:23–24) because, as apostle to the gentiles, he was responsible under God for them (1:14–15).[3]

However, before he could do that, he had another obligation to fulfill. Urged by the leaders of the Jerusalem church following his first missionary journey (Gal 2:9–10), Paul had devoted significant time and energy to organizing a collection among the churches he had founded in Galatia, Macedonia, and Achaia, and these churches had responded positively and contributed monies to the collection. Paul, along with representatives of the churches, had then to convey it to Jerusalem before he could pursue his ambition to preach in Spain and visit Rome on the way (15:25–28).

---

1. Manson, "St. Paul's," 3–15.
2. Bornkamm, "Letter," 16–28.
3. Unless otherwise indicated all scriptural citations are taken from Paul's letter to the Romans utilizing the New Revised Standard Version (NRSV).

THE SITUATION OF THE ROMAN CHURCHES

Many challenges were facing the believers in Rome. The churches there were originally predominately Jewish, most likely founded by Jewish believers returning from Jerusalem following religious festivals there. However, according to Acts 18:2, Claudius ordered all the Jews to leave Rome, an order believed to have been issued in AD 49. The Roman historian Suetonius (b. ca. 70 AD, d. ca. 130 AD) says "since the Jews constantly made disturbances at the instigation of Chrestus, he [Claudius] expelled them from Rome" (*de Vita Claudii* 25.4).

Following the edict of Claudius and the expulsion of Jews from Rome, the Christian community would have been comprised mainly of gentiles. When in 54 AD Claudius died and his edict lapsed, Jews began to trickle back into Rome. Believing Jews would have found a very different Christian community from the one they left. They were now a minority within a largely gentile Christian community, and there were significant tensions between the two groups, in particular tensions arising from different convictions concerning the observance of special days and food taboos (14:2–3, 5–6). This was one of the pastoral issues Paul had to address. But it was not the only one.

It is clear that some people had come to Rome and were criticizing the gospel that Paul preached on the grounds that it encouraged moral anarchy (3:8; cf. 6:1, 15), and the apostle had to refute strenuously these allegations by insisting that his gospel involved neither a license to sin nor any denigration of the law. On the contrary, he argued, it was only in the lives of those who accepted and believed the gospel that the power of sin could be broken, and the law's righteous demand find fulfillment (6:1—8:13).

Further, the Roman believers lived in the capital of the empire and their relations with civic authorities were an issue, particularly the matter of payment of taxes. Paul gives his advice concerning this matter in 13:1–7. These and other practical pastoral matters are addressed by Paul in Romans and the way he handled them will be explored shortly. However, before that it is important to take note of the way Paul understood the nature of his ministry and its spiritual dynamic.

PAUL'S UNDERSTANDING OF THE NATURE OF HIS MINISTRY

There are a few places in Paul's letters where he gives expression to his approach to and theological understanding of the nature of his pastoral ministry, and one of the more important expressions of this is found in 15:14–16:

> I myself feel confident about you, my brothers and sisters, that you yourselves are full of goodness, filled with all knowledge, and able to instruct one another. Nevertheless on some points I have written to you rather boldly by way of reminder, because of the grace given me by God to be a minister of Christ Jesus to the Gentiles in the priestly service of the gospel of God, so that the offering of the Gentiles may be acceptable, sanctified by the Holy Spirit.

These verses contain the only explicit statement by Paul of his purpose in writing Romans and it is related to his understanding of his pastoral ministry. Several matters deserve our attention. First, despite having to correct and exhort his audience earlier in the letter, Paul nevertheless expressed his confidence in them when he wrote: "I myself feel confident about you, my brothers and sisters, that you yourselves are full of goodness, filled with all knowledge, and able to instruct one another." He recognized that there is always good cause to affirm the work of God in believers' lives even when there still remain areas of concern (cf. his encouragement and affirmation of his audience in 1:8, 11–12; 15:14; 16:19–20).

Second, having strongly affirmed his audience, Paul adds: "Nevertheless on some points I have written to you rather boldly by way of reminder."[4] We have already noted what some of these points were, and we will look at a few of them in more detail shortly. Here we want to note that while Paul was a great encourager of his converts he was not prepared to stop with affirmation when other matters needed addressing.

Third, Paul says that it was only because of "the grace given" him by God that he was privileged to be a minister of Christ to gentiles. He knew it was as an act of the grace of God that he, a persecutor of the church, was called to faith in Christ and commissioned as his apostle (1 Cor 15:8–9), and that it was as the recipient of ongoing grace he was empowered to carry out that commission (Col 1:28–29).

Fourth, Paul describes his ministry as "the priestly service of the gospel of God."[5] Part of the function of priests in Israel was to preside over the sacrificial offerings brought by the people of Israel. Exploiting this priestly

---

4. Byrne, "Rather Boldly," 93, 95–96, suggests that Paul was speaking boldly when he informed those who were still clinging to the law in order to obtain eschatological righteousness that this was futile, and that only faith in what God has done in Christ makes salvation possible.

5. The verb used here (*hierourgeō*, "to serve as a priest") is found only in 15:16 in the NT, and in the LXX only in one manuscript of 4 Maccabees where it means to minister (to the law) (4 Macc 7:8). It is used by Josephus (Ant. 14.4.3 §65; 17.6.4 §166) and Philo (Cherub. 28 §96) without an object to mean "to offer sacrifice."

imagery Paul describes the purpose of his ministry as to ensure "that the offering[6] of the Gentiles may be acceptable, sanctified by the Holy Spirit."[7] In 12:1 he exhorts members of his audience: "I appeal to you therefore, brothers and sisters, by the mercies of God, to present your bodies as a living sacrifice, holy and acceptable to God, which is your spiritual worship." Paul saw it as his responsibility to ensure that the self-offering of gentile believers was acceptable to God. He carried out this responsibility through "the priestly service of the gospel of God," and we might add, by expounding the implications of the gospel for godly living. He presided, as it were, as priest over the self-offering of gentile believers to ensure that they continued to be an offering "holy and acceptable to God." It was a task to which he totally committed himself. It caused him great concern whenever he saw believers regressing into sinful behavior, or when he saw them under threat from false teachers, used by the devil to turn them away from their pure devotion to Christ (cf. 2 Cor 11:3).

It is significant that Paul saw the proclamation of the word of God as the primary means of a pastoral ministry that could promote godliness. Our Lord himself said of his teaching ministry: "It is the spirit that gives life; the flesh is useless. The words that I have spoken to you are spirit and life" (John 6:63). It was as the apostle proclaimed the word of God that he witnessed its transforming power in the lives of those he evangelized. In 1 Thessalonians 2:13 he writes: "We also constantly give thanks to God for this, that when you received the word of God that you heard from us, you accepted it not as a human word but as what it really is, God's word, which is also at work in you believers." It is a very great privilege to be entrusted with the preaching and

---

6. The "offering" is susceptible of two interpretations: (i) the offering consists of the gentiles themselves, and (ii) the offering consists of donations made by the gentiles, that is, their contributions to the collection. Downs, "'Offering,'" favors of the second interpretation arguing that the phrase h[set macron over e]ē prosphora t[set macron over o]ōn ethn[set macron over o]ōn in Rom 15:16 should be taken as a subjective genitive and therefore as a reference to an offering given by the gentiles, namely, the collection for the saints that Paul discusses in Rom 15:25–32. However, the former interpretation, which is adopted by the NIV, is preferable in the light of three facts: (i) the apostle has already urged the audience to offer their bodies (i.e. themselves) as living sacrifices, holy and pleasing to God (12:1); (ii) he speaks immediately of this offering being "sanctified by the Holy Spirit," not something that Paul would say about contributions to a collection; and (iii) Paul was heading for Jerusalem with the collection before his planned visit to Rome and therefore the Roman believers would not have opportunity to donate to the collection to which he refers in 15:25–32.

7. Witherington and Hyatt, *Paul's Letter*, 355, draws attention to the "Trinitarian progression here—Paul is a minister of Christ, serving the gospel of God, offering the Gentiles who have been consecrated by the Spirit."

teaching of the life-giving word of God and to witness its impact upon people as it is faithfully expounded and used by the spirit of God to shape their lives.

Fifth, Paul's reference to "the priestly service of the gospel of God" as the means by which he sought to ensure believers' self-offering was "acceptable to God is juxtaposed with a reference to the fact that this takes place as they are "sanctified by the Holy Spirit." Gospel ministry and the sanctifying work of the Spirit go hand in hand, and normally one does not occur without the other. In 1 Thessalonians 1:4-5 Paul again juxtaposes the proclamation of the word of God with the work of the Holy Spirit: "For we know, brothers and sisters beloved by God, that he has chosen you, because our message of the gospel came to you not in word only, but also in power and in the Holy Spirit and with full conviction." Paul's reference to the "power" (δυνάμις) of the Holy Spirit here has been variously interpreted but is best understood "as a reference to the sense of spiritual power attaching to the preached gospel so that it came to be accepted as the word of God."[8]

THE SPIRITUAL DYNAMIC OF PAUL'S MINISTRY

Also significant for our understanding of the nature of Paul's ministry and in particular the dynamic power of God released through it, is the passage that follows directly after the one we've been just considering, i.e. 15:17-19:

> In Christ Jesus, then, I have reason to boast of my work for God. For I will not venture to speak of anything except what Christ has accomplished through me to win obedience from the Gentiles, by word and deed, by the power of signs and wonders, by the power of the Spirit of God, so that from Jerusalem and as far around as Illyricum I have fully proclaimed the good news of Christ.

Here Paul insists that he will limit his boasting to "what Christ has accomplished through" him, adding that this has been achieved "by word and deed, by the power of signs and wonders,[9] by the power of the Spirit of God." This description of ministry is similar to the way the Synoptic Gospels depict the ministry of the historical Jesus which was effected by word (preaching of the kingdom of God), and accompanied by signs and wonders and with the power of the Holy Spirit (cf. Luke 7:22).

---

8. Cf. discussion in Kruse, *Foundations*, 92-93, n. 11.

9. Strauss, "Missions Theology," 461-62, notes that "the phrase 'signs and wonders' was the standard Old Testament way of referring to the miracles of the Exodus, and 'the expression regularly designates events surrounding the great redemptive acts of God.'"

When Paul describes his ministry as "what Christ has accomplished through me" he is recognizing the involvement of the risen Christ in his ministry. The ongoing involvement of the risen Christ in the ministry of his followers is implied in Luke's reference to "all that Jesus began to do and to teach" in Acts 1:1 (NIV). It implies that what is to follow in his account of the ministry of the early believers is what Jesus continued to do and to teach through them.

The passage 15:17–19 also reflects the purpose of Paul's ministry ("to win obedience from the [g]entiles"), the scope of his activities ("from Jerusalem and as far around as Illyricum"), and the fundamental nature of that ministry ("I have fully proclaimed the good news of Christ"). What this last element involved is perhaps best illustrated by Paul's statement to the Ephesian elders recorded in Acts 20:26–27: "Therefore I declare to you this day that I am not responsible for the blood of any of you, for I did not shrink from declaring to you the whole purpose of God." This is involved in the "priestly service of the gospel" in which Paul labored to ensure that gentiles became and continued to be an acceptable offering to God, sanctified by the Holy Spirit.

THEOLOGICAL DEFENSE OF THE GOSPEL

A significant part of Paul's pastoral ministry was ensuring that distortions of the gospel did not adversely affect believers for whom he felt responsible. That he needed to do so may be inferred from a number of texts. The first of these relates directly to slanderous accusations directed against him: "And why not say (as some people slander us by saying that we say), 'Let us do evil so that good may come'? Their condemnation is deserved!" (3:8). The apostle was aware that some were saying his preaching encouraged people to "do evil so that good may come,"[10] as if their falsehood would serve to put God's truthfulness into sharp relief and so enhance his glory. Paul dismisses the charges made by such people out of hand exclaiming, "Their condemnation is deserved!"

A similar notion underlies a second text: "What then are we to say? Should we continue in sin in order that grace may abound? By no means! How can we who died to sin go on living in it?" (6:1–2). Paul was responding to criticisms that his gospel encouraged people to "continue in sin" (lit.

---

10. Byrne, *Romans*, 110, comments: "the charge that surfaces here is clearly one that dogged the preaching of the Pauline gospel—one which he perhaps anticipated rising in the Roman community as his letter was being read."

"remain in sin")[11] so that God's grace might abound all the more and cover their sins. This charge Paul rejects out of hand also, arguing that those who have "died to sin" cannot "go on living in sin." He goes on to explain at some length that those who have been united with Christ through baptism cannot go on living in sin: "We have been buried with him by baptism into death, so that, just as Christ was raised from the dead by the glory of the Father, so we too might walk in newness of life."[12]

Paul's opponents who regarded the law as the primary deterrent to sinful behavior claimed his teaching that believers were no longer under the law as a regulatory norm was an encouragement to sin. A third text constitutes Paul's response to this charge: "Should we sin because we are not under law but under grace? By no means!" (6:15). Paul rejected out of hand also the insinuation his teaching provided a license to sin. Rather, he insisted that freedom from the law also meant freedom from sin so that people may become slaves of righteousness. He reminds members of his audience of the great change that took place when they became followers of Christ:

> When you were slaves of sin, you were free in regard to righteousness. So what advantage did you then get from the things of which you now are ashamed? The end of those things is death. But now that you have been freed from sin and enslaved to God, the advantage you get is sanctification. The end is eternal life. For the wages of sin is death, but the free gift of God is eternal life in Christ Jesus our Lord. (Rom 6:20–23)

Paul's responses to these distortions of the gospel were all written out of pastoral concern for the Roman believers in the hope that they would recognize the deceptive nature of these distortions and be encouraged to stand fast in the freedom provided by the gospel. He was contending theologically for the faith of his audience out of his deep pastoral concern for them, even though he had met only a few of them.

---

11. Wright, "Letter," 537 comments: "Of course, to 'remain in sin,' in English and for that matter in Greek, will mean to go on committing sin, but Paul is interested here in where one is first and foremost; it is like saying 'shall we remain in France,' with the assumption that if one does one will continue to speak French."

12. For a discussion of the relationship between baptism, death to sin, and new life in Christ see the additional notes on "Baptism in the Pauline Corpus" and "Dying and Rising with Christ" in Kruse, *Paul's Letter*, 270–72, 272–79.

THEOLOGICAL EXHORTATION

It is significant that in Romans, as elsewhere in Paul's letters, his ethical exhortations are not based upon the Mosaic law as we might expect from one who was trained as a Pharisee, but rather upon the implications of the gospel itself—what God has done in Christ for the redemption and restoration of humanity. The following will serve as examples of this.

Exhortations to Holy Living

In 6:1–23 Paul defends his law-free gospel against charges that it leads to moral anarchy (cf. 3:7–8). He does so by arguing that believers cannot continue in sin because they died to sin with Christ and now they are alive to God in him (6:1–14), and by pointing out that at their conversion they were set free from slavery to sin so as to become slaves of God (6:15–23). These fundamental gospel truths form the basis of his ethical exhortations to his audience not to let sin exercise dominion over them or to obey their sinful passions. Instead they are to present themselves to God as those who have been brought from death to life, and their members as instruments of righteousness (6:13–14).

In 7:1—8:13 Paul defends his gospel against charges that it involves a denigration of the law. He argues that those who accept the gospel are free from the law as a regulatory norm, and as they experience new life in the Spirit they see the "just requirement" of the law fulfilled in their lives (8:1–13). Based on the gospel truths of freedom from the law and new life in the Spirit, Paul reminded his audience that they were no longer debtors to the flesh to live according to the flesh, and encouraged them to put to death the deeds of the body by the Spirit (8:12–13).

The apostle did not explain what it means, in practice, to put to death the deeds of the body by the Spirit. It may perhaps be understood to involve asking the Holy Spirit, in times of temptation, to produce the fruit of the Spirit in their lives. John Stott said it was his prayer every day that the spirit of God would produce his fruit in his life.

An Exhortation for Gentile Believers

In 11:13–32 Paul addresses the gentile members of his audience directly, exhorting them not to look down upon unbelieving Jews. To support his exhortation he reminds them that although some Jews were presently like "branches" broken off from the "olive tree" of God's people because of unbelief, and as gentile converts they had been "grafted in" only through faith, and therefore they could not afford to be proud. Unbelieving Jews, for their part, could be grafted back into the "olive tree" if they did not persist in unbelief. Paul's exhortation to the Roman gentile believers not to look down on unbelieving Jews, then, was based upon his theological understanding of God's gospel purposes.

An Exhortation to Present Oneself to God as a Living Sacrifice

In 12:1 Paul exhorts his audience as follows: "I appeal to you therefore, brothers and sisters, by the mercies of God, to present your bodies as a living sacrifice, holy and acceptable to God, which is your spiritual worship." His appeal was based upon the extended theological exposition of "the mercies of God" in preceding chapters where he expounded and defended the gospel.

Presenting themselves to God would involve not being conformed to the world but being transformed by the renewing of their minds so as to discern what is the will of God (12:2). What follows in chapter 12 represents what Paul expected to be included in the outworking of the will of God in their lives. They would not think of themselves too highly (12:3), and as members of the one body exercise their differing gifts in accordance with the measure of faith God had assigned them, whether that be in prophesying, ministering, teaching, exhortation, generosity, leadership, or acts of compassion (12:4-8). Paul's exhortation is again theologically grounded, this time by an appeal to the mercies of God revealed in the gospel and the gifts of the Spirit activated in the lives of those who accept the gospel.

An Exhortation to be Subject to Governing Authorities

An important matter Paul had to address pastorally for the benefit of his audience was their attitude toward the Roman authorities, in particular their obligation to pay taxes.[13] So in 13:1, 7 the apostle exhorts them to "be subject to the governing authorities, and to pay to all what is due them—taxes to whom taxes are due, revenues to whom revenue is due, respect to whom respect is due, honor whom honor is due." Paul provided the following theological grounds for this exhortation: (i) the authorities that exist have been

---

13. Dunn, *Romans 9-16*, 766, comments: "We know from Tacitus (Ann. 13) that the year A.D. 58 saw persistent complaints against the companies farming indirect taxes and the acquisitiveness of tax collectors . . . so that some reform became essential. Presumably these complaints had been building up, or at least the occasion for them, in the years preceding 58, during the period when Romans was written."

instituted by God and therefore to resist them is to resist God (13:1–2); (ii) the authorities are God's servants for people's good—they are no terror to those who do good,[14] but execute God's wrath on wrongdoers (13:3–5)[15]; (iii) the authorities are "God's servants, busy with this very thing," and in this context "this very thing" is the collection of taxes, and for this reason people should pay "all what is due to them," and this included honor and respect as well as taxes (13:6–7). Once again Paul's exhortation is not merely pragmatic advice but is informed by his understanding of the role given to the governing authorities by God.

Exhortations for "the Weak" and "the Strong"

In 14:1—15:13 Paul addresses two groups in the Roman Christian community: "the strong" made up of predominately gentile believers, and "the weak" comprising mainly Jewish believers. There was tension between the two groups in relation to food taboos and calendrical rules. "The strong" who believed that they could eat anything and felt no compunction to observe special days tended to despise "the weak" who were bound by their scruples in both these matters. "The weak," on the other hand, tended to pass judgment on "the strong" for their failure to observe these rules and taboos.

Paul's exhortations to these two groups were more than just good advice intended to promote social cohesion. They were based on the theological significance of the gospel itself which he expected to be formational in the lives of members of his audience. "The strong" were not to look down upon "the weak" because of their scruples, remembering that God himself had welcomed them (14:3). Instead, they were to accommodate themselves to the scruples of "the weak." And "the weak" must not pass judgment upon "the strong" because they did not share their scruples, because, Paul says, "It is before their own lord that they stand or fall. And they will be upheld, for the Lord is able to make them stand" (14:4). And addressing both groups he says: "Why do you pass judgment on your brother or sister? Or you, why do you despise your brother or sister? For we will all stand before the judgment seat of God" (14:10).

---

14. The "good" (*ton agathon*) was understood to mean things that were useful for society, things of worth and social significance (cf. BDAG ad loc.)

15. Jewett, *Romans*, 793, comments: "the fact that Romans was drafted during a period of exemplary Roman administration led by Seneca and Burrus augments the likelihood that Paul's formulation would have resonated positively in Rome. However, before and after that period, Paul's unqualified formulation that officials punish the bad and praise the good seems far from accurate . . ."

Paul warned "the strong" that causing "the weak" to stumble by their example would be to "cause the ruin of one for whom Christ died" (14:15). He exhorted them not to become a stumbling block to "the weak" simply "for the sake of food," reminding them that "the kingdom of God is not food and drink but righteousness and peace and joy in the Holy Spirit" (14:15, 17). Rather than putting a stumbling block in the way of "the weak," Paul said, "each of us must please our neighbor for the good purpose of building up the neighbor. For Christ did not please himself; but, as it is written, 'The insults of those who insult you have fallen on me'" (15:2–3). Finally, he exhorted both groups to welcome one another, "just as Christ has welcomed you, for the glory of God" (15:7).

These five examples all reflect the fact that Paul's pastoral exhortations were grounded upon the gospel itself, its ethical implications and this understanding of the way God has ordered this world.

THEOLOGICAL ENCOURAGEMENT

In the process of his exposition and defense of the gospel Paul drew out its implications to encourage his audience. His encouragements, like his exhortations, were theologically based. There are many places in the letter where the apostle does this, drawing out, for example, the significance for his audience of the love of God for them (5:8–11), the fact that God has adopted them as his children (8:14–17), and the role of the Spirit in their lives (8:26–27). As a prime example of the way Paul employed theology for pastoral encouragement we may point to his application of doctrine of justification by faith to the needs of his audience.

In chapter 4 Paul explains how Abraham was justified by faith. In 4:3 he asks: "For what does the scripture say?" and provides the answer: "Abraham believed God, and it was reckoned to him as righteousness." And then in 4:23–25 he encourages his audience with this assurance: "Now the words, 'it was reckoned to him,' were written not for his sake alone, but for ours also. It will be reckoned to us who believe in him who raised Jesus our Lord from the dead, who was handed over to death for our trespasses and was raised for our justification." In what follows in 5:1–5, Paul draws out the benefits of justification: peace with God, a standing in God's grace, and the hope of sharing the glory of God. These things would enable them to endure suffering, for under God's good hand it will produce endurance, character, and a hope that would not disappoint them because God's love had been poured into their hearts by the Holy Spirit.

Paul's understanding of the *experience* of justification is best expressed in the climactic statements of 8:31–39. In this passage the apostle asks: "If God is for us, who is against us? He who did not withhold his own Son, but gave him up for all of us, will he not with him also give us everything else?" (8:31–32). What this involves is then teased out in the words: "Who will bring any charge against God's elect? It is God who justifies" (8:33). Believers may be sure that God will entertain no charges against those whom he has justified, whether such charges emanate from Satan, "the accuser of our comrades" (Rev 12:10), others who find fault, or even their own overscrupulous consciences. To drive home the great encouragement the doctrine of justification affords believers Paul adds: "Who is to condemn? It is Christ Jesus, who died, yes, who was raised, who is at the right hand of God, who indeed intercedes for us" (8:34). As God will entertain no charges brought against those whom he has justified, neither will Christ condemn them. For he has died for them, thus dealing with their sins once and for all, and he is now seated at the right hand of God where he intercedes for them. All this leads Paul to celebrate the experience of justification in the well-known words: "I am convinced that neither death, nor life, nor angels, nor rulers, nor things present, nor things to come, nor powers, nor height, nor depth, nor anything else in all creation, will be able to separate us from the love of God in Christ Jesus our Lord" (8:38–39).

THE CHALLENGE

The outstanding feature of Paul's pastoral ministry, as it is reflected in his letter to the Romans, is the extent to which is flows out of and reflects his theological understanding of what God has done in Christ for the salvation of humankind, and the implications of that for believers.

The challenge for us who seek to minister to God's people today is to likewise engage in "the priestly ministry of the gospel" trusting in the accompanying work of the Holy Spirit to sanctify his people so they become and continue to be acceptable "living sacrifices" well pleasing to God.

It is also a challenge for us to ground our exhortations and encouragements on the solid foundation of the theology of the gospel. This is not to deny the importance of Christian counselling, but to ensure that we do not shortchange people by failing to draw their attention to what God has done and continues to do for them, especially through the ministry of the indwelling Holy Spirit.

BIBLIOGRAPHY

Bornkamm, Gunther. "The Letter to the Romans as Paul's Last Will and Testament." In *The Romans Debate: Revised and Expanded Edition*, edited by Karl P. Donfried, 16–28. Peabody, MA: Hendrickson, 1991.

Byrne, Brendan. "'Rather Boldly' (Rom 15,15) Paul's Prophetic Bid to Win the Allegiance of the Christians in Rome." *Biblica 74* (1993) 83–96.

Byrne, Brendan, S. J. *Romans*. Sacra Pagina 6. Collegeville, MN: Liturgical, 1996.

Downs, David J. "'The Offering of the Gentiles' in Romans 15.16." *Journal for the Study of the New Testament* 29 (2006) 173–86.

Dunn, James D. G. *Romans 9–16*. WBC 38B. Dallas, Texas: Word, 1988.

Jewett, Robert. *Romans: A Commentary*. Hermeneia. Minneapolis: Fortress, 2007.

Kruse, Colin G. *New Testament Foundations for Ministry*. Marshalls Theological Library. Basingstoke: Marshall, Morgan & Scott, 1983.

———. *Paul's Letter to the Romans*. PNTC. Grand Rapids: Eerdmans, 2012.

Manson, T. W. "St. Paul's Letter to the Romans—and Others." In *The Romans Debate: Revised and Expanded Edition*, edited by Karl P. Donfried, 3–15. Peabody, MA: Hendrickson, 1991.

Strauss, Steve. "Missions Theology in Romans 15:14–33." *Bibliotheca Sacra 160* (2003) 457–74.

Witherington, Ben, III, and Darlene Hyatt. *Paul's Letter to the Romans: A Socio-Rhetorical Commentary*. Eerdmans: Grand Rapids, 2004.

Wright, N. T. "The Letter to the Romans: Introduction, Commentary, and Reflections." In *The New Interpreter's Bible X*, 393–770. Nashville: Abingdon, 2002.

13

Reflecting on a Wreck

The Book of Genesis and the Marginalization of Christianity in the West

Andrew Brown

THE DISSIPATION OF THE authority of the Christian church, Christian mindsets, and Christian Scripture in the European West over the past four centuries found one cause in disappointment in the inability of seminal biblical texts such as Genesis 1 to answer questions that inquisitive European scholars were asking about their world. The genre of "theories of the earth," which flourished especially between 1680 and 1750, with their most influential examples arising out of late seventeenth-century scholarly culture in Britain, provides a fitting case study. Attempting to integrate various kinds of available knowledge from classical texts and ancient philosophy through to current observations of nature with the text of Genesis 1–11, the story of their rise and fall demonstrates the source of this transient trend of harmonizing Christian Scripture with a general theory of the earth's formation in a misunderstanding about the purpose and nature of these early chapters of Genesis.

Failure is Not Final reads the title of the biography of MST's founder, C. H. Nash, written by Darrell Paproth.[1] As we reflect on one hundred years of history for MST/BCV/MBI, filled with events, achievements, personalities, and an enduring commitment to the gospel of Christ, Paproth's motto reminds us of the lasting value of Nash's determination to bounce back from failure and adversity. Had Nash not known how to bounce back this college would not exist.

The church of Christ could feel that it too has failed to salvage much social or intellectual influence out of its one-time cultural dominance in the West. Christians in Western-based cultures like contemporary Australia might feel like "marginal voices," despite occasional surprises such as the election of a prime minister who is a professing and apparently sincere Christian. Though fortunately the ethnic complexion of Australia is becoming increasingly diverse, Australian Christians know that in "Anglo" Australian company, talking about Christian faith is a reliable "barbeque stopper." With Theoden, King of Rohan, in *The Lord of the Rings: The Two Towers*, we are tempted to ask, "How did it come to this?"

We will never know how it came to this unless we study church history and, more broadly, the intellectual and cultural history of the West. I say the West, not because it is the only or the most important culture, but it is the major cultural heritage of the Australia into which most of us were born in the twentieth century. The Australia of the twenty-first will be able to talk about a much more diverse cultural heritage, and this may well prove a boon to the prosperity of the Australian church. But to understand the position of the church in today's Australia, we still need to study the Western legacy.

History gets a bad rap. Schoolteachers and Bible college lecturers alike are familiar with seeing many students' eyes glaze over once they realize that historical information is being communicated. That is a pity, because we can have no idea where we are or where we are going if we are not familiar with our past course. This was graphically illustrated in the Scilly naval disaster of 1707. Returning from a naval engagement with the French at the siege of Toulon, the British fleet encountered heavy weather after passing the Straits of Gibraltar into the North Atlantic. Without an established means to calculate longitude, and no horizon or view of the stars to confirm latitude, the fleet of twenty-one ships, led by Admiral Sir Cloudesley Shovell (no less), lost its bearings in the seas off Brittany. After consultation with his captains, Shovell directed the fleet north-east as if to make up the middle of the English Channel, but having wrongly guessed its position, instead ran the fleet into the shoals around the Scilly Isles west of Cornwall with the loss

---

1. Paproth, *Failure*.

of somewhere between 1,500 and 2,000 sailors.² Shock of the disaster, which saw wreckage and corpses washing ashore on the Scilly Islands long afterwards, helped to prompt the British government to pass the Longitude Act of 1714, offering a rich prize to anyone who could create the technology to permit more accurate measurement of longitude at sea. This was so difficult that it took John Harrison forty years and four versions of his chronometer to obtain the prize, and one of the purposes of Captain Cook's 1770 voyage was to test one of the final versions.³

It is little use, then, analyzing our present situation or prognosticating about the future if we have not taken the trouble to understand our past. In the words of that great oracle of modern culture, Mater from the movie *Cars* (2006), "Ain't no need to watch where I'm goin'; just need to know where I've been." Let us hope that our government can remain longsighted enough to know the value of protecting the place of humanities studies, such as history, within our university system. Let me, therefore, put this as a pointed statement: we will not understand the position of the Christian church in twenty-first-century Australia until we familiarize ourselves with the intellectual and cultural history of the past five hundred years in the West.

That statement is grandiose and oversimplified, but it is a plea to expand the work of understanding the past as a prerequisite to diagnosing the present. The following study hints at one reason for the intellectual and cultural marginalization of the church over the past five hundred years. Mistaken expectations of what the Bible was meant to do, explain all things, led to disappointment when data about the past that the Bible did not explain emerged. These mistaken expectations and the resultant disappointment are especially evident in relation to the early chapters of Genesis.

BACKGROUNDS: INTERPRETATION OF GENESIS IN RENAISSANCE EUROPE

Christian literature pertaining to Genesis 1 was already fairly abundant by the medieval period and increased exponentially in the Renaissance. Searching for the term "Moses" in English literature between 1500 and 1900 using Google's online tool, Ngram Viewer, reveals spikes in the line shortly after 1650 and before 1700, and rather sustained use until about 1750. Some of this would pertain, I would guess, to debates over Mosaic authorship of the Pentateuch that followed the 1651 publication of Thomas Hobbes's *Leviathan*, but it is the next spike that I believe pertains to a unique genre,

---

2. Eyers, *Final Voyage*.
3. Eyers, *Final Voyage*, 20–21; Truswell, *Memory of Ice*, 99–101.

concerned with the early chapters of the "first book of Moses," Genesis, that flourished for a while after 1680.

The book of Genesis, you see, had become in many quarters the authoritative frame for the accommodation of new knowledge. This trend had already been underway in the medieval period. If you ever need the doorstop to end them all, I recommend the four volumes of Vincent of Beauvais's *Speculum Maius*, or Great Mirror, dating originally to around 1240 CE.[4] Its four volumes are devoted to natural, doctrinal, moral, and historical truth. The "hexaemeron"[5] or six-day account of creation in Genesis holds a surprising prominence in this encyclopedic work as the gatekeeper text for all that can be known about the world.

Genesis 1 is rather suited to such a role, in one sense. Its extremely broad and generic creation categories provided cognitive boxes, ready to accommodate data obtained from other sources. Bring in more of the early chapters of Genesis, and you could read hints to the origin of the physical realm, humanity, marriage, culture, technology, food production, ethnic diversity, and linguistic diversity that might provide categories for all kinds of ongoing research. Consciously following the model of the patristic hexaemeral literature,[6] scholars of late medieval and Renaissance times generated an explosion of Genesis-related literature that engaged directly with the burgeoning learning of the day.[7]

Genesis commentaries therefore grew larger and larger, culminating in Catholic polymath Marin Mersenne's *Quaestiones Celeberrimae* (1623), which historian of science and Catholic apologist Stanley Jaki claimed, "remains the vastest commentary on Genesis 1 ever published."[8] Its coverage of Genesis 1:1–5 occupies 798 columns, as you may check for yourself via Google Books.[9] Beyond the thriving genre of Genesis commentaries and other encyclopedic works framed using Genesis, we find other genres under steerage from Genesis, including high literature (*belles lettres*) such as John Milton's *Paradise Lost*,[10] biblical chronologies, and associated univer-

---

4. Vincent of Beauvais, *Speculum Quadriplex*. I am capitalizing Latin titles in an English title case style, rather than as is usual in Latin.

5. Also seen with the Latinized spelling "hexameron."

6. Robbins, *Hexaemeral Literature*; Van Winden, "Hexaemeron."

7. Williams, *Common Expositor*.

8. Jaki, *Genesis 1*, 170.

9. Mersenne, *Quaestiones*. A possible rival for the title of the biggest ever Genesis commentary comes from a near-contemporary Protestant writer: Zanchius, *De Operibus*. See Kirkconnell, *Celestial Cycle*, 581.

10. Kirkconnell, *Celestial Cycle*; Evans, "*Paradise Lost*"; Ryken, "Paradise"; Banderier, "Fortunate Phoenix."

sal histories that cover events from creation to the present day,[11] "Mosaic philosophy,"[12] and finally the intriguing genre of "theories of the earth," to which we now turn.

THE CONTEXT OF THE THEORIES OF THE EARTH

Theories of the earth appeared on the scene when some of these other once-vigorous genres were beginning to wane. These theories were one attempt at the integration of knowledge at a time when scholars were beginning to struggle with sometimes conflicting data coming in from multiple sources. Consensus on the age of the world from documentary sources was delicate, given the greater length of the Septuagint chronology compared to the Hebrew, the unresolved status of Egyptian chronology, and new claims to cultural antiquity arising from Jesuit missions to China.[13] The discovery of a human-populated New World had bolder writers pondering whether all living humans might not necessarily descend from Adam and Eve.[14] Classical explanations of the cosmos and its origin were swirling in the air given the enthusiastic Renaissance drive back to antique sources (*ad fontes*), so that alongside well-established Aristotelian cosmology, Epicurean, Stoic, and Neoplatonic alternatives were making a comeback. Esoteric or mystical traditions (e.g., cabbalistic, hermetic, and gnostic) had revived in representatives of the southern Renaissance such as Ficino and Pico della Mirandola, as well as of the northern Renaissance, such as Jacob Böhme and Robert Fludd.[15] Copernican heliocentric cosmology was gaining traction after 1600 through the efforts of Johannes Kepler, Galileo, and others. Finally, Frenchman René Descartes (1596–1650) flirted with a hypothetical scenario whereby God might initially create uniform matter and leave it to form worlds by means of its natural properties.

The literature for this change, both primary and secondary, seems endless. A worldview metamorphosis was underway in the European West across the century between 1580 and 1680, without even mentioning the beginnings of modern biblical criticism associated with names like Thomas

---

11. Griggs, "Universal History"; Barr, "Created"; Grafton, "Joseph Scaliger."

12. Walton, *Genesis*; Blair, "Mosaic Physics"; Goudriaan, "Creation."

13. Grafton, "Joseph Scaliger," 170–80; McCalla, *Creationist Debate*.

14. Livingstone, *Adam's Ancestors*, 8–11, 26–51. The key primary source is La Peyrère, *Men before Adam*.

15. Forshaw, "Christian Kabbalah"; Forshaw, "Vitriolic Reactions"; Popkin, "Third Force"; Walton, "Genesis," 1–14.

Hobbes, Baruch Spinoza, and Richard Simon.[16] Every option was on the table, or perhaps sometimes under it, given that radical views were still difficult and dangerous to hold. Appropriately, John Donne's poem "An Anatomy of the World" (1611) is often cited to typify the sense of intellectual disorientation:

> So did the world from the first hour decay,
> That evening was beginning of the day,
> And now the springs and summers which we see
> Like sons of women after fifty be.
> And new philosophy calls all in doubt:
> The element of fire is quite put out;
> The sun is lost, and the earth, and no man's wit
> Can well direct him where to look for it.
> And freely men confess that this world's spent,
> When in the planets and the firmament
> They seek so many new; they see that this
> Is crumbled out again to his atomies.
> 'Tis all in pieces, all coherence gone.[17]

Into this disorienting, pluralistic environment arrived the "theory of the earth" literature. The name derives from the pioneering and most famous entry in the genre, the *Theory of the Earth* by Thomas Burnet (1635–1715),[18] although this intellectual project took some of its momentum from an earlier proposal by Descartes that an initially created chaos could be self-ordering according to God's ordained natural laws.[19]

Now in astronomy it was already accepted practice to postulate hypothetical mathematical models for the motion of the sun and planets that were not held to be literally true. This was called "saving the phenomena" and allowed one to adopt some measure of Copernican heliocentric modelling without incurring trouble from the authorities for actually claiming

---

16. These, too, fell in the same period, if we can stretch our century to reach Simon's *Critical History of the Old Testament* (1682).

17. Donne, *Anatomy of the World*, n.p., with antique spelling updated.

18. In later editions it sometimes goes by the title *Sacred Theory of the Earth*.

19. Descartes, *Descartes*, 40–43; Descartes, *World*, 21–23. The earlier work that is relevant here, *Le monde*, Descartes began in 1629, but abandoned in 1633 upon hearing of Galileo's condemnation: Descartes, *World*, viii. The later work, his major one, *Principia Philosophiae*, dates to 1644. In it he more cautiously summarizes the cosmogony he meant to propose in the earlier work. *World* was published posthumously in 1650.

that it was a physically true explanation.[20] Some thinkers suggest that this is roughly what Descartes and some of his followers (such as the English Platonist Henry More) meant to do: offer a model that explained why some elements of the physical world looked the way they do.[21]

The theories of the earth were different. They consciously claimed to explain how the world came to be in terms of physical processes, though not independently of the hand of God. These were not mere models. They were serious proposals for causation. This was still controversial, yet clearly there was a growing resistance to arbitrarily sidelining events like the Genesis flood as disallowed from human investigation. This prohibition was meant reverently by many, but it could imply that the biblical account was redundant. The earth theorists sought to show that the early chapters of the Bible still mattered for understanding world origins. We will look at the ideas of three Englishmen, not out of ethnic bias, I trust, but because they set the course for ensuing scholarly debate in early eighteenth-century Europe.[22]

THOMAS BURNET'S PHYSICAL EXPLANATION OF EARTH'S ORIGIN

Thomas Burnet had studied under the "Cambridge Platonists" Henry More (1614–1687) and Ralph Cudworth at Cambridge and showed signs of influence from these and numerous other thinkers, ancient and modern.[23] The part of Burnet's model of earth history pertaining to the past (books 1–2) was first published in Latin in 1681 and in English in 1684.[24] His model clearly leans upon Descartes's scheme but presents a more serious prehistory. Burnet sounds more orthodox than Descartes by clearly reinforcing the sub-six thousand-year biblical chronology for the earth's duration, yet clarifies that only the "sublunary world" is in view.[25] (The Cartesian-style formation of the wider cosmos from an initial formless chaos might have taken much longer, it is implied.) The work sounds apologetic: first, Burnet pits the earth's definite beginning against the eternal world of Aristotle's teaching.[26] Next, he seeks to explain the source of the vast quantity of wa-

---

20. Duhem, *Phenomena*.

21. Roger, "Cartesian Model," 98–102; Harrison, "Influence," 178–83 moderates Roger's position a little.

22. See the comments on this point in Rossi, *Dark Abyss*, 8.

23. Poole, *World Makers*, 15, 57, 158–59.

24. Poole, *World Makers*, 56.

25. Burnet, *Sacred Theory*, 2, 7, 34.

26. Aristotle's philosophy had until earlier in the seventeenth century been well

ter needed for Noah's flood to cover the globe, thus countering skepticism about the biblical flood narrative.

Burnet conceived of planet Earth as like an egg, a classical idea, to the point of having a longer polar axis. But he explained its arrival in this state using the naturalistic process postulated by Descartes: from an initial spherical chaos of minute, atom-like particles, the earth would form by settling according to density in a manner rather consistent with traditional ideas about the four elements, earth, water, air, and fire. However, he envisages an oily layer forming on the surface of the waters, collecting further falling particles like dust, and eventually forming the crust of the earth. This gravitational effect produces a smooth globe, lacking mountains, continents or oceans.[27] There is abundant water present, but this is contained as a vast subsurface ocean, the "abyss," out of sight. This was the antediluvian paradise enjoyed by the first humans created less than six thousand years ago.[28]

Burnet's major focus comes next: the deluge of Noah. This was a common part of a triad of reference points for world and redemptive history in the British intellectual culture of the time, along with initial creation and final "conflagration" or dissolution by fire, all supported by 2 Peter 3. Stoic influence was detectable both in the idea of a world that ends in fire and in the potential for a cyclical death and rebirth of the world.[29] Burnet's famous frontispiece arranges the stages of his physical history of the earth in a near-circle, which might almost imply that the world can be reborn from fire once again, despite Burnet's ostensible opposition to the idea of an eternal world.[30]

Returning to the flood, Burnet proposed that in time, through the drying effects of the sun on the earth's new-formed crust and increasing pressure from below the crust through evaporation of the subterranean waters, the crust ruptured and collapsed into the abyss in a worldwide cataclysm, survived by the providentially-protected occupants of Noah's ark. Classical writers, familiar with earthquakes, had also contemplated the potential collapse of vast subterranean caverns: most famously there was Plato's Atlantis

---

established and recognized, though his stance on the eternity of the world was commonly excised from it by Christian thinkers.

27. Burnet, *Theory*, 35–43.
28. Burnet, *Theory*, 2, 6, 8–9, 23, etc.
29. Magruder, "Theories," 193. "The hexameral tradition appropriated Stoic natural philosophy and in turn provided it in a sanctified form for appropriation by early modern natural philosophers who articulated Mosaic Theories of the dissolution of the world."
30. Burnet, *Theory*, 23–29; Gould, *Time's Arrow*, 21–22, 46; Magruder, "Theories," 447.

in the *Timaeus* and also Epicurean and Stoic examples.[31] More recent examples were available in Descartes's *Principia Philosophiae* (1644) and the proto-geological ponderings of Nicolaus Steno's *Prodromus* (1671).[32] Burnet's innovation was to integrate Descartes's and Steno's model of crustal collapse with the Genesis flood. As a result, the world as presently occupied by humanity was fallen in a very physical sense, with mountain ranges surviving as the most graphic evidence of this diluvial fall. Burnet saw our present landforms as a wreck attributable to preordained judgment for human sin. The world had literally been knocked off its primordial axis.[33]

Burnet's scheme at first blush seems quite biblical and gives pronounced attention to the flood as a real, globe-shattering event. "No one before Burnet had attributed such a mass deconstruction of the earth to the [biblical] Flood,"[34] despite the physical process being suggested by Descartes. Yet it rubbed many readers up the wrong way. One reaction would have been that he had transposed the central crisis of history: "The theologically significant moment in the history of sin is not the Flood but the Fall."[35] Similarly, in an age when whole treatises of natural philosophy could be framed using the hexaemeron or Genesis account of the six days of creation, Genesis 1 was conspicuous by its absence in Burnet's model. Worse, when one tried to integrate his model with Genesis 1, incompatibilities immediately revealed themselves. An obvious one was that a nearly spherical world lacking any surface oceans seemed to ignore the narrative of the third day of creation entirely, with its separate land and seas.

In fact, it became clear when Burnet subsequently published his more scholarly explanation in *Archaeologiae Philosophicae* (1692) that he regarded the hexaemeron as a rather low-grade creation myth tailored to the rudimentary intellectual level of its original Hebrew audience.[36] Publishing this work in Latin might have been a safety mechanism to conceal more radical ideas than were presented in the *Theory of the Earth*, but when Deist Charles Blount published the incriminating passage in English,[37] his disparaging attitude towards the early chapters of Genesis was apparent to all, and in the

---

31. In Lucretius' *De Rerum Natura* 6.535–47 and Seneca's *Natural Questions* 3.16 respectively: Magruder, "Theories," 180–86, esp. 182.

32. Magruder, "Theories," 476–77, 562–69. Gould, *Time's Arrow*, 53–58, esp. 58.

33. Poole, *World Makers*, 57.

34. Thomson, *Before Darwin*, 149.

35. Poole, *World Makers*, 59.

36. Burnet, *Archeologiae Philosophicae*, 297–314; Magruder, "Theories," 502, 553–55. The latter pages demonstrate Descartes's similar stance on Genesis 1.

37. Blount, *Oracles of Reason*, 52–76.

aftermath he lost his position as chaplain to the British monarch.[38] Burnet had very deliberately left his physical history of the world disconnected from Genesis 1, having satisfied himself (as had Descartes before him) that the biblical text had no meaningful content to offer in relation to what was called "natural philosophy," notably the physical origin of planet Earth.

JOHN WOODWARD'S CONTRIBUTION: CREATION 2.0

Many of the scholars of the day felt differently about the role of Genesis, so Burnet's publications generated a flurry of responses. Some writers, pained at the neglect of the early chapters of Genesis or the excessive naturalism of Burnet's scheme, proposed their own models for earth history. While they sought to correct his hermeneutic, they implicitly testified to the power of his proposal.

John Woodward (1665/8–1728)[39] was a member of the Royal Society and respected "professor of physic (medicine) at Gresham College, London."[40] There had already been several books published to counter and correct Burnet's *Theory of the Earth* by the time Woodward published his *An Essay toward a Natural History of the Earth* (1695), but it would be Woodward's work and that published in the following year by William Whiston (below) that would, with Burnet's work, form the trio of prominent earth theories that would set the terms of this debate for the next half century.

Woodward brought some new interests and qualifications to the debate. He certainly agreed with other critics who thought that Burnet had strayed too far from the text of Genesis, neglected and contradicted the details of the Mosaic creation week, and with an earth that remained an ideal paradise until the flood, "had ignored the entire scheme of sin and redemption" that was basic to traditional Christian theology.[41] So Woodward manifests apologetic motives, wanting to "assert the Superintendence and Agency of Providence in the Natural World: as also to evince the Fidelity and Exactness of the Mosaick Narrative of the Creation, and of the Deluge."[42]

He was also an increasingly devoted fossil collector, his collection still being available for viewing at Cambridge University, and demonstrated a commitment to empirical research and field work,[43] as opposed to the more

38. E.g. Gould, *Ever Since Darwin*, 145.
39. Poole, *World Makers*, 64.
40. Young and Stearley, *Bible, Rocks and Time*, 64.
41. Rappaport, *Geologists*, 143.
42. Woodward, *Essay*, viii.
43. Vaccari, "European Views," 30.

bookish basis of Burnet's work. His offering stands in contrast to Burnet's book for paying "constant attention to strata and fossils."[44] His biblical commitments and interest in the Genesis flood have gained him considerable disrepute in modern historiography, but he was at the cutting edge of research at the time (from our point of view), in acknowledging that fossils were the remains of living creatures rather than spontaneous productions within the rock as the dominant, Aristotelian view suggested.[45]

Woodward's own theory of the earth tacitly accepts Burnet's dramatic prioritization of the biblical flood as an agent of geological change. The flood therefore dominates his thesis. Woodward, like Burnet, also defends the global nature of the flood, an idea already facing questions at the time. The major change that Woodward makes in relation to Burnet's model is to *relocate the formation of the present world out of chaos* to a new historical position, *after Noah's flood*. The world's formation from chaos by a natural settling out of different kinds of matter was already a very old idea, but Descartes had renovated it as a more naturalistic way of thinking about the world's formation. Burnet had largely adopted Descartes's scheme as a model for *creation*, and in so doing had created a virtually irreconcilable breach with creation as Genesis 1–3 presented it, despite investing the biblical flood with tremendous, literally earth-shattering importance.

Woodward took the settling out of the chaos into natural layers, an Aristotelian commonplace, and identified it as a postdiluvial process! He did not say much about creation itself, holding himself to a natural-philosophical rather than expository discussion. What he did say seems to imply a world created in roughly its present form[46] by divine creative command. He does point out the statement in Exod 20:11 that God created the world in six days; the fact that this declaration falls in the epicenter of biblical law clearly holds special weight for Woodward, and he challenges "the Theorist" with his audacious bypassing of this clear statement of Scripture.[47]

That primordial world, then, was subjected to destruction by God as a punishment for sin, but in a way that would produce a renewed world well suited to life.[48] In the earliest edition of his book, Woodward attributes to the floodwaters the ability to erode the earth's material into a kind of slurry. In later writings, notably his *Naturalis Historia Telluris* (1714), he

---

44. Vaccari, "European Views," 30; Vermij, "Flood," 164–65.

45. Rudwick, *Fossils*, 35.

46. Note that Burnet's primordial world was imagined as very different from the postdiluvial one.

47. Woodward, *Essay*, 252.

48. Woodward, *Essay*, 90–94.

more clearly utilizes a Newtonian mechanism, the temporary suspension or reduction of the force of gravity.[49] The former process would delve "at least to the greatest depth we ever dig,"[50] whereas the latter would imply a radical and complete dissolution of the entire globe.[51] Only biological organisms would be structurally preserved, and as sediments settled out of suspension after the flood's climax according to specific gravity, different rock types would form as successive, level strata, studded with these fossil organisms.

The resultant world, despite its ordeal, was tailored to human life, rather than representing the ugly wreck that made Burnet shudder. It did, however, have to undergo a Burnetian-style crustal collapse to be fit for purpose, meeting the needs of its frail human occupants.[52] So, as with the concept of a formation of the world out of chaos, Woodward also moves Burnet's crustal collapse even later, not making it the cause of the flood disaster but part of its aftermath. Thus Woodward had taken over a great deal of Burnet's physical theory, but had injected a greater degree of empirical research, especially surrounding fossils, and also provided a scheme that was theologically safer and destined for the most favorable European reception of the three schemes.[53] Whether this sort of cosmogonic scheme deserves continued adherence in the twenty-first century is another question entirely.

WILLIAM WHISTON'S WORLDS IN COLLISION

Like Woodward, but even more so, as Newton's successor in his chair as Lucasian Professor of Mathematics at Cambridge, William Whiston (1667–1752) regeared Burnet's theory of the earth according to Newtonian rather than Cartesian physical principles. Whiston was a dedicated disciple of Newton, and whereas Woodward wrote like a fossil collector who had seen a great many landscapes, Whiston wrote like a mathematician interested in astrophysics. Nor was Whiston content with the apparent distance of Burnet's model from the biblical narrative, and he intended to draft a model of physical origins more amenable to the early chapters of Genesis.

49. Woodward, *Essay*, 74–80. Young and Stearley, *Bible, Rocks and Time*, 65–66. Poole, *World Makers*, 642; Magruder, "Theories," 642. Most writers conflate these two ideas, but the Newtonian mechanism is missing from the 1695 description. Young and Stearley recognize the distinction.

50. Woodward, *Essay*, 75.

51. Woodward, *Essay*, ii; Magruder, "Theories," 174, 191–92.

52. Woodward, *Essay*, 79–97; Magruder, "Theories," 191–92; Vaccari, "European Views," 32.

53. Harrison, "Influence," 175; Poole, *World Makers*, 65; Vaccari, "European Views," 30–32.

You will notice the implication: all three men clearly believe in the program of explaining the physical processes by which the present landscapes and natural resources of earth have come into being. Not every thinker of the day considered this a good idea or a godly idea, and it was a popular alternative position to regard either creation or the Genesis flood as pure miracle and immune from physical explanation.[54] Yet Burnet (a little ambivalently), Woodward, and Whiston thought that the credibility of Scripture could be shored up by showing how Genesis was endorsed by the latest theorizing and research into origins.[55]

Whiston's particular contribution in his *A New Theory of the Earth* (1696) would be to shift the limelight back to the narrative of the creation week. Burnet had indicated in his more radical statements that the hexaemeron could not be reconciled with a natural-philosophical account of physical origins, being a kind of "pop" publication for a people of little education and not very much intelligence—a primitive race living at a primitive time.[56] Whiston, like his mentor Newton, thought that a role for Genesis 1 could be retained in a theory of the earth so long as its genre was rightly identified: "not a Nice and Philosophical account of the Origin of All Things; but an Historical and True Representation of the formation of our single Earth out of a confused Chaos, and of the successive and visible changes thereof each day, till it became the habitation of Mankind."[57] This role could work only if it was also recognized that the hexaemeron only dealt with the origin of planet Earth, not of the wider cosmos, whose creation was only touched on from the point of view of its appearance to human view.

Thinking as he did, Whiston could only see the creation week narrative as a description of terrestrial origins if the days of creation were longer than twenty-four hours each. As early as this seems for the first appearance of this idea, coming in 1696, there were earlier precedents. Descartes had hinted in his 1644 *Principia*, and overtly stated in his correspondence with sympathizer Théodore Barin, that his envisaged settling-from-chaos process could not fit within the creation week, as Barin thought.[58] The

---

54. An example from the same time period is Keill, *Examination*. In the mid-eighteenth century (1749) comes the strong statement, Buffon, *Barr's Buffon*, 1.148–54. For a good explanation, see Poole, *World Makers*, 45–46.

55. Olson, *Science and Religion*, 168.

56. See above on Burnet, and the references in n. 37.

57. Whiston, *New Theory*, 3. Compare Newton's comment to Burnet: "As to Moses I do not think his description of ye creation either Philosophical or feigned, but that he described realities in a language artificially adapted to ye sense of ye vulgar." Newton, *Correspondence*, 331.

58. Magruder, "Theories," 544–45, 553–54.

Cartesian-influenced Henry More would follow up in *Conjectura Cabbalistica* (1653) by suggesting "that these *Six numbers*, or *days*, do not signify any order of time, but the nature of things that were said to be made in them.... [A]ll might be made at once, or in such periods of time, as is most suitable to the nature of the things themselves."[59] Matthew Hale combats the idea of extended creation days in his *The Primitive Origination of Mankind* (1677), demonstrating that the idea was already familiar.[60] Finally, Newton proposed to Burnet after 1681 that the creation week might see the earth brought up to speed beginning with one year-long third day of creation (the first day with a recognizable globe to rotate), followed by three days to the next year, and so on until the earth reached its present rotation speed. Otherwise, perhaps the earth would orbit the sun with the same face toward it during this week, creating year-long days.[61]

This latter idea was the one taken up by Whiston and worked out as a full cosmogonic scheme—one that, like Woodward's, incorporates a fresh and topical physical phenomenon, that of comets. Europeans were fascinated by comets around this time, having witnessed with the rest of the world the flyby of Kirch's (or the Great) Comet, first discovered November 14, 1680, and most spectacular in late December as it bypassed the earth a second time after perihelion, with a tail reaching halfway across the sky. The last observation of the comet was by none other than Isaac Newton on March 19, 1681.[62] Royal Society members Robert Hooke (in 1692) and Edmund Halley (in 1694) gave lectures on comets, while Newton was working on a theory about their contribution to creation events.[63]

It fell to Whiston, however, to incorporate this cutting-edge research systematically into his *New Theory*, where comets would feature prominently at the three recognized junctures of redemptive history: creation, deluge, and conflagration. The earth began as a comet, says Whiston;[64] it would be knocked off an upright axis and set rotating in twenty-four hour days by another comet passing nearby, then have its crust (still on the model of the shell of an egg) cracked by the sideswipe of another comet, and finally be impacted by a heated comet to produce the final dissolution in fire, leaving earth itself as a comet once again.[65] The creation week, restored

59. More, *Conjectura*, 148; Brown, *Days of Creation*, 146–49.
60. Hale, *Primitive Origination*, 293–95, 307.
61. Newton, *Correspondence*, 2:333–34.
62. Stoyan, *Atlas*, 77–81; Schechner, *Comets*, 156–57, 164–65.
63. Hooke, "Discourse"; Young, "Scripture," 16–17; Brooke, *Science*, 147–51.
64. Whiston, *New Theory*, 32–33.
65. Magruder, "Theories," 584–95; Harrison, "Influence," 174–75; Olson, *Science*

to theoretical importance after being bypassed by Burnet and Woodward, granted that its days were equivalent to solar years, would be long enough to permit the antediluvian world to settle out of its initial cometary chaos, so long as the sun, moon, and stars simply become visible on the fourth day as the atmosphere clears, rather than being first created on the fourth day.[66] Translating the verbs of speaking and creating in Gen 1:14–17 as pluperfects ("the LORD *had* said, and *had* made") was a device he advocated in support of this view, knowing that the Hebrew perfect form sometimes required this in Old Testament narrative.[67]

Thus, in Whiston's *magnum opus* was the hexaemeron restored to a place of natural-philosophical relevance, so long as its interpretation was carefully framed, a case Whiston took nearly one hundred pages to argue.[68] In contrast to Burnet, Whiston had come to the conclusion that there was no need to oppose "the Obvious and Natural, to the Rational and Philosophick Interpretations of the Holy Scriptures." The accommodated nature and commonsense language of Genesis did not prevent it from referring to the real origin of the world if rightly interpreted.

OUTCOMES FOR OUR UNDERSTANDING OF GENESIS

These and similar theories of the earth were highly influential in connection with early exploration of the history of nature (a new idea in itself) in the first half of the eighteenth century, and works entitled "Theory of the Earth" were published from about a century beyond Burnet's initial offering in 1681. Rather despised in the late nineteenth- and early twentieth-century mainstream historiography for seemingly representing an unholy blend of religious commitment, submission to Scripture and primitive science, this genre is now more recognized as having played an important role in framing and motivating early modern scientific research. Yet its relatively short period of prominence is historical demonstration that its way of synthesizing knowledge was not destined to last. It was not ultimately viable. The periodic and marginal reappearance of similar explanations of world origins ever since, along with the ongoing and important challenge of Christian

---

and *Religion*, 170–72; Cohn, *Noah's Flood*, 62–69, etc.

66. Whiston, *New Theory of the Earth*, 23–25, 33–38, 230–55.

67. Whiston, *New Theory*, 14–16. The New International Version (2011), for example, uses the same translation strategy in Gen 2:8 ("the LORD God had planted a garden") and 19 ("the LORD God has formed out of the ground"), though we might as easily question these translation moves as that of Whiston.

68. Whiston, *New Theory*, 2–96.

understanding of how Genesis relates to the real world, demand that we reflect on the significance of these theories. We focus here on the lessons for biblical interpretation. Theories of the earth often embodied a great respect for Scripture, but they also involved misunderstandings about what the early chapters of Genesis really do.

The Scope of Genesis 1–11

For anyone who still remembers the size of the print version of *Encyclopaedia Britannica* on someone's shelf, the opening chapters of Genesis will look like a rather compact explanation of the origin of all things. Prehuman history is covered on a single page, in Gen 1:1–25. Our children want to know where dinosaurs fit into the story. Did Adam and Eve have to duck for cover when Tyrannosaurus Rex went past, like a scene out of Jurassic Park? Patristic thinkers too felt that this brief account left out a vital part of created reality—angels! Augustine therefore concluded that "Let there be light" must have been an oblique reference to the creation of angels.[69] Otherwise, how could God leave out of his revealed account of the creation of everything the beginning of the most important category of reality after God himself?

There is a shared misunderstanding here. Genesis does not mention dinosaurs and it does not mention angels.

Genesis did not promise to cover the origin of everything. The Bible is not an encyclopedia. If it is supposed to be, it is far too short, and that inadequacy grows by the day. But it is not. We have misunderstood its purpose. What could be judged a lack of coverage is no failing in a written text that never promised to tell us all that we ever wanted to know about origins but were afraid to ask. "The secret things belong to the LORD our God, but the things revealed belong to us and to our children forever," says Deut 29:29, reminding us not to assume entitlement to know everything about everything. God has clearly not intended to use Genesis to tell ancient Israel, let alone us, everything there is to know about origins.

This does not rule out the validity of scientific enterprise; in fact, it may help to provide warrant for it. A creation account that does not address physical causal processes or indicate that the cosmos and the globe, like human society, show clear marks of a history of their own, will not be able to arbitrate directly on the validity of one theoretical construction of physical

---

69. Augustine, *De Genesi ad litteram*, II.8.16: Augustine, *Literal Meaning*. The other possibility he considered was that the "heavens" mentioned with the earth in Gen 1:1 referred to angels.

origins versus another. Genesis by its brevity and bypassing of process leaves us to seek answers elsewhere to legitimate questions about how the world we know came into being. A scientific epistemology with its theological basis anchored in Scripture is capable of warranting and clarifying the enterprise of understanding God's world through empirical study, and such study can be sanctified by a motivation to acknowledge God's glory in creation.[70] These are all venerable ideas and easily researched elsewhere. However, biblical revelation does not leave the Christian free to say just anything about God's world and be free of all fear of error. We clearly cannot exclude purpose, design, and a personal God from our operating metaphysic without doing violence to the biblical presentation of creation.

The Genre of Genesis 1–11

What, then, is early Genesis meant to do? One approach to this question is to narrow down the kind of literature it is, because it is easy to misconstrue purpose when we misinterpret genre. Late Enlightenment thinker J. G. Herder (1744-1803) protested in his reverent if overambitious *Oldest Document of the Human Race* (1774) that the rationalistic systems that sought a full integration of Genesis and all physical knowledge of origins misunderstood an Eastern, emotive, and very early text by treating it like the kind of intellectual Western document they themselves represented.[71] He explains Genesis 1 as an Eastern text that portrays creation through the imagery of sunrise, hence the appearance of light as the first event. It is a provocative presentation of the text and still worth reading,[72] but the point here is that Herder recognizes that Genesis 1 and following chapters were not written according to contemporary literary rules. It is both an ancient text and an Eastern text.

I wish we could learn this lesson today. The genre of Genesis 1 is hard to define; scholars are sometimes forced to admit, despite some connections with other ancient Near Eastern literature (e.g. the Atra-hasis Epic),

---

70. Epistemology is the study of the process of knowing itself. Before we try to learn things about the world scientifically, it is important, and has long been a study of philosophy and theology, to ask how we "know" at all. The Bible has strong theological claims to make about the way that humans in God's world are enabled to "know." Already in Genesis 1, the claim that human beings bear the image of God (vv. 26-27) offers warrant for some confidence that God's human creatures can have some hope of interpreting aright the nature of other things God has created.

71. Herder, *Älteste Urkunde*, 1.8-21. Bultmann, "Creation," 25-26, 30. (There is not yet an English translation to my knowledge.)

72. E.g. see Herder, *Älteste Urkunde*, 1.27-37 on the light of the first day.

that it is one of a kind without any direct analogue.[73] It is technically not poetry, because it lacks the basic identifying elements of Hebrew poetry, notably parallelism. It is highly structured prose. Nor does it fit our familiar category of history because there is no human witness to narrate events, and there are no historical events to narrate. A divine decree of creation is an ontological reality and a causal factor, but not an event in history in any recognizable way. Can we imagine God reflecting on these days to Adam, saying, "... and then I said, 'Let there be a sun and moon,' and no sooner had I said the words, there they were! So, I said, 'Let them operate as lights,'" and so forth. We are dealing with the language of analogy: the constructive work of God portrayed on the analogy of a human work week.[74] Yet although the work is constructive, there is no real labor involved; like an ancient Near Eastern monarch, what God wants, God gets. He simply has to speak, and his will is done.

So, the text of Genesis 1 is full of willing and achieving, a complete matching of intention and result. But it is empty of process. There is no intention to explain how God achieves his will here in terms of physical, causal mediation.[75] Perhaps everything God does is instantly complete! Perhaps God never uses "process" to achieve his will, so there is nothing to describe. I would challenge this either/or thinking. For it is my conviction that it is both biblically justified and pastorally vital to see every human individual as the creation of God. This could be established from Psalm 139, or Job 10, or Job 31, or from James 3:9. Individual human createdness shows that not all of God's works are completed instantly or without mediating processes.[76] The same is true of the nation of Israel, frequently described as the creation of God in Isaiah 40–55. Did God create the mountains? I want to say yes! Why are they like layer cakes inside, rather than homogenous? Why do they contain fossil trees and fish? They, too, have a history. Science may investigate it. It is just that Genesis 1 does not set out to describe it, because it does not tell us everything there is to know about origins. And their development does not rule out God's creative oversight.

---

73. Waltke, "Literary Genre," 2–10.

74. Waltke, "Literary Genre," 7–8; Collins, "How Old," 17–18; Collins, "Reading Genesis 1:1"; Collins, "Reading Genesis 1–2," 73–92. This is a little different from Kline's "upper register" representation of the creation week, which is more dependent on a kind of Platonist subtext than I think we need to be: Kline, "Space and Time."

75. A subtle exception to this statement is the possible subtle nod to mediating agency in the wording, "Let the land produce vegetation" (Gen 1:11) or "Let the water teem with living creatures" (Gen 1:20).

76. Immediately or im-mediately.

A later Christian geologist, William Buckland, clarified this in his contribution to an apologetic lecture series, the Bridgewater Treatises, in 1836:

> The disappointment of those who look for a detailed account of geological phenomena in the Bible, rests on a gratuitous expectation of finding therein historical information, respecting all the operations of the Creator in times and places with which the human race has no concern.... [at] what point ... short of a communication of Omniscience [might] such a revelation ... have stopped?
>
> The above supposed communication of omniscience would have been imparted to creatures, utterly incapable of receiving it ...[77]

The Groundedness of Genesis 1–11

On the other hand, I find another mistaken either/or antithesis in John Walton's position that biblical creation, understood in its ancient Near Eastern setting, concerns only function and not physical origins.[78] It is unclear to me that an ancient audience would understand Genesis 1 *only* in terms of functional origins to the complete exclusion of physical origins. The things described as commanded into existence in Genesis 1 are physical realms, physical objects, and living beings. The subject is not simply what these things do, as important as that is. It is also that they come to be. The misguided science-and-religion battleground cannot so easily be sidestepped by claiming that Genesis does not concern physical *origins*. Physical *process*, yes: Genesis 1 does avoid commenting on that.

But this has primarily concerned Genesis 1 alone, defying our subheadings. Let me return attention to the flood of Noah. In Genesis 6–8 we see a different face of Genesis 1–11, still concerned with the real, tangible, physical world occupied by humans, but now with an eye on physical process and physical agency. There is rain, there is rising water, there is subterranean water contributing,[79] and then as the flood wanes, the water retreats just as it would in a familiar, everyday kind of flood. Nature takes part and the process takes time. Now this narrative falls within the broad and still

---

77. Buckland, *Geology*, 14–16.

78. Walton, "Reading Genesis, 147–50. Compare the frequent questioning of his antithetical thinking by other contributors, e.g. pp. 170–74, 180–81.

79. However, five Hebrew words about the rupturing of the "great deep" (הָבְּר מוֹהָת) in Gen 7:11 hardly provide an adequate basis for constructing a theory of the earth with crustal displacement and deposition.

vaguely-defined genre of "cultural memory," and cultural memory accounts are not like the court reports of a stenographer. They are heavily filtered through local experience, long oral transmission, and cultural recoloring.[80] But viewing Genesis 6–8 as cultural memory is saying that it concerns the real world, rather than some mythical scene, and finds its source in some event in history that could be placed on a timeline. In the latter sense it is even more "grounded" than Genesis 1.

To revisit our theorists of the earth, then: their models are obsolete for many reasons, not just in using scientific models destined for obsolescence as the years passed, but for putting too much faith in human reason to grasp the entire process of earth's formation. Whiston erred in treating Genesis 1 as if it described an origins process, as have many since. Burnet erred in placing too much confidence in the naturalistic cosmogonic model of Descartes. Woodward overread into the flood narrative a global *geological* catastrophe that the reader of the plain sense would never have seen—a global dissolution and redeposition. Yet I am not willing to call these thinkers wrong for daring to incorporate *some* account of the flood of Noah into their physical history of earth. The story of a nearly civilization-ending event is likely to stem from genuine collective memory of group trauma passed down the ancestral chain.[81] For there is an earthy reality about the early chapters of Genesis that should not be lost, even as we cater for an ancient cosmology, a distant culture, and the constrained task of Genesis 1–11 as they begin to relate the story of God's saving involvement with the humans he made.

Genesis and the Wreck of the Western Church

We have seen that from medieval times and into the Renaissance and Reformation, the Bible was understood in the West as an authoritative source for discovering truth. Early Genesis, with its global tone and topics, and in particular the universal statements of Genesis 1, could function as the master frame for all knowledge. Yet Genesis 1 had the risky role of a party balloon in its cultural application. Genesis commentaries grew larger and larger, and practitioners across many fields, historical, philosophical, chemical, astronomical, medical, and geological, took on the responsibility of showing how current theories were reconcilable with the Genesis text.

---

80. For instance, various cultures' flood myths not uncommonly describe the kinds of boats they know how to make and have survived the flood on their highest local mountain peak.

81. Although it is not necessarily the same memory or the same event for each cultural group that preserves such a story.

Eventually there was too much data to fit within the scope of the Scriptural framework, so that it was increasingly questioned and left aside as irrelevant to research. The progressive discarding of Genesis as the arbiter of truth may be observed across many fields of study in the West between 1650 and 1850. In its encyclopedic use, Scripture was a burst balloon. What our case study of theories of the earth has taught us is that Genesis was expected to be all things to all men in the domain of knowledge, to say everything about the world that could be said or needed to be said.

The lesson of the theories of the earth is that we need to let the Bible itself set our expectations of what the Bible is going to do for us. Genesis 1–11 reveals a tightly focused purpose that does not include acting as an encyclopedia. Genesis 1 for its part insists on *authority*: one God is in creative charge of the cosmos. It insists on *agency*: this God is the active cause of the existence of the cosmos, in part and in whole. It insists on *purpose*: the world and its living occupants, above all humans, are present because God wished them to be present. Our existence is fully intended. It is then a short step to *design*, perhaps more an implication of purpose than an outright statement of the text of Genesis, although the intellectual history of the idea of design is highly contested. Finally, Genesis 1–11 initiates the story of God's quest to pursue human beings—in Milton's words, now centuries old, of paradise lost and paradise regained.

Good things can be salvaged from a wreck.

BIBLIOGRAPHY

Augustine. *The Literal Meaning of Genesis*. Edited by John Hammond Taylor. 2 vols. New York: Newman, 1982.

Banderier, Gilles. "A 'Fortunate Phoenix'? Renaissance and Death of the Hexameron (1578–1615)." *Neuphilologische Mitteilungen* 102, no. 3 (2001) 251–67.

Barr, James. "Why the World Was Created in 4004 BC: Archbishop Ussher and Biblical Chronology." *Bulletin of The John Rylands Library* 67 (1985) 575–608.

Blair, Ann. "Mosaic Physics and the Search for a Pious Natural Philosophy in the Late Renaissance." *Isis* 91, no. 1 (2000) 32–58.

Blount, Charles. *The Oracles of Reason: Consisting of 1. A Vindication of Dr. Burnet's Archiologiae. 2. The Seventh and Eighth Chapters of the Same. 3. Etc.* London, 1693.

Brooke, J. H. *Science and Religion: Some Historical Perspectives*. Cambridge History of Science. Cambridge: Cambridge University Press, 1991.

Brown, Andrew J. *The Days of Creation: A History of Christian Interpretation of Genesis 1:1—2:3*. Leiden: Brill, 2012.

Buckland, William. *Geology and Mineralogy Considered with Reference to Natural Theology*. 2 vols. London: William Pickering, 1836.

Buffon, Georges Louis Leclerc, Comte de. *Barr's Buffon. Buffon's Natural History, Containing a Theory of the Earth, a General History of Man, . . . From the French. With Notes by the Translator*. 10 vols. London: J. S. Barr, 1792.

Bultmann, Christoph. "Creation at the Beginning of History: Johann Gottfried Herder's Interpretation of Genesis 1." *Journal for the Study of the Old Testament* 68 (1995) 23-32.

Burnet, Thomas. *Archeologiae Philosophicae, sive Doctrina Antiqua de Rerum Originibus*. London, 1692.

———. *The Sacred Theory of the Earth, Containing an Account of the Original of the Earth, and of All the General Changes Which It Hath Already Undergone, or Is to Undergo, till the Consummation of All Things*. Glasgow: R. Urie, 1753. http://books.google.com/books?id=-aQvAAAAYAAJ.

———. *The Theory of the Earth: Containing an Account of the Original of the Earth, and of All the General Changes Which It Hath Undergone, Or Is to Undergo Till the Consummation of All Things*. London, 1697. https://books.google.com.au/books?id=a-NBAQAAMAAJ.

Cohn, Norman. *Noah's Flood: The Genesis Story in Western Thought*. New Haven: Yale University Press, 1996.

Collins, C. John. "How Old Is the Earth? Anthropomorphic Days in Genesis 1:1—2:3." *Presbyterion* 20 (Fall 1994) 109-30.

———. "Reading Genesis 1:1—2:3 as an Act of Communication: Discourse Analysis and Literal Interpretation." In *Did God Create in Six Days?*, edited by Jr. Joseph A. Pipa and David W. Hall, 131–50. White Hall, WV: Tolle Lege, 1999.

———. "Reading Genesis 1-2 with the Grain: Analogical Days." In *Reading Genesis 1-2: An Evangelical Conversation*, edited by J. Daryl Charles, 131–50. Peabody: Hendrickson, 2013.

Descartes, René. *Descartes: Selected Philosophical Writings*. Translated by John Cottingham and Robert Stoothoff. Cambridge: Cambridge University Press, 1988.

———. *The World and Other Writings*. Translated and edited by Stephen Gaukroger. Cambridge Texts in the History of Philosophy. New York: Cambridge University Press, 1998.

Donne, John. *An Anatomy of the World*. London: S. Macham, 1611. https://books.google.com.au/books?id=ihMzAQAAMAAJ.

Duhem, Pierre. *To Save the Phenomena: An Essay on the Idea of Physical Theory from Plato to Galileo*. Translated by Edmund Doland. Chicago: University of Chicago Press, 1969.

Evans, J. M. *"Paradise Lost" and the Genesis Tradition*. Oxford: Clarendon, 1968.

Eyers, Jonathan. *Final Voyage: The World's Worst Maritime Disasters*. London: A&C Black, 2013.

Forshaw, Peter J. "The Genesis of Christian Kabbalah: Early Modern Speculations on the Work of Creation." In *Hidden Truths from Eden: Esoteric Readings of Genesis 1-3*, edited by Caroline Vander Stichele and Susanne Scholz, 121–44. Atlanta: SBL, 2014.

Forshaw, Peter J. "Vitriolic Reactions: Orthodox Responses to the Alchemical Exegesis of Genesis." In *The Word and the World*, 111–136. Basingstoke: Macmillan, 2007.

Goudriaan, Aza. "Creation, Mosaic Physics, Copernicanism, and Divine Accommodation." In *Reformed Orthodoxy and Philosophy, 1625-1750*, 85–141. Leiden: Brill, 2006.

Gould, Stephen Jay. *Ever Since Darwin*. Harmondsworth: Penguin, 1980.

———. *Time's Arrow, Time's Cycle. Myth and Metaphor in the Discovery of Geological Time*. Harvard: Harvard University Press, 1987.

Grafton, A. T. "Joseph Scaliger and Historical Chronology: The Rise and Fall of a Discipline." *History and Theory* 14 (1975) 156–85.

Griggs, Tamara. "Universal History from Counter-Reformation to Enlightenment." *Modern Intellectual History* 4 (2007) 219–47.

Hale, Matthew. *The Primitive Origination of Mankind, Considered and Examined According to the Light of Nature*. London, 1677.

Harrison, Peter. "The Influence of Cartesian Cosmology in England." In *Descartes' Natural Philosophy*, edited by S. Gaukroger, J. Schuster, and J. Sutton, 168–92. London: Routledge, 2000.

Herder, Johann Gottfried. *Älteste Urkunde des Menschengeschlechts*. 2 vols. Riga: J. F. Hartknoch, 1774.

Hooke, Robert. "A Discourse of the Nature of Comets." In *The Posthumous Works of Robert Hooke, . . . Containing His Cutlerian Lectures, and Other Discourses, Read at the Meetings of the Illustrious Royal Society. . . . Illustrated with Sculptures. To These Discourses Is Prefixt the Author's Life, . . . Publish'd by Richard Waller*, 149 [marked 194]–192. London: Sam. Smith and Benj. Walford, 1705.

Jaki, Stanley. *Genesis 1 through the Ages*. 2nd ed. Royal Oak, MI: Real View, 1998.

Keill, John. *An Examination of Dr. Burnet's Theory of the Earth*. Oxford, 1698.

Kirkconnell, W., ed. *The Celestial Cycle*. New York: Gordian, 1967.

Kline, Meredith G. "Space and Time in the Genesis Cosmogony." *Perspectives on Science and Christian Faith* 48, no. 1 (March 1996) 2–15.

La Peyrère, Isaac de. *Men before Adam: Or a Discourse upon the Twelfth, Thirteenth and Fourteenth Verses of the Epistle of the Apostle Paul to the Romans*. London: F. Leach, 1656.

Livingstone, David N. *Adam's Ancestors: Race, Religion, and the Politics of Human Origins*. Baltimore: Johns Hopkins University Press, 2008.

Magruder, K. V. "Theories of the Earth from Descartes to Cuvier: Natural Order and Historical Contingency in a Contested Textual Tradition." PhD diss., University of Oklahoma, 2000.

McCalla, Arthur. *The Creationist Debate: The Encounter between the Bible and the Historical Mind*. London and New York: Continuum, 2006.

Mersenne, Marine. *Quaestiones Celeberrimae in Genesim, Cum Accurata Textus Explicatione*. Paris: Sebastiani Cramoisy, 1623. https://books.google.com.au/books?id=mUFEAAAAcAAJ.

More, Henry. *Conjectura Cabbalistica*. London: James Flesher, 1653.

Newton, Isaac. *Correspondence*. Vol. 2. Edited by H. W. Turnbull. Cambridge: Cambridge University Press, 1960.

Olson, Richard. *Science and Religion, 1450–1900: From Copernicus to Darwin*. Westport, CT: Greenwood Press, 2004.

Paproth, Darrell. *Failure Is Not Final: A Life of C. H. Nash*. Macquarie Centre, NSW: Centre for the Study of Australian Christianity, Macquarie University, 1997.

Poole, William. *The World Makers*. Oxford: Peter Lang, 2010.

Popkin, Richard H. "The Third Force in Seventeenth-Century Thought: Scepticism, Science and Millenarianism." In *The Third Force in Seventeenth-Century Thought*, edited by Richard H. Popkin, 90–119. Leiden: E. J. Brill, 1992.

Rappaport, Rhoda. *When Geologists Were Historians 1665-1750*. Ithaca and London: Cornell University Press, 1997.
Robbins, F. *The Hexaemeral Literature: A Study of the Greek and Latin Commentaries in Genesis*. Chicago: University of Chicago Press, 1912.
Roger, Jacques. "The Cartesian Model and Its Role in Eighteenth-Century 'Theory of the Earth.'" In *Problems of Cartesianism*, edited by Thomas M. Lennon, John M. Nicholas, and John W. Davis, 95-112. Kingston and Montreal: McGill-Queen's University Press, 1982.
Rossi, Paolo. *The Dark Abyss of Time. The History of the Earth and the History of the Nations from Hooke to Vico*. Chicago: University of Chicago Press, 1984.
Rudwick, M. J. S. *The Meaning of Fossils*. London: Macmillan, 1972.
Ryken, Leland. "Paradise Lost and Its Biblical Epic Models." In *Milton and Scriptural Tradition*, 43-81. Columbia, MO: University of Missouri Press, 1984.
Schechner, Sara J. *Comets, Popular Culture, and the Birth of Modern Cosmology*. Princeton, NJ: Princeton University Press, 1997.
Stoyan, Ronald. *Atlas of Great Comets*. Cambridge: Cambridge University Press, 2015.
Thomson, Keith. *Before Darwin. Reconciling God and Nature*. New Haven: Yale UP, 2005.
Truswell, Elizabeth. *A Memory of Ice: The Antarctic Voyage of the Glomar Challenger*. Canberra: ANU Press, 2019.
Vaccari, Ezio. "European Views on Terrestrial Chronology from Descartes to the Mid-Eighteenth Century." In *The Age of the Earth from 4004 BC to AD 2002*, edited by C. L. E. Lewis and Simon J. Knell, 25-38. GS Special Publications 190. London: Geological Society, 2001.
Van Winden, J. C. M. "Hexaemeron." In *Reallexikon für Antike und Christentum* 14:1250-1269. Stuttgart: Anton Hiersemann, 1988.
Vermij, R. "The Flood and the Scientific Revolution: Thomas Burnet's System of Natural Providence." In *Interpretations of the Flood*, edited by Florentino García Martínez and Gerardus Petrus Luttikhuizen, 150-66. Leiden: Brill, 1998.
Vincent of Beauvais. *Speculum Quadriplex, sive, Speculum Maius*. 4 vols. Graz: Akademische Druck- und Verlagsanstalt, 1964.
Waltke, B. "The Literary Genre of Genesis, Chapter One." *Crux* 27 (December 1991) 2-10.
Walton, John H. "Reading Genesis 1 as Ancient Cosmology." In *Reading Genesis 1-2: An Evangelical Conversation*, edited by J. Daryl Charles, 141-69. Peabody: Hendrickson, 2013.
Walton, Michael T. "Genesis and Chemistry in the Sixteenth Century." In *Reading the Book of Nature: The Other Side of the Scientific Revolution*, edited by Allen G. Debus and Michael Thomson Walton, 1-14. Kirksville, MO: Truman State University Press, 1998.
———. *Genesis and the Chemical Philosophy: True Christian Science in the Sixteenth and Seventeenth Centuries*. Brooklyn, NY: AMS, 2011.
Whiston, William. *A New Theory of the Earth, from Its Original, to the Consummation of All Things*. London: R. Roberts, 1696.
Williams, Arnold Ledgerwood. *The Common Expositor: An Account of the Commentaries on Genesis 1527-1633*. Chapel Hill: University of North Carolina Press, 1948.
Woodward, John. *An Essay Toward a Natural History of the Earth*. London: R. Wilkin, 1695.

Young, Davis A. "Scripture in the Hands of Geologists." *Westminster Theological Journal* 49 (1987) 1–34, 257–304.

Young, Davis A., and Ralph Stearley. *The Bible, Rocks and Time: Geological Evidence for the Age of the Earth*. Downers Grove: InterVarsity, 2008.

Zanchius, Hieronymus. *De Operibus Dei intra Spacium Sex Dierum Creatis Opus*. Neustadt, 1591.

Cultural Insights

14

Making Christ Offensive Again

A Kierkegaardian Polemic against Soft-Pedal Evangelicalism

Ernie Laskaris

IT HAS BEEN OBSERVED that evangelicalism in the twenty-first century has largely followed the pattern of the culture within which it exists, and it is a culture that excludes that which may be considered offensive to a person's sensibilities. As such, evangelicalism has largely censured the offensive aspects of Christianity. As Kierkegaard argued, however, offence is *essential* to biblical Christianity, and to remove what is essential to Christianity it is to abolish Christianity. In order to reintroduce biblical Christianity into *soft-pedal evangelicalism*, then, it is necessary to recover the following: (1) the doctrine of the "infinite qualitative difference" between God and humanity; (2) the doctrine of the forgiveness of sins; and (3) the call to a discipleship that is characterized by Christian suffering.

THE PARASITIC

A centennial year for a theological institution in this day and age is certainly a cause for celebration, and as the students and faculty of Melbourne School of Theology prepare for another hundred years of theological research (Lord willing), we find ourselves confronted once again with the question of the current state of *evangelicalism*.[1] The question, however, has too often been answered with reference to the numerical, asking questions like, "How many Australians marked the 'Christian' box on this year's census?" Instead, we ought to answer the question with reference to the marks of true Christianity (by which I mean Christianity as it is presented in the New Testament), and this might require that we reframe the question. Perhaps we can borrow an approach from the work of Michael Horton, who—despite the commercial, political, and media success of evangelicalism—once asked, "Is it still *Christian*?"[2] His own answer is a negative one, arguing that the broad category of evangelicalism is "becoming theologically vacuous," a "Christless Christianity."[3] Tragically, a significant body of research stands in support of this assessment.[4]

In an extensive study on the religious beliefs and spirituality of teenagers in the United States, Christian Smith and his team of sociologists from the University of North Carolina concluded that the *de facto* dominant religion among the youth of the day was not any one of the world's established religions, but a kind of amorphous, "melting-pot" religion —they gave it the name "Moralistic Therapeutic Deism" (MTD).[5] Greg Sheridan, an Australian journalist, recently described it as the belief that "there is a God" who "exists to solve your problems and make you feel happy," commanding only that you "be nice to people."[6] This is not a God who wishes to be particularly involved in the lives of believers, unless he is in some way needed to solve a problem (to be fair, the fact that this God can be called upon at all disqualifies MTD from the category of "deism").[7] This is a God, rather, who offers to grant people comfort, to bolster their self-esteem, and

---

1. Of course, the sheer breadth of this category is sufficient to eliminate almost all of its functional utility, which is perhaps why the term itself has become a pejorative among many lay Protestants. For the purposes of this chapter, "evangelicalism" will simply refer to the body of churches that profess fundamental Protestant doctrines (e.g. the supreme authority of Scripture alone, justification by grace alone through faith alone, etc.).

2. Horton, *Christless Christianity*, 19.

3. Horton, *Christless Christianity*, 23, 27.

4. For example, see Pearce and Lundquist Denton, *Faith*. For an earlier work that anticipated much of what we are seeing today, see Hunter, *Evangelicalism*.

5. Smith and Lundquist Denton, *Soul Searching*, 162–63. For a similar project with a specific focus on Australian teenagers, see Mason, "Spirituality."

6. Sheridan, *Good for You*, 10.

7. As noted by Stackhouse, "Post-Christian," 1165.

to lubricate all of their interpersonal relationships by encouraging a general (albeit relative) moral goodness.[8]

It is tempting to write this off as another passing fad, but the greatest danger of MTD, aside from the fact that it deafens the youth of today to the true gospel of grace, is that it functions *underneath the surface* as a "parasitic" faith. It is "Christian Parasitology," as one scholar describes it, for it is the weaker organism drawing life from the stronger organism (biblical Christianity) by inhabiting its "space" (namely, the local evangelical churches).[9] In the words of Christian Smith and Melinda Lundquist Denton:

> It cannot sustain its own integral, independent life; rather, it must attach itself like an incubus to established historical religious traditions, feeding on their doctrines and sensibilities, and expanding by mutating their theological substance to resemble its own distinctive image . . . This religion generally does not and cannot stand on its own, so its adherents must be *Christian Moralistic Therapeutic Deists* . . . [MTD] is colonising many historical religious traditions and, almost without anyone noticing, converting believers in the old faiths to its alternative religious vision of divinely underwritten personal happiness and interpersonal niceness.[10]

What we are dealing with, then, is something that is "only *tenuously Christian* in any sense that it is seriously connected to the actual historical Christian tradition"—something that, through its "parasitic" attachment to biblical Christianity, has "substantially morphed into Christianity's misbegotten step-cousin, Christian Moralistic Therapeutic Deism."[11]

Of course, we are now in a new year—a new decade—but much has stayed the same, with numerous theologians and sociologists highlighting the ongoing danger of the MTD parasite within the structures of contemporary evangelicalism even in the past five years.[12] This is by no means to suggest, however, that this parasite has not evolved. The form of evangelicalism that this chapter will be addressing is not the pure MTD described above, but a certain sociopolitical, sociocultural mutation of this MTD that we might call "soft-pedal evangelicalism" (SPE). This mutation has largely been the product of the ongoing politicization of the "safe space" concept, which

---

8. Dean, *Almost Christian*, 29.
9. Dean, *Almost Christian*, 12–15.
10. Smith and Lundquist Denton, *Soul Searching*, 166, 171 (emphasis original).
11. Smith and Lundquist Denton, *Soul Searching*, 171 (emphasis added).
12. See, for example, Ward, *Liquid Ecclesiology*, 125–141; Hiebert, "Subjective Turn"; Travis, *Metamorphosis*, 59–61.

was first formulated during the civil rights movement to describe a place where members of various identity-based collectives could meet and talk about their experiences without the possibility of criticism.[13] In the past decade, however, it seems that the physical safe space has been expanded to include virtually every "space" imaginable—the university campuses, the schools, the libraries, and even the internet. Netflix, for example, recently received quite an ideological beatdown from millennial viewers who were offended that a popular sitcom, *Friends*, included a few lighthearted jokes that they deemed to be "sexist," "fat-shaming," and "transphobic."[14] Notwithstanding, I still think it is a great show.

By "safe space," then, I am referring primarily to the political and cultural implications of the "safe space" concept *qua* politicized, rather than to an actual physical space as originally formulated (I do believe that a case can be made for the original "safe space" concept being a good idea). Consider the university campuses, which seem to have been hit particularly hard, as an example. Monash University recently required all of their faculty members to review all course content and remove anything that might be considered "emotionally confronting material."[15] In 2016, faculty at the University of Edinburgh (as well as that of various other universities across the United Kingdom) were required to have "trigger warnings" prior to lectures on the topic of Christianity, for such lectures are "potentially distressing."[16] Simply put, students are to be protected from the possibility of offence, criticism, and anything that might make them somewhat uncomfortable. This, of course, is shocking behavior from the institution that was once heralded as the bastion for free enquiry, and as a recent report by the American Association of University Professors highlights, "The presumption that students need to be protected rather than challenged is at once infantilising and anti-intellectual."[17] Such behaviors and attitudes, however, are indicators of a cultural shift. What we are seeing develop before our eyes is a "soft-pedal culture," a culture that excludes the "unsafe"—and by "unsafe," we mean something that may be considered *offensive* to a person's sensibilities. In other words, soft-pedal culture is the censuring (and, at times, censoring) of the offensive aspects of culture. In that same vein, then, we may also define SPE as the censuring (and, at times, censoring) of the offensive aspects of Christianity (we will consider some of these below).

13. Wexelbaum, "Safe Space," 39.
14. Pike, "Netflix."
15. Campbell and Manning, *Victimhood Culture*, 77–78.
16. Campbell and Manning, *Victimhood Culture*, 77.
17. Wiener, *Microaggressions*, 70.

In this chapter, I will argue that removing the offence from Christianity is to remove something that is *essential* to Christianity—and thus, it is to abolish Christianity. In making this argument, I will draw particularly from the work of Søren Kierkegaard, history's most outspoken Christian apologist of the gospel as essentially offensive. Then, as a conclusion, I will present something of a Kierkegaardian vision for the future of theological studies; a call for the recovery of the *unsafe gospel* of Jesus Christ—or, in Kierkegaardian terms, a call for the introduction of Christianity into contemporary SPE.

A brief word of caution is necessary here, however, considering recent developments in the world of Australian evangelicalism. When I speak of the gospel as "essentially offensive," I am strictly referring to the offence contained *within its content*. Therefore, I am by no means advocating insensitive, thoughtless, or coldhearted approaches to proclaiming Christianity. As Christians have argued for centuries, nothing is to be added to the gospel of Jesus Christ by the preacher/evangelist (e.g. Gal 1:6–9), and that "nothing" includes offence that is not inherent to its content.[18] I stand in agreement with this position, and as such, this chapter will be a call for the recovery of the inherent offence of the Christian message *alone*, and thereby excluding any and all impudence, abusiveness, and insensitivity from the lips of those who only claim to "speak the truth in love" (Eph 4:15), but truly speak from the "restless evil" (Jas 3:8) of their untamed tongues.

THE UNSAFE GOSPEL

It would not be too far of a stretch to suggest that the Bible is full of offence—both to the characters in its actual narrative, as well as to its readers. "You only need to quote selected passages from the Bible," writes the controversial ex-professor Barry Spurr, "and the shrill cries of the censorious will ring out to the ends of the earth."[19] A now infamous example of this is a heated exchange between Democrat Senator Bernie Sanders and Russell Vought (the president's nominee for the position of deputy director of the White House's Office of Management and Budget) in 2017. Vought, being a devout Christian, wrote an article for the purpose of critiquing the comments of a former Wheaton College employee, Larycia Hawkins, which sought to establish a sense of solidarity between Christians and Muslims (claiming that Christians and Muslims "worship the same God").[20]

---

18. See, for example, Calvin, *Sermons*, 41.

19. Spurr, "Cultural Curse," 9.

20. Her full statement, posted on her Facebook page, was as follows: "I stand in religious solidarity with Muslims because they, like me, a Christian, are people of the

In his response, Vought cited Jesus's words, "Whoever believes in [the Son of God] is not condemned, but whoever does not believe is condemned already, because he has not believed in the name of the only Son of God" (John 3:18).[21] Senator Sanders would draw attention to this during the confirmation hearing for Vought, stating before congress,

> In my view, the statement made by Mr. Vought is indefensible. It is hateful, it is Islamophobic, and it is an insult to over a billion Muslims throughout the world . . . I would simply say, Mr. Chairman, that this nominee is really not someone who is what this country is supposed to be about—I will vote no.[22]

According to Senator Sanders, one must reject a fundamental doctrine of Christianity, the exclusivity and necessity of Christ for salvation (cf. John 14:6), in order to be the deputy director of the Office of Management and Budget. Fortunately, this was not how the case turned out, and Vought was eventually confirmed by the senate in 2018.

Nonetheless, the point stands—historical Christian beliefs are increasingly considered too offensive to be broadcast in this soft-pedal culture, and this includes even the most stock standard of them all. For example, this past Christmas, the headmaster of a London primary school changed the lyrics to *Away in a Manger* for the school's annual Christmas carols, ordering that the students no longer sing of the "little Lord Jesus," but only of the "baby boy Jesus."[23] Why? Because the lordship of Jesus was not deemed to be "inclusive" enough, and so it needed to be "sanitized" for the soft-pedal culture. What we are now seeing, however, is the growing persuasion that Christianity can only exist in a soft-pedal culture if it becomes soft-pedal Christianity—one without the possibility of offence. As Sarah Travis explains,

> In a time of fear, despair, and uncertainty, church leaders and preachers may abandon deep and meaningful theologies in favour of a gentle and *unoffensive* gospel . . . Preachers might be tempted to speak "safe" words that do not upset or challenge.[24]

The fatal problem for the SPE advocates is that there is an *essential* relation between offence and understanding when it comes to the gospel. As

---

book, and as Pope Francis stated last week, we worship the same God." For more on this, as well as a critique of this sentiment, see Qureshi, "Same God?"
21. See the article at Vaught, "Wheaton College."
22. Bernie Sanders, quoted in Buckles, "Unashamed, 817.
23. Dieppe, "Too Offensive."
24. Travis, *Metamorphosis*, 60 (emphasis added).

Mark Dever once said, "A gospel that in no way offends the sinner has not been understood."[25] Or, on the other side of this coin, a gospel that has been understood, but in no way offends the sinner, cannot be said to be the true gospel—as Paul says, "The word of the cross is folly to those who are perishing" (1 Cor 1:18). To sanitize the gospel, then, is to do away with the gospel.

I intend now to further this case against SPE through the lens of a particular Christian thinker; one who is, as noted above, perhaps the staunchest defender of the Christian faith as, like its Christ, essentially offensive.

THE ESSENTIALLY CHRISTIAN

Søren Kierkegaard (1813–1855) was an author and philosopher during the "golden age" of Danish literary, ecclesiastical, and artistic life. In his final few years before his early death, Kierkegaard—interpreting the mass social unrest caused by the 1848 revolutions in Europe as an opportunity for reformation—began assessing and criticizing the Danish "established church" (by which we mean the official state Lutheran church of Denmark). According to his own witness, he had done this for his entire career as a religious author, claiming that his "whole authorship pertains to Christianity . . . with direct and indirect polemical aim at that enormous illusion, Christendom."[26] Central to his thinking is this distinction that he makes between "Christianity" and "Christendom"—the former referring to the Christianity we see portrayed in the New Testament, and the latter referring to the "established church" of Denmark. By "illusion," he means that the state of nineteenth-century Christendom led its citizens to "the blasphemous assumption that everyone was Christian."[27] It was a time, in his own words, that being a Christian was "as simple as pulling on one's socks," rather than taking up one's cross (Mark 8:34).[28] He goes on to say, "Christendom has abolished Christianity without really knowing itself. As a result, if something must be done, one must attempt again to introduce Christianity into Christendom."[29] In what exact way, however, did Christendom abolish Christianity? Why exactly is it that these two categories no longer had anything in common? Kierkegaard's answer would come in *Practice in*

---

25. Dever, *Gospel*, 64.
26. Kierkegaard, *Point of View*, 23.
27. Kapic and Madueme, "Practice in Christianity," 661.
28. Kierkegaard, *Practice in Christianity*, 35.
29. Kierkegaard, *Practice in Christianity*, 35–36.

Christianity, the book he believed to be "the most perfect and the truest thing" that he had ever written.[30]

Originally, this work was not intended to be an outright indictment against the Danish state church. It was meant as a "corrective," rather—a "potential defence for an established order if it understands itself."[31] In other words, the goal was not to overthrow it, but to call it to repentance. The church's response, however, was dispassionate. Neither repentance nor outrage came out of it, not even from Kierkegaard's childhood pastor Jacob Peter Mynster (a key figure in the Danish church at the time).[32] One disappointment after another would only lead Kierkegaard to publish a second edition of *Practice in Christianity*, prefaced with the assertion that "the established order is Christianly indefensible," and that every single day that Christendom persists to exist, "it is Christianly a crime."[33] Why? Simply, it is because Christendom has removed from Christianity that which is *essentially Christian*, that without which Christianity can no longer truly be called Christianity—the "possibility of offence."

Kierkegaard's understanding of the possibility of offence as something that is *essentially Christian* is informed by the words of Jesus Christ himself— "Blessed is the one who is not offended by me" (Matt 11:6). This beatitude toward those who are not offended by Jesus necessitates the possibility of those same people being offended by Jesus (as many indeed were—e.g. Matt 13:57; 15:12; Mark 6:3; John 6:61). It is at the place where one encounters this possibility of offence, however, that one is faced with the call to faith and repentance. Kierkegaard describes it as a kind of crossroads:

> Just as the concept "faith" is an altogether distinctively Christian term, so in turn is "offence" an altogether distinctively Christian term relating to faith. The possibility of offence is the *crossroad*, or it is like standing at the *crossroad*. From the possibility of

---

30. Kierkegaard, *Practice in Christianity*, 287, 308. At one point, Kierkegaard considered giving it a far more provocative title, *A Contribution to the Introduction of Christianity into Christendom*. He believed that this title was "categorically correct; nothing is said about Denmark or Germany or Sweden, etc., nor about whether it is the present or the past—no, it is a purely dialectical definition, the relation between the two concepts: Christianity and Christendom, with the purpose of introducing Christianity. It is a spiritual fencing" (Kierkegaard, *Practice in Christianity*, 307). Eventually, however, he decided against it—"This title was not used; if it were used, it would, after all, be merely poetic, and that is too much. The original title was used, *Practice in Christianity*." See also the historical introduction written by Howard V. Hong and Edna H. Hong in Kierkegaard, *Practice in Christianity*, xi–xx.

31. Kierkegaard, *Point of View*, 18–19.

32. Kapic and Madueme, "Practice in Christianity," 664.

33. Kierkegaard, *Practice in Christianity*, xvii.

offence, one turns either to offence or to faith, but one never comes to faith except from the possibility of offence.[34]

In other words, the possibility of offence is the dialectical element in the Christian concept of faith. Christian believers are not offended by Christ, but they still must have encountered the possibility of offence in order to come to faith in the first place.[35] Kierkegaard calls this the "guardian" of faith—or "Christianity's mortal weapon"—refusing to grant entrance to any counterfeit doubles by way of *frastød* ("repulsion").[36] As Sylvia Walsh puts it,

> This repulsion, however, is designed first and foremost to guard against the misunderstanding of Christianity's true nature, and taking its attractiveness lightly or in vain . . . It thrusts everyone backward in order to prevent a direct communication of, or transition to, *becoming a Christian*. In its deepest sense, the possibility of offence is an expression for the necessity of emphasising the great attention required in the [passionate resolve] to become a Christian.[37]

It is this repulsion essential to Christianity, then, that drives the offended away from faith, while also functioning as the mechanism through which a person is brought to faith. Walsh goes on to suggest that Christianity attracts believers, but "it sets about this task inversely by first repelling, then attracting them . . . It repels in order to attract."[38] It is the task of every believer, then, not to avoid the possibility of offence, but rather to "go through it" with the "infinite passion" that finds its ultimate culmination in eternal blessedness—for blessed are they who are not offended when they stand at the crossroads.[39]

For Kierkegaard, though, this talk of *frastød* and the possibility of offence is profoundly christological. Jason Mahn suggests that *Practice in Christianity* can be read as though it is asking a question that is akin to that of the heavenly accuser in Job 1:9, "Do Christians love Christ for naught?"[40]

---

34. Kierkegaard, *Practice in Christianity*, 81 (emphasis added).
35. As noted by Walsh, *Living Christianly*, 51.
36. Kierkegaard, *Practice in Christianity*, 102, 105, 121.
37. Walsh, *Living Christianly*, 52 (emphasis added).
38. Walsh, *Living Christianly*, 52.
39. Kierkegaard, *Practice in Christianity*, 97–98, 111.
40. Mahn, *Fortunate Fallibility*, 139. Of course, I am aware that the traditional view is that the devil was the one asking this question, but there are significant reasons to doubt this identification. This, however, is not the place for an exposition on the text of Job, but I will recommend to the reader the following resources: Longman, *Job*, 82–83;

The fundamental problem of Danish Christendom, the illusion, is that it was *disinterested*, and disinterested religion is possible only insofar as the possibility of offence is removed; and if the possibility of offence is removed, Jesus is not being rightly presented. The New Testament presents the Christ, Jesus of Nazareth, as a sign of offence (e.g. Luke 2:34; 1 Cor 1:23; 1 Pet 2:8), but this sign of offence, according to Kierkegaard, had "become the most fabulous of all fabulous characters, a divine Mr. Goodman."[41] Jesus was seen as the prototypical "jolly good fellow (pause), and so say all of us!"[42]

To a large degree, the Jesus of SPE is the same—though perhaps with an added touch of romance and sentimentality, which has proven to be extremely marketable (cf. the sheer number of published books by a *New York Times* best-selling author at your local Christian bookstore).[43] We hear songs sung in churches that profess a Jesus who "didn't want heaven without us," and so he "brought heaven down."[44] Is there truth to this statement? You be the judge, but at the very least, we might call it an incomplete picture of the gospel, one in which there is no possibility of offence. Of course, presenting Christ as the sign of offence would probably not have won this song a Grammy. Kierkegaard's words in *Works of Love* might be directly applicable to our SPE context here: "Woe to the one who ingratiatingly, panderingly, commandingly, convincingly preached to the people some *unmanly something* that was supposed to be Christianity!"[45] Some may consider these words to be too serious for the present context (especially if we take the word "woe" in the biblical sense), but this is a *serious* issue. The argument here is that, apart from the possibility of offence (or, rather, if the possibility of offence is removed), it becomes impossible to recognize Christianity in Christendom—that is how *essential* offence is to Christianity. Hence, Kierkegaard goes on to make the following suggestion: "Take away from the essentially Christian the possibility of offence . . . and

---

Clines, *Job 1–20*, 19–20; and Pope, *Job*, 9–11.

41. Kierkegaard, *Practice in Christianity*, 35–36. Mr. Goodman is an allusion to the protagonist of a German children's book by Karl Traugott Thieme, *Gutmann oder der Dänische Kinderfreund*. He is presented as a rather exaggeratedly hearty and foolish man. Kierkegaard here asserts that Danish Christendom had reduced Jesus to such a man—exaggeratedly hearty and foolish.

42. Trad., "Jolly Good Fellow," in Cryer, *Love Me Tender*, 14.

43. For an in-depth study on this, see Brenneman, *Homespun Gospel*.

44. Hillsong Worship, "What a Beautiful Name," track 5 on *Let There Be Light* (Hillsong Music, 2016).

45. Kierkegaard, *Works of Love*, 200 (emphasis added).

then close the churches, the sooner the better, or turn them into places of amusement that stand open all day!"[46]

Kierkegaard drew attention to the fact that, when Jesus came into the world, and when he actually walked on the earth in the first century AD, Christianity "did not itself need to point out (even though it did do so) that it was an offence, because the world, which took offence, certainly discovered this easily enough."[47] In other words, Christ's contemporaries took him as he truly was—the sign of offence. Almost two thousand years later, and Christ is (and has been for quite some time) understood to be the antonym of offensive. The tragic corollary of this is that "many 'Christians' in these times miss out on Christianity," and if this is to stop, "then first of all the possibility of offence must be thoroughly preached back to life again," for it is this alone that "is able to revoke the enchantment so that Christianity is itself again."[48] As Walsh would ask, however, "Exactly what in Christianity occasions the possibility of offence? And why is it unavoidable in becoming a Christian?"[49]

Originally, Kierkegaard planned to write a new book—*Thoughts That Cure Radically*—which would consist of two parts. In the end, the two parts were published separately, the second being *Practice in Christianity* in 1850. His answer to Walsh's questions asked above, however, are made explicit in the first part, *The Sickness Unto Death*, published in 1849. The thesis of this work is that a Kierkegaardian concept of *fortvivlelse* ("despair") is equal to the biblical concept of ἁμαρτία ("sin"). According to Kierkegaard, while not all kinds of despair involve being offended, being offended (by Christianity) is always a symptom of a kind of despair—and thus, is always sin. The crossroads, therefore, which is only the *possibility* of offence, is the intersection between faith on the one side and sin on the other. In the latter parts of *The Sickness Unto Death*, however, Kierkegaard specifically outlines three (at least) negative movements of offence (i.e. reasons that Christianity offends).

THE CHASMIC QUALITATIVE ABYSS

Firstly, Christianity offends because it asserts that there is an *uendelige kvalitative forske* (an "infinite qualitative difference") between humanity and God as a result of sin. "At this point lies the most extreme concentration of offence," Kierkegaard writes, "[that] as sinner, man is separated from

---

46. Kierkegaard, *Works of Love*, 201.
47. Kierkegaard, *Works of Love*, 199.
48. Kierkegaard, *Works of Love*, 199–200.
49. Walsh, *Living Christianly*, 54.

God by the most chasmic qualitative abyss."[50] He would go on to suggest that, "humanly speaking, any teaching that disregards this difference is demented; divinely speaking, it is blasphemy."[51] Indeed, God himself makes this indictment, for he says to the wicked, "You thought that I was altogether one *like you*, but now I rebuke you and lay the charge before you" (Ps 50:21). In other words, the guilty party here is being charged with attempting to "domesticate" God, and this is arguably the most flagrant problem with SPE in the twenty-first century. The chasmic qualitative abyss between God and humanity has been bridged by "the domestication of transcendence," to borrow from William Placher's 1996 book title.[52] Matthew Barrett explains:

> The last two centuries have demonstrated that the modern and postmodern person is quick to substitute a God who is like us, a God we can domesticate, for the "high view of God" affirmed by figures like Augustine, Anselm, and Aquinas . . . a God in our own image, a God whose immanence has swallowed his transcendence, a God that can be controlled by the creature because he is not that different from the creature.[53]

What does this "domestication" of God look like? Or, rather, what does it sound like from the pulpits of our churches? In her study of what is being preached from evangelical pulpits in the early 1990s, Marsha Witten observed that there seems to be a tendency for preachers and/or evangelists to "present God through characterizations of his inner states, with an emphasis on his emotions, which closely resemble those of human beings."[54] That is, we are more likely to hear about the way God *feels* than what God *commands* (for example). It is to prefer thinking of Jesus as *friend* rather than as *King*.[55] It is to believe that God is love in such a way that the love of God is abstracted from his other attributes (e.g. his holiness, his sovereignty, his justice, etc.).[56] Hence Witten's lament: "The transcendent,

---

50. Kierkegaard, *Sickness Unto Death*, 122. This idea would become central to the theological works of Karl Barth, who spoke of the *unendliche qualitative Unterschied* ("infinite qualitative difference") between God and man.

51. Kierkegaard, *Sickness Unto Death*, 126.

52. Placher, *Domestication*.

53. Barrett, *None Greater*, xvi.

54. Witten, *All Is Forgiven*, 40.

55. One study in the late 1980s found that 75 percent of survey participants shared this preference—see Greeley, *Religious Change*, 37.

56. Carson, *Difficult Doctrine*, 11.

majestic, awesome God of Luther and Calvin . . . has undergone a softening of demeanor."[57]

The offence, then, is rooted in the fact that God is wholly distinct, or "wholly other," and not just in an abstract or disinterested sense—God is "wholly other *for me*, a stranger to myself . . . due to sin."[58] The "otherness" of God is not merely that he is a greater version of ourselves, but that he is nothing like ourselves.[59] This, for Kierkegaard, is what underlies the importance of the incarnation, for "no teaching on earth has ever really brought God and man so close together" as that of Jesus as the God-man.[60] The grace of Christianity is seen in God's willingness to make himself a man, only "to debase himself, take a servant's form (cf. Phil 2:5–7)," and in this paradoxical manner, to bridge the "chasmic qualitative abyss" between himself and the objects of his love. The offence of Christianity, however, is seen in the event of our sin being so great that God had to do the paradoxical to save us.

> First of all, Christianity proceeds to establish sin so firmly as a position that the human understanding can never comprehend it; and then, it is this same Christian teaching that again undertakes to eliminate this position in such a way that the human understanding can never comprehend it . . . [Christianity] seems to be working against itself by establishing sin so securely as a position that now it seems to be utterly impossible to eliminate it again—and then, it is this very Christianity that, by means of the Atonement, wants to eliminate sin as completely as if it were drowned in the sea.[61]

Herein is the "infinite" nature of the abyss, and herein is the paradox, that Christianity fixes sin so securely, so powerfully, that removing it is wholly impossible—much like the way climbing out of an infinite abyss is impossible. And yet, through the atonement, Christianity raises the sinner out of that infinite abyss, removing the very sin that it proclaimed impossible to remove, and doing so to such a degree that we can think of it as cast into the deepest sea.[62]

---

57. Witten, *All Is Forgiven*, 53.
58. Podmore, *Kierkegaard*, 45.
59. Barrett, *None Greater*, xvi.
60. Kierkegaard, *Sickness Unto Death*, 117.
61. Kierkegaard, *Sickness Unto Death*, 100.
62. Cappelørn, "Movements of Offence," 100.

THE DESPAIR OF DEFIANCE

This leads to a second reason why human beings are offended by Christianity, which is by no means independent from the first—Kierkegaard called it "the despair of the forgiveness of sins."[63] Central to the Christian message is the historical proposition that the God-man, Jesus Christ, accomplished the forgiveness of sins for all who believe in him by his atoning death on the cross. To believe in Jesus is to receive the forgiveness of sins (Acts 10:43). In this proposition, however, is the underlying suggestion that a given person stands in need of forgiveness.[64] Calling someone to faith in Jesus for the forgiveness of their sins, therefore, is to call that someone a "sinner"—and this, of course, is offensive. As the street evangelist Ray Comfort once said, "[Preaching the gospel] will be offensive because I am insinuating that [the person listening] is a sinner when he doesn't think he is. As far as he is concerned, there are a lot of people far worse than him [sic]."[65]

Words like "sin" and "sinner," however, seem to be somewhat taboo in contemporary SPE. Of course, a biblical hamartiology is necessary for understanding the nature and the effect of the cross—and therefore, in order to keep "Christ crucified" central to its theology, it became necessary for SPE to reinterpret the cross event, to develop its own hamartiology. While there are subtle differences between the various reinterpretations, there is a particular uniform feature, and this feature is a kind of soteriological narcissism—an egocentric view of salvation. Christopher Lasch, in *The Culture of Narcissism*, said of evangelicalism in the 1970s, "People today hunger not for personal salvation . . . but for the *feeling*, the momentary illusion, of personal well-being, health, and psychic security."[66] Of course, infusing such narcissism into a church existing in a narcissistic culture is a ticket to ecclesial success. As Todd Brenneman once noted, "The narcissism that evangelical ministers offer provides an opportunity for evangelicals to resolve all the *psychological* tensions that contemporary life creates."[67] Consider, for example, the emphasis on self-esteem/self-worth in contemporary psychological research, with some even calling the last five or six decades the "Age of Self-Esteem."[68] Such an emphasis has permeated the teaching of

---

63. Cappelørn, "Movements of Offence," 113.
64. Walsh, *Living Christianly*, 63.
65. Comfort, *Wonderful Plan*, 53.
66. Lasch, *Narcissism*, 7.
67. Brenneman, *Homespun Gospel*, 34 (emphasis added).
68. Miller and Cho, *Self-Esteem*, 21.

SPE, as demonstrated well by the following statement of Todd White (who is something of an SPE popstar):

> The cross isn't the revelation of my sin. The cross is actually the revealing of my value. Something underneath that sin must have been of great value for heaven to go bankrupt to get me back . . . Jesus paid such a high price for me on that tree, and when I see that, I see my value.[69]

This is the basic message of the SPE movement, that the cross of Christ was not designed to atone for sin (at least not primarily), but to establish once and for all the inherent value of the human being. It is salvation not from God's judgment against sinners, but from one's low self-esteem. The call of the gospel, then, is not for you to deny yourself, take up your cross, and follow Jesus (Matt 16:24), but to embrace this divine assessment of you as one who is worthy of the death of Christ.[70] Celebrity pastor Charles Stanley, for example, once said, "The one Person with the authority to judge your value—the one who owns and rules everything in all creation—made this eternal assessment: you are worth dying for."[71] But the one who removes sin and atonement from the gospel, Kierkegaard contends, displays a symptom of a type of despair (the offended and unwilling to believe "despair of defiance"):

> This is defiance, for here it is indeed the defiance of not willing to be oneself, what one truly is—a sinner—and for that reason, wanting to dispense with the forgiveness of sins . . . What is the situation of Christendom with regard to the forgiveness of sins? Even the consciousness of sin is not reached, and the only kinds of sins recognized are those that paganism also recognized—and life goes on happily in pagan peace of mind.[72]

This, we could say, is the heart-wrenching reality of the SPE framework. Thousands, even millions, of professing Christians have never reached the consciousness of sin because sin has been reduced to matters

---

69. Todd White, quoted in Drummond, "Revelation."

70. June Hunt, for example, once wrote, "By [the cross event], your worth was forever established by God . . . Without a doubt, he established your worth—you were worth his life, you were worth dying for." Hunt, *Emotions*, 309. Similarly, Jason C. Dukes wrote, "You and I are declared worth dying for! The living God thinks that we are worth dying for, regardless of how we think of ourselves, and since he made us, we probably ought to adopt *his perspective* of us and live in that view." Dukes, *Live Sent*, 44.

71. Stanley, *Confront the Lies*, 154.

72. Kierkegaard, *Sickness Unto Death*, 113, 117.

of self-worth—matters which offend nobody. As such, Christ "becomes just a part of 'self-esteem' therapy, and grace is swallowed like a 'happy pill.'"[73]

THE ABASED LIFE

Finally, a third reason that human beings are offended by Christianity, interwoven between the first and the second, is the Christian conception of the single individual, the lonely self, and its standing in contradiction with the self-understanding of the natural human being.[74] Consider the fact that individual human beings project for themselves various life goals—designing for themselves the ideal "end" to their pilgrimage on the earth. Christianity is no respecter of such ends, Kierkegaard asserts, for Christianity designs for believers an "end" that reaches far beyond the depths of the individual's noetic capacities. He writes,

> There is so much talk about being offended by Christianity because it is so dark and gloomy, offended because it is so rigorous, etc., but it would be best of all to explain that the real reason that men are offended by Christianity is that it is *too high*, because its goal is not man's goal, because it wants to make man into something so extraordinary that he cannot grasp the thought.[75]

To illustrate, Kierkegaard presents a parable of a poor day laborer and a mighty emperor (indeed, the mightiest emperor who ever lived). The latter sent for the former, declaring that he wanted him for a son-in-law, but the former "had never dreamed . . . that the emperor knew he existed," considering himself "indescribably favoured just to be permitted to see the emperor once . . . A little favour, that would make sense to the labourer . . . But this, this plan for him to become a son-in-law, well, that was far too much."[76] The question, then, is whether this laborer would have sufficient courage to dare to believe it.

> The person lacking this courage would be offended; to him the extraordinary would sound like a jibe (i.e. a taunt) at him. He would then perhaps honestly and forthrightly confess: "Such a thing is too high for me, I cannot grasp it; to be perfectly blunt, to me it is a piece of folly."[77]

73. Castleman, "Soothing Sin," 52.
74. Walsh, *Living Christianly*, 63.
75. Kierkegaard, *Sickness Unto Death*, 83.
76. Kierkegaard, *Sickness Unto Death*, 84.
77. Kierkegaard, *Sickness Unto Death*, 85.

So it is with the one offended by Christianity, for Christianity teaches that the human being "is invited to live on the most intimate terms with God" through Jesus Christ and his work of redemption, and such a reality is "too high" for the human being.[78] The reason it is "too high," however, is grounded in the point of departure between Christianity and the parable of the poor day laborer and the mighty emperor—namely, that although Christ is indeed the King of kings and Lord of lords (Rev 19:16), "it is Jesus Christ in his abasement who stands at the crossroads," and this abased Jesus Christ summons all who would approach him to a life of abasement.[79]

Here, Kierkegaard demonstrates his typically Christocentric theology, at the center of which stands Jesus Christ as *Gud-Mennesket* (the "God-man"), "the Absolute Paradox."[80] What is the paradox? That the human single individual, Jesus of Nazareth, claimed to be God—acting and speaking as though he were God—and yet this human single individual claiming divinity was the lowly, poor, suffering, and ultimately executed human being. In beautiful succinctness, Kierkegaard summarizes the Absolute Paradox, speaking of Jesus as "the lowly human being, yet God."[81] This is the one who stands at the crossroads, and thus, when one arrives at the possibility of offence, they must reckon with Christ as he was to his contemporaries—simultaneously *wholly other* to humanity and *wholly alike* to humanity, for the wholly other God became wholly man.[82] In other words, they must reckon with Christ as the "God-man," wholly God and wholly man, in his loftiness and lowliness.[83] Now, this is "too high" as it stands, but the offence is radically intensified when "it becomes manifest" to the hearer "that the follower is not above his master, but is like him" (cf. Luke 6:40).[84] It is worth quoting Kierkegaard at length here.

> [T]o be a Christian, truly to belong to Christ—when Christ truly is who he claims to be—to be a Christian must indeed be the highest for a human being (humanly speaking), and then that truly to be a Christian is to mean, in the world, to human eyes, to be the abased one, that it is to mean suffering every possible evil, every mockery and insult, and to be punished like a criminal!

78. Kierkegaard, *Sickness Unto Death*, 85.
79. Walsh, "Crossroads," 146.
80. For a study on the Christocentricity of Kierkegaard's theology, see Rose, *Christocentric Theology*.
81. Kierkegaard, *Practice in Christianity*, 75.
82. Larson, "Absolute Paradox," 36. See also Kierkegaard, *Philosophical Fragments*, 37–48.
83. Kapic and Madueme, "Practice in Christianity," 666.
84. Kierkegaard, *Practice in Christianity*, 106.

> Here, again, is the possibility of offence. Ah, and it holds true of this offence that it can be avoided if you, either hypocritically or out of whining human compassion for yourself and for others, want to be a Christian of sorts only to a certain degree, a Christian of sorts according to the pagan *ne quid nimis* (nothing too much)... To be a Christian certainly does not mean to be Christ (what blasphemy), but means to be *his imitator*, yet not a kind of prinked-up, nice-looking successor who makes use of the firm and leaves Christ's having suffered many centuries in the past. No, to be an *imitator* means that your life has as much similarity to his as is possible for a human life to have.[85]

To be a true Christian, in other words, is to come into *samtidighed* ("contemporaneity") with Christ (which is Kierkegaard's understanding of discipleship)—"not to make observations at the foot of the cross," but to carry the cross up the mountain beside him.[86] According to Kierkegaard, contemporaneity with Christ involves taking upon oneself the contradictions that constitute the possibility of offence in Christianity. Once again, he provides a parable. A man in sickness goes to a physician, and the physician prescribes treatment to the man that will necessitate some degree of suffering. There is no contradiction if the man accepts this treatment and thereby suffers. If the man suddenly finds himself an object of suffering simply for going to *that particular* physician, however, there is a contradiction:

> The physician has perhaps announced that he can help me with regard to the illness from which I suffer, and perhaps he can really do that, but there is an *aber* (a "but") that I had not thought of at all. The fact that I get involved with this physician, and attach myself to him, that is what makes me an object of persecution—here is the possibility of offence.[87]

The contradiction here is that a person goes to Christ in faith to seek help, and then comes to suffer on account of the helper. Suffering, in other words, is essential—or intrinsic—to the Christian cure, which distinguishes Christianity from all other forms of therapy.[88] This is the offence: that, as Dietrich Bonhoeffer puts it, "When Christ calls a man, he bids him come and die."[89] And yet, it is precisely this summoning unto death that also paradoxically promises life (cf. Matt 10:39; 16:25; John 12:25). Such teaching,

---

85. Kierkegaard, *Practice in Christianity*, 106.
86. Kierkegaard, *Practice in Christianity*, 171.
87. Kierkegaard, *Practice in Christianity*, 115.
88. Mahn, *Fortunate Fallibility*, 150.
89. Bonhoeffer, *Cost of Discipleship*, 79.

of course, is offensive to practical reason, for "it is like being told that one wins by losing," and there is perhaps no gospel truth as unattractive to the contemporary soft-pedal culture—the culture in which everybody is a winner—than this.[90]

To borrow the words of the Christian statistician George Barna, SPE can be described as the proclamation of a "costless faith."[91] There is no abased Jesus Christ; there is only a "comfortable Jesus to whom we sing affectionate valentines," a Jesus who is sold to us "as fire insurance."[92] The heart of SPE (and perhaps the spark that brought SPE into being) is, as Ronald Sider puts it, a "one-sided, unbiblical, reductionist understanding of the gospel," which presents Christ as accomplishing everything necessary for salvation (which is true), but as demanding nothing (which is blatantly false).[93] It is like being told that one just wins, period. It is to believe that *Christ suffered*, "and now the rest of us will have it easy."[94] There is no possibility of offence here, for there is no "contemporaneity" with Christ—there is no discipleship. What, then, needs to be recovered? Simply, that Christ, willing himself to be the lowly one, came to save sinners, and yet also to "express what the truth would have to suffer, and what the truth must suffer in every generation."[95] Contemporaneity with Christ, that is, demands a volitional willing to go to *that particular* physician; "Whether it is a help or a torment, I want only one thing, I want to belong to Christ, I want to be a Christian."[96]

THE CURE

Having now established a "theology of offence," so to speak, wherein offence is understood as *essentially* Christian, and having also considered the ways in which SPE has "abolished Christianity" through its removal of the possibility of offence (which, in effect, nullifies the gospel), we find ourselves in a position to speak of a solution—a cure to the SPE parasite. As students and faculty of Melbourne School of Theology embark on this centennial year, which will become the hundred and first year before we know it, how might we go about the task of introducing Christianity into soft-pedal evangelicalism? How might we go about the task of recovering the unsafe gospel of

---

90. Gouwens, *Religious Thinker*, 176.
91. Barna, *State of the Church*, 126.
92. Castleman, "Skim-Milk Gospel," 52.
93. Sider, *Scandal*, 57.
94. Kierkegaard, *Journals and Papers*, 4:431.
95. Kierkegaard, *Practice in Christianity*, 34–35.
96. Kierkegaard, *Practice in Christianity*, 115.

Jesus Christ? Such tasks, of course, must begin with a reverence for God, and as Kierkegaard warns us, "Act just once in such a manner that your action expresses that you fear God alone and man not at all—you will immediately in some measure cause a scandal."[97] Our first step, therefore, must be to encourage a deep willingness to embrace the *essentially* Christian in spite of the certainty of the scandal that it will cause. "The only thing that manages to dodge scandal," Kierkegaard continues, "is that which out of the fear of men and deference to men is completely conformed to the secular mentality."[98] In other words, removing the scandalizing aspects of Christianity can and ought to be considered the compromising of Christianity, and doing so on the basis of fear of and deference to mere humankind can and ought to be considered irreligious—even idolatrous. In the fear of God alone, then, a Kierkegaardian cure to the SPE parasite is for the Christian—the theology student, the lecturer, the pastor, and the average churchgoer—to recover the three aforementioned movements of offence.

First, we must recover the doctrine of the "infinite qualitative difference" between God and humanity; doing away with the purely horizontal relation that is characteristic of both MTD and SPE. In a journal entry, Kierkegaard wrote, "To call Christ a friend in heaven" is "a sentimentality which has made a thorough mess of Christianity."[99] Of the historical Christian thinkers, Kierkegaard would be the first to assert the personal and the emotional aspects of one's relating to God, but never at the expense of the lordship and the kingship of Christ—yes, he is Lord even in his abasement. Second, we must recover the biblical and historical Christian doctrine of the forgiveness of sins—and in so doing, we also recover a biblical and historical Christian understanding of the love and grace of God. To make the SPE claim that Christ died for those worth dying for is to abolish grace (which, by definition, is unmerited) completely, and it is to trample underfoot the love of God. Indeed, these divine attributes are demonstrated not in the worthiness of the objects, but in the fact that Christ died despite the unworthiness of the objects. As it is made clear in the Epistle to the Romans, Christ died not for his friends, but for his enemies (Rom 5:6–10). Third, we must recover a New Testament model of Christian discipleship. It has often been said that Jesus "suffered so that we don't have to."[100] This, however, confounds Jesus's suffering the wrath and judgment of God with his suffering the scorn and the

---

97. Kierkegaard, *Journals and Papers*, 3:703.

98. Kierkegaard, *Journals and Papers*, 3:703.

99. Kierkegaard, *Journals and Papers*, 2:80. Kierkegaard would go on to qualify that he is not referring to the notion of Jesus Christ as the "friend of sinners" (Matt 11:16–19), for "this is the same as Saviour and Redeemer."

100. For example, see McDonald, *Lent*, 31.

hatred of the world. The former alone is relevant to the substitutionary death of Christ, but the latter is a normative aspect of Christian existence (e.g. John 15:18–20; 1 Pet 2:19–21). As many have pointed out, Jesus Christ did not suffer so that we would not have to suffer; he suffered, rather, so that when we do suffer, we will become more like him.[101] If we truly seek to disciple the nations (Matt 28:19), then, it is necessary for us to recover the call of the abased Christ to an abased life, for this abased life in fellowship with Christ is the meaning of Christian discipleship.

These three aspects of Christianity—these movements of offence—are seen as mortal wounds for SPE proponents, who seek to patch up anything that might drive people away from the faith—i.e. to "improve" Christianity, or to try and adorn it with whatever would qualify as "safe." As Kierkegaard would say with his characteristic poetic simplicity, however, "Patching simply does not make something better . . . [and therefore], a patch is the worst of all mistakes."[102] The cure to SPE, then, is the removal of these patches, and the revealing of the glorious truths that have been suppressed underneath. In this way, we not only make Christ offensive again, but we present Christianity as itself again.

It is fitting, I believe, to conclude this paper with Kierkegaard's prayer for his readers, that they may come to the possibility of offence, seeing *Jesus as he is*, and there turn to faith.

> Lord Jesus Christ, would that we too might become contemporary with you in this way, might see you in your true form . . . not in the form in which an empty and meaningless, or a thoughtless-romantic, or a historical-talkative remembrance has distorted you . . . Would that we might see you as you are, as you were, and as you will be until your second coming in glory—as the sign of offence and the object of faith—the lowly man—yet the Saviour and Redeemer of the human race, who out of love came to earth to seek the lost, to suffer and die, and yet, alas, every step you took on earth, every time you called to the straying, every time you reached out your hand to do signs and wonders, and every time you defenselessly suffered the opposition of people without raising a hand—again and again, and in concern, you had to repeat, "Blessed is the one who is not offended at me." Would that we might see you in this way, and would that we then might not be offended at you![103]

---

101. For example, see Powlison, "God's Grace," 173.
102. Kierkegaard, *Journals and Papers*, 3:691.
103. Kierkegaard, *Practice in Christianity*, 9–10.

BIBLIOGRAPHY

Barna, George. *The State of the Church 2002*. Ventura, CA: The Barna Group, 2002.
Barrett, Matthew. *None Greater: The Undomesticated Attributes of God*. Grand Rapids, MI: Baker, 2019.
Bonhoeffer, Dietrich. *The Cost of Discipleship*. New York: Macmillan, 1960.
Brenneman, Todd M. *Homespun Gospel: The Triumph of Sentimentality in Contemporary American Evangelicalism*. Oxford, UK: Oxford University Press, 2014.
Buckles, Johnny Rex. "Unashamed of the Gospel of Jesus Christ: On Public Policy and Public Service by Evangelicals." *Harvard Journal of Law and Public Policy* 41, no. 3 (2018) 813–899.
Calvin, John. *Sermons on Galatians*. Edinburgh: Banner of Truth Trust, 1996.
Campbell, Bradley, and Jason Manning. *The Rise of Victimhood Culture: Microaggressions, Safe Spaces, and the New Culture Wars*. New York: Palgrave Macmillan, 2018.
Cappelørn, Niels Jørgen. "The Movements of Offence: Toward, Away From, and Within Faith." In *International Kierkegaard Commentary: Practice in Christianity*, edited by R. L. Perkins, 95–124. Translated by K. Brian Söderquist. Macon, GA: Mercer University Press, 2004.
Carson, D. A. *The Difficult Doctrine of the Love of God*. Wheaton, IL: Crossway, 2007.
Castleman, Robbie. "Skim-Milk Gospel of Cheap Grace." *Themelios* 30, no. 1 (2004) 52–53.
———. "Soothing Sin of Self-Esteem." *Themelios* 30, no. 2 (2005) 52–53.
Clines, David J. A. *Job 1–20*. Word Bible Commentary 17. Dallas, TX: Word, 1989.
Comfort, Ray. *God Has a Wonderful Plan for Your Life: The Myth of the Modern Message*. Bellflower, CA: Living Waters, 2010.
Cryer, Max, ed. *Love Me Tender: The Stories Behind the World's Favourite Songs*. Auckland, NZ: Exisle, 2008.
Dean, Kenda Creasy. *Almost Christian: What the Faith of Our Teenagers is Telling the American Church*. Oxford, UK: Oxford University Press, 2010.
Dever, Mark. *The Gospel and Personal Evangelism*. Wheaton, IL: Crossway, 2007.
Dieppe, Tim. "'Lord Jesus' Too Offensive for School Nativity." *Christian Concern*, December 18, 2019. https://christianconcern.com/comment/lord-jesus-too-offensive-for-school-nativity.
Drummond, Taylor. "Is the Cross a Revelation of My Value? A Response to Todd White." *The Chorus in the Chaos: Relevant and Reformed*, January 19, 2017. https://www.patheos.com/blogs/chorusinthechaos/cross-revelation-value-response-todd-white.
Dukes, Jason C. *Live Sent: You Are a Letter*. Tucson, AZ: Wheatmark, 2009.
Gouwens, David. *Kierkegaard as Religious Thinker*. New York: Cambridge University Press, 1996.
Greeley, Andrew. *Religious Change in America*. Cambridge, MA: Harvard University Press, 1989.
Hiebert, Dennis. "The Massive Subjective Turn: Sociological Perspectives of Spirituality." *Journal of Sociology and Christianity* 8, no. 2 (2018) 55–75.
Horton, Michael. *Christless Christianity: The Alternative Gospel of the American Church*. Grand Rapids, MI: Baker, 2008.
Hunt, June. *How to Handle Your Emotions: Anger, Depression, Fear, Grief, Rejection, Self-Worth*. Eugene, OR: Harvest House, 2008.

Hunter, James. *Evangelicalism: The Coming Generation*. Chicago, IL: University of Chicago Press, 1987.

Kapic, Kelly M., and Hans Madueme. "Practice in Christianity." In *Reading Christian Theology in the Protestant Tradition*, 661–72. London: Bloomsbury, 2018.

Kierkegaard, Søren. *Philosophical Fragments*. Kierkegaard's Writings 7. Edited and translated by Howard V. Hong and Edna H. Hong. Princeton, NJ: Princeton University Press, 1985.

———. *The Point of View*. Kierkegaard's Writings 22. Edited by Howard V. Hong and Edna H. Hong. Princeton, NJ: Princeton University Press, 1998.

———. *Practice in Christianity*. Kierkegaard's Writings 20. Edited and translated by Howard V. Hong and Edna H. Hong. Princeton, NJ: Princeton University Press, 1991.

———. *The Sickness Unto Death*, Kierkegaard's Writings 19. Edited and translated by Howard V. Hong and Edna H. Hong. Princeton, NJ: Princeton University Press, 1980.

———. *Søren Kierkegaard's Journals and Papers*. Edited and translated by Howard V. Hong and Edna H. Hong. 7 vols. Bloomington, IN: Indiana University Press, 1967–1978.

———. *Works of Love*. Kierkegaard's Writings 16. Edited and translated by Howard V. Hong and Edna H. Hong. Princeton, NJ: Princeton University Press, 1995.

Larson, R. E. "Kierkegaard's Absolute Paradox." *The Journal of Religion* 42, no. 1 (1962) 34–43.

Lasch, Christopher. *The Culture of Narcissism*. New York: W. W. Norton, 1979.

Longman, Tremper, III. *Job*. Baker Commentary on the Old Testament Wisdom and Psalms. Grand Rapids, MI: Baker Academic, 2012.

Mahn, Jason A. *Fortunate Fallibility: Kierkegaard and the Power of Sin*. Oxford, UK: Oxford University Press, 2011.

Mason, Michael. "The Spirituality of Young Australians." In *Religion and Youth*, Theology and Religion in Interdisciplinary Perspective Series, edited by Sylvia Collins-Mayo and Pink Dandelion, 55–62. Burlington, VT: Ashgate, 2010.

McDonald, David. *Lent: Giving Up Guilt for Forty Days*. Seasons of Christian Spirituality 3. Littleton, CO: Samizdat, 2011.

Miller Peggy J., and Grace E. Cho. *Self-Esteem in Time and Place: How American Families Imagine, Enact, and Personalise a Cultural Ideal*. Oxford, UK: Oxford University Press, 2018.

Pearce, Lisa D., and Melinda Lundquist Denton. *A Faith of Their Own: Stability and Change in the Religiosity of America's Adolescents*. Oxford, UK: Oxford University Press, 2011.

Perkins, Robert L., ed. *Practice in Christianity*. International Kierkegaard Commentary 20. Macon, GA: Mercer University Press, 2004.

Pike, Molly Rose. "The One with Homophobic Jokes, Sexism, and Body-Shaming: Friends' Arrival on Netflix Reveals Storylines That Are Very Problematic for a New Millennial Audience." *Daily Mail Australia*, January 12, 2018. https://www.dailymail.co.uk/femail/article-5258829.

Placher, William C. *The Domestication of Transcendence: How Modern Thinking about God Went Wrong*. Louisville, KY: Westminster John Knox, 1996.

Podmore, Simon D. *Kierkegaard and the Self Before God: Anatomy of the Abyss*. Bloomington, IN: Indiana University Press, 2011.

Pope, Marvin H. *Job*. AB 17. New York: Doubleday, 1965.
Powlison, David. "God's Grace and Your Sufferings." In *Suffering and the Sovereignty of God*, eds. John Piper and Justin Taylor. Wheaton, IL: Crossway, 2006.
Qureshi, Nabeel. "Do Muslims and Christians Worship the Same God?" *Ravi Zacharias International Ministries*. https://www.rzim.org/read/rzim-global/do-muslims-and-christians-worship-the-same-god.
Rose, Tim. *Kierkegaard's Christocentric Theology*. Ashgate New Critical Thinking in Theology and Biblical Studies. Burlington, VT: Ashgate, 2001.
Sheridan, Greg. *God is Good for You: A Defence of Christianity in Troubled Times*. Sydney: Allen and Unwin, 2018.
Sider, Ronald J. *The Scandal of the Evangelical Conscience: Why Are Christians Living Just Like the Rest of the World?* Grand Rapids, MI: Baker, 2005.
Smith, Christian, and Melinda Lundquist Denton. *Soul Searching: The Religious and Spiritual Lives of American Teenagers*. Oxford, UK: Oxford University Press, 2005.
Spurr, Barry. "The Cultural Curse of the New Censorship." *Quadrant* 63, no. 11 (2019) 9–13.
Stackhouse, John G. "What Has Happened to Post-Christian Canada?" *Church History* 87, no. 4 (2018) 1152–70.
Stanley, Charles. *Emotions: Confront the Lies, Conquer with Truth*. New York: Howard, 2013.
Travis, Sarah A. N. *Metamorphosis: Preaching after Christendom*. Eugene, OR: Cascade, 2019.
Vaught, Russell. "Wheaton College and the Preservation of Theological Clarity." *The Resurgent*, January 17, 2016. https://theresurgent.com/2016/01/17/wheaton-college.
Walsh, Sylvia. *Living Christianly: Kierkegaard's Dialectic of Christian Existence*. Philadelphia, PA: The Pennsylvania State University Press, 2005.
———. "Standing at the Crossroads: The Invitation of Christ to a Life of Suffering." In *Practice in Christianity*, edited by R. L. Perkins, 125–60. International Kierkegaard Commentary 20. Macon, GA: Mercer University Press, 2004.
Ward, Pete. *Liquid Ecclesiology: The Gospel and the Church*. London: Brill, 2017.
Wexelbaum, Rachel S. "The Library as Safe Space." In *The Future of Library Space, Advances in Library Administration and Organisation 36*, edited by S. S. Hines and K. M. Crowe, 37–78. Bingley, UK: Emerald, 2017.
Wiener, Gary, ed. *Microaggressions, Safe Spaces, and Trigger Warnings, Current Controversies*. New York: Greenhaven, 2018.
Witten, Marsha G. *All Is Forgiven: The Secular Message in American Protestantism*. Princeton, NJ: Princeton University Press, 1993.

15

Jesus and Modernity

Why the Twenty-First Century is the Most Christian Ever

Rikk Watts

MANY MODERNS MISTAKENLY REGARD Christianity as a religion. Often marginalized as a matter of private faith over against public science and reason, it can be seen as a crutch for the weak and largely irrelevant to the everyday pluralistic and global world. This chapter argues to the contrary that the gospel is better understood as a comprehensive "grammar of life" that in fact provided the foundations for much that the global world now takes for granted. In particular, the modern world's assumption of the possibility of genuine change and transformative innovation, that knowledge comes through the senses and testing, that cities should be dynamic, that all people have equal value, that the body is not the enemy, and that compassion and love are key to a genuine humanity, all derive from the gospel. In these respects, the gospel has already won.

A POST CHRISTIAN WORLD?

We often hear we live in a post-Christian world, and one gets the impression that many of us feel under siege. It is easy to understand why. We have witnessed significant declines in church attendance and seismic shifts in, for example, *mores* of sexual behavior. We face not only ignorance of, but increasing hostility toward, Christianity. Nor has the cause of the gospel been helped by horrific child abuse, and even less by subsequent denials and/or coverups.

All this makes it even more important that we do not lose sight of the larger picture. Several years ago, Tom Holland, a popular historian of the early Roman Empire, wrote a piece for the *New Statesman* entitled, "Why I Was Wrong about Christianity." He began by explaining that as a young boy he was obsessed with dinosaurs—weren't we all?—finding them glamorous, ferocious, and extinct. This evolved into a love of the ancient Greeks and Romans, who were likewise glamorous, ferocious, and extinct. Compared to the God of Israel, with all his rules and condemnation of other gods, Apollo, Athena, and Dionysus were far more charismatic. They enjoyed themselves. And if they were vain, selfish, and sometimes cruel, it only endowed them with rock star allure. For him, Christianity had ushered in a dark age of superstition, myth, and "po-faced puritanical killjoys" who drained all the color and excitement from the world.

But apex predators in children's books are one thing; a living, salivating Tyrannosaur six feet in front of you is quite another. The more Holland immersed himself in that ancient world, the more alien and disturbing he found it. The Spartans trained their young men to kill uppity peasants by night. Julius Caesar slaughtered a million Gauls, enslaved a million more and left 250,000 families with neither home nor hearth for the coming winter—and remember we are talking about first century BC and hence far smaller total populations—and no one really cared. It was not just the cruelty, endemic violence, and callousness that concerned Holland, but the complete absence of any sense that the poor or the weak might have any value at all.

When Paul declared, "We preach Christ crucified, a stumbling block to the Jews and foolishness to the Greeks," he was not exaggerating. It is almost impossible for us to grasp how unspeakably offensive was his preaching of the cross. In antiquity, order was maintained by inflicting punishment, not by suffering for the world; by imposing leadership, not by washing others' feet. Yet, as Holland noted, even in the so-called post-Christian West, most of us still think it is nobler to suffer than to inflict suffering, and that every human life is of equal value. Holland concluded by saying that he has now come to accept that in his morals and ethics he is neither Greek nor Roman but thoroughly and proudly Christian.

It seems to me that this argument is irrefutable. The morality of the West is irreducibly Christian—but then what would one expect after two thousand years of pervasive Christian influence? However, as significant as it is, does the argument go far enough? I initially trained as an aeronautical engineer. And while I knew every Sunday that God was real, each Monday I was confronted by the question: what does any of this have to do with turbofans at thirty thousand feet?

In this chapter I want to respond with an emphatic "Everything!" One cannot participate in our global twenty-first-century world without being fundamentally Christian. In spite of how things might look, I want to argue that the twenty-first century is, in many respects, the most Christian the world has ever seen. In terms of our basic worldview, the gospel has already won. Since these are huge claims and we have relatively little space, this chapter will necessarily be more illustrative than comprehensive. Nevertheless, we hope the basic contentions will be clear enough.[1]

THE GOSPEL'S FAR-REACHING IMPACT

Recent scholarship has highlighted the gospel's radical impact on antiquity.[2] For example, Rodney Stark, one of American's leading sociologists of religion and writing as a non-Christian, concluded it was the early Christians who gave the ancient world, for the first time, its humanity. Australia's own Mark Strom traced Paul's uncompromising challenge to ancient notions of personhood and social hierarchies, which has shaped Australian society to a degree perhaps unmatched in the rest of the world. Ian Scott outlined Paul's championing of historical experience as a way of knowing over against Hellenistic philosophy/theology, while Larry Hurtado reminded us of Christianity's astonishing achievement in ridding the world of the "gods," something that modernity takes for granted. The renowned classicist Edwin Judge delineated key areas in which Christianity transformed not just morality but, and at the very least of equal importance, how we understand and structure the world. Consequently, as Kavin Rowe has shown, it is not surprising that wherever the earliest Christians went, they encountered hostility. They proclaimed a radically new view of reality.

However, long before the gospel, those Scriptures from which it originated had already laid some remarkable foundations. Wholly against the

1. See the more in-depth discussion in Watts, "Christianity."
2. I readily acknowledge my indebtedness throughout to the scholars listed below.

grain of its ancient Near Eastern neighbors, Genesis almost nonchalantly disenchanted the entire cosmos in asserting that creation was not divine.[3] Fully realized, the implications would be world changing. No longer feared (e.g. Ps 121:6) nor worshipped—and, make no mistake, there was nothing even faintly romantic about either—creation was now free to be studied and understood. It also claimed that creation was "good," not perfect. We will return to this, but that distinction has profound consequences. Then, almost as a word of prophetic promise, it claimed that creation was intended for flourishing—which was not most people's subsistence experience—and for all—not merely for a handful of elites. Perhaps most radically, it was clear from the Torah that Yahweh was not human. He was not merely a larger, more powerful version of ourselves. Furthermore, far from being relatively uninterested in human affairs (just so long as he was sated with sacrifices), Israel's Yahweh was deeply interested in our behavior, and especially in how we treated one another. He much preferred mercy to burnt offerings, which in any case he did not really need.

Arguably, Israel's "living against the grain" came to a head in the nation's second-century BC clash with Hellenism (the ancient Greeks called themselves Hellenes). Alexander's ultimate project was to create one humanity, partly by incorporating the various nations' gods into a single Hellenic pantheon, introducing his own canon of Hellenic texts and building model Hellenic cities. Against this program of creeping cultural homogeneity, the translation of the Hebrew Bible into Greek (the LXX) can be seen as a deliberate act of cultural resistance. There was no pantheon, only Yahweh; no canon but Scripture; and Zion alone was the city of the Great King. Underpinning the Maccabean revolt, however mixed its motives and unhappy its outcomes, was a mortal clash between two very different ways of seeing the world. And, given that the Romans at the end of the first century AD were more Hellenized than the Hellenes, it foreshadowed the hostility to which, as we saw earlier, Acts bears witness.

It is vital, however, to understand that this conflict was not a matter of different religions. Although debated, it is highly doubtful that anyone in the ancient world thought they were practicing "religion." Assuming we could even define the term (an exercise far more difficult than we might initially imagine), seeing "religion" as merely an optional adjunct to one's identity is a very recent Western conceit. They were simply being Roman, Hellenic, Egyptian, Jewish, and so on. Appeasing their ancestral gods was as much who they were as was their family, ethnicity, and culture. The gospel was never simply a matter of merely removing Zeus's nameplates from his

---

3. For further reading see Provan, *Seriously Dangerous Religion*.

temples and replacing them with dedications to Jesus. Even if the ancients could not fully articulate it, they sensed the profound threat. And they were right. The gospel mounted a fundamental and radical challenge to the entire social fabric and substructure of antiquity, hence the Thessalonians' maddened outburst: "These people who have been turning the world upside down have come here too!" (Acts 17:6). This was a life-and-death struggle between, to use Kavin Rowe's helpful phrase, two radically and profoundly incompatible "grammars of life."

Why "grammar"? Although stories, treatises and poems are surely more than grammar, they would, nevertheless, be impossible without it. Grammar enables us to frame, clarify, and communicate our thoughts. Its structure is what facilitates our creativity and personal agency. The gospel, as John so well understands, is God's grammar for living out his eternal life in his creation. Not only so, but as surprising as it might sound, the gospel was apparently designed to overthrow antiquity, which in the first century meant Hellenism. And to the extent that it has succeeded, Jesus's relevance could not be greater: his gospel provides the "grammatical structure" for life in the modern world.

THE GOSPEL ORIGINS OF MODERNITY[4]

With all this in view, the remainder of this chapter outlines the gospel's radically different views of cosmology (what reality is), epistemology (how we know), sociology and politics (nature of society), anthropology (what it means to be human), and virtue/ethics (how we should behave). In particular, the gospel claimed that change was a gift, knowing was about the senses and testing, cities should be dynamic, all people were of equal value, the body is not the enemy, and that love and compassion are central.

THE GIFT OF GENUINE CHANGE

In antiquity, change was highly problematic. For the Egyptians, the only good pharaoh was the one in whose reign nothing happened. The turbulent history of the Hellenes, characterized by violent swings between extremes and an unstable geography, gave an even greater impetus to finding something stable. Parmenides had declared that the true could not change; after all, one plus one must always equal two. If something changed, it was not true, and

---

4. Defining "modernity" and locating its origins are remarkably difficult and lie well outside the narrow confines of this chapter.

hence not real, at least in any fundamental sense. The truly real was unchanging and therefore perfect, as mirrored in the beautiful and static heavens (hence the word *cosmos*, whose root meaning is "ordered" and "beautiful").

Of course, they realized things around them changed. Heraclitus had early recognized that one could not step into the same river twice. Empedocles solved the tension by arguing that all change was merely rotation. So for the Stoic Chrysippus (which school challenged Paul in Athens, Acts 17:18), there could never be anything new; everything was repeated down to the very last detail. Genuine change was not merely impossible, it was illogical and inconceivable. A perfect cosmos ultimately became a prison where human agency and significance were at best marginal. (One of the pagan philosophers' complaints against Christians was that they made people too important.) This is why no one in antiquity ever discussed innovative thinking. If something was "new" or radically different, it must be wrong; hence the opposition to the gospel.

Of course, people still invented things—that is what people do—but among the elites such "distractions" were rarely applied practically. Invention *per se* never became the focus of serious scientific knowledge, not least because it concerned the things that could be otherwise.

But for the early Christians, genuine change was not only possible; it was a gift to be celebrated. As we saw earlier, Genesis from the very beginning made the remarkable claim that creation was good, meaning, deliberately, not perfect. A perfect cosmos, the moment it changes, is no longer perfect. But in a good world—formed and filled (Gen 1)—there is space for flourishing, growth, discovery, creativity, and consequently, human agency and significance. Accordingly, one of the key features of early Genesis, even if regularly missed, is human creativity, even among those of us who rebelled against God (4:2, 17, 20–22). Whatever else we do, humans "make"; our worldview merely facilitates or hinders the making. Paul, so far as we know, was the first person in antiquity to speak of "transformation" in the sense of genuine, positive change (Rom 12:2). It is difficult for us, in a world so thoroughly Christianized, to grasp just how radical these ideas were. But all of our modern talk about innovation, designing for change and creativity—which we take so much for granted—is only possible because of the gospel. In one sense, you really can thank Jesus for your smartphone.

Knowing through the Senses and Testing

Perhaps the Hellenes' greatest achievement was their speculative leap that the cosmos could be understood solely through the resources of the human mind. Since the only things in human experience that could be perfect and unchanging were ideas, only the "rational" could be true. This is why they loved geometry, with its perfect theoretical shapes, none of which existed in the changeful world of the senses. The philosophers' "logos"—with which many of us are familiar because of John's radically transvaluative usage, that is, of a first-century Jew, Jesus!—was essentially mathematical, implying a rigidly determined outcome. For this reason, while changeful history could be helpful in offering general principles by which to live (for Aristotle poetry was better because it at least distilled those principles), truth was confined to philosophy whose universal timelessness and strict logic ensured certainty. As a side note, this might give the lie as to why some forms of "Christian" theology look far more like philosophy—*theologia* is, after all, Plato's ad hoc word for the "rational science of the divine"—than the Scriptures with their profound historical and cultural particularity of narrative and letter. This might also explain why neither the Greek translation of the Hebrew Bible nor the NT ever described what they did as "theology."

The resultant conviction was that if something was "rational"—that is, made sense in appropriately trained human minds (characteristically male)—it must be true. It was a brilliant idea, except that it was wrong. Consider, for example, Aristotle, one of the brightest people who ever lived. In his view, it was perfectly rational that heavier objects should fall faster than light ones. But they do not. All he had to do was systematically test his theory by dropping a range of objects. But why test a perfectly rational explanation against a world that, because of its changefulness, was already suspect? It would take another eight hundred years for John Philiponus, another Greek but now a Christian, to prove Aristotle wrong—by experiment. (It turns out that Galileo, he of the Leaning Tower of Pisa fame and a thousand years later, had read Philiponus; but, humble chap that he was, he refrained from mentioning it.)

This is not to say that the Hellenes never got it right. Heliocentrism—the idea that the Earth revolves around the Sun—was early proposed by Aristarchus of Samos. But it *is* why they never developed science, at least not in the sense that we now recognize it. The cosmos is not "rational." It does not conform to what we speculate it should "logically" be, at the very least because it does not start with us. It is apparently "intelligible," but only insofar as we start outside ourselves, allowing the cosmos to be what is, carefully observing, and then holding our ideas to account against its reality.

This is why, in the gospel's cosmos, gifted as it was with change, using the senses and testing is exactly the way the Scriptures say we should learn. We have to look first, think second, and test what we think we have understood against what we see and hear. This applies equally and especially to

Israel's God. Whatever else, Yahweh's celebrated "I AM who I AM" response to Moses implies that Israel has never met a "god" like him, and hence must not speculate. Instead, what we have throughout the Exodus is a thoroughgoing emphasis on the senses, on what Israel saw and heard, thereby confirming through their experience Yahweh's power, wisdom, faithfulness, justice, and compassion.

The same applies to Jesus. Christians understood that which was from the beginning by what they had heard, seen, looked at, touched and testified to (1 John 1:1–3). This is not Hellenistic speculative "rationality." But nor it is blind "faith." It is what was tested through experience.

Although the Scriptures speak of history and personal agency, and science addresses impersonal matter, the epistemological parallels are nevertheless clear. This is why science as we now know it, and the technological explosion that accompanied it, developed only in the Christian West and nowhere else. Certainly not in Hellenistic antiquity. From this perspective, to pit the gospel against science not only makes a category error—Christianity is neither a religion nor "rational" speculation—but also fails to recognize that seeing, hearing, touching, handling, and testing lies at the very heart of both.

Dynamic Societies

For the Hellenes, it was logical that the ideal society should mirror the unchanging rational cosmos. This notion was epitomized in Plato's ideal Republic, with its rigid hierarchy of the best elite males at the head, descending down through the lesser ranks of women, artisans, slaves, non-Greeks, and barbarians. Of course, in the everyday world, reality *will* have its way. Elite families became impoverished and the lesser-born very occasionally did well—though the latter were never allowed to forget the stigmata of their lowly origins.

Even so, anchored to its conception of a static and perfect cosmos, we are not surprised that Hellenistic culture essentially goes nowhere. If the true and real is expressed only in the single ideal form, where is the imperative to innovate, to experiment or to try new ideas? In spite of the perfections of classical Hellenic art, in one sense, to have seen one statue is to have seen them all. But this is not just a Hellenic trait. The Shanghai cultural history museum is not dissimilar. One only has to compare both to the Louvre to notice the stark differences in creativity and manifold diversity. Nor is this a question of race. Humans do make things, and the Chinese had early on invented printing, water clocks, gunpowder, primitive blast furnaces, and much longer keel lines on their ships. Instead, it is a matter of whether one's "grammar of life" inspires or inhibits human creativity, goes with or against the grain of the cosmos, and what it means to be human.

In contrast, the gospel's "grammar" transformed the Hellenic body metaphor. No longer was the head made up of elite males backed by their extensive genealogies of power-hungry "noble" families. There was now only one head: a self-sacrificing, foot-washing servant Christ. And after this, everything is a gift. We cannot, on the basis of status, race or gender, "know" in advance someone's gifts or contribution to society, that merely being prejudice. Like the cosmos, we have to pay attention to all people, and to each individual, regardless of his or her origins.

Furthermore, if everything is a gift, where is boasting? Not only is society dynamic, but everyone is, ultimately, of equal value. Thus, Paul writes some of the most radical words in the Hellenistic world: in Christ, there is no longer Jew nor gentile, slave nor free, male nor female. The eye cannot say to the hand, I have no need of you. And why? Because, in the gospel's grammar of life, all are made in God's image, Christ died for all, and all, in him, can be indwelt by the one and the same Spirit.

Why did the ancient world never give rise to movements for the betterment of the poor, the worker, the disabled, the disadvantaged, and the slave? Because it was the gospel, not reason, that told us the world really could be different, and that all people mattered.

Being Human

For the Hellenes, the body was a problem. In their folk culture, that the word for body, *soma*, sounded much like the word for tomb, *sema*, helped launch the remarkably resilient idea of the battle between the pure eternal soul and its tomblike body. (This is a conflict that continues, alas, to infect various forms of Christianity.) And if the true and real could not change, what does this say about the body, which obviously ages, leading inevitably to the corruption of death? Even those exercises aimed at building the ideal body were primarily motivated by the desire to have the body reflect the trained mind and purified soul, not because of any particular value attributed to the body itself. Consequently, bodies were either abused or indulged, both of which extremes Paul had to confront early among his converts (e.g. Col 2:16–23; 1 Cor 6:12–30). In either case, the presupposition was the same: the body had no eternal significance.

But according to the Scriptures, humans cannot be in the image and likeness of God without a body. The word "image" always meant something physical, three-dimensional, and in the round. This is why Yahweh declares himself to be Israel's healer (Exod 15:6); why Jesus, the Lord among us, heals people; and why bodily resurrection is central to Israel's and the gospel's hope—one simply cannot be human without a body. One might, therefore, need to be careful of talk about "saving souls." If by soul we intend the Scriptural idea of "lifedness," then fine. But any sense of the soul being an independent superior substance defiled by physical existence is clearly out of court. After all, God himself saw that creation was in and of itself "very good" (Gen 1:31), and through which he has given us all things richly to enjoy (1 Tim 6:17).

The Scriptures' high view of the body also undergirds Christians' well-known constraints around sexual behavior, especially when compared to the general laxity, if not oppression, of the surrounding cultures. For example, the primary sexual *more* for elite first-century males was, "Whose body can I enjoy with impunity?" But for Christians, the issue was neither "gender," orientation, love, monogamy nor commitment. Instead, the body was for the LORD, and the LORD was for the body (1 Cor 6:13–20). Since the very physicality of maleness and femaleness came from God's own creative word, which word reflects his character, and since God is eternally faithful, the only appropriate venue for sexual expression is between one man and one woman in lifelong commitment.

Paul's implication that people who sleep around do not know God (1 Thess 4:1–8) does not come from his being a bigoted first-century Jew who could not cope with more tolerant Roman practices. It was based on the creation account of the one true God, and that emphatically over against the dehumanizing idolatry of an oppressive antiquity (Rom 1). In this he is simply following his Lord, for whom the only options are one man and one woman for life or being a eunuch, meaning no sexual activity (Matt 19:3–12). Not only were his Jewish disciples taken aback; it is deeply offensive, if for other reasons, to our culture too.

Shockingly in the first century, this concern was not only for elite male bodies. Everybody's body mattered, including the slave girl whose master could no longer use as he wished, the seven-year-old boys sold as sexual playthings for exorbitant prices on the slave markets (this fact alone makes the current child abuse scandals in the church unspeakably sickening), and the disabled person who was compelled to dance for the general merriment of wealthy guests. The poor, the weak, the discarded: they all matter. The gospel alone gave the West and modernity the notion of universal human rights, grounded in our being made in God's image.

This last point bears some expansion. It seems from the Scriptural perspective that one cannot separate respecting one's own body from respecting someone else's body or respecting the body sexually and respecting it politically; after all, having bodies is what makes us all human. One wonders how long it will be before the idea that I can do with my body whatever I please bleeds over into treating other people's bodies also as I please; before dishonoring my own body leads to my dishonoring the bodies of others?

A New Way of Life

In the world of Homer, virtue was essentially an expression of elite male virility: buffed up warriors, courageous in vicious battle, and able to speak well. As his *Iliad* illustrated, the result was terrible conflict, cycles of revenge, and, as we saw earlier, a brutal carelessness of the lives of the masses. I suspect many of our summer blockbusters are, in one way or another, recycled "heroic" Greek myths: not a great model for world peace then or now. It could be argued that Aristotle intended his "nothing to excess" ethics to bring some stability to this tumultuous bloodletting. But since his ethics were essentially about maintaining the *status quo*, his idea of, for example, justice meant keeping the elites where they belonged. Compassion was not just weak, hence marginally acceptable in females; it was potentially immoral because it transgressed justice. In the first century, virtue had mutated into an elitism of status, education, and wealth. Even so, it often devolved into vicious and vengeful competition.

But in the gospel's "grammar of life," matters were radically different. Worshipping at the feet of a crucified God, Christians were about neither virtue—courage is not a Christian idea; we are strong not in ourselves but in the Lord—nor ethics—there was nothing of the "untroubled, aloof and self-composed golden mean" in the cross.

Instead, the gospel emphasized trust, hope, and care, which are neither self-focused nor of our own effort but directed toward others and effected through the Spirit. Christians were generous and compassionate because that is what unique Yahweh, a god unlike any other, is like.

In sum, those folks who proudly boast of their sole reliance on "reason" would do well to remember that it was Hellenic "reason" that produced the endemic violence, injustice, devaluation of the masses—including women, slaves, the poor, the weak and the disabled—and hopelessness of the changeless ancient world.

THE QUESTION

So now we come to the question. Having briefly surveyed some characteristic features of antiquity—and, so as not to be misunderstood, I am not at all suggesting that everything from antiquity is worthless—consider now the modern world with its emphases on innovation and change, where genuine knowledge comes through the senses and testing, where cities are dynamic, in which all people (at least putatively) are said to be of equal value regardless of race, gender or social status, where the body is not the enemy, and compassion and love for others are seen as hallmarks of genuine humanity. What does the modern world most resemble: Hellenistic antiquity or the gospel?

It seems clear to me that one cannot genuinely participate in the modern world without inhabiting the gospel's grammar of life—and this includes modern China (as several of their most highly placed intellectuals admit). The gospel has in many large respects already won. And it has won, not because we started with unaided human reason, but because we first trusted the gospel. I am on occasion quizzed as to why I believe this stuff. After all, what relevance could these ancient Jewish texts have in our modern world? To this I sometimes cheekily reply: "Well, do you like your iPhone?" The proof of the gospel is everywhere in the modern world's eating. Let the "new money" parade its flashy bling. We are the "old money," who in one sense have nothing to prove. After all, we own, as it were, "most of England."

WHERE TO FROM HERE?

Why have most of us Christians not seen this, or if we have, seen it almost solely in moral terms? I suspect, partly because for many of us Scripture starts with the fall, our grammar is fundamentally about good and evil, which leads us, if we are not careful, to traffic in guilt and shame. This is ironic—not least for those who regularly champion Scriptural inerrancy—since it is not where the Scriptures themselves start. They start with life and creativity (as John's Gospel, with its emphasis on eternal life, well understands). Perhaps, too, having dallied in the Hellenistic agora, we have been seduced by the attractions of logic and perhaps, if we are honest, by the vanity of being among the educated, rationalistic elite. I suspect the latter is why it took so long for the gospel to work its new creational wonders. It was not long into the patristic period that the elites of the church sought to marry the gospel with Plato and then, in the medieval period, with Aristotle, both of whom needed to be discarded for the modern to be born. But by then, alas, we had already saddled the gospel with those unhelpful allegiances, effectively putting it "on the wrong side of history."

Having spoken of these matters in several settings, I know the immediately pressing question: why is the modern world in such mess? I think the answer is relatively straightforward. Designers tell us that every decision reflects our character. The incredible freedom and unimaginable agency offered by the gospel only brings life when we humans reflect the character of unique Yahweh, who created this entire cosmos. Since that character is most fully expressed in Jesus, the continued flourishing of modernity depends utterly on our imitating him. In such a case, never has Jesus been more relevant. This of course raises at least two more searching questions—how well do we who own his name understand his gospel, and even more importantly, ourselves reflect his character? But time has gone, and these questions will have to be addressed at another time.

BIBLIOGRAPHY

Holland, Tom. *Dominion: How the Christian Revolution Remade the World*. New York: Basic, 2019.

———. "Why I Was Wrong about Christianity." *New Stateman*, August 25, 2016.

Hurtado, Larry. *Destroyer of the Gods: Early Christian Distinctiveness in the Roman World*. Waco, TX: Baylor University Press, 2016.

Judge, Edwin. *Gospel Conversations*. https://www.gospelconversations.com/speaker/edwin-judge.

Provan, Iain W. *Seriously Dangerous Religion: What the Old Testament Really Says and Why it Matters*. Waco, TX: Baylor University Press, 2014.

Rowe, Kavin. *World Upside Down: Reading Acts in the Graeco-Roman Age*. Oxford: Oxford University Press, 2009.

Scott, Ian. *Paul's Way of Knowing: Story, Experience, and the Spirit*. Grand Rapids: Baker Academic, 2008.

Stark, Rodney. *The Rise of Christianity: How the Obscure, Marginal Jesus Movement Became the Dominant Religious Force in the Western World in a Few Centuries*. Princeton: Princeton University, 1996.

Strom, Mark. *Reframing Paul: Conversations in Grace and Community*. Downers Grove: Intervarsity, 2000.

Watts, Rikk. "Christianity and the Ancient World." *Crux* 53, no. 1 (2017) 2–26.

Woodberry, Robert D. "The Missionary Roots of Modern Liberal Democracy." *American Political Science Review* 106 (2012) 244–74.

16

Mindsets and Muslims

Richard Shumack and Peter Riddell

IN THIS CHAPTER, ROMANS 10:1–4 provides a framework for engaging with Islam. In these verses, the apostle Paul considers the interaction between zeal and righteousness, or between believing passionately and believing truly. While his point of reference is Jewish belief, his framework provides fertile ground for exploring Muslim belief and piety. Through an examination of statements and reflections of noted Muslim scholars and practitioners, we assess the extent to which Muslim claims of rationality, certainty, and righteousness satisfy a biblical understanding as expressed by Paul in Romans 10. This examination points to an Islamic framework that leans toward legal righteousness, which can very easily metamorphose into enforcement, a far cry from the true righteousness and zeal of Romans 10.

Some approaches to Christian engagement with Muslims are shaped by media exaggerations while others are formed on the basis of personal experience with Muslims or the world of Islam. Our approach in this paper will base its foundations on biblical perspectives on Muslim religious mindsets.

From our perspective, the Scriptures approach this missional question with nuance and a deep appreciation of the nature of human spirituality. A short passage exploring important ideas around this is Romans 10:1–4. In this chapter Paul is referring to Jewish belief, but his ideas could equally be applied to the traditional outlines of Muslim belief. The key dynamic being explored by Paul here is the interaction between zeal and righteousness; that is, between believing passionately and believing truly.

MUSLIM ZEAL FOR RIGHTEOUSNESS—ROMANS 10:2-3

It soon becomes obvious to any who have engaged with Islamic communities that, like firstcentury Jews, a significant proportion of Muslims are both passionate about their faith and extremely confident that their beliefs are true. So it is important to understand the traditional Islamic belief framework (or epistemology) that (supposedly) undergirds this confidence.[1]

So, first, Islam teaches that religion is properly *rational*. Many times throughout the Qur'an, the readers are challenged: "Do you not comprehend?" (*a fa la ta'qilun?*) (Q.12:109) and "Will you not take heed?" (*fa la tadhakkarun?*) (Q.11:24,30). The idea here is that all religious beliefs should be sensible, clear, and without contradiction. Sudanese scholar Jaafar Sheikh Idris states this clearly in an interview he gave as part of the series *The Rational* on Huda TV:

> . . . some people say that they do not accept religion because religion is not something rational and they describe themselves as being rational and some of them think that it is only the soft headed people who will accept religion. But in fact religion, a true religion must be rational. Why should a religion be rational? Because reason is the only means by which we decide whether a certain claim is right or wrong . . . Usually we ask for evidence and if this is so then it should apply to religion also. And in fact wise people don't accept the claim of someone who calls himself a prophet just because he comes and tells them I am Abraham, I am sent from God, I am Jesus, I am Moses; they must have asked them for evidence to show that they are what they claim, so this is the reason why (a true) religion must be rational.[2]

Second, Islam claims that religious beliefs must be *certain*. In Islam doubt is viewed negatively in the sense that doubting or questioning one's beliefs leads away from faith and not towards it. Happily, for Muslims, Islam

---

1. For more detailed discussion of the issues addressed in this paper, see Shumack, *Wisdom of Islam*.

2. Idris, "Religion and Rationality."

claims to offer that degree of certainty. So Muslim Palestinian American philosopher Ismail al-Faruqi (1921–1986) makes the very strong claim that:

> Unlike the faith of Christians, the imân (faith) of Islam is truth given to the mind, not to man's credulity. The truths, or pr[o]positions, of imân are not mysteries, stumbling blocks, unknowable and unreasonable but critical and rational. They have been subjected to doubt and emerged from the testing confirmed and established as true. No more pleading on their behalf is necessary. Whoever acknowledges them as true is reasonable; whoever persists in denying or doubting is unreasonable. (Islam) . . . comes to us armed with logical and coherent arguments and expects our acquiescence on rational, and hence necessary grounds.[3]

Clearly, being told, and believing, that Islam is necessarily true leads to a very great felt confidence—even if this [necessary truth] isn't the case.

Third, classical Islamic religion views righteousness primarily as *legal righteousness*. Both to be right before God and to live a righteous life are to fulfill all God's commands as they are revealed in the Qur'an and the *Sunna* (the words and example of Muhammad). It is important to recognize that just because Islam centers on law, that need not make it legalistic. Many Muslims will enjoy keeping the *Sharia* from their heart—not just because they are ordered to. Nevertheless, it is true that the traditional Islamic conception of the divine-human relationship is viewed essentially in legislative, not personal, terms. In Islam, Allah is a distant king, not an intimately involved father. This sense underlies the following statement by the famous Shi'ite cleric Murtadha Mutahhari (1919–1979):

> What, then, is "nearness" to the being of al-Haqq [Allah]? Is it literal nearness or figurative nearness? Are the slaves of Allah, through submission, worship, conduct and purity moving up towards Allah, and thus becoming nearer to Him? Is the distance between them becoming shorter; to that point at which distance vanishes, and, in the Qur'anic expression, "meeting with the Lord" (*liqa'u'r-rabb*) takes place?
> . . . Of course, Allah has no nearness or distance. Nearness to Allah is exactly like closeness to someone of social eminence; that is to say, Allah acquires satisfaction from His slave, and, in the end, His grace and favor is returned and it increases.[4]

---

3. Al-Faruqi, *Islamic Theory*. See also al-Faruqi, *Al Tawhid*, 41.
4. Mutahhari, "Nearness to Allah."

This logically leads to a fourth idea: that good religious laws can properly be *enforced* on society. The logic here is simple and sensible. If the laws of Islam are good and truly divine, then it is best for all people for them to form the legislative basis upon which society is built. As Iranian American scholar Seyyed Hossein Nasr (b. 1933) puts it:

> Technically speaking, the Islamic ideal is that of a nomocracy, that is, the rule of Divine Law. It is true that all power, including political power belongs ultimately to God . . . in the case of Islam, the rule of God . . . is associated with that of the Shari'ah.[5]

It is easy to see how this sort of belief leads to the sort of extreme enforcement of the *Sharia* seen in the actions of groups like the Taliban and ISIS. For most Muslims, these forms of enforcement are extreme. Instead, they argue that Muslim laws can be enforced with compassion and within proper political systems. Perhaps it can. But, in any case, the whole idea of a nomocracy implies that Islam is *inherently* universal, political, and enforceable.

Lastly, and importantly, traditional Islam teaches that proper religion is *successful*. The understanding of success here is wide. It incorporates God assisting the believers to be successful against unbelievers in this world as they build a society (Q61:14):

> We supported the believers against their enemy and they were the ones who came out on top.

Muslims are told in the Qur'an that they are the best of all people (Q 3:110).

> [Believers], you are the best community singled out for people: you order what is right, forbid what is wrong, and believe in God. If the People of the Book had also believed, it would have been better for them. For although some of them do believe, most of them are lawbreakers.

But more importantly it involves humans being religiously successful before God. That is, Islam teaches Muslims that it is within their natural, unaided capacity to obey the divine law successfully enough to stand proudly before God on the last day pointing at their good works as meriting his gracious favor.

It is easy to see how, in combination, these fundamental beliefs can lead to an extraordinary zeal. If someone thinks their religious beliefs are *sensible, achievable, universal, enforceable*, and on top of that *unquestionable* and *necessarily true*, that is a recipe for extreme conviction. It is also easy to

---

5. Nasr, *Heart of Islam*, 148–50.

see how Muslims can undermine Christian confidence with these zealous claims.

However, Christians need not be intimidated by any of these Muslim claims. The framework of a Muslim mindset described above is not simply a recipe for zeal, it is a recipe for *misplaced* zeal for it erodes an impetus toward carefully examining the truth of one's beliefs. As it happens this is a tragedy for Muslims, since their beliefs can be subjected to very stern challenges.

So firstly, Islamic doctrine is *not at all obviously rational*. Take, for example, the most fundamental of Muslim doctrines: *Tawhid* or divine unity. Islam teaches an extreme version of divine simplicity in which God is allowed no complexity or division whatever. This is held with great pride as being obvious—in contrast to the incoherence of the notion of Trinity. University of Cambridge scholar Dr. Abdal-Hakim Murad (a.k.a Dr. Tim Winter, a convert to Islam) demonstrates this:

> Reading Muslim presentations of the Trinity one cannot help but detect a sense of impatience. One of the virtues of the Semitic type of consciousness is the conviction that ultimate reality must be ultimately simple, and that the Nicene talk of a deity with three persons, one of whom has two natures, but who are all somehow reducible to authentic unity, quite apart from being rationally dubious, seems intuitively wrong. God, the final ground of all being, surely does not need to be so complicated.[6]

Even a superficial reading of the philosophy of religion around this idea will reveal that it is not at all clear that the Muslim take on divine simplicity is coherent. The idea is greatly challenged in the literature. However, we do not need to engage in deep philosophical thinking about this, as there is a much simpler problem for Islam around *Tawhid*. Traditional Islam also teaches that the Qur'an is an eternal book. But here's the problem: if the Qur'an is eternal, and God is eternal, and God is simply one, then how can the Qur'an be eternal? This is one of many similar problems where something superficially simple is, on reflection, very complicated. As stated succinctly by Geisler and Saleeb, citing Goldziher:

> Orthodox Islam describes the relation between God and the Qur'an by noting that "speech is an eternal attribute of God, which as such is without beginning or intermission, exactly like His knowledge, His might, and other characteristics of His infinite being." But if speech is an eternal attribute of God that is not identical to God but is somehow distinguishable from him,

---

6. Murad, "Trinity."

then does not this allow the very kind of plurality within unity that Christians claim for the Trinity?[7]

Now, even if Muslim beliefs can be shown to be sensible, they are in *no way necessarily true and absolutely certain*. There are multiple reasons for this including the following: that the textual evidence shows Muslim claims around the reliability of the Qur'an are false;[8] that the historical records about Muhammad's life are notoriously unreliable;[9] and that there is no way of claiming that any limited human understanding of the eternal, infinite God eliminates any mysteries or unknowns. However, what's most ironic about al-Faruqi's appeal to certainty is his claim that the core beliefs of Islam have been properly subjected to rigorous historical and philosophical examination. This is simply untrue. Sophisticated philosophical questioning was largely shut down by Muslim religious authorities almost a millennium ago and even today philosophy departments are absent from many Muslim universities.

Moreover, beliefs to do with the supposedly pristine textual history of the Qur'an have *never* been carefully examined in the history of Islam. It is only in the last few decades that the Qur'an has been subjected to detailed textual analysis where some of the most searching questions about the history of the qur'anic text are being asked. This analysis is revealing texts riddled with intentional changes[10] and a text development that cannot be squared with the traditional account found in centuries of Islamic scholarship. Clearly, core beliefs to do with the inerrancy of the qur'anic text and reliability of the records of the *Sunna* are very far from being certain. Sadly, because Muslim scholars have left this unexamined, the Muslim masses are in the dangerous epistemic position of feeling extraordinarily certain about beliefs that are desperately *un*certain. This situation is compounded by the fact that in Islam's key text, believers are discouraged from asking questions for fear that they might lose their faith (Q.5:101–2):

> You who believe, do not ask about matters which, if made known to you, might make things difficult for you—if you ask about them while the Qur'an is being revealed, they will be made known to you—for God has kept silent about them: God

---

7. Geisler and Saleeb, *Answering Islam*, 139–40.

8. For a fascinating study arguing that the qur'anic text is sourced in oral tradition see Bannister, *Oral-Formulaic Study*.

9. Cf. the critical scrutiny of the earliest biography of Muhammad in Spencer, *Truth about Muhammad*, 27–32.

10. Brubaker, *Corrections*.

is most forgiving and forbearing. Before you, some people asked about things, then ignored [the answers].

Third, it is unclear how the laws of Islam show the proper signs of being divine, or even good. In our experience of living among Muslims, the Sharia when followed closely *appears oppressive* rather than life-giving. Here's one example "from below" (i.e. in the lives of ordinary Muslims). The *Sharia* teaches that fasting in Ramadan is obligatory, but that you do not need to fast if you are breastfeeding or pregnant. Nevertheless, if you skip the fast, you need to make it up at some stage in the future. There are personal stories of women who had been either breastfeeding or pregnant for around twelve years straight, and so had more than a year's worth of straight fasting to catch up on. All of them found this unreasonable and oppressive. Is this sort of demand really the sign of a loving and most gracious God?[11]

The problem becomes clear when examined "from above" too. If the *Sharia* really does produce the best of people, then why is the track record of Muslim nations so dire when it comes to matters of human flourishing? On most measures of human rights, countries that seek to enforce Islam on their population overwhelmingly rank poorly—in particular, in their treatment of the weak and vulnerable, including Christian minorities.[12] Muslim apologists might respond that this is due to these countries not taking their Islam seriously enough. But that simply raises the question why, if Islam is all it's claimed to be in terms of success, can't it be successfully adopted by any nation? The track record of the enforcement of Islam should lessen the zeal of Muslims rather than increase it!

Paul captures all this when he suggests that the sort of religion represented by Judaism and Islam displays a zeal that fails to be grounded in true knowledge:

> For I bear them witness that they have a zeal for God, but not according to knowledge. For, being ignorant of the righteousness of God, and seeking to establish their own, they did not submit to God's righteousness. (Rom 10:2–3)

Islam bears all the hallmarks of a religion that hungers after righteousness, but from a biblical perspective lacks the true knowledge of God's righteousness that can lead to a truly transformative life. This becomes all the more pointed when it comes to the person of Jesus.

---

11. Cf. Riddell, "No Mere Legal Code."

12. See, for example, the Open Doors *World Watch List* where, of the top twenty countries in which it is most dangerous to be a Christian, fifteen are Muslim majority.

TRUE RIGHTEOUSNESS—ROMANS 10:3

When Paul speaks of the righteousness of God, he means the righteousness found in Jesus (e.g. Phil 3:9). The central message of the gospel of Christ is that his righteous sacrifice secures righteousness for humanity—both in terms of being right with God and living right lives. It is precisely this Christ-focused righteousness that is absent in Islam.

Of course, traditional Islam claims to embrace truth about Jesus. It recognizes Jesus as the Messiah[13] and teaches a range of ideas to do with his miracle working[14], his virgin birth[15], and his prophetic role.[16] It is this that leads to the common Muslim notion that they hold Jesus in very high regard. Indeed, a young Muslim friend was once wearing a T-shirt with the claim "I Love Jesus" emblazoned across the front. On the back, it also said: "because I am a Muslim, and he was too!" When asked just what it was about Jesus that he loved—which of Jesus's actions, and which words—he smiled and confessed that it was merely a free T-shirt from the mosque and that he knew very little about Jesus's life. This amusing story is instructive: most Muslims, in fact, know very little of the historical Jesus and next to nothing about what it meant for him to be the Messiah.

However, the problem here is not simply ignorance of the biblical Jesus. What is most telling is not what Islam affirms or ignores about Jesus but what it denies. A little later in Romans 10, Paul reaches the nub of how to secure righteousness, proclaiming that:

> . . . if you confess with your mouth that Jesus is Lord and believe in your heart that God raised him from the dead, you will be saved. (Rom 10:9)

The core truths about Jesus that pertain to humans achieving righteousness are his divine lordship and his atoning death and resurrection. These are the two truths about Jesus that enable his fulfillment of the role of Messiah and, ironically, these are precisely the two truths Islam denies. The verse often cited by Muslims in support of their views is Q4:157, which flies in the face not only of the biblical record but also of secular writings dating from the decades after the crucifixion of Christ:

> Q4:157: and [they] said, "We have killed the Messiah, Jesus, son of Mary, the Messenger of God." They did not kill him, nor

---

13. By referring to him as 'Isa al-masih on multiple occasions; e.g. Q4:171.
14. E.g. Q3:41; Q3:49; Q5:109–10; Q5:112–115.
15. Q19:20.
16. Q19:30.

did they crucify him, though it was made to appear like that to them; those that disagreed about him are full of doubt, with no knowledge to follow, only supposition: they certainly did not kill him.

What this means is that while Muslims are happy to accept a wide range of truths to do with Jesus, they remain steadfastly "... ignorant of the righteousness of God" for salvation.

The upshot of all this is that many ordinary traditional Muslims are left in a philosophically compromised mindset whereby they are holding their religious beliefs with extreme confidence, with reticence to question or doubt, and with a basic ignorance of a subject thought to be familiar—Jesus.

CHRISTIAN ZEAL—ROMANS 10:1

Understanding traditional Islamic religious mindsets, and Islam's teaching to do with Jesus, helps Christians recognize a range of epistemological barriers that need to be overcome in sharing the gospel with Muslims. For Muslims to accept Christian claims about Jesus will require them to make a massive shift in mindset. This sort of shift is difficult for all of us. It is a huge thing to be faced with the realization that your passions are not lined up properly with reality. Sometimes this is merely disappointing. Consider the example of golf. Felt confidence often belies true abilities; we try to play unachievable shots. When it comes to religion, though, a fundamental mindset shift is scary since it involves deeply core belief. For any Muslim to make this sort of epistemological shift he or she will need to question fundamentally matters they have historically taken to be unquestionable. They will need to embrace a humbling recognition that perhaps Islam isn't the best of religions or Muslims the best of people. They may need to do some very hard and unfamiliar thinking about the true rationality of Islamic doctrine.

The challenge for Christian mission amongst Muslims is finding the appropriate sort of approach to trigger just this sort of existential wrestling in the Muslim mind. Here, obviously, apologetic arguments have their place. There is a right place to offer merely intellectual challenges to why others believe what they do and whether their beliefs are truly warranted. But in the case of Muslim belief, their closed epistemology, with its resistance to questioning, often resists argument.

In addition to an intellectual discussion, Christians need to dent supreme Muslim confidence that they hold absolute truth by displaying the sort of godly and Spirit-filled life over time that leads to the possibility that a Muslim might recognize them as an epistemic authority on religion. So, for example, an encounter with a Spirit-filled, and grace-living, Christian community might naturally lead a Muslim to question whether Islam really did produce the "best of all people," or whether they have been told the truth about Christianity. Similarly, any Muslim witnessing God answering the prayers of Christians will have no choice but to be confronted with the possibility that their beliefs about to whom God listens are incorrect. In these, and so many areas, the key realization is that when confronted with a zealous and largely closed mindset, it is important to not just *tell* people they are ignorant of truth but to show them they are in ways that will crack through psychological confidence.

Now of course, this model of engagement requires deep and long-term commitment from Christians to building substantial relationships with Muslims. Here, the attitude of our hearts is far more important than the adoption of correct ministry models. Again, Paul's discussion in Romans is helpful. All through the book of Romans he displays just the sort of missional heart that is required in reaching out to those who are naturally resistant to recognizing Jesus as Lord. Indeed, the passage we have been focusing on comes in the middle of chapters 9–11, a section which begins with the lament:

> I am speaking the truth in Christ—I am not lying; my conscience bears me witness in the Holy Spirit—that I have great sorrow and unceasing anguish in my heart. For I could wish that I myself were accursed and cut off from Christ for the sake of my brothers, my kinsmen according to the flesh. (Rom 9:1–3)

Crucially, Paul's missiological discussion is undergirded and framed by his love for his people. His deep longing for his neighbors to discover God's true righteousness is repeated in our passage:

> Brothers, my heart's desire and prayer to God for them is that they may be saved . . . (Rom 10:1)

Paul's example reminds us that the best response to Muslim religious zeal is Christian zeal! Partly this is because Christian zeal for the truth about Jesus is grounded in a long history of humble and rich examination of the reasons for our confidence. That is, Christian confidence that we believe the truth corresponds to the evidence better than Islam does. More importantly, though, proper Christian zeal is necessary, for it should lead not to unquestioning pride in being right but to unwavering perseverance in loving Muslims deeply and sharing our lives with them. The degree to which we exhibit this sort of zeal is the degree to which our love will show Muslims that Jesus is real (John 13:35).

BIBLIOGRAPHY

Al-Faruqi, Ismail. "Towards an Islamic Theory of Meta-Religion, Part 1" (n.d.). http://islamicstudies.islammessage.com/ResearchPaper.aspx?aid=572.

Al-Faruqi, Ismail Raji. *Al Tawhid: Its Implications on Thought and Life*. Herndon, VA: IIIT, 1992.

Bannister, Andrew. *An Oral-Formulaic Study of the Qur'an*. Lanham: Lexington, 2014.

Brubaker, Daniel. "Corrections in Early Qurʾān Manuscripts: Twenty Examples." *Think and Tell* (2019).

Geisler, N. L., and Abdul Saleeb. *Answering Islam: The Crescent in the Light of the Cross*. Grand Rapids, MI: Baker, 2002.

Idris, Jaafar Sheikh. "Episode 01—Religion and Rationality." *The Rational*. Huda TV (n.d.). http://www.jaafaridris.com/rational-episode-01/.

Murad, Abdal-Hakim. "The Trinity: A Muslim Perspective." 1996. http://masud.co.uk/ISLAM/ahm/trinity.htm.

Mutahhari, Murtadha. "What Does Nearness to Allah Mean?" (n.d.). https://www.al-islam.org/wilayah-station-master-ayatullah-murtadha-mutahhari/what-does-nearness-allah-mean.

Nasr, S. H. *The Heart of Islam*. San Francisco: HarperOne, 2004.

Open Doors. *World Watch List*. https://www.opendoors.org.au/persecuted-christians/world-watchlist?gclid=CjwKCAjwqdn1BRBREiwAEbZcR8Quu1ju42V28GBm74c8h2olSTk_ZsxJpy2xEk3Wk2jS8VuVOlEYDxoCXoIQAvD_BwE.

Riddell, Peter. "No Mere Legal Code: The Harshness of Shari'a Law." *Biblemesh*, March 30, 2011. https://biblemesh.com/blog/no-mere-legal-code-the-harshness-of-sharia-law/.

Shumack, Richard. *The Wisdom of Islam and the Foolishness of Christianity*. Sydney: Island View, 2014.

Spencer, Robert. *The Truth About Muhammad: Founder of the World's Most Intolerant Religion*. Washington, DC: Regnery, 2006.

17

From Receiving to Sending

Healthy Principles to Mobilize the Church for CrossCultural Service—Insights from Ukrainian Evangelicalism

Eric Oldenburg

OVER THE PAST TWENTY years, the Evangelical church in the country of Ukraine has undergone a radical reorientation around Jesus's Great Commission to reach the ends of the earth with the gospel. Rather than viewing themselves solely as an unreached people in need of assistance and training from the global body of Christ, Ukrainian believers are gaining a vision and a passion to take Jesus faithfully to the unreached people groups of the world. This cross-cultural worldview shift did not happen overnight, nor was it a flawless or fluid process. And the task is not complete. Conflict-ridden conversations still take place, some meetings continue to end in frustration, and misunderstanding abounds on all sides, i.e., the missionary mobilizers, the Ukrainian missionaries and supporting churches, as well as the receiving fields, all struggle to figure out whether and how Ukrainians can participate in the charge to make God's name great among the nations. What are the lessons that the Evangelical church in sending countries should learn from the swell in cross-cultural mission work that continues in

Ukraine to this day? What are the driving missiological truths that capture the hearts of Ukrainians and should similarly excite brothers and sisters in Christ in young and/or developing churches around the world? Which mistakes in fanning the cross-cultural flame can be avoided, either from the mobilization side, or from the missionary trainee side, in other, similar contexts? Finally, what are the kingdom successes over which we can all rejoice that God is realizing through the Ukrainian church? God desires every member of the body of Christ to play a part in the fulfillment of his global gospel plan. The positive and negative missional experience of the Ukrainian evangelical church has much to teach the rest of God's people as we all navigate our place in that plan.

INTRODUCTION: SETTING EXPERIENTIAL PARAMETERS

My wife, Josie, and I arrived in Ukraine in the summer of 2004, eager to learn language so that I might eventually teach theology, philosophy, and apologetics at a Ukrainian seminary or Bible college.[1] Fellow missionaries showed us how to exchange money, where to buy groceries and furniture, and how to navigate the public transport system. We also plugged into a local Ukrainian church, and even though we understood almost nothing in those early months, the young adults in that congregation embraced us as their own, especially once we opened our apartment to them for weekly meetings. I consider our cultural transition quite smooth compared to some stories I have heard, even from missionaries within our own relatively healthy mission.

Shortly after our arrival, a leader in our mission reached out to Josie, a trained and experienced writer/editor who had left a career in journalism to serve in Ukraine, asking her to help with a promotional piece for a relatively new ministry to educate and equip Ukrainians to become cross-cultural missionaries.[2] There were three American missionaries and one Ukrainian on this new ministry team, and they were convinced that the Ukrainian Evangelical church was poised to become a hub of missionary activity, sending Ukrainians throughout Eurasia and the world to places where Westerners are not welcome. In all of our preparation to move to

---

1. We served with the interdenominational, multinational, Evangelical mission, SEND International. SEND's mission, "is to mobilize God's people and engage the unreached in order to establish reproducing churches." To find out more about SEND, visit www.send.org.

2. Josie still serves in SEND's US office as a writer.

Ukraine, we had never heard of this ministry of Great Commission training. It was an exciting and promising possibility. But during the course of our two-year language training, we watched several teammates transition from mobilization to other ministries; the Ukrainian moved to the West; and, most devastatingly for the movement, the Ukrainian church, by and large, responded coldly to the idea of mobilization for cross-cultural service. The typical response was something like, "There are so many unbelievers in Ukraine; we need to take the gospel to them. Others will have to take the gospel to the unreached in other countries and cultures."[3]

Today, less than twenty years after these initial hardships, Ukraine is experiencing a strong surge in the momentum of cross-cultural missions. We moved back to the United States in 2016, but our former missionary team has more members serving either directly with non-Ukrainian unreached people groups (hereafter UPGs) within Ukraine, or with the mobilization of Ukrainians to reach the unreached both inside and outside Ukraine, than with any other ministry. Among Ukrainians, countless churches are aware of and praying for the unreached, dynamic missions conferences are held each year with hundreds of participants, leading seminaries have cross-cultural missions programs and majors, and the Evangelical church supports dozens of cross-cultural missionaries in countries all over the world. The Ukrainian Evangelical church is an active and growing partner in the cross-cultural, Great Commission work that Jesus commanded his followers to carry out, rather than a mere recipient of the cross-cultural, Great Commission work of others.

My goal in this chapter is to reflect on this ongoing transformation among Ukrainian followers of Jesus to an ends-of-the-earth mindset, and to offer suggestions that missionaries from sending countries might follow when assisting newly established churches to shift similarly to this mindset. Inasmuch as these reflections are based on my personal experience as a missionary and mission field leader, and on interviews with other such leaders,

---

3. This sentiment is also attested to by a SEND International missionary in Alfie Mossé's report, *Mobilization Analysis*, 7, shared with author on April 5, 2020. The report, a survey of field missionaries, leaders, and representatives, aims to help missionaries become more resilient and agile and to have greater gospel impact. Phase I (November 2019–February 2020) included ninety minute interviews with fifty-one SEND Eurasia field members. Topics discussed included member care, mobilization, and national partnerships. For Phase II (February–March 2020), similar interviews were done with SEND leadership. These interviews indicated that globalized mobilization was of great interest to the members and leaders, both as an area of excitement and an area that needs improvement. The analysis cited is based on comments and responses specifically related to questions concerning globalized mobilization. As of the writing of this chapter, the Eurasia study has entered Phase III.

they are understandably limited.[4] It should also be noted that the Ukrainian Evangelical church is at her own unique place in the ecclesial development process, as is any church. Thus, these reflections may not be helpful or appropriate in every context where the church has yet to develop or is in the initial stages of developing a cross-cultural missions vision. Building an all-nations ethos is important in any church plant, but not every new Christian movement needs to think about what its missions training philosophy for seminaries should be, especially if there is not or will not be traditional seminaries among those peoples. My thoughts are directed at those who are working in contexts where the church is ready to educate, train, send, support, and strengthen her own missionaries in cross-cultural contexts. Where such mobilization opportunities are available, may others glean from what those of us working with our beloved Ukrainians have learned as we have watched them embrace the gospel and take it to the ends of the earth.[5]

PATIENT EMPOWERMENT: REALIZING THE TIME AND EFFORT NECESSARY FOR MISSIONAL WORLDVIEW TRANSFORMATION

Institutional change in the modern world can be difficult and painful, whether in a church or in a Christian organization. Given all of the integrated elements of organizational function, there are many ways that change, even when administered well, can prove difficult. Branson and Martínez's words powerfully capture the common reality:

> Church transformation is never smooth—experiments fail, people are offended, some of the most promising leaders get weary.

4. From 2011 to 2014, I served as the area director for SEND's Ukraine team, directing the ministries of twenty missionary families in six different cities. A significant component of the area director role is to represent the ministries of the SEND Ukraine team both to the sending offices in the US, as well as to our Ukrainian co-laborers. Because missions mobilization among Ukrainians is a major ministry focus for the SEND Ukraine team, I spent much of my time advocating for and serving alongside the missionaries working in this area.

5. Throughout I make mention of how the cross-cultural missions movement in Ukraine might be helpful to young and developing churches among newly reached people groups. This is not because the Ukrainian Evangelical church is young and developing; it has been alive and growing for well over one hundred years. However, since the Ukrainian Evangelical church came out from under the restrictive, persecuting hand of the Soviet Union only thirty years ago, she bears certain similarities to young and developing churches in newly established mission fields. In my mind, these similarities serve as the basis for comparison and legitimize the drawing of conclusions from the Ukrainian experience for the young and developing churches.

In a society where monthly reports and quick fixes are expected, the complex and slower work of transformation will be discouraging for many. Developing intercultural life, in which cultural diversity is apparent internally and externally—in relationships, language, structures, activities, decision making and leadership—is never done. Challenges will always appear. Humans will hurt each other. Sin messes every initiative. Good ideas will lack resources.[6]

These stark circumstances surrounding change are no less true in young and developing churches when faced with the prospect of gaining a global, all-nations vision. Of course, if churches are raised up with such a vision, many of these difficulties can be avoided, if not mitigated significantly. But that does not seem to be the case today with most young, developing churches that were planted or co-planted by Evangelical missionaries. As Ralph Winter notes, "Protestant missions have been so focused on planting churches that they have neglected to instill within these new churches the same missions vision—the very reason these missionaries came with the gospel!"[7] While pioneer missionaries planting new churches among UPGs have the advantage of discipling them in this way from the outset and avoiding some of these difficulties, cross-cultural workers in young but established churches should brace themselves for the slow process of transition from a sole focus on their immediate context to an inclusive, global and local focus.

As mentioned in the introduction, we arrived on the field to find our mission already in the process of missions mobilization among Ukrainian churches. A team was working to create cross-cultural missions awareness and, as the Lord called Ukrainians to the task, to train up missionaries to take the gospel to the ends of the earth. Because the Ukrainian church's primary focus was local, many of our cross-cultural missions mobilization efforts were not broadly or warmly received.[8] In one instance, after years

---

6. Branson and Martínez, *Churches*, 230–31.

7. Cited in Living Springs, *Kairos*, chaps. 5, 16. The original source for this quote by Ralph Winter is not provided in the document.

8. Among many Ukrainian Evangelical churches, there did and does exist a passionate zeal for "missions." The definition of missions, however, often centers on taking the gospel to the many Ukrainian villages that do not have an Evangelical presence. This is a distinct need and a worthy call. But it is not, in many cases, a cross-cultural work. The Ukrainian church can and should exhibit both this local and a global missionary zeal. For an in-depth study of the spread of the gospel across the Slavic world by Ukrainians in the 1990s, see White, "Factors," 134–44. While there was engagement with non-Slavic people groups during this time, the majority of the work involved Slavs planting churches among Slavs where there was no church. As White notes, Pentecostal

of investment into a young woman who clearly understood God's heart for the nations, our team approached the local church where this woman was a member. For months they discussed a process whereby our mission and this church could jointly send her to the people group in another nation for which the Lord had given her a passion. In what was a sharp blow to this first wave of our cross-cultural mobilization efforts, the leadership of the church decided that this woman was too valuable to send away to serve others; they required her to stay put and serve in ministry among her local congregation.

Branson and Martínez discuss the following types of leadership needed to transition a church or organization to an ethnically inclusive and culturally diverse worldview. Interpretive leadership equips members to understand and interpret themselves and their surrounding context properly. Relational leadership listens to and cares for members while also looking for opportunities to connect with those outside the church or organization. Implemental leadership works with members to enact positive change that preserves previously established core values while developing new values through open dialogue and experimentation.[9] SEND Ukraine's initial missions mobilization team was practicing all three types of leadership; however, in hindsight, it seems that they had not given enough time for their interpretive and implemental work to take effect, nor had they established their relational roots deeply and broadly enough for their efforts to take hold. Today, almost twenty years down the missions mobilization road, the situation is reversed. There has been such a widespread transformation that some churches sacrifice their ministries in other areas in order to support cross-cultural work. Chad Wiebe, SEND Ukraine missionary and director of 3M (Missions Mobilization Ministry), recounts with tears a special moment that illustrates the worldview shift that has occurred in some churches.[10] Chad, along with 3M, had trained and helped send a Ukrainian family to a remote village in Central Asia for six months. As their six months were drawing to a close, a pastor from a neighboring village in that same country called Chad, recounted the gospel impact the Ukrainian couple was having, and asked if their stay could be extended so that their village could benefit

---

missionaries were more involved in reaching UPGs in the Slavic world than were Baptists during this time.

9. Branson and Martínez, *Churches*, 212–26. This so-called "Leadership Triad" is introduced in chapter one, pages 54–57, but is developed in much more detail in this latter, penultimate chapter.

10. Chad Wiebe, e-mail message to the author, May 2, 2020. I heard Chad recount this story a number of times while we were serving together in Ukraine, but he confirmed the details in this latest e-mail exchange.

from the Ukrainian missionaries as well. This required more funding, and so Chad reached out to his contacts of missions-minded churches throughout Ukraine, seeking support for this three-month extension. After several days of silence, the small home church that had sent this couple contacted Chad and announced that they had funds to pass on. When Chad met up with the church deacon, he handed Chad an envelope bursting with Ukrainian *hryvnia*,[11] saying, "This is for the missionaries. It's everything. It's all we have in our strong box, everything from our annual giving, everything from our latest offerings. We don't want the proclamation of the gospel to this unreached group to cease due to lack of resources." SEND Ukraine's initial missions mobilization efforts were not at all unsuccessful; they were merely seeds planted that needed time to bear the dynamic fruit of a global vision that is capturing the Ukrainian church today. Any cross-cultural worker serving a young but established church, who is desiring to disciple that church into commitment to the Great Commission, should know that the process will likely take sustained effort over a long period of time. Yet the kingdom results are worth it.

ONE COUNTRY, MANY CULTURES: DISCOVERING THE UPGS WITHIN A GEOPOLITICAL NATION

Regardless of whether we speak of politics, the economy or the media, everyone can agree that we live in a globalized world. It is not difficult for most, even if they are unable to travel to other parts of the planet and visit unique cultures and peoples, to learn about them via the Internet.[12] In spite of the seeming ubiquity of access to cultural education, geopolitical nations are the reductionistic, ethnocultural boundary markers to which we often refer. Kenyans are from Kenya, Brazilians are from Brazil, and Ukrainians are from Ukraine. This one-to-one geopolitical correspondence approach to the determination of cultures/people groups would mean that there are 195 cultures/people groups in the world, i.e., one for each country.[13] Compare this gross oversimplification with Joshua Project's largest people group count of 17,423.[14] Simple observation requires us to acknowledge that large numbers

11. *Hryvnia* is Ukrainian currency.
12. Moreau et al., *Introducing World Missions*, 265.
13. Hayes, "How Many."
14. Joshua Project, "Global Statistics." This statistic counts a people group once for every geopolitical county in which that people group resides. If each people group is counted only once, regardless of how many geopolitical countries may be home to that people group, the number reduces to 10,434.

of people groups and cultures will be found in each geopolitical nation-state; we must strive to move away from the latter as our default category.

Missionaries and cross-cultural workers must prioritize teaching a people group mindset in the developing Evangelical churches with which they work. Doing so will have, at least, the following two results. First, it will teach the developing church the clear scriptural emphasis on God's passion for people groups. While it is the case that Jesus's Great Commission in Matthew 28:19 to make disciples πάντα τὰ ἔθνη, "of all the nations," may appear general and unspecific, by contrast, John's picture in Revelation 7:9, that a multitude ἐκ παντὸς ἔθνους καὶ φυλῶν καὶ λαῶν καὶ γλωσσῶν, "from all the nations and tribes and peoples and tongues," will be worshipping Jesus, is pointed and clear.[15] So a people group mindset aligns followers of Jesus with God's revealed word regarding the larger, national context, without neglecting the more specific, tribal group, people group, and language group foci. Second, a people group mindset will open the eyes of those willing to see that there are, very likely, various people groups all around them. For the eschatological picture in Revelation 7:9 to become reality, the church must take the gospel to not just the nations, but to the tribes and peoples and tongues in those nations, as well. And if each geopolitical nation today contains large numbers of distinct people groups, a developing Evangelical church can exhibit God's heart for all people groups without necessarily leaving their own country. Some, but certainly not all, followers of Jesus are called to cross-cultural missions in a nation other than their own. Others, for a myriad of reasons, may not be able to leave their home country. With a people group mindset and some rudimentary investigation, such Jesus followers can spread the gospel cross-culturally without crossing a border. When we moved to Ukraine, we knew that there were both Ukrainians and Russians living there. In the first few years, it became obvious that there was a strong contingent of people from Central Asian countries residing there as well (everyone knows that the best spices at the open-air markets are those sold by the Azerbaijani). I was later quite shocked to learn, as are most Ukrainians when they discover this fact, that there are approximately eighty people groups in Ukraine, with about thirty of them categorized as unreached.[16]

---

15. In missions mobilization contexts, ἔθνος is typically pointed to as the word from which we get "ethnicity" or "ethnic groups." While ethnicity/ethnic group is within the semantic range of ἔθνος, it bears other meanings, including geopolitical nations. A fuller biblical theology is necessary to interpret ἔθνος as ethnic groups in Matthew 28:19. John 7:9 is a part of that fuller biblical theology. Bietenhard, "People," 790–95.

16. Joshua Project, "Country: Ukraine."

I became aware of Ukraine's non-national people groups, specifically their UPGs, through the work of my friend and fellow SEND-missionary, Kyle Eipperle.[17] Kyle developed a prayer guide for the unreached peoples of Ukraine in order to inform Ukrainians of the many UPGs in their country.[18] I had just stepped into the area director role for SEND Ukraine when I learned these facts and, as is common for someone in such a leadership role, my calendar began to fill up with preaching appointments. Since missions mobilization is an aspect of SEND Ukraine's ministry focus, I desired to develop a sermon that I could preach regularly with an end to informing people about the UPGs in Ukraine. The Spirit led me to Luke 14:7–24 and the story and parable there about kingdom inclusion of the outcast and marginalized. Approximately a dozen times, I preached this message, closing with a presentation of Ukraine's UPGs, making the point that, by and large, these peoples are considered and treated as outcasts and are marginalized in Ukrainian society. Once the church service was over, I would hand out an unreached peoples of Ukraine prayer guide to each attendee, encouraging them to ask God how he might be calling each of them to reach out to the outcast and marginalized among them. I am still overwhelmed with joy every time I recall the follow-up stories that I would hear from pastors about how their churches are now regularly praying for UPGs, for people they never even knew existed before. Kyle estimates that, to date, close to five thousand prayer guides have been printed and distributed in seminary classes, at missions conferences, and during church services, all with similar results. Ukrainian Evangelicalism now has an army of prayer warriors interceding on behalf of the unreached in their country, serving them in various ways as the Lord opens the door. While not every cross-cultural missionary team serving young Evangelical churches will have a person like Kyle to do this kind of research and publication, each team can and should do the initial work necessary to inform the churches they are serving to develop a people group mindset. The minimal result will be a biblically-faithful foundation for a global perspective and, perhaps, some in the developing church may be called to engage the unreached around them.

Information dissemination for the purpose of prayer is important, but figuring out how to minister to UPGs in contextually appropriate ways is another question altogether. More than once, I heard Ukrainian pastors,

---

17. Kyle Eipperle is currently a research associate at Operation World, seconded from SEND International. The information in this paragraph is from either our personal field experience together or from Kyle Eipperle, interview by author, Zoom video conference, March 25, 2020.

18. Find both the unreached peoples of Ukraine prayer guide and the unreached peoples of Russia prayer guide at https://joshuaproject.net/pray/guides.

after learning the UPG statistics in Ukraine, say something like the following, "The [members of a particular UPG in their area] know that our Evangelical church is here. Let them come to us if they want to hear the gospel." This culturally insensitive and presumptuous sentiment displays the general need for cross-cultural church planting strategies for developing churches that may be trying to reach unbelievers of different cultures and ethnicities than their own. Our missions organization sensed this need and tasked two missionary units with starting up an international ministry, particularly targeting the non-Ukrainian people groups in an area, including those in the university system. Over the course of just a few years, this ministry grew from a Friday night meeting to a Sunday morning service that, at one point, represented ten different people groups, most of them UPGs. Of course, engaging a student population carries the challenge that student visa status is precariously unstable in many nations and, at best, students graduate and move on in just a few years. Nevertheless, this international ministry continues today with Ukrainians having served on the leadership team; it is at least one model of UPG engagement within the country. While skepticism about this approach still exists, it continues to proliferate and Ukrainians are reaching UPGs by these means. Innovative, cross-cultural ministry strategies like this should be part of the outreach options considered by developing churches when strategizing how to reach the unreached with the gospel.

SURPRISED BUT NOT SHAKEN: LEARNING TO EXPECT POSITIVE AND NEGATIVE CHANGES IN DIRECTION

The cross-cultural missionary life, like any Christian life, is a both/and rather than an either/or. We do not experience a life of abundant blessing or a life of painful suffering; we experience both. We are not met with hostile opposition to the message of the gospel or warm, appreciative reception of it; we are met with both. And we do not find that our ministry plans work out perfectly or that they are upended in life-altering ways; we find both. Jesus's very own teaching substantiates this both/and reality. In John 14:12, after attempting to help the disciples understand who he is and in what his mission consists, Jesus declares that they will do greater things than even he had done. Thus, we should expect God to do amazing and even miraculous work as we labor to make his name great among the nations. Robert Coleman expresses this expectation in terms of a spiritual revival today.

> All of us should join in . . . prayer, even as we look expectantly to what lies ahead. Something great is on the horizon. You can almost feel it in the air. Though forces of evil are becoming more

> sinister and aggressive, there is a corresponding cry for spiritual awakening. Across the world there has never been more yearning by more people for spiritual reality, nor has the Church ever had the means it now has to take the glad tidings of salvation to the lost, unreached peoples of the earth. What a day to be alive![19]

Later in the same discourse, John 15:18, Jesus essentially tells the disciples that the world will end up hating them because of him.[20] Josef Tson describes such a life as sacrificial.

> To clarify this concept, suffering for Christ is not a self-inflicted suffering. The disciple of Christ seeks to do the will of Christ and to promote the cause of Christ. However, the suffering for Christ does mean that the disciple will voluntarily involve himself in suffering and sacrificial living for Christ and His gospel.[21]

So, in the teachings of our Lord, in our everyday life, and from the pen of mission leaders, we see that a life of great power, yet a life of hardship, is a standard experience. This both/and characteristic of Christian living should bring a sober realism to what cross-cultural workers should expect on the field.

This dual expectation, if truly incorporated into the ethos of a missionary team, can serve as a stabilizing factor through the ups and downs of cross-cultural service. For our mission mobilization efforts in Ukraine, it has done just that. Quite recently, several Ukrainian and American mission representatives gathered together with key Roma leaders—the Roma are one of Ukraine's highest population UPGs—to strategize a Bible translation project for their people group.[22] The common language for the roundtable discussion was Russian. But as the Roma leaders began to speak Roma with one another, it was immediately evident that all five Roma leaders were speaking different, very distinct dialects. They could not understand one another. This was quite an unexpected surprise to everyone, yet the result was even more surprising. The Ukraine Bible Translators organization, rather than deciding to focus on one or two of these dialects, is committed to translating the Bible into all five Roma dialects. The Lord has provided

---

19. Coleman, "Hope," 203.
20. See Matthew 24:9 for Jesus's prophetic word that such opposition will only increase as the church approaches the end of the age. One's eschatological viewpoint will affect the exegesis of this passage. Nevertheless, no one should deny that today the message of Jesus is embraced in some contexts and rejected in others.
21. Tson, "Suffering and Martyrdom," 195.
22. This story was shared with the author by Kyle Eipperle, who was present at the meeting. Interview by author, Zoom video conference, March 25, 2020.

the vision, the passion, and the means for these projects to move forward. To date, the Christmas story, the Easter story, and the Gospel of Luke have been translated into these dialects. God certainly uses surprising challenges to stimulate positive change.

At the same time, some surprising challenges rock our worlds. The Crimean Tatar are Ukraine's largest UPG; there are approximately 300,000 of them in Ukraine and only three hundred (0.10%) are Evangelical believers. In an effort to both take the gospel to this people group and to model to Ukrainian Evangelicals a contextually appropriate and culturally sensitive mission effort, SEND Ukraine sent a family of four and a single woman to minister in Crimea in the summer of 2013. It was not easy to form the team, to discern the right ministry platform or to establish trusting relationships with Crimean Tatar. But the team was launched, and we were trusting God to do something extraordinary. Our hopes were sky high and our prayers were reaching higher still. Yet, less than one year after this unique work began, Russia occupied and then annexed the Crimean Peninsula.[23] This led to a rapid and rushed evacuation of that team from the peninsula, a splitting of that team and one unit ultimately transitioning back to their home country. After years of prayer and preparation, our efforts in Crimea came to a missionally heartbreaking and emotionally devastating halt. As hard as this experience was for us, however, the SEND Ukraine team continues to mobilize God's people in Ukraine, knowing that there are many other opportunities to exemplify God's heart for the nations.

The grounding element that keeps missionaries stable in both positive and negative changes in direction, and the lesson that should be passed on to young, developing churches as they wade into the uncertainties of cross-cultural service is that we are doing God's work at his bidding. The successes come because he has orchestrated them, and the seeming failures may have little to nothing to do with us. This is one of a number of theological realizations that, when it permeates our missions mobilization, will mark our efforts with a mature humility and a deep expectation.[24]

> Being chosen by God to be sent may seem to carry great honour and responsibility, but the more pressing reality is that it normally also involves suffering, rejection, persecution and sometimes

---

23. As with most of the world, I consider the occupation and annexation of Crimea by Russia to be a gross violation of international law; Crimea is rightly considered a territory of Ukraine.

24. Some other theological realizations that must be present to ground our work in the midst of both difficulty and victory are: sense of calling for oneself, understanding that others are called, appreciation of God's global plan and work, ministry competence, peer-support, encouragement from various sources and a life of dependent prayer.

death. God's mission involves a host of sent-ones, deliverers, messengers, but ultimately the accomplishment of God's mission does not depend on human agents, but on the sovereign power of God Himself, through His Spirit and his Word.[25]

UNITED IN MISSION, DIVIDED IN VISION: NAVIGATING A VARIEGATED MISSIOLOGY IN THEOLOGICAL EDUCATION

As the global center of Christianity continues to shift from the West to the East and South, theological education is undergoing a related shift.[26] Many seminaries and Bible schools in countries and regions where the Evangelical church is young and developing were originally modelled after Western theological institutions in everything from curriculum design, to textbook use, to classroom structure. While God certainly has used and continues to use the Western model in non-Western contexts, two negative consequences of such imitation serve as the basis for the shift toward more contextualized models for theological education. First, as Michael Ortiz notes, studying in Western-styled theological institutions can tempt students to emigrate to the West to receive the "real thing," leaving the local church with even fewer leaders.[27] Secondly, newly developing seminaries and Bible colleges typically need broad and integrated coverage of the whole sweep of theology, yet they are modelled after the siloed, specialist approach to scholarship, so ubiquitous in Western academia. This can hinder schools from training up leaders for all areas of life who have a holistic approach to their calling; they are missing the missional component of the theological endeavor. Perry Shaw captures well the ideal toward which developing seminaries and Bible colleges should aim.

> The role of theological education is not merely to equip those preparing to serve *in* the church, but those called to serve *as* the church in the world, to prepare people who are able to claim the

---

25. Wright, "God's People," 209. Original verb tense changed from past to present.

26. Moreau, *World Missions*, 270. Moreau merely notes the global shift in Christian majority, not the shift in theological education. For more on the global shift, see the widely influential work of Jenkins, *Next Christendom*.

27. Ortiz, "Missiology." This emigration reality was painfully present in the post-Soviet Slavic world, including Ukraine. Only recently, thanks in part to the presence of Talbot School of Theology's accredited degree program at Kyiv Theological Seminary and significant scholarly steps forward in a number of Ukrainian institutions, is emigration becoming less of the heartbreaking issue that it has been.

whole of private and public life for Christ and his Kingdom. . . . The central missional message of the Scriptures is of a God who seeks to reconcile and restore. Consequently our curricula should give substantial space to training students to lead God's people in being restorative agents in this broken world.[28]

Inasmuch as cross-cultural training and missiology are vital to the mission of God, an integrated world missions curriculum must be part of contextualized theological education.

An exciting development of the past decade is the formation of world missions departments in a number of Ukraine's theological education institutions. As a result, hundreds of young Slavic believers now grasp God's heart for the nations and are serving UPGs, both within Ukraine and across the globe in Asia, Africa, Europe, and South America. This shared understanding of the mission of God and strong commitment to carrying out that mission cross-culturally is cause for great celebration. Yet this progress in mobilization among seminaries and Bible schools is not without its complications. For instance, at a missions conference I attended in 2012, one denominational leader was charged with promoting the missions programs of three schools, all of which were represented at the conference. He spoke glowingly about the one-year intensive program run by the school with which he was most closely associated. He was similarly positive about the two-year program of a second school. But when it came time to speak about the four-year bachelor of theology program of the conference's host school, this leader said, "Of course, you could study missions for four years here at this institution, but who wants to take that long when you can study at one of these other schools for just one or two years?" More shocking than the disrespect shown to the host school of this conference is the shortsightedness of publicly undermining a program that is equally as passionate about training cross-cultural workers as the other programs, is filling the need for training within a full undergraduate curriculum, and can disciple students missiologically with longer-term strategies than the other programs. A national church needs multiple training options in order to develop both practitioners and theoreticians, both missionaries and mission leaders, if it is to realize a biblical, global vision.

The previous episode illustrates the challenge Ukrainian theological institutions have in working together. Each institution should be free, of course, to develop her programs according to God's calling, the needs of her constituency, and the resources available to her. But none of that logically translates into the seeming inability, even aversion, that Ukraine's

---

28. Shaw, "Holistic and Transformative," 211–12.

seminaries and Bible schools have toward forming partnerships. With the number of potential missionaries increasing with each graduation, the need is great for financial and prayer support as they move into cross-cultural work. One possible way to meet that need would be for the theological institutions, each of which represents a significant number of churches, to network together to provide the needed support. I echo what one missionary expressed, as reported by Alfie Mossé, that SEND's missions mobilization ministry could extend its work to include integration and collaboration with the missions programs of Ukrainian schools.[29] The move to missions education and training in Ukrainian seminaries and Bible schools is a significant step in the process of carrying out the mission of God. Strategic thinking in how these institutions can mutually support one another in the process is a definite goal toward which to strive.[30]

THE POWER OF PRINCIPLE: SETTING MOBILIZATION EFFORTS UP FOR SUCCESS AT ALL LEVELS

There is no church, past, present or future, in any part of this world that is exempt from cultivating an all-nations perspective. As David Platt stated with passion recently, "There is actually a type of person who is zealous for the spread of the gospel and the glory of God among the nations—their hearts beat for this—but they don't become a missionary. . . . They're called Christians."[31] If this is true, then missions mobilization efforts among young and developing churches cannot focus solely on those whom God is calling from those churches to serve in cross-cultural contexts. Teaching about God's heart for every people group in the world and training to express that heart must reach all levels of the body of Christ, from preaching pastor to praying parishioner. Of course, robust missions programs in theological institutions should produce those equipped to do this work. But in a national church's development stage, as missionaries partner with their leaders to help them understand the importance of a Great Commission

---

29. Mossé, *Mobilization Analysis*, 5.

30. Jason Gupta is a missionary with World Venture and is currently the director of the world missions program at Kyiv Theological Seminary. He reported that the current leadership for missions in the largest Evangelical denomination in Ukraine has a robust understanding of the mission of God and desires a healthy working relationship with Ukraine's theological institutions. This bodes well for the future of cross-cultural efforts in the Ukrainian theological landscape. Interview by author, Zoom video conference, March 26 and April 23, 2020.

31. Platt, "Goal of God."

vision, there are two vital principles that, if realized, will go a long way to seeing the whole church mobilized.

First of all, there is no substitute for wholehearted support by the missions organization in the home or sending country for the missionaries engaged in mobilization efforts on the field, or receiving, country. This may seem odd even to mention, but in today's world of metrics and analyses, some ministries in some missions experience high levels of scrutiny, which can be disheartening for those engaged in those ministries.[32] Of course, some evaluation is warranted; a mission should always be asking whether it should be doing what it is doing and missionaries should know when it is time to hand their work on to nationals. Yet, from experience, I can testify to the boost in morale and freedom of spirit that accompanies deep trust from the sending country in the work of mobilization.[33] During the time that I served as area director of SEND Ukraine, our team was involved in roughly ten distinct ministries. We worked on metrics and exit strategies for all of the ministries, and so we thoroughly discussed how we would know when the Ukrainian church was sufficiently mobilized for cross-cultural work. But at no time did I, as the area director, feel that the leadership of our organization questioned the work of casting vision and developing strategies with and for Ukrainians as they learn how best to engage the unreached. Such work is active and ever-changing, but rather than defending our initiatives or working through excessive amounts of bureaucracy before jumping into projects and ideas, we felt empowered and trusted by the sending offices to participate in what seemed most advantageous in our efforts.[34] Mobilization work in young and developing churches is much more likely to thrive when personnel experience this kind of backing and encouragement from the home office.

---

32. This is especially the case if a missionary does not see the value of such evaluation or feels disconnected from the driving mission and vision behind the metrics and analyses.

33. Even in Mossé, *Mobilization Analysis*, where the focus is primarily on gaps and disconnects in the ministry, the underlying premise is that mobilization is a vital and valuable work. The goal of the report is to determine how to improve the ministry, rather than whether the ministry is viable.

34. One long-standing ministry for SEND Ukraine is theological education; it was one of the initial ministries our team was involved in when our work in Ukraine began in the early 1990s. Very understandably, having been at the theological education task for twenty years, the home office of SEND International was asking many questions about the necessity of continuing that ministry and a plan for transitioning out of theological education. I, along with many other teachers, spent significant time justifying our continued work with Ukrainian seminaries and Bible colleges. And while it was good to ask ourselves hard questions, we couldn't help but feel that our mission was questioning our very involvement in theological education. Our missions mobilization ministry has had a radically different experience.

Secondly, in order to mobilize the church at all levels, a commitment to do so must be built into the vision, and work that touches all sectors of the church must be given adequate attention. Compelling invitations from national, organizational leaders and pastors of large, influential churches could easily occupy all of a missionary's time. It will take the kind of dedication expressed in Christopher Wright's "pastoral task" question to avoid spending time on only the most high-profile opportunities. "Are we mobilizing, training and supporting people . . . for mission—not only by sending some overseas as 'missionaries,' but seeing the whole church engaged in mission in the world every working day of their lives?"[35] SEND Ukraine has prioritized this whole church commitment through a precise definition of mobilization. "Missions mobilization is not recruitment, but the process of helping believers and churches everywhere understand and find their unique role/calling in the Great Commission. In other words, we strive to mobilize the whole body of Christ, not just recruit individuals."[36] Yes, SEND Ukraine's Missions Mobilization Ministry organizes multi-denominational missions conferences attended by hundreds each year. But they also assist small churches of less than one hundred members to hold missions conferences for their congregations. Yes, they do spend significant time meeting with denominational leaders, strategizing about how to mobilize and send missionaries. But they also meet with individual churches, coaching them on what it takes to rework a budget to support cross-cultural work or develop a missions committee. By exemplifying this principle of whole church mobilization through working with congregations of all sizes in various contexts, Ukrainian brothers and sisters are learning from SEND Ukraine how to recognize and value the unique make up of each individual body of Christ. As Sharon Hoover wisely notes, biblically grounded guidelines "shape the model for missional engagement, but the church family provides the means for action. The expression of mission will look different for every church and every person. The men, women, and children who make up the local church bring the unique gifts, talents and passions to serve."[37] Missionaries can and should work hard to ensure that they are diversifying their missions mobilization efforts. Doing so will both model a whole church missions focus and impact national churches across all levels.

---

35. Wright, *God's People*, 272.
36. Chad Wiebe, e-mail message to author, March 27, 2020.
37. Hoover, *Mapping Church Missions*, 151. Hoover's term for "biblically grounded guidelines" is "continuums." But without the development of her argument, such a term is difficult to comprehend.

CONCLUSION: FROM EVERY NATION TO EVERY NATION

In God's good timing, Jesus will return and establish his kingdom with worshippers from every tribe, tongue, people, and nation gathered in unity around his throne. Until that day, the task of the global church is to share his saving name with those who have never heard. My goal in this chapter has been to encourage missionaries who are currently serving people groups where the church is young and developing to prioritize the mobilization of those people groups to have and live out an all-nations vision. Inasmuch as the whole of Scripture testifies to God's heart for every people group he created, so teaching this foundational truth must be part of the fulfillment of Jesus's Great Commission. It is non-negotiable. My suggestions here may be a precise fit for some missionaries and they may be utterly inapplicable to others. But I trust that the underlying and driving motivation to mobilize God's people to take the gospel to the ends of the earth is both evident and, I hope, infectious, since it is what God wants from his people.[38]

BIBLIOGRAPHY

Bietenhard, Hans. "People." In *The New International Dictionary of New Testament Theology*, vol. 2, G—Pre, edited by Colin I. Brown, 790–95. Grand Rapids, MI: Zondervan, 1986.

Branson, Mark Lau, and Juan F. Martínez. *Churches, Cultures and Leadership: A Practical Theology of Congregations and Ethnicities*. Downers Grove, IL: IVP Academic, 2011.

Coleman, Robert E. "The Hope of a Coming World Revival." In *Perspectives on the World Christian Movement: A Reader*, edited by Ralph Winter and Steven C. Hawthorne, 199–203. 4th ed. Pasadena, CA: William Carey Library, 2009.

Hayes, Marques. "How Many Countries Are There in the World?" *WorldAtlas*. https://www.worldatlas.com/articles/how-many-countries-are-in-the-world.html.

Jenkins, Philip. *The Next Christendom: The Coming of Global Christianity*. 3rd ed. Oxford: Oxford University Press, 2011.

Joshua Project. "Country: Ukraine." https://joshuaproject.net/countries/UP.

———. "Global Statistics." https://joshuaproject.net/people_groups/statistics.

Hoover, Sharon R. *Mapping Church Missions: A Compass for Ministry Strategy*. Downers Grove, IL: IVP, 2018.

Living Springs International. *Kairos: God, the Church and the World*. 4th ed. Manukau: World Outreach, 2011.

---

38. I am grateful to Dr. Michael Bräutigam for the invitation and encouragement to write this chapter. I am deeply indebted to Jason Gupta, Alfie Mossé, Chad Wiebe, Lois Cox, and Kyle Eipperle, all current or former missionaries to Ukraine, for insightful and constructive comments that made this chapter much better than it would have been without their input.

Moreau, A. Scott, et al. *Introducing World Missions: A Biblical, Practical and Historical Survey*. 2nd ed. Grand Rapids, MI: Baker Academic, 2015.

Mossé, Alfie. *Mobilization Analysis for Eurasia Hub Workgroup. Report*. Farmington, MI: SEND International, 2020.

Ortiz, Michael A. "Missiology: A Contextualization Framework." *Didaktikos Journal of Theological Education* 3, no. 4 (February 2020) 38–39.

Platt, David. "The Goal of God and the Goal of Your Life." Resurrection Chapel message, Talbot School of Theology, March 10, 2020. https://www.youtube.om/watch?v=Yo acjkozauY&list=PLVHY3HvnI6yPNw_JGApyBv6Q7b4BFlwn2.

Shaw, Perry. "Holistic and Transformative: Beyond a Typological Approach to Theological Education." *Evangelical Review of Theology* 40, no. 3 (2016) 205–16.

Tson, Josef. "Suffering and Martyrdom: God's Strategy in the World." In *Perspectives on the World Christian Movement: A Reader*, edited by Ralph Winter and Steven C. Hawthorne, 195–98. 4th ed. Pasadena, CA: William Carey Library, 2009.

White, John E. "Factors Behind the Ukrainian Evangelical Missionary Surge from 1989–1999." PhD diss., Biola University, 2016.

Wright, Christopher J. H. *The Mission of God's People: A Biblical Theology of the Church's Mission*. Biblical Theology for Life. Edited by Jonathan Lunde. Grand Rapids, MI: Zondervan, 2010.

18

Why Does Theology Still Matter for Chinese Christianity?

A Theological Reflection on Contemporary Christian Mission in China

Jason Lam

THIS CHAPTER FIRSTLY PRESENTS an "actualistic" typology of Chinese Christianity in the PRC for the last few decades. This is to capture several dimensions including the relationship between the church and the state, the interest of Christians in producing a public voice, and the urbanization, educational background, and other related factors contributing to the present shape of Chinese Christianity. The author contends in the second part that the future development cannot only be projected with the aid of sociopolitical analysis: theology should be considered a significant factor contributing to the future transformation. Hence how to develop a form of theology appropriately informed by other disciplines is a task to be accomplished. Some points are articulated for producing a "possible" and "responsible" theological "imagination" under the present sociopolitical situation.

INTRODUCTION[1]

This title may look strange at first glance. Isn't theology an integral part of Christianity? If yes, then how can Chinese Christianity be an exception? Nevertheless, in view of the developing trends of scholarship in Chinese Christianity, especially those that have emerged in the People's Republic of China (PRC) during the last decade, this question is not superfluous. Statistics show that the total number of articles and dissertations on Christianity peaked in the years 2011–2012. After that the number declines year by year and even more sharply after 2015.[2] This phenomenon coincides with the apparent increase of state harassment against Christianity in the socialist country. In this way, the phenomenon has invited studies from the sociopolitical perspective. It is a natural development, which has its own set of justifications. Nevertheless, if scholarship keeps on developing on an unevenly distributed path, then it would not only affect the future of theoretical studies in Chinese Christianity (e.g. dogmatic theology and biblical studies), but even the practical level, including the development of the church, would be affected.

In view of this issue, we will not in this chapter produce a direct study on the social and political factors influencing the development of Chinese Christianity in recent years. We will, however, attempt to develop an "actualistic" typology of Chinese Christianity in the PRC for the last few decades. This typology is to capture several dimensions, including the relationship between the church and the state, the interest of Christians in producing a voice in the public, and the urbanization, the educational background, and other related factors contributing to the above characteristics. We will find that the younger the type of Christian church/community emerged, the more likely it is to have urbanized people involved and a larger proportion of intellectuals intending to produce a Christian voice in the public. It is, needless to say, seen as a threat by the Chinese Communist Party (CCP) government and it could be a factor affecting the state-church relationship. Nevertheless, from an insider or theological perspective, I contend that the future development of Chinese Christianity cannot be projected only from sociopolitical analyses; theology must also be considered a significant factor contributing to the future transformation. This is because theology shapes the thoughts and actions of the communities involved, which are in continuous interaction with other groups in the society, including the government.

---

1. Thanks to Dr. Justin Tan and Dr. Naomi Thurston for their sincere comments on the early drafts of this chapter. Thanks also due to Diana Summers for her proofreading of the revised draft. All errors that remain, of course, are the author's sole responsibility.

2. Huang and Hu, "Trends and Reflections," 45–70, 49–51.

Therefore, the future is, of course, something even interdisciplinary studies cannot comprehend completely. Hence how to develop a form of theology appropriately informed by other disciplines is a task to be accomplished for both theorists and practitioners of Christianity in contemporary China.

EXISTING MODELS OF CHINESE CHRISTIANITY IN THE PRC

In 1949 the CCP took control of Mainland China. It is no secret that the orthodox state teaching is atheism, which is in ideological conflict with Christianity and all forms of theistic faith. As a result, the Christian churches and in fact all institutional religions were suppressed and experienced a difficult time during the early reign of the regime, especially during the Cultural Revolution. But since the end of the 1970s the policy of Reform and Opening Up has been implemented and, at least to some extent, religions have been tolerated over the last forty years. This is not to say that the conflict between communism and religion is settled. Rather, when the regime declares its primary target as developing economy, the issue of ideological conflict is often treated as secondary. It may even go so far as to consider taking religion as a means for social cohesion, as long as the religious communities in question are not seen as making trouble for the government.

In view of this we may have a better understanding of the present landscape of Chinese Christianity (in the PRC). Undoubtedly, the sociopolitical situation is just one of the many dimensions affecting the shape of Christianity in a given place and time. Nevertheless, no one can escape from this background and the Christians living in the context must try to accommodate to it. Therefore, in what follows we will first offer an overview of the existing types of Chinese Christianity presented in an "actualistic typology." And we will find that they are not just discrete types emerging by accident but have shown characteristics related to the context in which they are living.

"Actualistic typology" is a paradoxical term because we usually expect a "typology" to be collectively exhaustive from a theoretical perspective with various models described; but adding "actualistic" here means that we are just articulating what is actually there at hand. In other words, we are not going to describe exhaustively all possible Christian responses theoretically but only what has already been embodied as a spectrum in the specific context, along with the reasons behind this.

For some years we have not lacked modern ecclesiologies composed of typological articulation. However, Nicholas M. Healy reminded us that being satisfied with a seemingly comprehensive blueprint of the church is precisely the issue to be cautious about. It is because in this way one may easily develop merely empty talk on some essential and perfect features of the church; but they could be too far away from the concrete situations of the Christians in a particular time and place.[3] In this light, a responsible theological discernment of the church should be made not only against some perfectionist models, but also from the concrete life situation of the practicing community. Therefore, the following exercise is not just going to pour out some free-floating agendas; otherwise we cannot understand why Chinese Christianity has arrived at the present situation and cannot really be informed by the expertise of other disciplines in our theological reflection. Only in this way may we truly offer an "imaginative" and "responsible" agenda—with critical reflection, responsive to the concrete situation that can be implemented by Christians in that context.

What are the "actualistic" possibilities that have already been embodied in the PRC for the last seventy years, especially after the Reform and Opening Up policy? And why are they present in the context now? Although we are only describing and explaining the existing models (probably in a reduced form), it is still a huge task for a single chapter. Thanks to the recent work *Chinese Public Theology* by Alexander Chow,[4] we can have a convenient means for building our discussion. Needless to say, this book or any other would not have exactly the same objective as this chapter. But in the first part of Chow's work, several major types of Chinese public theology are described in chronological order, which is very useful for our purpose here of articulating an "actualistic typology," especially when it is to be examined against the sociopolitical context.

A State-Sanctioned Church

We understand that since 1949 religions, including Christianity, have been suppressed in the PRC. Nevertheless, a state-sanctioned church has still remained and continues to operate under the two national committees (*lianghui*, the two bodies of the Three-Self Patriotic Movement [TSPM] and the China Christian Council [CCC]). This is the first model of Chinese Christianity in the PRC, usually understood as the "registered church,"

---

3. Healy, *Church*, chap. 2, 25–51.
4. Chow, *Chinese Public Theology*. This book starts with Christian intellectuals speaking for the church in the public realm prior to CCP rule, but we are more interested in how the church responded to the specific situation as described above. Thus, the typology to be presented will not closely follow his analysis.

to be articulated under this severe situation. Needless to say, this officially sanctioned community must conform to everything the state deems good, which is quite often a political judgment by the regime rather than a religious decision by the church. Therefore, it would encounter at times the problem of serving "two masters" and making concessions in order to retain its legal status. In addition, according to the regulations, this church is confined to specific locations, and outside of these registered sites the transmission of Christian faith is not allowed. This "spatialization" (*kong jian hua*) constraint has hindered the Christian voice from being heard, not to say from doing comprehensive missional work or taking responsible actions in the society.[5] In this way, apart from reinforcing some of the claims of the state, the possible response to the society that can be practiced by this model of Chinese Christianity is greatly hindered. But we can understand with empathy that it is in a sense an unavoidable compromise in struggling for survival during persecution.

Unregistered Churches

Contrasting with the state-sanctioned church, there have been "house churches" or "unregistered churches" existing since the reign of the CCP in Mainland China, which is the second model to be examined. The Christians involved do not find it right to make so many concessions to the state and do not feel comfortable in serving "two masters" at the same time. Therefore, they do not operate under the umbrella of the state administration system and have been deemed illegal by the government. Hence in the old days their activities took place in private houses owned by Christian families and thus they are often called "house church," "family church," and "underground church." But it is interesting that for quite a long period the local governments have employed a more relaxed approach toward these "illegal" congregations.[6] A few of them have thrived in recent years to become literally megachurches with more than one thousand congregants, such that sometimes one can hardly use the terms "house church," "family church" or even "underground church" but only "unregistered church." They are allowed to exist as long as they do not bring "troubles" to the local governments,

---

5. "Spatialization" is a term coined by Li Xianping to describe the performance of religions in China; cf. his *Zhongguo Dangdai Zongjiaode Shehuixue Quanshi* [*Sociological Interpretation*], 123–24; "'Place' Centered."

6. Chow in his book drew our attention to Wu and Cui, "House Churches," an article published in *China Daily*. Chow, *Chinese Public Theology*, 92. Another very distinguished work in this area is Reny, *Authoritarian Containment*.

which are busy boosting the economy. They have enjoyed a peaceful time; but there would be an issue if the Christians wanted to respond to the cry of society in public, including the exploitation of human and natural resources, and sometimes even reporting improper use of money and power by officials and enterprises. Obviously, if they want to dwell peacefully on earth, then some form of compromise is still to be made.[7]

Sino-Christian Studies Movement

As a matter of fact, even if some Christians dare to risk their lives in producing a prophetic voice in society, they need a public platform to do so. But the present regulations basically bar all religious voices from the public realm if they present themselves as visible communities. Therefore, the rise in academia of intellectuals who are empathic to the Christian faith has attracted many people's attention for the last few decades. Chow named this "Cultural Christianity" while it is often recognized as a "Sino-Christian Studies" movement.[8] Previously Christian churches in the PRC were characterized by a disproportionate demographic of the elderly (especially women) in rural areas, and most of them were illiterate. But as time went on, with the help of the developing economy, people generally had better education, and more and more intellectuals in big cities have been attracted by the Christian faith. Some of them have even converted. They are scattered across all professions and may produce their voices in the public realm (mainly in academia or broadly in the cultural and educational sector) and reflect Christian values in the society. Certainly, this has only been possible in recent times when the economic and political situation allows, which was quite unimaginable in the past. But these new-generation intellectuals understand very well the so-called red lines (*hong xian*; unspoken rules) of the government. Therefore, most of them would not openly identify themselves as Christians; and for this reason, some of them may not become genuine believers (from the perspective of the institutional church) but only conform to Christian values in their studies and practices. Nevertheless, this is already a breakthrough compared with the past; at least some Christian voices are heard in the public space, though a Christian community cannot be easily identified.

---

7. Therefore, Chow did not find a distinguished type of public theology produced by those churches that did not produce provocative actions in his book.

8. For a concise and comprehensive view, cf. my article, "Faith Identity"; also Lai and Lam, *Sino-Christian Theology*.

Urban Intellectual Churches

It was not until recently that some committed Christians felt the need of producing a prophetic voice against injustice in Chinese society. Most of them are intellectuals emerging from the unregistered churches. Some are even lawyers and legal scholars involved in the rights defense movement (*weiquan yundong*). Because of their social vision, many of them have claimed attachment to some form of Calvinist theology.[9] Obviously, this recent development is possible only if there are Christians who are highly educated and who understand their rights both in theory and in reality. They have gathered in cities and have sufficient resources to develop their religious communities as "Urban Intellectual Christianity," as Chow called them. It can also be perceived as a by-product of the economic growth of the last few decades. Therefore, they have acquired an attitude like that of middle-class citizens in a liberal society; but, unfortunately, they do not really live in such a situation. At the moment it seems that this layer of people is still not strong enough to produce a crucial change in the PRC, as the state has still grasped hold of most resources to monitor and control the country, including the religious sector. Nevertheless, these Christians have already developed a strong sense of responsibility to produce not only voices but also actions in society. Whether in the end they will succeed or make a contribution to a more extensive transformation of their society remains to be seen.

The above four types are the existing "actualistic" models in the "typology" of contemporary Chinese Christianity in the PRC. The distinctiveness of Chow's work is not only in articulating these types but in arranging them in chronological order of emergence and regarding them as different generations of public theology in China. This development is possible because there has been a sociopolitical change through the years. Since a (quasi-) free market is established and some resources (economic and political) are shared by the people, a (quasi-) open and liberal society has been felt in the last few decades in the PRC; hence more progressive types of public theology have emerged. Now as Christians we come to a point at which many people are asking a similar question: what if China's economy stops growing or grows less rapidly? This is no longer a conditional clause but a matter of fact; the economic and political situation of the country has become less stable than before. Therefore, various phenomena have occurred more often, e.g. provocative Christians are arrested, unregistered churches of large

---

9. One of the representatives is undoubtedly the pastor of the Chengdu Early Rain Reformed Church (*Qiuyu zhi fu guizheng jiaohui*), Wang Yi, who was recently sentenced to prison for nine years. For a recent survey of the whole trend, cf. Fällman, "Calvin, Culture and Christ?"

size are raided, the crosses and even buildings of some official churches are pulled down, and intellectuals find that the space for producing their voices in academia shrinks. This is also a reason why we have had an ambivalent view of China's economic impact and the related explanations for the last ten years or so.[10] Truly, what should be the Christian response in view of this present situation?

RETHINKING THE ROLE OF THEOLOGY

Stephen B. Bevans and Roger P. Schroeder in their renowned work *Constants in Context* articulated three types of theology of mission on the basis of several theological models before them:

1. Mission as saving souls and extending the church
2. Mission as discovery of the truth
3. Mission as commitment to liberation and transformation.[11]

Needless to say, in actual practice the three types are not mutually exclusive but cooperative. From the above articulation, we could see that the existing types of Chinese Christianity in the PRC may also map onto the different models articulated. The state-sanctioned church, and to a large extent even the unregistered churches, can only focus on saving souls and church extension in order to avoid suppression from the state. Yes, even the unregistered churches would find that at times they may have to keep silent and make compromises if the truth they learn from the Christian tradition is in conflict with the interests of the state. Cultural Christianity or the Sino-Christian Studies movement obviously concerns discovering the truth from the Christian tradition, and some participants may have a heart to commit to social liberation and transformation, as they write in the public realm about their findings. Nevertheless, some concessions still have to be made, and thus it is not easy to identify a visible community for this type of Chinese Christianity. In order words, expansion can hardly be a primary concern, and they may even be reluctant to go too far in social liberation and transformation lest they put themselves in danger. Thus, their responses can at most be in theoretical articulation rather than in concrete actions. It seems then that the urban intellectual Christians have tried to actualize all

10. This is too vast a topic to be addressed here. The author is preparing another essay on the issue.

11. Bevans and Schroeder, *Constants in Context*, chap. 2; it is mainly built upon the models suggested by Sölle, *Thinking about God*, and González, *Christian Thought Revisited*.

missional models. But that is why they often live at high risk of being raided by the regime. In recent years, when the sociopolitical situation has become less stable than before, news about persecution of individual Christian leaders and churches has become more frequent. Some people ask whether Chinese Christians should use their tactics more wisely. But in this way, are we making further compromise and concessions in the face of injustice?

From the above "actualistic typology" articulated, it is not difficult to find that, apart from some urban Christian political activists, all other types are seeking ways of surviving under the rule of an authoritarian regime with atheist ideology by self-limiting in some ways. Marie-Eve Reny described this phenomenon in her recent book as "containment" (*ezhixing*)—the conditional and bounded toleration of a group outside state-sanctioned institutions:

> Toleration is *conditional* insofar as it involves a bargain. State security actors grant religious leaders some autonomy in exchange for complying with a set of conditions. Rules may be implicit or explicitly stated. The authorities expect religious leaders to keep a low profile and share information about their internal activities with public security bureaus. They further expect unregistered pastors to refrain from crossing red lines (*guo hongxian*) deemed unacceptable by the regime . . .[12]

In other words, the CCP, or perhaps the local government officials, can tolerate the existence of different kinds of Christianity in the PRC, insofar as they do not threaten the political security of the regime (it perceives). Nevertheless, in the last few years, when the economic and political pressure on the state has increased, we have seen the augmentation of strikes on Christianity in the PRC. Obviously, this kind of bargain in exchange for survival space is largely controlled by the hand of the regime. In view of this increasing harshness, some people may ask whether engaging in this bargain is a wise tactic for the long run. Taking the question to another level, one may even ask if it is right to exchange (part of) the autonomy of the church for survival in the face of unjust persecution. Agreeing to enter this perverted game, as interpreted by Reny, is a risk-averse behavior that usually pays off. Nevertheless, this kind of informal agreement would also isolate those communities that do not see it as appropriate and produce distrust between both sides. On top of that, it may even strengthen the resilience of the authoritarian regime.[13] Whether it is worthy and ethical for Christians in the PRC to do so is truly a difficult question.

12. Reny, *Authoritarian Containment*, 6.
13. Reny, *Authoritarian Containment*, 16.

Making a Possible and Responsible Answer

Looking at the issue from another perspective, the later the generation of Christians involved, the greater is the tendency to address social issues in the public arena, regardless of whether it is directly related to the church or not. Christians in the PRC surely understand the potential hazards of doing so, but the younger generation still has the courage to take action. We may wonder whether the churches have gradually reached the threshold of self-limitation and hence survival, such that they become fearless to speak out. But this is precisely the way of looking at things from the "containment" perspective. These Christian intellectuals could have the courage to do so, not completely due to the issue of their own survival, but because of a prophetic vision to speak for the good for themselves and for society at large.[14] This is also the point urged for a Christian response that is not only "possible" but also "responsible."

After articulating the "actualistic" models, it is easy for us to fall prey to just projecting "possible" responses that can be easily actualized on this basis without bringing in our "imagination." Empirical studies, including history and the social sciences, however, do not provide us the only reality, whereas the theological discipline is sometimes regarded as transcendent or even unreal. But the church is precisely such a theological reality and at the same time a political, ethical, and eschatological one.[15] Therefore, we cannot understand it, including the Chinese one in question, merely from the "actualistic" perspective, lest we forget its pluralistic nature. In addition, the church is not merely the sum total of its phenomena already shown in this world; it is an eschatological entity, from a theological perspective, to be practiced by the people of God and on its way to being shaped by the Lord. That is why we need theological discernment at the same time of doing empirical analysis, and thus any model, be it actualistic or ideal, can be evaluated and improved. Therefore, we claim that theology still matters for Chinese Christianity even in this difficult situation.

As a matter of fact, trying to combine two perspectives or different approaches together is not a practice unique to theological studies. Even if we turn to the social sciences after the Second World War, a similar kind of struggle could be found. As early as 1959, C. Wright Mills suggested the notion of "sociological imagination" against the dichotomy between practitioners and intellectual craftsmen for his colleagues.[16] He thought that

---

14. For example, cf. Wang, "我的聲明"; Qiuyu, "95 Theses."
15. Cf. Huen, "會何以另類?," 54.
16. Mills, *Sociological Imagination*, 5–8.

the particular "troubles" felt by some individuals or communities should be transformed to become public "issues." This is not only for the sake of making it information to be constructed by remote intellectuals or of trying to solve some particular problems from a teleological drive. But in such a process, since one wants to understand better or resolve the troubles in question, he or she has to transcend that particular context to make it an issue of concern to a wider audience. Conversely, unless an issue could attract a wide variety of readers and thus address multiple concrete situations, it would not become a topic to be investigated in-depth. In other words, the sociological imagination is aimed at reconstructing the theory but not merely as an intellectual game. Mills even summoned his fellow scholars to make their studies a "public intelligence apparatus" and hence producing history-making theory.[17] If social scientists had already developed this sense of making dual efforts eighty years ago, then academics working on Chinese Christianity and all kinds of theological studies should have embraced it more readily and wholeheartedly from the "transcendental" theological point of view.[18]

Historically, it is true that in the interaction with the world, especially with political powers, the church has not usually been in control. Nevertheless, it does not mean that Christians have no choice but to conform to all of the world's demands. Otherwise, the church would become merely one more human grouping in this world. Arne Rasmusson reminded us that the politics of the church are different from the politics of the world. We should not merely endorse some existing political agenda; otherwise the church would become just another agent for a political circle or ideology. In other words, we should be aware that the church is not a political party and has no intention of offering an agenda for solving the political matrix at hand. We are not a political alternative but an alternative to politics.[19] That is why we are also asking for a "responsible" answer on top of the possible ones—bringing in our "imagination" through a critical theological reflection, such that we would not be satisfied with merely what we are at present but challenging ourselves to become the people we should be as God wills for us. However, in the face of a complicated sociopolitical situation in the PRC, what sort of responsible theological "imagination" can be produced?

17. Mills, *Sociological Imagination*, 181.

18. John Milbank's *Theology and Social Theory* can be seen as an effort working from the other direction, but we cannot explore it and other materials here.

19. Rasmusson, *Church as Polis*, 208–19, 331–34; also cf. Huen's concise explanation, "教會何以另類?," 52–53.

Reactions in the Actual World

Turning back to our Chinese theological scene, although we have emphasized that the typology articulated above is an "actualistic" one, it is to a large extent comprehensive and may have covered nearly the whole possible spectrum concerning the community's attitude toward the government. In a sense all models have tried to make responses in their own contexts according to what they see as good in balancing "possible" and "responsible." From an outsider's perspective, one easily tends to think that, since the later the model the more perspectives of missional action are taken, thus it is going on a better route; the older the model the more concessions are made, thus it is obsolete. In reality the mechanism behind the church and the state in the PRC is not as simple as is perceived. Needless to say, it is too huge a topic to be examined in one single chapter. But even from the surface, we know that many urban intellectual churches in the PRC have tried to build their thoughts on a Calvinist political theology, hoping for a kind of theonomous governance. It is good for Christians to hope for the best in spite of the present misery, but whether it is relevant and appropriate to apply an eschatological model for the present situation is worth pondering from the ecclesial history.[20] Conversely, it looks to many people as if the registered church has been conceding too much in exchange for a peaceful survival. There have been reports, however, telling us that the exchange between the church and the government, especially the regional ones, is not so straightforward. On occasion the local churches may have opportunities to "educate" the local officials on religious matters and may even gain "negotiating capital" in cooperation and hence could implicitly affect the policy-making process.[21] The Sino-Christian studies movement seems to be a little dissociated from churchgoers and thus only exists among scholars. Nevertheless, as the education level of the people in the PRC has been raised in recent years, the publications related to Christianity are transmitted widely such that some people would find interest in learning more from this faith. Hence the movement may also help transmit Christian faith outside of the church without missionaries.[22]

Having said all this, does it mean that Chinese Christianity and the related scholarship has already been running on a very good track? Certainly, there is ample room to develop. But I am just trying to say that a response could only be made appropriately according to its own situation. We should

---

20. Cf. Chow, "Calvinist Public Theology"; Starr, "Wang Yi."

21. Cf. Liu and White, "Old Pastor."

22. Cf. Lam, "Emergence of Scholars"; Xin, "Preliminary Survey"; Thurston, *Studying Christianity*.

not neglect the fact that the church is still a community on earth and not yet taken to heaven. Nevertheless, we are not only informed by experts in economic, finance, sociology, politics, and the like; the church is seen and taken as a social and political entity as we have our influences not only within the religious community but also on society at large through our interaction with the world. That is why the CCP has had a concern with Chinese Christianity, just as all worldly governments have concerns with religious communities in their respective contexts, especially in the modern pluralistic age. Therefore, the responses from the church should be "actualistic" on one hand, as we are not isolated from the world to produce any free-floating agenda. Any response produced is to be truly followed and executed by Christians in the world. Yet on the other hand, one should beware lest the response is merely an earthly projection without any "imaginative" element.

Christianity living in sociopolitical tension is indeed not a rare phenomenon. The Confessing Church in Nazi-ruled Germany, liberation theologians since the 1950s, black Christians in the US afterwards, the churches in South Africa during the period of Apartheid, and Minjung theologians in recent South Korea are all concrete examples of Christian communities under oppression within a century. They produced distinguished theologies amid their struggles. Conversely, the respective theologies produced have empowered those Christians in their reactions in the unfavorable situations and inspired others in different contexts as well. As a matter of fact, the Christian church from the day of her birth has been living in a sociopolitical situation not favorable to her. She has still marched on until today, and although many witnesses have given up their lives on the way, she has staggered to grow. Nevertheless, the early church did not only produce a theology of martyrdom; most classical doctrines were constructed in that period. They are often seen as cold, abstract, and remote theories in modern eyes, but they are in fact crystallized through the interaction with the practical world, and even the theological models and movements mentioned above have to take them as reference.

Needless to say, we cannot articulate a grandiose theological agenda for Chinese Christianity in the PRC in this chapter. Nonetheless, after examining the "actualistic" situation and consulting recent theological examples, some points can be made for producing a responsible theological "imagination" under the present sociopolitical situation.

Firstly, as the younger generation of Chinese Christians is more willing to speak out in public, there is the age-old adequacy issue of the message produced by the Christian community. It is too simple merely to differentiate whether a theological imagination produced is for or against the government or the state; but the point is that Christians are supposed to speak the will of God from the situation of the people and for the people. How one can insist on doing so in the unfavorable situation of the PRC is truly a big issue.

The second point follows: that this imagination should carry a transformative power rather than just an act of grumbling, and thus to some degree it can be accompanied by performative actions or praxis. It can be but need not be a rigorous activist type, but it should be able to empower the people involved in the situation in question. Otherwise, it would really become idle words without life. We can understand that the sociopolitical tension for Christians in the PRC may not vanish within a short time, but still one may try to articulate the meaning and mission of God's people living in such a context. That is why previous examples under sociopolitical tension could be taken as references.

Lastly, there must be a balance between the usage of the local resources and the continuity with the Christian tradition. In the abovementioned twentieth-century theological examples, most have tried to link the people to the oppressed image of Christ and hence his salvific power. A similar route can be invoked today; but how to relate the present situation in the PRC to Jesus's story truly requires imaginative effort. Perhaps we may still need to address why the people of God are suffering and for what purposes and how one can still proclaim hope in such a situation.

In a nutshell, a transformative vision must be communicated appropriately from the gospel through relating to the present situation. If it succeeds, then echoes may be heard from other contexts and reinforce the imagination and produce further influences. Thus our "actualistic" typology provides only a schematic capture of the "possible" as a first step and requires refined analysis in carrying out further "responsible" actions, especially from a concrete and complicated situation in the PRC.

FINAL REMARKS

In the end we must admit that Christians are not completely free to actualize their faith, especially in the special situation in the PRC today. Sometimes it is regrettable to see that some forms of compromise and concession may have to be made for Christians to survive. Nevertheless, the theological discernment that the church is an eschatological entity precisely tells us that at present it is not perfect but is a pilgrim on its way. Having said all this, obviously no one can provide a comprehensive missional response to the present situation in the PRC. Quite the contrary, we must admit that Christians in such a situation very often do not have the upper hand in the world. Any response must be considered concretely, taking the sociopolitical situation with ethical and theological reflection together seriously. An attempt to universalize a single strategy for all situations could be grandiose but impractical. In the end, Christians may still be caught in the dilemma between taking compromise and holding principles and values without a viable outcome. In such a situation the words of T. S. Eliot in addressing the relation between Christianity and culture still haunt us:

> The fact that a problem will certainly take a long time to solve, and that it will demand the attention of many minds for several generations, is no justification for postponing the study. And, in times of emergency, it may prove in the long run that the problems we have postponed or ignored, rather than those we have failed to attack successfully, will return to plague us. Our difficulties of the moment must always be dealt with somehow: but our permanent difficulties are difficulties of every moment.[23]

Nonetheless, we can be assured that the church is not destined to be controlled by a political entity. Much to the contrary, in a difficult situation we easily forget that it is the Lord of the church rather than any earthly authority who has the last word. In fact, the church as an entity in the world by itself is not possible. The fact that it exists is already a miracle made possible by the power of the Spirit through the salvific work laid by Jesus Christ.[24] Returning to the concrete situation of Chinese Christianity in the PRC, we should hence not only see an "actualistic typology" but perceive the miracles made possible by the Spirit. The Triune God will work out his plan in human history, and we who are called to engage in related missional works and theology are charged to be faithful servants in spite of facing any difficulties.

BIBLIOGRAPHY

Bevans, Stephen B., and Roger P. Schroeder. *Constants in Context: A Theology of Mission for Today*. Maryknoll: Orbis, 2004.
Chow, Alexander. "Calvinist Public Theology in Urban China Today." *International Journal of Public Theology* 8, no. 2 (2014) 158–175.
———. *Chinese Public Theology: Generational Shifts and Confucian Imagination in Chinese Christianity*. Oxford: OUP, 2018.
Eliot, T. S. *Christianity and Culture*. NY: Harcourt Brace & Co., 1960.
Fällman, Fredrik. "Calvin, Culture and Christ?: Developments of Faith Among Chinese Intellectuals." In *Christianity in Contemporary China: Socio-Cultural Perspectives*, edited by Francis Khek Gee Lim, 153–68. NY: Routledge, 2012.

---

23. Eliot, *Christianity and Culture*, 5.
24. Hauerwas, *Peaceable Kingdom*, 98, 106.

González, Justo L. *Christian Thought Revisited: Three Types of Theology*. Maryknoll: Orbis, 1999.

Hauerwas, Stanley. *The Peaceable Kingdom: A Primer in Christian Ethics*. London: SCM, 2003.

Healy, Nicholas M. *Church, World, and the Christian Life: Practical-Prophetic Ecclesiology*. Cambridge: CUP, 2000.

Huang, Jianbo, and Mengyin Hu. "Trends and Reflections: A Review of Empirical Studies of Christianity in Mainland China Since 2000." *Review of Religion and Chinese Society* 6 (2019) 45–70.

Huen, Freeman. "教會何以另類？超越社會實在論的教會觀." In *The Church Being Church*, edited by Andres Tang, 25–62. HK: Logos, 2012.

Lai, Pan-chiu, and Jason Lam, eds. *Sino-Christian Theology: A Theological qua Cultural Movement in Contemporary China*. Frankfurt: Peter Lang, 2010.

Lam, Jason. "The Emergence of Scholars Studying Christianity in Mainland China." In *Sino-Christian Theology*, edited by Pan-chiu Lai and Jason Lam, 21–33.

———. "The Faith Identity of Sino-Christian Theology: An Inquiry from a Comparative Perspective." In *Confucianism and Christianity: Interreligious Dialogue on the Theology of Mission*, edited by Edmund Chia. London: Routledge, 2021.

Li, Xianping. "The 'Place' Centered 'Space of Religious Activity': The Changes of 'Religion System' in China." *Logos and Pneuma* 26 (2007) 93–114.

———. *Zhongguo Dangdai Zongjiaode Shehuixue Quanshi* [A Sociological Interpretation of Contemporary Chinese Religions]. Shanghai: Renmin, 2006.

Liu, Jifeng, and Chris White. "Old Pastor and Local Bureaucrats: Recasting Church-State Relations in Contemporary China." *Modern China* 45, no. 5 (2019) 564–90.

Milbank, John. *Theology and Social Theory*. Oxford: Blackwell, 2006.

Mills, C. Wright. *The Sociological Imagination*. NY: OUP, 2000.

Qiuyu, Zhifu Jiaotang. "我們對家庭教會立場的重申 (九十五條)" ["95 Theses: The Reaffirmation of our Stance on the House Church"]. 《生命季刊》第75期 (2015年9月). https://www.cclifefl.org/View/Article/4248.

Rasmusson, Arne. *The Church as Polis: From Political Theology to Theological Politics as Exemplified by Jürgen Moltmann and Stanley Hauerwas*. Notre Dame: University of Notre Dame Press, 1995.

Reny, Marie-Eve. *Authoritarian Containment: Public Security Bureaus and Protestant House Churches in Urban China*. NY: OUP, 2018.

Sölle, Dorothee. *Thinking about God: An Introduction to Theology*. London: SCM, 1990.

Starr, Chloë. "Wang Yi and the 95 Theses of the Chinese Reformed Church." *Religions* 7 (2016) 142–56.

Thurston, Naomi. *Studying Christianity in China: Constructions of an Emerging Discourse*. Leiden & Boston: Brill, 2018.

Wang, Yi. "我的聲明：信仰上的抗命." *Christian Times*, December 12, 2018. https://christiantimes.org.hk/Common/Reader/News/ShowNews.jsp?Nid=156491&Pid=104&Version=0&Cid=2053&Charset=big5_hkscs.

Wu, Yiyao, and Cui, Xiaohuo. "House Churches Thrive in Beijing." *China Daily*, March 17, 2010. http://www.chinadaily.com.cn/cndy/2010-03/17/content_9600333.htm.

Xin, Gao. "Preliminary Survey on the New Generation of Scholars of Christian Studies in Mainland China." In *Sino-Christian Theology*, edited by Pan-chiu Lai and Jason Lam, 225–37.

www.ingramcontent.com/pod-product-compliance
Lightning Source LLC
Chambersburg PA
CBHW050615300426
44112CB00012B/1518